# China, the Developing World, and the New Global Dynamic

# China,
# the Developing World,
# and the
# New Global Dynamic

edited by
**Lowell Dittmer**
**George T. Yu**

LYNNE
RIENNER
PUBLISHERS

BOULDER
LONDON

Published in the United States of America in 2010 by
Lynne Rienner Publishers, Inc.
1800 30th Street, Boulder, Colorado 80301
www.rienner.com

and in the United Kingdom by
Lynne Rienner Publishers, Inc.
3 Henrietta Street, Covent Garden, London WC2E 8LU

**Library of Congress Cataloging-in-Publication Data**
China, the developing world, and the new global dynamic / edited by Lowell
Dittmer and George T. Yu.
    p. cm.
  Includes bibliographical references and index.
  ISBN 978-1-58826-700-9 (hc : alk. paper) — ISBN 978-1-58826-726-9 (pb :
alk. paper)
  1. China—Foreign economic relations—Developing countries. 2. Developing
countries—Foreign economic relations—China. I. Dittmer, Lowell. II. Yu,
George T., 1931–
  HF1604.Z4D445 2010
  337.510172'4—dc22
                                                2009032150


**British Cataloguing in Publication Data**
A Cataloguing in Publication record for this book
is available from the British Library.


Printed and bound in the United States of America

      The paper used in this publication meets the requirements
∞     of the American National Standard for Permanence of
      Paper for Printed Library Materials Z39.48-1992.

5  4  3  2  1

*To Helen and Priscilla*
*for their encouragement and support*

# Contents

10   China's Rise, Global Identity, and the
Developing World, *Lowell Dittmer*                      203

# 1

# China and the Developing World

## Lowell Dittmer

For the past three decades, the People's Republic of China (PRC) has taken a renewed interest in the five-sixths of the world that is still developing, famously christened the "Third World" in the dawn of the Cold War to refer to those still-developing countries whose political and economic trajectories remained uncertain.[1] And although at times it seemed to have been eclipsed by security concerns superimposed by threatening superpowers or by lucrative economic opportunities elsewhere, China's identification with the developing world has never wavered. Indeed, we hope to establish that China's developing world "identity" has intensified since the Cold War ended, removing some of the urgency of security competition with the superpowers and providing an alternative reference group to fill the vacuum left by the collapse of the Communist bloc.

However, it is a new developing world, and a new China. The developing world has split in two: a Fourth World of about 50 "least-developed countries" (with a cumulative population of about a billion people) whose gross domestic product (GDP) has grown hardly at all in the past forty years, and a developing world of over 100 developing countries (totaling about four billion people) whose economic growth rate has for the past several decades outpaced that of the developed world.[2] Although China still "belongs" to this self-selected reference group in terms of per capita GDP and standards of living, in aggregate terms its inclusion there has become problematic. First, the extraordinarily swift pace of its economic development is lifting it from the ranks of other less-spectacular developers. Second, because its sheer size and population endow progress with such enormous scale effect, China has been able to loom as one of the world's largest economies (third largest by exchange rate measures, second according to purchasing power parity) within one generation.[3] Thus, by the turn of the millennium, China had become East Asia's lead-

1

ing regional growth locomotive, generating a fourth of the world's growth since 1995, able to put a man into orbit, regain Hong Kong and Macau, stymie Taiwan's drive for independence, subsidize much of the US domestic and foreign exchange deficit, help manage the incipient North Korean nuclear threat, and open wide to globalization while containing any outbreak of Islamic terrorism or Buddhist "splittism" among its national minorities. As symbolized by the triumphant 2008 Olympics, if China is still a developing country, surely it is a formidable one indeed.

This book is organized into three sections. The first explores the macro political and economic dimensions of China's new or revised role vis-à-vis the developing world. It consists of two chapters: the first, by Mel Gurtov, reviews the chronological vicissitudes of China's evolving relationship with the Third World, beginning at a time when ideology was typically an indispensable railway switchman signaling just how far and how fast China's relations with these only occasionally socialist countries might proceed. In the second, David Zweig undertakes a systematic analysis of that dimension of Chinese foreign policy that has since the death of Mao transformed its relations with the developing world more dramatically than any other: its own booming economy, specifically its trading sector (now the world's largest, comprising over half of China's GDP).

The second part of the book focuses on those developing countries in China's immediate geopolitical "neighborhood," from which vantage point they may be expected to loom large on Beijing's security horizon, whatever their economic or political significance. The third section turns to those parts of the global south that are more geopolitically removed from China and whose cultural-historical ties tend to be more recent and superficial, requiring somewhat greater Chinese rhetorical emphasis on shared political-economic interests in order to foster a "harmonious world." While this may have constrained any PRC strategic aspirations, it seems to have had very little impact on burgeoning economic relations.

## China's Neighbors

Located in the heart of Asia, sharing its long national border with more countries (sixteen) than any other country in the world, China has always been particularly concerned with cultivating and preserving good relations with these borderlands (from which attacks have periodically been launched throughout Chinese history), sometimes going so far as to launch limited offensive operations in order to preserve a favorable balance of power or to enhance deterrence.[4] The end of the Cold War has considerably expanded China's policy options, assuaging ideologically based apprehension in South and Southeast Asia and creating a proliferation of new sovereign identities in the north (viz., Mongolia) and west (Kazakhstan, Kyrgyzstan, Tajikistan, and slightly more removed, Uzbekistan and Turkmenistan). In South Asia, the advent of nuclear weapons in Pakistan and India has complicated an already long, tense tangle of relations with calculations of deterrence via mutually assured destruction.

The region in which China's strategic designs are most ambitious, according to the chapter by Jörn Dosch, is Southeast Asia. There is ample historical precedent for this—most of the "tributary" or client states making up the traditional Chinese international system were located in this region. The role to which China aspires, according to Dosch, is that of a leading but benign regional power, possibly displacing the US role of offshore balancer (the "outside in" model) with an "inside out" model. And there is growing empirical evidence to suggest that this goal is not unrealistic. China's role as hub in the emerging multinational manufacturing and assembly chain puts it in an indispensable economic position, which it has augmented with interest-free loans, outgoing foreign direct investment (FDI), and developmental aid to its partners, and trade is beginning to cluster around the region's new economic "locomotive." Though still smaller than Japan's, China's GDP is much bigger than that of Southeast Asia (which barely exceeded that of South Korea in 2007), absorbing more trade and FDI and growing faster. From 1991 to 2007, trade volume between China and Association of Southeast Asian Nations (ASEAN) increased twenty-three times, from US$8.408 billion to $202.55 billion, making each the other's fourth-largest trade partner. Beginning in the 1990s, China has become much more active in those multilateral regional forums in which the United States is not involved, such as the ASEAN+3 caucus and of course the ASEAN-China Free Trade Agreement (ACFTA, formally launched in 2002 and scheduled for completion by 2010), moving from strictly economic associations to joint political and even security forums.

Regarding security, Beijing would like to eliminate the US bilateral "hub-and-spokes system" that it deems an obsolescent holdover from the Cold War era in favor of its "new security concept," a multilateral framework based on mutual trust, mutual benefit, equality, and coordination and directed largely against nontraditional security threats. China has accordingly established various military links with seven of the ASEAN ten involving various forms of security coordination—joint training exercises, defense memoranda of understanding, military aid and loans, and bilateral talks on security affairs. As in the previous US-led "hegemonic security" arrangement, leadership derives from the hegemon's ability to assure both economic and military well-being,[5] and although the former is nearer to hand than the latter, China's signature on the ASEAN's Treaty of Amity and Cooperation and the Declaration on the South China Sea, as well as such bilateral or trilateral accords as the 2005 oil exploration deal with the Philippines and Vietnam (lapsed in November 2008), are steps in this direction. Yet China is not only an impartial adjudicator but an interested party in some of these disputes: the Spratly Island territorial issue is not yet fully resolved, perhaps awaiting only discovery of more large subsurface oil deposits to resurface, and the issue of hydropower development upstream of the Mekong and other rivers is one in which China is seeking bilateral hydropower-sharing deals with its neighbors in hopes of disarming trepidation about adverse downstream environmental consequences. Yet "smile" or "charm" diplomacy, accompanied by Confucius institutes, tourism, and other manifestations of soft power, have thus far been paying rich dividends.

The PRC has long taken an active interest in South Asia, initially as friend of India (which was among the first to recognize Beijing) in forming the nonaligned bloc, an early landmark in the formation of a distinct Third World identity. In these early years, India still led China in developmental indicators (though both were among the world's least-developed countries), and in developing the Panchsheel, or Five Principles of Peaceful Coexistence, they jointly molded the ideological content of peaceful nonalignment and established the basis for the noninterventionist, latitudinarian strain of Chinese foreign policy that coexisted with the militant Maoist revolutionary strain and has since constituted the enduring cornerstone of Chinese foreign policy (having been written into the 1982 PRC Constitution). Following the flight of the Dalai Lama entourage to its Indian sanctuary in Daramsalah and the 1962 Sino-Indian border clash (in which India sustained significant territorial losses), the relationship soured, as Lawrence Saez and Crystal Chang relate in their chapter. China now assumed the role of outside balancer, helping to counterbalance subregional bipolar hegemony by supporting Pakistan, then Bangladesh, Nepal, and other smaller powers against India, which in turn signed a friendship treaty with the Soviet Union in 1971. Beginning in the 1980s, there have been serious attempts to negotiate the border dispute, especially after Rajiv Gandhi's 1988 visit to China (the first prime ministerial visit since 1954), which resulted, among other things, in the establishment (in 1991) of a regular meeting forum to discuss such difficult issues. Despite slow but steady progress on many bilateral issues (India has recognized Chinese sovereignty in Tibet, and China recognized Indian sovereignty in Sikkim, though the latter remains somewhat equivocal), the territorial dispute remains unresolved, and India's May 1998 nuclear test, initially justified (by Defense Minister George Fernandes) in terms of a "China threat," revived old suspicions. The nuclear issue continues to freight the relationship, Saez contends, particularly in the context of recent US attempts to accommodate at least some of India's nuclear ambitions in exchange for facilitating nuclear fuel supply and diffuse security support. Thus China pursues "a policy of *reluctant competition* with India, *contingent cooperation* with Pakistan, Bangladesh, and Sri Lanka, and *secretive co-optation* with Nepal, the Maldives and Myanmar."[6] China continues to cultivate Myanmar (Burma) and Nepal and to cooperate with Pakistan and other subcontinental rivals, but no longer at the risk of peripheral destabilization (e.g., no longer backing Islamabad's position on Kashmir). There have already been three wars between India and Pakistan, and China's more cautious stance since 1998 reflects calculations that another would be more risky now that both have a nuclear first-strike capability. Traces of the old rivalry for leadership of the Third World are still visible but now in more realist form—in the cultivation of Myanmar, for example; in competitive bids for energy stakes throughout the Third World (which China has been winning); or in India's quest for a permanent seat on a reorganized UN Security Council (which China has quietly opposed). Meanwhile, despite old rivalries, bilateral trade has been expanding rapidly, though as in many other such cases the balance of payments tilts in China's favor.

China has been engaged in Central Asia at least as long as in South or Southeast Asia, Niklas Swanström attests, though its neighbors to the west were hardly tributary states: The "journey to the west" was to a wild and exotic land, home of "barbarian" mounted nomad warriors who continually menaced China's frontiers, sometimes even seizing the reins of national leadership. Even after imperial Russia absorbed this region in the eighteenth and nineteenth centuries, some of this perilous aura survived, as in the defection of some 200,000 Uighurs into Kazakhstan during the catastrophic post–Great Leap famine. Yet this was also the route of the ancient Silk Road to the fabulous wealth of the Middle East and beyond that to Europe. Though Beijing finds Central Asia far less threatening since the Soviet Union disintegrated into fifteen sovereign states in 1991, five of which share China's border and can be dealt with separately (viz., Russia, Mongolia, Kazakhstan, Kyrgyzstan, and Tajikistan), some of its double-edged character survives. Unmoored from Soviet sovereignty, the region is now the source of both vast subterranean mineral wealth and Islamic revivalism emerging under the uneasy auspices of postcommunist secular authoritarianism. These features are, however, also of interest to both the Russian Federation to the north and the European Union, and the picture is further complicated by the unfulfilled aspirations for democratization still latent in the wake of the region's incomplete liberation upon the dissolution of the Soviet Union (as manifested in "color" or "flower" revolutions in Ukraine, Georgia, and Kyrgyzstan). In deference to Russia's still-dominant security role and ownership of most of the energy pipelines, China's strategy has been opportunistic. Beijing's bottom line is strategic denial, that is, to coordinate effective suppression of the forces of transnational terrorism/splittism, which in present circumstances entails robust support for the authoritarian status quo and deep mistrust of US or international nongovernmental organization (INGO) meddling. For the Central Asian states, China's keen new interest in the region's commercial potential dovetails nicely with Western energy needs to evoke the visionary prospect of swift enrichment. Access to this wealth has also excited multilateral interest in constructing a new land bridge integrating the Eurasian heartland with its more dynamic Asian and European peripheries.[7] Meanwhile, cross-border trade is thriving (again, balanced in China's favor), the Atasu-Alashankou oil pipeline to Kazakhstan is now in operation; a natural gas pipeline from Turkestan is planned; and in Tajikistan and Kyrgyzstan, China has invested in hydroelectric projects. In terms of soft power, Beijing has contributed developmental aid and subsidized loans to these countries.

## China and the World

Though Sino-African relations can be traced all the way back to the Tang Dynasty (618–896 AD), antedating even the famous voyage of Zheng He to the eastern coast of the continent in 1415 (from whence he sent two giraffes home for Emperor Yong'le), China first became intensively engaged during the early 1960s, when most of these erstwhile colonies became independent republics. As George Yu makes clear in Chapter 7, the PRC has always felt a strange special kinship with Africa, and it was here that many of the basic tenets of China's revolutionary Third World strategy first took operational effect. China's radical liberation rhetoric struck a sympathetic chord with Robert Mugabe's Zimbabwe African National Union liberation movement and other newly emerging African regimes, and China invested in several showcase infrastructure projects (most famously, the Tanzania-Zambia Railroad). But the subsequent Sino-Soviet dispute also split the African community between Chinese and Soviet variants of socialism, largely at Beijing's expense. Without abandoning these principles entirely, Beijing has all but abandoned its revolutionary iconoclasm since 1979 in favor of a more flexible, multifaceted policy of mutual cooperation and development. President Jiang Zemin made a tour of Africa in May 1996 in which he presented a "Five Points Proposal" establishing the terms of a new relationship with the continent, centering around reliable friendship, sovereign equality, nonintervention, mutually beneficial development, and international cooperation. The ministerial meeting Forum on China-Africa Cooperation (FOCAC), which launched in Beijing in October 2000, was the first collective dialogue between China and African countries and has since been held biennially; the third and largest Ministerial Conference and FOCAC Summit was convened in Beijing November 3–5, 2006, bringing China's "Year of Africa" to a spectacular climax. China awards from 1,500 to 2,000 scholarships to African students each year; in 2003, 1,793 African students accounted for 2.31 percent of all international students in China, while some 14,000 African officials have been trained in China since 2004; and 110,000 Chinese tourists visited Africa in 2005, double the previous year. Whereas in 1999, the total Sino-African trade volume was only US$6.5 billion, by 2007 this had mushroomed to US$74 billion, balanced (unusually) in Africa's favor since 2005, as China leapfrogged France to become Africa's second-largest trade partner (China aims to replace the United States as Africa's biggest trade partner at $100 billion by 2010). Investment seems to have accelerated significantly (with extensive government encouragement) since 2006. According to research done by Chatham House, from 1995 to 2006, Chinese national oil companies invested some $8 billion in Africa, anticipating a continuing rise in Chinese petroleum imports.[8] Investments tend to focus on areas rich in natural resources and to be linked to the export sector. Nearly a third of China's total oil imports as of 2006 come from Africa, and Beijing has skillfully used infrastructure investments, high-level visits, swift and nonconditional grants and loans, and "noninterference in internal affairs" (appreciated by African democrats as well as dictators) to facilitate access to resource rights. At the same time, China quietly overlooks human rights abuses by some of the regimes with which it does business—indeed some are in partnership with China's own state-owned enterprises (SOEs).[9] No longer backstopped by any ideological vision other than short-term mutual benefit, the relationship remains vulnerable to economic and political vicissitudes: can "win-win" suffice if those at the bottom feel the only real winners are those at the top? Though hesitant to violate its old taboo against domestic interference, China has become more sensitive to such downside risks; it now has 1,300 servicemen and police on the ground in six UN peacekeeping operations in various African states, hoping to straddle its support for African sovereign self-reliance with its commitment to be a "responsible great power."[10]

China's growing presence in the Middle East, according to Yitzhak Shichor in Chapter 8, teems with contradictions: ambivalence about the US presence there, ambivalence about Islam (because of its recent terrorist excrescence, to which China is exposed in Xinjiang) yet avid interest in economic cooperation, and last but hardly least, ambivalence about what has become the defining subregional cleavage, the Israeli-Palestinian embroilment. Shichor divides Chinese involvement in the Middle East chronologically into three phases. During the first, the Maoist national liberation phase (ca. 1950–1980), China spurned proffered Israeli recognition on ideological grounds and embraced the cause of the Palestine liberation movement, an ideologically impeccable policy so out of touch with strategic realities that it achieved very little. Of course, China at this point had very little it needed to achieve, aside from world revolution: China was economically "self-reliant" with very little commercial intercourse.

During the second phase, from the 1980s until the early 1990s, China abandoned ideological exclusivity in its foreign affairs, wresting recognition of "feudal" Saudi Arabia away from Taiwan and undertaking cooperation with even Israel for high-tech weapons development (still sub rosa at this stage, not so much for ideological reasons as to avoid breaching the Arab and Third World united front on the Palestinian issue). Although China was not yet interested in Middle Eastern oil, it saw great opportunities in construction and in the export of labor crews to these rich but underpopulated economies; it also took advantage of internecine wars (particularly the long, deadly Iran-Iraq struggle) to promote weapon sales.

During the third phase, China suddenly found itself no longer self-sufficient in oil (and within a decade, the second-largest importer in the world) and hence increasingly dependent on the major oil-producing states (particularly Iran). Chinese oil companies have been careful to diversify purchases widely and to buy production sharing agreements, using market mechanisms to lock in supply. Meanwhile, having resolved that worldwide class war is no longer inexorable, China found it ideologically possible to urge peaceful resolution of the Palestinian issue, thereby bridging (at least theoretically) the yawning split between two politically interesting and economically lucrative relationships. Despite an energy dependency (60 percent of its oil came from the Middle East by 2005) that Shichor expects only to grow, China's now fully normalized relations with Israel—a far more advanced economy than its Arab neighbors, particularly in marketable weapons technology—continues to thrive. Since normalization in 1992, annual growth in trade has averaged 40 percent, rising to US$3 billion in 2005 and projected to reach US$10 billion by 2010; China has surpassed Japan to become Israel's largest Asian trading partner. The Middle East thus perhaps best exemplifies China's postrevolutionary capability to compromise the bitterly entrenched cleavages of the world while profiting from both sides.

Nicola Phillips notes in Chapter 9 that, whereas China took Latin America into peripheral account during the Maoist era, supporting Fidel Castro (until paths diverged during the Sino-Soviet split) and Che Guevara in the late 1950s, for example, and taunting Nikita Khrushchev with cowardice after the Cuban missile crisis, the relationship was thereafter somewhat neglected relative to (say) Africa due to the obviously vast geographical and cultural distance (and sensitivity to the US Monroe Doctrine). Even after the reform and opening to the outside world, the region remained preoccupied throughout the 1980s with the mounting debt crisis economically and the third wave of democratization politically, while China initially focused on relations with the newly opened advanced market economies. Since the mid-1990s, however, China has launched an ambitious drive for economic trade and cooperation, while remaining careful not to provoke the superpower to the north. China has thus quietly ignored the recent leftward turn among half a dozen Latin American neoauthoritarian regimes, also playing down any ideological affinity with Cuba or Venezuela.[11]

Despite its recent advent, bilateral trade has expanded explosively (from US$12.6 billion in 2000 to $107 billion in 2007), as China leaped from nowhere to rank second or third among these countries' trade partners, outdistancing even Sino-African trade. In 2009, China outdistanced the United States to become Brazil's leading trade partner. Trade was initially imbalanced in favor of Latin America, driven by China's drive to import oil, tin, copper, soybeans, and other natural resources to feed its second wave of heavy industrialization in the late 1990s, but China then began to flood Latin American consumer markets with cheap, labor-intensive manufactures, triggering a shift in the balance in China's favor—and a raft of antidumping suits. While Latin American governments and exporters have been delighted by the consequent bidding up of commodity export prices, they have had three problems with the emergent China boom: First, China's reserves of cheap labor (and low currency valuation) have made it a ferocious price competitor, enabling Chinese exports to crowd Latin American products out of many of their export markets. This has been especially noticeable in the case of Mexico, which has been displaced by China as second-largest US trade partner (despite membership in the North American Free Trade Agreement). Second, by providing a good price and seemingly boundless market for resource-based Latin American exports while at the same time competitively driving them out of various higher value-added markets, China trade tends to trap these economies in the primary sector, in effect imposing the same "dependent development" of which advanced Western capitalist "core" economies have long stood accused.[12] Third, unlike in Africa, China has not yet invested much in Latin America, leading to cries of neoimperialism. Though this gives rise to some trepidation about the future, for the time being Latin American delight with booming export markets trumps anxiety about stunted long-term future developmental implications.

## Conclusion

China has changed, but the developing world has also changed. In the 1960s and 1970s, in the early dawn of postcolonial modernization, the Third World was more truly a peer group with shared dark memories of underdevelopment and brightly envisioned national futures. Yet even in this context, the path of a violent People's War advocated by Beijing found few takers. China spilled much ink and spent millions of dollars in support of national liberation, only to find that shared ideological commitment offered no reliable guide to mutually beneficial economic and political relationships.

Developing countries are now more diverse both politically and economically than ever before, and it has become more complicated to characterize China's developmental path as well. Even though China has been a brilliant economic success story, neither China nor any of the developing countries has expressed much interest in a whole-cloth appropriation of a "Beijing consensus" or Chinese developmental "model"—though China's economic success story is certainly respected, and selected aspects of China's pragmatic developmental approach have aroused growing interest. The relationship, thriving economically as never before, has grown in many ways disenchanted, secularized, commercialized. But China seems to retain from its revolutionary heritage a genuine if ideologically obscure conviction that the future of the world still lies with the less developed countries. Thus China has been quietly responsive in its own way to calls to become a "responsible stakeholder." China's bureaucratically uncomplicated loans and aid, its proliferating infrastructure investment projects, its participation in UN peacekeeping operations have made a substantive contribution to Third World development. Beijing's renewed economic commitment to the less developed—bolstered, it is true, by its own developmental needs—may have even had a certain bandwagon effect on eleemosynary efforts in advanced Western democracies as well—bolstered in this case by a jealous concern with China's geostrategic inroads. In the wake of the current financial meltdown in the Western capitalist economies, China's bet on development may prove most prescient, both for China and for the developing world.

## Notes

1. The term "Third World" (*le tiers monde*) was coined by French demographer Alfred Sauvy in an article published in *L'Observateur* on April 14, 1952. Like the commoners of the Third Estate in the French Revolution, he wrote, the Third World was "ignored, exploited, scorned." First gaining currency after being used at the Bandung Conference of African and Asian countries at Bandung in 1955 to characterize a new direction in world politics, the term has remained controversial.

2. Paul Collier, *The Bottom Billion: Why the Poorest Countries Are Failing and What Can Be Done About It* (New York: Oxford University Press, 2007).

3. According to 2008 figures from the International Monetary Fund.

4. See Allen S. Whiting, *The Chinese Calculus of Deterrence: India and Indochina* (Ann Arbor: University of Michigan Press, 1975).

5. See Robert Gilpin, *War and Change in World Politics* (New York: Cambridge University Press, 1981), inter alia.

6. Lawrence Saez, "China's Emergence and South Asia: Theoretical Linkages Between Multilateralism and Peripheral Stability," Paper presented at the Instituto do Oriente conference, Lisbon, Portugal, June 17–19, 2008.

7. Nicklas Norling and Niklas Swanström, "The Virtues and Potential Gains of Continental Trade in Eurasia," *Asian Survey* 47 (2007): 351–373.

8. Alex Vines, "China in Africa: A Mixed Blessing?" *Current History* 106, no. 700 (May 2007): 213–219.

9. For example, the Mineworkers Union of Zambia has estimated that at least seventy-one people died in Zambian mining accidents in 2006, many of them in copper mines controlled by Chinese businesses. Hu Jintao was forced to cancel a visit to the Chinese-run Chambesi copper mine during his February 2007 visit to Zambia because of fears of demonstrations by workers protesting low wages, unsafe working conditions, and so on. Vines, "China in Africa".

10. Bates Gill and James Reilly, "Tenuous Hold of China Inc in Africa," *Atlantic Quarterly* 30, no. 3 (Summer 2007): 37–52.

11. Which does not lead China to ignore obvious commercial opportunities. Cuba is turning to Chinese companies rather than Western ones to modernize its crippled

transportation system at a cost of more than US$1 billion, continuing a trend that has made Beijing Cuba's second-largest trading partner after Venezuela in 2005.

12. There are some exceptions, of course—Volkswagen's branch factories in Brazil, for example, produce components for assembly of the Santana 2000 and Polo models in the Shanghai plant, linking Brazil to a multinational manufacturing and assembly chain.

# 2

## Changing Perspectives and Policies

### Mel Gurtov

At a time when China's economic rise has enabled it to become a true global political force for the first time since 1949, it may be useful to recall that for the first generation of Chinese communist leaders, China's world was considered threatening and insecure. The revolution had succeeded against all odds, and in the aftermath of a world war, an emerging cold war was making the task of rebuilding the country along socialist lines daunting. "New China" faced monumental political and economic challenges similar to those faced by many underdeveloped countries. In addition, the United States, having "lost" China to Mao Zedong's forces, was determined to do all that it could to make life difficult for Mao. The faithfulness of China's principal ally, the Soviet Union, was in doubt despite rhetoric of proletarian solidarity and "leaning to one side." China would have to find its place in Asian and international affairs by somehow integrating different roles: as a developing country, a socialist country, and a revolutionary country. That proved a difficult juggling act.

### China First

The Third World has always occupied a special, almost mythical place in Chinese communist thinking about world affairs. Early on, Chinese communist leaders viewed their revolution in global terms. National liberation, Mao explained, would mean not only the defeat of Japanese aggression; it would also "help the people of other countries. Thus in wars of national liberation, patriotism is applied internationalism."[1] The Chinese perception was that the country's extreme poverty, class differences, and history of capitalist penetration as well as resistance to imperialism all created special ties with the developing world. This view also lent itself to the belief that China was a more appropriate development model for Third World countries than the Soviet Union—a belief that helped shatter the Sino-Soviet alliance.

A second component of early Chinese ideas about the developing world was its centrality in the struggle between East and West. As Mao famously predicted in 1946, the United States could not attack the Soviet Union until it had "subjugated" the "vast zone which includes many capitalist, colonial and semi-colonial countries in Europe, Asia and Africa."[2] This "intermediate zone," as later Chinese commentaries identified it, lent strategic importance to the developing world in two senses: as a barrier to US imperialism's ambitions of global domination, and as an element of support of China's own defense against the United States. Here, the Chinese relied as always on their own experiences. US imperialism would come to no good end in trying to dominate the developing world because, like the Japanese who invaded China, "all reactionaries . . . are paper tigers."[3] Resistance to such external pressures was the appropriate response, and thus to the extent China could support revolutions against colonial or proimperialist governments abroad, China would become more secure. This was not meant to convey blanket Chinese commitments to antigovernment groups abroad, however. Self-reliance, another product of China's revolutionary experience, was proposed as the guideline for both making revolution and developing a country's economy.

Beyond shared experiences lay shared interests. Mao and his colleagues saw in the developing world opportunities to promote common political stands in international fora, such as opposition to great-power interventions, elimination of nuclear weapons, peaceful settlement of international disputes, equitable North-South relations, recovery of Taiwan, and the Chinese seat in the UN.

These three functions of the developing world—as a reflection of the Chinese model of revolutionary development, as a deterrent of China's enemies, and as a supporter of China's international policies—should be understood within the context of China's *domestic* political and economic priorities. As a former People's Republic of China (PRC) foreign minister once put it, "diplomacy is the extension of internal affairs."[4] From the vantage point of China's modern history, this view makes perfect sense: China's constant struggle for international acceptance, independence, and security from foreign intervention always depended above all on the legitimacy and stability of its domestic institutions, and on the success of its economy. Thus, whether in 1919 at the time of the May 4 Movement, or in Mao's duels with the United States and the Soviet Union, or since the start of Deng Xiaoping's policy of reform and opening (*gaige kaifang*), Chinese leaders have been fixed on the notion that the purpose of foreign policy is *to protect and promote China's socialist development and thus its security and recognition of its important place in the world.* Regardless of how Chinese leaders have defined socialist development, and no matter which political themes have dominated in particular times—from

"never forget class struggle" in Mao's day to "harmonious society" today—
they have conducted foreign policy in ways that seek to maintain control over
the pace, methods, and strategy of economic development and political
change. The foreign-policy dimension of that determination has consistently
been to avoid dependence and protect China's freedom of action—to "keep the
initiative in our own hands," as a slogan of the 1970s put it.

## United Front

Central to China's identification of the developing world in Mao's time was
the concept of "contradictions" with China's enemies. The chief enemy was
"imperialism" (referring to the United States and its allies, and later to the
Union of Soviet Socialist Republics [USSR]), and the analysis of contradictions with imperialism usually identified primary and secondary types. The developing world's place in this schema was always important and sometimes
primary; Mao's prediction in 1946 that the intermediate zone would be the
chief contesting ground of US-Soviet rivalry proved accurate. Consequently,
until the Suez crisis of 1956, when contradictions "among the imperialists"
(the United States, Britain, and France) became acute, Chinese analyses depicted the primary contradiction in the world as being the one between imperialism and the developing world. Mao would say in those days that
Washington's "main purpose is to be the tyrant of the intermediate zone."[5]
With war raging in Vietnam throughout the 1960s, the contradiction between
imperialism and developing countries invariably stood out in Chinese analyses, necessitating—as in revolutionary times—formation of a united front.[6]

The escalation of Sino-Soviet tensions throughout the 1960s extended the
primary contradiction to one between imperialism and "social-imperialism"
(i.e., the USSR) on one hand and the developing world on the other. In fact,
during that decade the competition with Moscow for Third World leadership
gradually overtook concern about building a united front against "US imperialism."[7] Soviet troops invaded Czechoslovakia, justified by the Brezhnev
Doctrine that Chinese leaders believed was ultimately aimed at them. Meantime, the Vietnam War moved toward defeat for the United States and eventual withdrawal, and President Richard Nixon prepared the way for a historic
visit to Beijing. Mao thus proclaimed his "three worlds" thesis in which the
USSR was depicted as China's most dangerous adversary.[8] China's revised
worldview now was that the chief contradiction was between the USSR and
the United States on one hand and all Second and Third World countries on the
other, with China belonging to both the socialist and developing world camps.[9]

China's identification with developing world concerns reached its height
at that time. Mao proclaimed that "revolution is the main trend in the world
today,"[10] and Premier Zhou Enlai said in 1975: "The Third World is the main

force in combating colonialism, imperialism and hegemonism."[11] Only after the start of the reform period, when the notion of class struggle *within* China was jettisoned, did Beijing's international view evolve to embrace more generalized contradictions, such as between "hegemonism" and the people of the world in the 1980s.

China established a hierarchy of the developing world. Although in the early days of the People's Republic, Chinese officials would frequently proclaim a two-worlds thesis in which countries were urged to follow China's example of choosing between the socialist and "imperialist" camps—"to remain neutral or sit on the fence is impossible," according to Liu Shaoqi[12]—in reality there were three Third Worlds: one of friends, one of enemies, and one of "genuine" neutrals. Friendly countries included not only socialist North Korea and North Vietnam, but also countries whose policies supported Chinese interests—such as diplomatic recognition of the PRC, agreement on the "five principles of peaceful coexistence" (such as noninterference and "equality and mutual benefit"),[13] support of a PRC seat in the UN in place of Taiwan, and rejection of security ties with the United States. In Asia, these countries included Burma, Ceylon, Cambodia, Pakistan, and Nepal.[14] China rewarded them with aid, trade, official visits, and in some cases friendship treaties.

Countries such as Thailand, Philippines, South Korea, and Malaysia fell into the unfriendly category, mainly due to their close relations with the United States. Chinese propaganda railed against their oppressive governments and proclaimed support of communist insurgents there. As Zhou put it in 1959, China was "ready to give support and assistance to the full extent of our capabilities to all national independence movements in Asia, Africa, and Latin America."[15] But the reality was quite different: China's actual support of revolution was more rhetorical than substantive and depended above all on the nature of state-to-state relations. In Asia, only the Vietnamese communists who fought the French and then the Americans received significant and consistent weapons support for "making revolution."[16] Likewise in Africa, the Chinese provided small amounts of aid to groups seeking independence in British Rhodesia and Portuguese Angola and Mozambique. As discussed below, China's main advice to would-be revolutionaries was to practice self-reliance.

The neutrals—countries that belonged to the nonaligned group—were the most difficult for Beijing to deal with. Here is where the penalty for "lacking a clear recognition of objective facts," as a Chinese specialist has written, was most apparent. And the penalty was "unprecedented isolation."[17] Between the major gatherings of the nonaligned countries at Bandung, Indonesia, in 1955 and Algiers in 1965, Chinese diplomats moved from quiet but effective diplomacy, emphasizing support of the five principles of peaceful coexistence, to demanding hard-line policies toward imperialist and colonialist countries. Nonalignment, in Beijing's view, meant a commitment by developing countries to joining an "international united front" but not being "a bloc by themselves."[18] The ideological and political battle with the Soviet leadership had much to do with this shift, since the competition for Third World loyalties was quite keen. Algiers was a disaster—China's effort to prevent Soviet participation failed, and the meeting had to be "postponed"—and China's tough line lost it considerable support in the developing world.[19]

China's definition of "genuine" neutrals as those countries that had "forged good relations" with the socialist camp also did not resonate well with many developing countries. Here, the Chinese drew on the Soviet experience with Marshall Tito in Yugoslavia—a false socialist whose neutrality in the Cold War represented a dangerous third force in world politics. To Mao, India was Tito's Asian equivalent, despite Delhi's early recognition of the PRC and incorporation of the five principles of peaceful coexistence in an April 1954 agreement on the status of Tibet. India's close relations with the USSR proved the undoing of relations with China. Clashes along the India-China border starting in 1959 led to escalating acrimony and open fighting in 1962. "It's no fun being a running dog," Mao would later privately say of Prime Minister Jawaharlal Nehru.[20] Indonesia, on the other hand, fit the model of a friendly neutral, at least until the crackdown on its Chinese community in 1965 amidst the abortive coup attempt by the PRC-supported Indonesian communist party. Unlike India, Indonesia was not a rival of China's for Third World leadership. It signed a friendship treaty with China in 1960, accepted the dual nationality of its Chinese population, and joined China in denouncing "neocolonialism" in Malaysia and West Irian.[21]

China during the Mao years saw itself as the most appropriate model and most reliable friend of the underdeveloped countries. "The path taken by the Chinese people in defeating imperialism and its lackeys and in founding the People's Republic of China is the path that should be taken by the peoples of many colonial and semi-colonial countries in their fight for national independence and people's democracy," said Liu Shaoqi.[22] He also said: "The Chinese revolution has a great attraction for peoples in all the backward countries that have suffered, or are suffering, from imperialist oppression. They feel that they should also be able to do what the Chinese have done."[23] These early statements seemed largely born of postrevolutionary idealism. But they also reflected a *moral* dimension of PRC foreign policy that continues to this day: the belief, shared by early Chinese self-strengtheners, that the Chinese model of international politics, articulated in the 1950s in terms of the five principles, represented a viable and ethical alternative to Western models based on power politics, the use of force, and lack of respect for sovereign equality.[24]

In later years, the self-reliance of China's revolutionary victory would be the overriding theme, both with respect to making revolution and nation-building.[25] Chinese leaders came to recognize that neither China's revolution nor its economic model could be easily copied. They may also have learned a lesson from the diplomatic disaster of the Cultural Revolution period (1966–

1976), when Red Guard factionalism played havoc with China's foreign ministry, disputes erupted with more than thirty countries (a number of which broke relations with China), and all but one PRC ambassador was recalled to Beijing.[26] Noteworthy about *both* aspects of self-reliance is how much they reflected changing domestic as well as international developments—domestically, China's shift from reliance on the Soviet development model to self-reliant development by 1958, and Mao's attempt to perpetuate the revolutionary heritage thereafter; internationally, China's simultaneously hostile relationships with Moscow and Washington.

Indeed, one cannot escape the conclusion that even as Third World events were closely followed and heavily influenced Mao's and his colleagues' foreign-policy strategy, their thinking and their highest priority grew out of internal political and economic circumstances. The PRC's overriding objective was to create external conditions conducive to carrying out Mao's radical socialist development program. Its revolutionary rhetoric, assistance to the Vietnamese communists in their wars against France and the United States, intervention in Korea, Bandung diplomacy, and criticisms of Soviet international policies were all designed out of defensiveness against "US imperialism" and later, Soviet "social-imperialism."[27] Protecting the revolution at home, in a word, always had priority over projecting the revolution abroad. It still does.

## The Reform Period, 1978–1989

> *China is a major country as well as a minor one. . . . China is one of the permanent members of the Security Council of the United Nations. Its vote belongs firmly to the Third World, to the underdeveloped countries. We have said more than once that China belongs to the Third World. It will still belong to the Third World even in the future, after it is developed. China will never become a superpower.*[28]
>
> —Deng Xiaoping, 1984

According to Deng, China's entry into the new era of "reform and opening" at the end of 1978 meant that the country would require a "peaceful international environment."[29] "Without a peaceful environment, how much construction can there be?" Deng asked.[30] "A trillion US dollars [in GNP]! That will be our national strength."[31] In a talk with Japanese industry leaders in 1985, Deng stressed the need for long-term peace and observed, in contrast with Mao, that the danger of a major war had receded, allowing China to move forward. The two great issues in world affairs, Deng said, were "first, peace, and second, economic development. The first involves East-West relations, while the second involves North-South relations. Of these, "North-South relations are the key question" because "unless their economic problems are solved, it will be hard for all the Third World countries to develop and for the developed countries to advance further." Here, he said, is where China's own development entered the picture, since a China that expands its role in international trade would be able to import more from the developed countries.[32] In addition, increased South-South exchanges were important. "The developed countries should appreciate that greater development of their economies is impossible without growth in the economies of Third World countries."[33]

Deng's theme of peace and development signaled dramatic changes in China's foreign policy based on a fairly optimistic reading of international prospects. First, it meant an "independent and autonomous" (*duli zizhu*) policy stance, with a commitment for the first time to multilateralism in foreign affairs (*duobian waijiao*) and a reaffirmation of the five principles of peaceful coexistence as China's fundamental foreign-policy guideline.[34] These positions became evident in several concrete ways: support of the UN Charter and processes; alignment with the New International Economic Order being demanded by the nonaligned community, though now in terms of making economic globalization work for underdeveloped countries; Chinese membership in the World Bank and the International Monetary Fund (IMF); attention to transnational security problems; and adoption of policies toward the USSR parallel with (but not in alliance with) the United States.[35] Second, peace and development also meant acceptance of "one world, two systems"—that is, globalization of the world economy, but with national interests rather than global integration still determining the policies of states.[36] What this idea portended was that the common ground for national security would be economic security—in China, based on the "four modernizations." Close PRC economic ties and active diplomatic engagement with the West were now essential features of foreign policy; a strong China was simply impossible without the West's help. "The world today has become [a single] entity and no country can practice economic isolationism," a Chinese commentator said early in the 1980s. "The new technological revolution which is emerging in the world makes it all the more necessary for us to build closer economic relations with all countries. . . . "[37]

Third, in terms of the developing world, China's new diplomacy promised pragmatism. It meant, first of all, that China would work to restore international relationships that had been damaged by the Cultural Revolution and other mistaken "leftist" policies. At the start of the 1990s, Chinese leaders such as Premier Li Peng journeyed around China's rim in a largely successful effort at normalizing ties with neighbors. This *zhoubian* (omnidirectional) diplomacy repaired relations with India, Indonesia, and Vietnam; implemented confidence-building measures with the USSR/Russia; and established new relationships with the Central Asian post-Soviet states and with South Korea. Another aspect of diplomacy was identifying shared development interests with the Third World in multilateral settings. Deng Xiaoping's theme of widening development gaps between North and South became a mainstay of Chinese commentaries. Lastly, the new diplomacy meant that China, considering itself a nonaligned country as well as an emerging great power, would adopt policies toward the Third World "according to the rightness or wrongness of each international situation" rather than "by dividing Third World states into 'progressive' and 'reactionary'" categories.[38]

Taken together, these were indeed far-reaching departures from the Chinese perspectives and policies of previous decades. They were accompanied by equally dramatic changes in China's military-industrial complex, including troop and budget cuts in the People's Liberation Army and a major military-to-civilian (*jun zhuan min*) industrial conversion program. China by no means abandoned ongoing military programs related to developing world interests: It was an important contributor to Iran's and Pakistan's nuclear- and chemical-weapons programs,[39] for example, and it was among the top five sellers of conventional weapons to developing countries.[40] But as events in the next decade would show, there was now a clear emphasis in China's foreign policy on challenging the new global order while working within it: "one world, two systems; multi-polarization in politics and economics; competition and coexistence," as Huan Xiang said.[41]

## Beijing Consensus?

The 1990s began with two extraordinary developments: the last days of the Soviet system, and war in the Persian Gulf. Whereas for the United States, these events signaled the start of a "new world order" (in the words of President George H. W. Bush), for China they meant a "new *international* order."[42] Once again Chinese analysts drew a distinction between the old order characterized by power politics (the Yalta System) and hegemonism, on one hand, and the new order that should be governed by the five principles and "peace and development" on the other. Deng Xiaoping was quoted as having said: "I recommend that the Five Principles of Peaceful Coexistence, which were formulated by us Asians in the 1950s, should serve as the norms for the New International Order for a very long period of time to come."[43] In that new order, the stress was on two trends: preserving state sovereignty[44] and working within a *multipolar* world.[45]

Despite their high degree of interdependence with the world economy, the Chinese still find themselves at odds with a US-dominated world order. Again, too, they look to support from within the developing world, where many governments reject liberal political tenets such as the rule of law and respect for human rights, and instead hold fast to the idea of the strong state and unqualified sovereignty—a "world without the West":

This world rests on a rapid deepening of interconnectivity within the developing world—in flows of goods, money, people and ideas—that is surprisingly autonomous from Western control, resulting in the development of a new, parallel international system, with its own distinctive set of rules, institutions and currencies of power. This system empowers those within it to take what they need from the West while routing around the American-led world order. The rising powers have begun to articulate an alternative institutional architecture. . . . This alternative order . . . proposes to manage international politics through a neo-Westphalian synthesis comprised of hard-shell states that bargain with each other about the terms of their external relationships, but staunchly respect the rights of each to order its own society, politics and culture without external interference. . . . Inviolable sovereignty in the World without the West rejects key tenets of "modern" liberal internationalism and particularly any notion of global civil society or public opinion justifying political or military intervention in the affairs of the state.[46]

The alternative order has been christened the "Beijing Consensus" by some writers. It is framed as a counterpoint to the so-called Washington Consensus: the coordinated efforts of the World Bank, the IMF, and the US Treasury Department to ensure that development assistance flows only to governments that lower tariffs, open their doors to foreign investment, cut state subsidies, and privatize state-owned firms.[47] Ideologically, the Washington Consensus presumes that marketization will lead to democratization. By contrast, the Beijing Consensus avoids rule making and (at least in theory) the imposition of rigid standards of political or economic conduct on China's partners. It is guided by a proclaimed noninterference in the affairs of other states (specifically, their civil wars and human-rights violations), support of state-centered development, and removal of conditionality from trade, aid, and investment policies. China's economic diplomacy in Africa is a perfect illustration.[48]

## The New Security Concept

China's "new security concept" links the principles of the Beijing Consensus with a foreign-policy platform that clearly aims at offering an alternative to a Western-dominated world order. PRC leaders give particular attention to three principles: respect for the sovereignty of all nations, emphasis on "mutual interest and common prosperity," and promotion of mutual trust and nonhegemonic behavior among states.[49] Speaking in Indonesia in 2003, Hu Jintao called for "a new security concept that embraces the principles of equality, dialogue, trust and cooperation, and a new security order should be established to ensure genuine mutual respect, mutual cooperation, consensus through consultation and peaceful settlement of disputes, rather than bullying, confrontation, and imposition of one's own will upon others. Only in that way can countries coexist in amity and secure their development."[50] Here is another variation on the theme of the five principles of peaceful coexistence—"multilateralism with Asian characteristics,"[51] as one analyst has characterized it. The security dimension is the centerpiece here: Beijing has been busy forming strategic partnerships of a consultative character (such as the Shanghai Cooperation Organization [SCO] and ASEAN+3),[52] and in each instance "noninterference" is proclaimed to be the guiding principle.

Distinct from Western alliances, these partnerships do not involve binding security commitments and basing rights. Instead, China seeks to promote ties founded on confidence building, consultation, and mutually beneficial economic development. But there remains a "realist" dimension here: the cultivation of positive relations with those states that either resist or do not fully accept US foreign-policy leadership or the values that underlie the Washington Consensus. China is still an arms supplier to select developing countries—in recent years, the main recipients have been (in order) Pakistan, Bangladesh, Iran, and Namibia—though arms exports are much less now than in the 1990s and thereafter than in the 1980s.[53] The People's Liberation Army (PLA) has extended its reach in a different way, establishing military attaché offices (ninety-nine in 1999) abroad and many more military exchange programs and official visits than previously.[54]

The new security concept may be considered a repetition of earlier appeals to developing world governments on the basis of a common political and moral interest in preventing great-power interference in their internal affairs. The noninterference principle, newly empowered by the US "war on terror" and the invasion of Iraq, essentially urges governments to reject US hegemony even if they retain diplomatic and commercial ties with the United States. It is no less a moral choice than a political choice, one prominent PRC scholar has written—but not the kind of morality associated with Western thought, and not the kind of "noninterference" that would keep *China* from profiting. Whereas the Western system of international relations remains founded on power politics and unequal sovereignty, this scholar asserts, the "East Asian" system is based on China's stability and the Confucian notion of reciprocity.[55]

The concept of an East Asian system is hardly adequate, however—first, because the alternative order China seeks goes beyond East Asia and Confucian values, and second, because (contrary to the view quoted at length above) it encompasses states that have liberal political institutions. In fact, China's new global reach spans two groups of Third World states. One consists of the Central Asian states in the SCO: Sudan, Equatorial Guinea, Angola, and Zimbabwe in Africa; Myanmar (Burma) and North Korea in East Asia; Iran in the Middle East; and Cuba, Venezuela, Bolivia, and Ecuador in Latin America.[56] Notable about this group is that it includes a number of pariah states—those whose policies on human rights and/or nuclear-weapon proliferation have made them international outcasts, except to China. These governments obviously welcome the Chinese doctrine of absolute sovereignty. From Beijing's point of view, although concessions to international opinion may sometimes be unavoidable—for example, China has agreed to UN sanctions against Iran and North Korea, has criticized North Korea's missile and nuclear-weapon tests in July and October 2006, and has supported a peacekeeping force in the Darfur region of Sudan—the weight of its policies falls heavily on the side of noninterference, which translates to inaction and obstructionism. Thus, while China supported the mission in Darfur, and mildly criticized the Burmese military's crackdown on human-rights protesters, these were no more than gestures. When the International Criminal Court voted to issue a warrant for the arrest of Sudan's president on war crimes and other charges, China opposed it; and China vetoed a US-backed Security Council resolution in January 2007 that condemned the Burmese junta.[57] Worse yet, as two writers who argue that China *has* changed its policies nevertheless acknowledge, China continues to sell arms and transfer military technologies to these dictatorships. "By 2007," these writers observe, "China had become the largest trading partner of Iran, North Korea, and Sudan and the second-largest of Burma and Zimbabwe."[58] (One senior PRC official has justified this by stating that politics and business must be kept separate.[59])

In the second group of Third World friends are countries that are on good terms with the United States, may even have military ties with it, and in some cases are democratizing. Regardless, all have developed significant economic partnerships with Beijing. These include Thailand, South Korea, Vietnam, and the Philippines in East Asia;[60] Pakistan and Sri Lanka in South Asia; Saudi Arabia in the Middle East; Nigeria and South Africa in Africa; and Brazil and Argentina in Latin America.[61]

These categories suggest the usual workings of political and economic self-interest as China reaches out. What is truly new about the new security system is the extent to which it has promoted China's involvement in multilateral diplomacy. Although Chinese leaders retain some suspicion of regional and international organizations that act mainly at the behest of the United States, they have come to believe that working through such institutions will often enhance Chinese influence and China's image among developing countries more than will the usual bilateral diplomacy. Thus we find China operating in multilateral settings such as the Montreal Protocol and the Kyoto Protocol on global environmental problems;[62] the ASEAN process—including the ASEAN Regional Forum and accessions to a code of conduct on the disputed South China Sea islets (in 2002) and to the Treaty of Amity and Concord (in 2003)—and the SCO on regional security and political issues; the China-ASEAN Free Trade Agreement, World Trade Organization, World Bank, Asian Development Bank, and IMF on regional and international trade, aid, and investment matters; the Six-Party Talks on North Korea's nuclear-weapons program; and the Comprehensive Test Ban Treaty. In the UN, China has come round to support peacekeeping operations: It now has about 2,000 troops in ten UN peacekeeping operations, second only to France among the five permanent members.[63] And China has used its veto in the Security Council far less often than has the United States. "Multilateralism is the only choice for solving global problems," a Chinese foreign ministry official told a conference of the nonaligned states.[64] To be sure, China does not act through multilateral groups more than other major countries; but its willingness to trust in a multilateral process on many important issues to produce gains for its national interests represents something of a revolution in Chinese thinking.[65]

## A Concluding Assessment

The central argument in this chapter is that we should understand China's developing world policies in essentially domestic terms—that is to say, as a source of support for China's sovereignty and internal security. "Foreign affairs serves domestic politics," one Chinese scholar has written, and the question for leaders has always been how to realize that "longstanding strategic objective."[66] As Deng said in 1987, "Without political stability and unity, it would be impossible for us to go on with construction, let alone to pursue the open policy."[67] Today, of course, China is in position to capitalize on domestic stability, unparalleled external security, and new wealth to devote enormously greater attention and resources to Third World and other international affairs than it could in the Mao years. At the same time, the developing world's strategic role is no longer as vital to China as it had once been. Hegemonism still exists, but imperialism is gone, and the need of a "broad united front" against it is no longer necessary or even possible. Besides, China no longer need assume a defensive stance in world affairs. "In essence," one Chinese scholar has said, "the whole concept of national security (including economic security) manifests departure from the previous one which was based on security of existence. What China pursues now is a security of sustained development."[68]

Thus, while China's policy options and capabilities in the developing world have changed significantly over time, its perspective and aims under Mao, Deng, and their successors have remained fairly constant:

- *To gain political support against threats to sovereignty ("hegemonism") and in favor of staples of Chinese foreign policy such as "one China" and the five principles of peaceful coexistence.* China still regards itself as a Third World and developing-country leader. The five people's principles remain the gold standard of Chinese diplomacy, even as the principles have been reinvented in forms such as the new security concept, China's "peaceful rise," "harmonious world," and the Beijing Consensus. Protection of sovereignty is central to China's appeal and its identity.[69]

- *To present an alternative model of political and economic development: managed globalization.* China sees itself as a model for Third World development, but not through self-reliance. Instead, it is a model of how economic globalization can be tied to the national interest of rapid, controlled, export-led but state-protected development.
- *To acquire resources for China's own economic development.* No matter to which Third World region one turns, figures on Chinese investments abroad, trade, and aid generally are dramatically higher since 2000 than ever before.[70] Energy and industrial resources have become the driving forces behind China's economic diplomacy, supplemented by strong PRC assistance programs for public works projects.[71] Oil is the centerpiece of China's resource extraction: It is importing somewhat less than half its oil from the Middle East, but is busy diversifying sources, with rising oil imports from Africa (led by Angola), Europe (Russia), and Asia-Pacific (Vietnam). In exchange for multibillion dollar loans, Chinese oil companies have also bought stakes in a number of oil companies in developing countries, such as in Kazakhstan, Brazil, and Venezuela.[72] These latter two deals reflect another new Chinese reality: Latin America has become a major economic target, with development loans and investments that have helped elevate China to second place behind the United States as a trade partner.[73]
- *Bilaterally and through multilateral groups, to acquire leverage against Western-dominated groups.* Chinese strategic thinking is no longer framed by contradictions, class analysis, formation of a united front, or an obsession with "imperialism." A secure China is a self-confident and less vituperative China. "Hegemonism" still threatens; but China now has various means to contend with it. Seeking the support of friendly developing countries remains useful for strategic purposes: The SCO, with its joint military exercises, is a good example.[74] But increasingly, China is relying on its soft power to exert influence. Its checkbook diplomacy has become prominent in the developing world: China's aid to Africa is comparable to US, British, and French assistance, and possibly is second to Japan's in Southeast Asia.[75] Since the start of the global economic recession in late 2008, moreover, China has aimed its economic power at its chief partners in the developed world. Aligning with the so-called BRIC countries (Brazil, India, Russia, China), China is becoming ever more insistent on the need for policy changes such as those noted immediately below. We can expect to hear China's voice even more frequently in the future from within other such loose multilateral groups, such as the Group of Twenty Finance Ministers and Central Bank Governors (G-20) economic group, China-ASEAN Free Trade Agreement, and the China-Africa Forum.
- *To speak with one voice as a developing-country leader.* Where its own interests are served, China will unite with other developing coun-

tries against the policies of the major economic powers. We see this in China's stand on developed-country trade protectionism,[76] global warming,[77] and reform of the international financial order.[78]

## Potential Issues

China's successful identification with Third World interests and goals is by no means problem-free, however. For one thing, PRC policy rests on the assumption that the sovereignty issue is a winning formula for getting and keeping friends in the Third World. Appealing on the basis of "respect for sovereignty" is surely welcome by neighbors that have had to deal with a revolutionary China in the past. But the appeal does not square with China's notion of being a "good global citizen." Supporting international norms, such as nonproliferation of weapons of mass destruction, protection of the environment, and respect for human rights are issues that may require, as Kofi Annan constantly stressed when he was UN secretary-general, accepting limits on state sovereignty. China's friendly and profitable dealings with oppressive regimes such as in Sudan, Iran, Zimbabwe, and Myanmar are also irresponsible from a global-community viewpoint. (Needless to add, China is not alone in disregarding international norms in favor of narrow self-interest.) "Sovereignty" is largely a smokescreen behind which China can hide, all the while engaging in the pretense that it is a Third World loyalist. Inevitably, some Third World governments will agree, but among those governments are perhaps the worst offenders when it comes to humane governance and lawful behavior.

Second, the China model of development cannot be easily emulated for obvious reasons such as China's size and international influence, presocialist history of entrepreneurship, and attractiveness to foreign investors. While Chinese officials pointed out during the Asian financial crisis that foreign direct investment (FDI) was a much more reliable way than short-term portfolio funds to finance economic growth,[79] FDI has a history of creating dependent development in Third World countries. Further, the Chinese model seeks to spur production and consumption, with much built-in waste, pollution, and income inequity. To be sure, China has lifted millions out of poverty, a marvelous achievement for so large a population. But the costs in public health, regional and rich-poor disparities, resource depletion, and local-level corruption may be—in fact, *should* be—unacceptable at international *and* national levels. Thus, if one wants to talk about the Chinese model's appeal to the developing world, it would be to their elites far more than to their farmers, miners, and factory workers.

There are still other limitations. China's "soft power" has markedly improved its image in and beyond the Third World, particularly in Southeast Asia. Strong economic ties, including aid programs, have generally helped erode the notion of a China threat.[80] But the picture of China as a good Third World citizen is sometimes bound to clash with China's insistence on being treated as a great power, for example, on nuclear-weapons testing, territorial disputes (such as in the South China Sea[81]), and trade.[82] In the future, China's all-out search for energy may be blunted by nationalistic regimes demanding a higher price. Furthermore, a falling out with Third World countries such as happened in the 1960s and 1970s—war with India, the diplomatic setback at Algiers, tense relations during the Cultural Revolution, and war with Vietnam—could happen again. China's strategic competition with India presents one such possibility.[83] Another is in Southeast Asia, where regional organizing via the ASEAN process may find China at odds with its neighbors over how an "East Asian Community" should evolve and which countries should be included.[84]

China, after all, may say it is a Third World country, and it certainly has many characteristics typical of one, but it is becoming richer, and its embrace of rules-based globalization and outward economic orientation (as an investor nation, aid giver, and global marketer, for instance) fits the profile of a First World state.[85] As such, China may have to make economic decisions based on the bottom line rather than follow the no-strings-attached practice under the Beijing Consensus. This shift already seems to be occurring in China's investments in Africa.[86] In that and other ways, China may run afoul of the kinds of problems that have come to bedevil the Washington Consensus: local nationalism, popular hostility, and negative international reputation.[87] Governments that receive Chinese assistance may regret having to depend so heavily on it. "Aid" is never free (in China's case, aid mainly means loans and government-backed investments, both of which can be called in); there is a price to be paid that goes beyond repayment of principal and interest. Beijing will want some kind of political payoff on its money, and some recipients may resist giving it. These governments, even the most repressive among them, also have to keep an eye on their publics. There is always a tipping point beyond which too close an association with a foreign government carries major disadvantages. Chinese money and Chinese workers may become a target of local dissatisfaction in economically difficult times, and when the right to organize is denied. At that point, people might protest the Chinese presence in the same way people rioted against the IMF in Latin America when the price of basic commodities skyrocketed.[88] China's appeal to sovereignty may just backfire, particularly during times of worldwide economic hardship.

A final consideration is the meaning of China's Third World policies for the West—the United States in particular—and the global community. The Beijing Consensus clearly resonates with Third World governments as they seek to come to grips with globalization. It also feeds Chinese nationalism in its own (and latest) encounter with the West. Many Chinese intellectuals, including students,[89] see the United States as again seeking to contain China. But they also see China as uncontainable, the rising star in the international firmament. The developing world's support is, once more, an important part of China's resistance to a world dominated by the United States and its developed-country allies. China is not, however, seeking to establish an alternative, renminbi-denominated "world" or "balance" against the United States. Beijing is still operating very much within the parameters of a single world economy and the international institutions that were created after World War II. But if China's preferences are not met creatively and sympathetically by the West, a virulent, confrontational Chinese nationalism tied to supportive Third World countries might quickly surface, leading us back to the future: another cold war.

As of yet, China has failed to show that the Beijing Consensus does better than the Washington Consensus in addressing the deepest *human and environmental* sources of global insecurity. At bottom, China's approach to the Third World is just as self-interested as the West's, and perhaps more so. For Beijing makes no pretense at giving priority to environmental decline, rich-poor and male-female income and opportunity gaps, and human-development problems that flow from widespread poverty, such as lack of access to drinkable water, education, and basic health care. Nor has Beijing's consensus sought to embrace problems of governance that typically underlie human-security issues, such as official corruption, excessive military spending, repression of dissent, and suppression of ethnic and other minorities and religions. Proponents of the strong state will care little about such omissions from Chinese policy, arguing that it shows the PRC's respect for the noninterference principle. But other state leaders, and their domestic opponents, will see in these omissions the Achilles heel of the Beijing Consensus: the sacrifice of real long-term security for immediate, and unequal, advantages.

## Notes

1. "The Role of the Chinese Communist Party in the National War" (October 1938), in Mao Zedong, *Selected Readings from the Works of Mao Tsetung* (Peking: Foreign Languages Press, 1971), p. 140.

2. "Talk with the American Correspondent Anna Louise Strong" (August 1946), ibid., p. 348.

3. Ibid., p. 349.

4. Qian Qichen, quoted in "China's Important Role in World Affairs," *Beijing Review*, no. 42 (October 15–21, 1990), p. 12.

5. *Mao Zedong sixiang wansui* [Long Live Mao Zedong Thought], vol. 1, unpubl. ms. (Beijing: 1967), p. 245.

6. See Mao Zedong, *The Chinese Revolution and the Chinese Communist Party* (Peking: Foreign Languages Press, 1967). Mao wrote this essay in 1939 to promote the idea of a united front of all nationalistic, anti-imperialist social classes.

7. This may have been the case, for example, in Chinese policy toward Indonesia. See the vitriolic attack on Soviet policies by Peng Zhen (Peng Chen), *Speech at the Aliarcham Academy of Social Sciences in Indonesia* (Peking: Foreign Languages Press, 1965), and J. D. Armstrong, *Revolutionary Diplomacy: Chinese Foreign Policy and the United Front Doctrine* (Berkeley: University of California Press, 1977), pp. 136–137.

In any event, it is clear that China did not order and probably did not support the October 1965 coup attempt in Jakarta by the Indonesian communist party (the PKI), which led to a rupture in Indonesia-PRC relations. See Peter Van Ness, *Revolution and Chinese Foreign Policy: Peking's Support for Wars of National Liberation* (Berkeley: University of California Press, 1970), pp. 106–108.

8. *Chairman Mao's Theory of the Differentiation of the Three Worlds Is a Major Contribution to Marxism-Leninism* (Beijing: Foreign Languages Press, 1977).

9. See *Peking Review*, no. 45 (November 5–11, 1972) and no. 31 (July 29–August 4, 1973), p. 7.

10. Mao's statement was made on May 20, 1970, in response to the US intervention in Cambodia. It was repeated by China's representative to the UN, Qiao Guanhua, in a speech to the General Assembly on October 2, 1973; see *Peking Review*, no. 40 (October 5, 1973), pp. 10–11.

11. It was Zhou who also said in August 1973: "Countries want independence, nations want liberation, and the people want revolution." This became a frequently repeated slogan too.

12. Liu Shaoqi (Liu Shao-chi), *Internationalism and Nationalism* (Beijing: Foreign Languages Press, 1951), pp. 32–33. Liu was relying on Mao's 1940 essay, "On New Democracy," in which Mao had said that in the global competition between the Soviet Union and the United States, "it is inevitable that China must stand either on one side or the other. . . . in the world today 'neutrality' is becoming merely a deceptive phrase." Mao, *Selected Readings*, vol. 3, p. 135.

13. The other principles are mutual nonaggression, sovereignty and territorial integrity, and peaceful coexistence.

14. The fact that Burma's government faced various communist-party and ethnic insurgent movements was not as important to China as was its government's early recognition of Beijing.

15. Zhou Enlai, "Report on the Work of the Government," April 18, 1959, in US Consulate-General, Hong Kong, *Current Background*, no. 559 (1959), p. 59.

16. See Van Ness, *Revolution and Chinese Foreign Policy,* and Melvin Gurtov, *China and Southeast Asia—The Politics of Survival: A Study of Foreign Policy Interaction* (Lexington, MA: D. C. Heath, 1971). Of course, China's intervention in the Korean civil war in 1950 is a different matter, in that the intervention turned on what PRC leaders regarded as a direct threat to China's own security.

17. Chu Shulong, *Zhongguo waijiao zhanlue he zhengci* [China's Foreign Strategy and Policy] (Beijing: Shishi chubanshe, 2008), pp. 96–97.

18. See the *Renmin ribao* editorial of September 9, 1961, which followed conclusion of the Conference of the Heads of State or Government of Nonaligned Countries in Belgrade, Yugoslavia; translated in *Peking Review*, no. 37 (September 15, 1961), p. 5.

19. Charles Neuhauser, *Third World Politics: China and the Afro-Asian People's Solidarity Organization, 1957–1967* (Cambridge, MA: Harvard East Asian Monographs, 1968).

20. Stuart Schram, ed., *Chairman Mao Talks to the People: Talks and Letters, 1956–1971* (New York: Pantheon, 1974), p. 198.

21. See Armstrong, *Revolutionary Diplomacy*, chap. 4, and David Mozingo, *Chinese Policy Toward Indonesia, 1949–1967* (Ithaca, NY: Cornell University Press, 1976).

22. Quoted in John Gittings, *The World and China, 1922–1972* (New York: Harper & Row, 1974), p. 159.

23. Liu Shaoqi, *Ten Glorious Years* (Beijing: Foreign Languages Press, 1950), p. 1.

24. See John Cranmer-Byng, "The Chinese View of Their Place in the World: An Historical Perspective," *The China Quarterly*, no. 53 (January–March 1973), p. 69.

25. Among numerous official Chinese statements on self-reliance in revolution, surely the most prominent was Lin Biao's "Long Live the Victory of People's War!" *Peking Review*, no. 36 (September 3, 1965), which appeared at the height of US escalation of the war in Vietnam. On self-reliance in nation-building, see for example Qiao Guanhua's opening speech to the UN General Assembly on November 5, 1971, in *Peking Review*, no. 47 (November 19, 1971), p. 6.

26. For an authoritative account, see Ma Jisen, *Waijiaobu wenge jishi* [The Cultural Revolution in the Foreign Ministry] (Hong Kong: The Chinese University Press, 2003).

27. Byong-Moo Hwang and I explore this theme in *China Under Threat: The Politics of Strategy and Diplomacy* (Baltimore, MD: Johns Hopkins University Press, 1980).

28. Deng Xiaoping, *Fundamental Issues in Present-Day China* (Beijing: Foreign Languages Press, 1987), p. 83.

29. Ibid., p. 84.

30. Ibid., p. 107.

31. Ibid., p. 90.

32. Ibid., pp. 99–100.

33. Talk of May 29, 1984; ibid., p. 47.

34. Chu, *Zhongguo waijiao zhanlue*, p. 317. An "independent foreign policy" was officially adopted by the PRC leadership at the twelfth party congress in December 1982. Among numerous sources, see Foreign Minister Qian Qichen, "*Guoji xingshi xianzhu gaishan de yi nian*" [A Year of Remarkable Improvement in the International Situation], *Renmin ribao* (overseas ed.), December 17, 1988; the report on Premier Li Peng's address to an Afro-Asian conference in *Renmin ribao*, March 13, 1990; and the comments of Huan Xiang in the following notes.

35. Huan Xiang, "On Sino-US Relations," *Foreign Affairs* 60, no. 1 (Fall 1981): 35–53.

36. Huan Xiang, "World Prospects for the Years Ahead," *Renmin ribao*, December 31, 1987, and an interview of Huan Xiang in "*Dongdang, biange, bupingjing de yi nian*" [A Turbulent, Changing, Unquiet Year], *Renmin ribao*, January 2, 1988. See also the discussion by Samuel S. Kim, "China and the Third World: In Search of a Peace and Development Line," in Kim, ed., *China and the World: New Directions in Chinese Foreign Relations*, 4th ed. (Boulder, CO: Westview, 1989), pp. 153–157.

37. Tang Hualiang, "Safeguarding World Peace Is the Primary Objective of China's Foreign Policy," *Hongqi* [Red Flag], no. 11 (June 1, 1984); trans. JPRS/CRF No. 84-014 (August 3, 1984), pp. 26–33.

38. Xue Mouhong, "*Wo guo waijiao de xin jumian*" [The New Situation in Our Country's Foreign Policy], *Hongqi*, no. 6 (1986), pp. 19–24.

39. Chinese chemical and nuclear-energy corporations were apparently the key players in these sales. On Iran, see Patrick E. Tyler, "China Reports New Problems in Atom Deal with Tehran," *New York Times*, May 18, 1995, and R. Jeffrey Smith, "Chinese Firms Supply Iran with Gas Factories," *Washington Post*, March 8, 1996. China was the main foreign contributor to Pakistan's nuclear bomb project, providing technical experts and equipment. See R. Jeffrey Smith, "U.S. Aides See Troubling Trend in China-Pakistan Nuclear Ties," *Washington Post*, April 1, 1996. This cooperation continued well into the 1990s. See Tim Weiner, "Atom Arms Parts Sold to Pakistan by China, U.S. Says," *New York Times*, February 8, 1996, p. 1.

40. R. Bates Gill, "Curbing Beijing's Arms Sales," *Orbis* 36, no. 3 (Summer 1992): 379–396.

41. Huan, "World Prospects for the Years Ahead."

42. See Hu Sheng, "On the Establishment of a New International Order on the

Basis of the Five Principles of Peaceful Coexistence," *Social Sciences in China* 13, no. 1 (January 1992): 5–12.

43. Ibid., p. 9.

44. Said Hu Sheng (ibid., p. 11): "Any cooperation that is mutually beneficial and conducive to shared development in the genuine sense will be possible only with sovereign equality as its premise. Can anything be more obvious?"

45. "The decline of the Soviet Union, the relative weakness of the strength of the United States, and the growing economic strength of Germany and Japan as well as the rise of a number of developing countries have demonstrated that the world is trending, more than ever before, towards multipolarization." Qian Qichen, "Adhering to Independent Foreign Policy," *Beijing Review*, no. 52 (December 30, 1991–January 5, 1992), pp. 7–10.

46. Nazneen Barma, Ely Ratner, and Steven Weber, "A World Without the West," *The National Interest* 90 (July–August 2007).

47. On the Washington Consensus, see Joseph E. Stiglitz, *Globalization and Its Discontents* (New York: W. W. Norton, 2002).

48. In addition to the sources in George Yu's chapter in this volume, see Richard Behar, "China in Africa," *Fast Company* (June 2008), online at www.fastcompany. com. Some writers have interpreted the Beijing Consensus as simply neoliberalism with Chinese characteristics, that is, a classic developmental-state approach not all that different from the model preached and practiced by Western states and multilateral institutions. (See, for example Wei-Wei Zhang, "The Allure of the Chinese Model," *International Herald Tribune*, November 2, 2006.) But clearly, the Chinese have a different political as well as economic agenda even while operating within the global capitalist economy.

49. Chu, *Zhongguo waijiao zhanlue*, pp. 278–279.

50. Quoted in Carlyle A. Thayer, "China's New Security Concept and ASEAN," *Pacific Forum*, online at www.csis.org/pacfor/cc/003Qchina_asean.html.

51. Michael Yahuda, *The International Politics of the Asia-Pacific*, 2nd rev. ed. (London: RoutledgeCurzon, 2004), p. 342.

52. The SCO, established in 2001, includes China, Russia, Kazakhstan, Kyrgyzstan, Tajikistan, and Uzbekistan. ASEAN+3 is the ten-member Association of Southeast Asian Nations plus China, Japan, and South Korea. It is an informal network that began in 1997.

53. Total Chinese arms exports declined 75 percent in the 1990s, and by 1998 were down to less than US$200 million in value. The decline was due mainly to lower quality and a shrinking market (especially in the Middle East). For the first time, the PRC also began to impose stricter regulations on arms exports. See Evan S. Medeiros and Bates Gill, *Chinese Arms Exports: Policy, Players, and Process* (Carlisle, PA: US Army War College, Strategic Studies Institute, 2000). From 2001 to 2007, China ranked eighth among arms exporting countries, with a total value for those years of about US$3.1 billion. Thus, whereas China accounted for around 8 percent of global arms sales by 1990, today its share is around 2 percent. Figures were compiled from the Stockholm International Peace Research Institute (SIPRI) databases at http://armstrade.sipri.org/arms_trade/toplist.php and http://armstrade.sipri.org/arms_trade/values.php.

54. Kenneth W. Allen and Eric A. McVadon, *China's Foreign Military Relations* (Washington, DC: Henry L. Stimson Center, 1999).

55. Bin Yu, "China's Rise and the West's Bias," *Asia Policy*, no. 6 (July 2008): 166–168, online at http://nbr.org/publications/asia_policy/AP6/AP6_BRRT_China Rising.pdf.

56. Belated Chinese advice to the Sudanese government in early 2008 to accept a

UN peacekeeping force in the Darfur region does not detract at all from this criticism. China has too much at stake economically to go beyond quiet diplomacy with Khartoum, and the fact that China continues to provide arms to Sudan makes clear its self-limiting role there. (See Hu Jintao's statement while in Sudan on the need for "peaceful resolution through dialogue and equal consultation" [Embassy of the People's Republic of China in the United Kingdom, September 27, 2007, at www.chineseembassy .org.uk/eng/zt/features/t367458.htm] and Lydia Polgreen, "China, in New Role, Uses Ties to Press Sudan on Troubled Darfur," *New York Times*, February 23, 2008, p. A7. On China's economic and military relations with Sudan, see the Human Rights First report, "Investing in Tragedy: China's Money, Arms, and Politics in Sudan" (March 2008), at www.humanrightsfirst.info/pdf/080311-cah-investing-in-tragedy-report.pdf; and on arms shipments in violation of UN restrictions, see the BBC report, "China Breaking Arms Ban in Sudan," at www.thestar.com/article/460253.) In Sri Lanka, China also provides military assistance to a government that, in the course of a civil war, has engaged in widespread human-rights violations, as noted later in this discussion. And in Zimbabwe, China along with Russia vetoed a UN Security Council resolution proposed by the United States that would have imposed an arms embargo and sanctions against the government of Robert Mugabe in the political crisis of summer 2008.

57. The exception, an important one, is North Korea: Despite Beijing's disenchantment with Pyongyang after its missile and nuclear tests, it still brokered the October 2007 package deal at the Six-Party Talks.

58. Stephanie Kleine-Ahlbrandt and Andrew Small, "China's New Dictatorship Diplomacy," *Foreign Affairs* 87, no. 1 (January–February 2008): 42. These writers further acknowledge (p. 50), with reference to Myanmar: "Ultimately, China's leaders acted largely in response to the threat to China's energy security and the potential loss of a closely allied neighboring government to what they saw as a pro-US democracy movement."

59. David Zweig and Bi Jianhai, "China's Global Hunt for Energy," *Foreign Affairs* 84, no. 5 (September–October 2005): 32.

60. China has supplied small arms to Thailand for many years, and most recently has enhanced its defense relationship with the Thai government by expanding the range of arms deliveries and establishing military-to-military ties. See Ian Storey, "China and Thailand: Enhancing Military-Security Ties in the 21st Century," *China Brief* 8, no. 14 (July 3, 2008), online at www.jamestown.org/china_brief/article.php?articleid=2374283. The booming South Korean–PRC commercial relationships have put China in first place as Korea's trade partner. PRC economic aid to the Philippines, such as for road construction, has upstaged World Bank, US, and Japanese assistance. See Ian Storey, "Trouble and Strife in the South China Sea, Part II: China and the Philippines," *China Brief* 8, no. 9 (April 28, 2008), online at www.jamestown.org/china_brief/article.php ?articleid=2374130.

61. For studies of these relationships, see the special issue of *Asian Perspective* guest-edited by Jean-Pierre Cabestan, vol. 30, no. 4 (2006).

62. See Elizabeth Economy, "The Impact of International Regimes on Chinese Foreign Policy-Making: Broadening Perspectives and Policies . . . But Only to a Point," in David M. Lampton, ed., *The Making of Chinese Foreign Policy in the Era of Reform, 1978–2000* (Stanford, CA: Stanford University Press, 2001), pp. 230–253.

63. See the International Crisis Group report, "China's Growing Role in UN Peacekeeping," April 17, 2009, at www.crisisgroup.org/library/documents/asia/north _east_asia/166_chinas_growing_role_in_un_peacekeeping.pdf.

64. Quoted by Chu, *Zhongguo waijiao zhanlue*, p. 305.

65. See Jeremy T. Paltiel, *The Empire's New Clothes: Cultural Particularism and Universal Value in China's Quest for Global Status* (New York: Palgrave Macmillan, 2007), pp. 220–225. As the case studies in Lampton (*The Making of Chinese Foreign Policy*) make clear, moreover, one reason for this acceptance of multilateral approaches is the pluralization of the Chinese policymaking process itself, with greater roles than ever before for bureaucratic and regional interests as well as expert opinion to assert themselves.

66. Chu, *Zhongguo waijiao zhanlue*, p. 114.

67. Deng, *Fundamental Issues*, p. 169.

68. Wu Baiyi, "The Chinese Security Concept and Its Historical Evolution," *Journal of Contemporary China* 10, no. 27 (May 2001): 281.

69. Paltiel, *The Empire's New Clothes*. As Chu Shulong writes (*Zhongguo waijiao zhanlue*, p. 321), Chinese leaders reached the firm conclusion in the 1990s that "no country can be allowed to interfere in our country's internal affairs and threaten national security and territorial integrity."

70. For useful charts and maps for the 1990s and early 2000s, see Phillip C. Saunders, *China's Global Activism: Strategy, Drivers, and Tools*, Occasional Paper No. 4 (Washington, DC: National Defense University, Institute for National Strategic Studies, October 2006).

71. See Zweig and Bi, "China's Global Hunt for Energy," pp. 25–38; Thomas Lum et al., "China's Foreign Aid Activities in Africa, Latin America, and Southeast Asia," Report R-40361 (Washington, DC: Congressional Research Service, February 25, 2009), table 5, p. 8.

72. Eugene Tang, "China, Kazakhstan, Sign $10 Billion Loan-for-Oil Agreements," Bloomberg, April 16, 2009, in NAPSNet, April 17, 2009. China has also signed such agreements with Russia.

73. Simon Romero and Alexei Barrionuevo, "Deals Help China Expand Its Sway in Latin America," *New York Times*, April 16, 2009.

74. In August 2007, SCO military forces staged counterterrorism exercises. The PLA's participation probably relates to China's concern about its own ethnic minority unrest, as well as the perceived need to play a more forceful role in Central Asian security. China had been quick to support the Uzbek government in 2005 when it violently suppressed antigovernment dissent. Later in 2005, China and Russia led the way in calling on the United States to set a date for withdrawal from bases in both Uzbekistan and Kazakhstan, showing that another PRC objective in the SCO is to erode the US presence in Central Asia. See Roger N. McDermott, "Rising Dragon: SCO Peace Mission 2007," Jamestown Foundation report, October 2007, at www.jamestown.org/uploads/media/Jamestown-McDermottRisingDragon.pdf.

75. Lum et al., "China's Foreign Aid Activities," pp. 9–10, 16–17. As this source cautions, what constitutes Chinese "aid" makes an accurate accounting difficult, as does the reliability of the reported aid figures.

76. Chu Shulong, *Zhongguo waijiao zhanlue*, p. 320, cites a September 2003 meeting of developing countries that called on the World Trade Organization to demand changes in US and European Union protectionist agricultural policies detrimental to Third World exports.

77. Most recently, in response to the G8 meetings in Japan in July 2008, which accepted the US insistence on cuts in carbon emissions by China and India as part of any new global compact on climate change, China and India led a group of Third World countries in making their own proposals on global warming.

78. Both on its own and alongside other governments, China criticized US financial management for its role in the global economic recession of 2009. PRC leaders,

notably Hu Jintao, asked for "guarantees" of the stability of China's investments in US securities. Prior to the first-ever meeting of G-20 finance ministers and central bank governors in March 2009, a statement of the PRC, Russia, Brazil, and India ministers urged stronger financial regulations, avoidance of trade protectionism, and a revamping of IMF voting and financing—all aimed at US and European practices. The statement (March 14, 2009) may be found at www.g20.utoronto.ca/2009/2009-bric090314. html.

79. See, for instance, Dai Xiaohua, "'East Asian Model': A Few Problems, but It Works," *Beijing Review*, no. 12 (March 23–29, 1998), pp. 7–9.

80. See Thomas Lum et al., *China's "Soft Power" in Southeast Asia* (Washington, DC: Congressional Research Service, January 4, 2008) and the Pew Global Attitudes Project report of June 12, 2008, "Global Economic Gloom—China and India Notable Exceptions," at http://pewglobal.org/reports/display.php?ReportID=260. For a more nuanced assessment of poll results that reflects some concern in Asia about a rising China even while seeing China as the wave of the future, see the Chicago Council on Global Affairs report, "Soft Power in Asia: Report of a 2008 Multinational Survey of Public Opinion," at http://www.thechicagocouncil.org/UserFiles/File/POS_ Topline%20Reports/Asia%20Soft%20Power%202008/Chicago%20Council%20Soft %20Power%20Report-%20Final%206-11-08.pdf.

81. See Mark Valencia, "The South China Sea Hydra," NAPSNet, July 24, 2008, at www.nautilus.org/fora/security/08057Valencia.html. Valencia points out the need for a legally binding code of conduct—beyond the 2002 joint declaration that China signed—to avoid new confrontations involving China and the ASEAN countries with territorial claims in the South China Sea area.

82. For example, China was invited in mid-2008 to join a new Group of 7 on global trade talks. The group includes Brazil and India, both of which reportedly are concerned about opening their markets to a flood of Chinese goods. See Stephen Castle, "China Emerges as Major Player in Global Trade Talks," *New York Times*, July 29, 2008, p. C2.

83. Despite the "strategic partnership" that China and India agreed to in November 2006, when Hu Jintao visited New Delhi, and the resumption of border talks in 2008, both countries remain wary of each other's intentions. China's military and economic assistance to India's neighbors—Pakistan, Myanmar, Sri Lanka, and Thailand— and the evident interest of both China and India in naval development make for strategic competition in the Indian Ocean. See Somini Sengupta, "Take Aid from China and Take a Pass on Human Rights," *New York Times*, March 9, 2008 (Week in Review).

84. See Shaun Breslin, "Supplying Demand or Demanding Supply? An Alternative Look at the Forces Driving East Asian Community Building," Stanley Foundation Policy Analysis Brief (November 2007).

85. Wei Liang, "China: Globalization and the Emergence of a New Status Quo Power?" *Asian Perspective* 31, no. 4 (2007): 125–149.

86. With commodity prices plummeting and political circumstances chaotic, the investment climate for China in some African countries, such as Guinea and Congo, has turned too risky. See Lydia Polgreen, "As Chinese Investment in Africa Drops, Hope Sinks," *New York Times*, March 26, 2009.

87. For example, China was apparently forced by the protests of African dock workers and numerous governments to recall an arms shipment to the Mugabe government in Zimbabwe, just when he was refusing to step down after being defeated for re-election. See Celia W. Dugger and David Barboza, "China May Give Up Attempt to Send Arms to Zimbabwe," *New York Times*, April 30, 2008, p. 1.

88. On some instances of criticism of China's aid and labor policies, see John C. K. Daly, "Feeding the Dragon: China's Quest for African Minerals," *China Brief* 8, no. 3 (January 31, 2008), pp. 7–13, online at www.jamestown.org/terrorism/news/uploads/cb_008_003e.pdf.

89. See for example Evan Osnos, "Angry Youth," *The New Yorker*, July 28, 2008, pp. 28–37.

# 3

## The Rise of a
## New "Trading Nation"

### David Zweig

In 1978, Deng Xiaoping recognized that the only way to rebuild China's economy, enhance its comprehensive national power, and return to its former leadership position in the world was through engaging in domestic economic reform and "opening to the outside world." Strengthening relationships with the developed world was central to this strategy. China sought capital, technology, management skills, and to educate a "lost generation" of scientists who had been cut off from the creative minds of the world by the Cultural Revolution.[1] The initial reform movement, therefore, ignored the developing world and placed most of China's eggs in the basket of the developed world.

Emphasizing ties to the developed world was a major shift in Chinese foreign policy. Mao had seen the path to world revolution passing through the Third World. By leading the developing world to surround the developed world, he had internationalized the strategy of the Chinese revolution—"using the countryside to surround the cities." But by the mid-1990s, particularly after China became a net importer of oil, China's leaders recognized that the country needed strong ties with both the developed and the developing world, and since then, has made ties to the Third World a pillar of its global strategy. As this volume demonstrates, China has rediscovered the developing world. China's leaders travel frequently to Africa, Latin America, Southeast Asia, and the Middle East.

China's booming economy and its emergence as the world's newest "trading nation," drives much of these enhanced relations.[2] As a "trading nation," China's need for oil and gas, raw materials and minerals, and foreign markets, and its position in globalized manufacturing networks that are closely tied to Southeast Asia, strengthen its ties to developing economies. And while economic ties to the Third World are only one part of China's global economic strategy, three aspects form the core of its economic relations with the Third World:

1. As a "trading nation," China challenges many developing countries for export markets in the developed world, even as it swamps the developing world with low-cost, quality products.
2. China competes with other developing nations for technology and foreign direct investment (FDI) from the developed world, consolidating its dominance over most of the developing world's economies.
3. China's need for resources, particularly energy and a variety of raw materials, sent Chinese firms on a whirlwind shopping spree, buying companies, mines, and oil fields around the world. Especially since the global "tsunami" in 2008, China's huge dollar reserves have allowed it to buy foreign assets even more aggressively. These purchases affect China's selection of partners and allies.

## China as a "Trading State": The Theory

Since World War II, few states have expanded their national power through territorial acquisition.[3] Instead, trade allows states to turn labor power into value, create greater wealth, enhance technology, and grow rich. Trade surpluses become the road to national wealth, as states accumulate foreign exchange with which they can buy resources, companies, technology, and increase their influence worldwide. And while Ricardian economics stresses that states engage in successful trade based on their comparative advantage, the East Asian model shows that states can "create comparative advantage,"[4] doing what Alice Amsden calls, "getting the prices wrong."[5] Even within a liberalizing world trading system, states employing mercantilist strategies—protectionism, export subsidies, suppressed labor costs, and cheap energy prices—gain significant advantage in an open trading system.[6]

Engaging the global economy has been a major boon to China. No state has benefited more than China from trade liberalization and globalization. To enter the World Trade Organization (WTO), China had to meet strict targets imposed by the United States and the European Union (EU), opening the Chinese economy to the outside world more than any other WTO entrant. According to Nicholas Lardy, China's real tariffs in the 1990s were as low as 6 percent, making China's domestic market more open than South Korea or Japan.[7]

Dependency theorists would predict the failure of such a strategy, due largely to the structure of the international economy. They note that Latin America failed to break out of the dependency trap. Even in China, some nationalists criticize China's export-led growth strategy as "dependent," rather than "autonomous."[8] But the East Asian "miracle" fundamentally challenged the dependency model, as China's trade has enhanced its industrial structure, helped it move up the product cycle, and strengthened its global competitiveness.[9]

Admittedly, China has become the final assembly "hub" for products designed and manufactured by enterprises owned or operated by ethnic Chinese in Southeast Asia, Taiwan, and Hong Kong, rather than the initiator of such products. Similarly, it has become the "world's workshop" for firms throughout the developed world. And by producing goods that are subsequently resold to the developed world, it challenges the developing world for those markets. Moreover, the enormous capital reserves accumulated through exports has enhanced China's state power, as the "trading nation" theory would predict. Still, according to Homi Kharas, "if economic liberalization allowed China to post 9 percent growth over three decades and lift 300 million people from poverty during that time, then surely other countries can make significant gains by knocking down barriers."[10]

## China as a "Trading State": The Data

China's trade has grown at an annual rate of 15–17 percent for almost thirty years, well above the 7 percent growth rate for world trade over the same period.[11] Trade, as a share of gross domestic product (GDP), is far greater than for any country of similar size (Figure 3.1).

**Figure 3.1    China's Exports and Imports as a Share of GDP, 1978–2006**

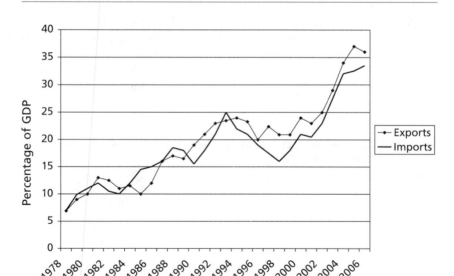

*Source:* Barbara Stallings, "China's Economic Relations with Developing Countries," unpublished paper, Brown University, December 12, 2007.

Despite Albert Keidel's assertion that China's growth has been driven predominantly by the domestic market,[12] since 2004, the role of exports in China's overall growth has increased significantly (Table 3.1). China's emergence as a "trading nation" has enormous implications for its economic policy, particularly as it relates to the developing world. These implications are addressed in the remainder of this chapter.

## "Resource Diplomacy" and China's "Going Out Strategy"

Both domestic demand and its transformation into a "trading nation" have led China to adopt a strategy of "resource diplomacy." As the "world's factory," China needs raw materials, in particular nickel, copper, iron ore, and aluminum, making China deeply dependent on states that possess such materials. According to Credit Lyonnais Securities of Asia's aptly named report, "China Eats the World,"[13] China's combined share of world consumption of aluminum, copper, nickel, and iron ore doubled from 1990 (7 percent) to 2000 (15 percent), and by 2004 was about 20 percent. Chinese demand for these commodities expanded throughout the decade until the 2008 global economic downturn. The domestic drivers behind this demand for commodities—housing and infrastructure construction, consumption of appliances and autos, and transportation of goods and people—also persisted through 2008, "leaving the Chinese dragon very, very hungry."[14] And according to Stallings, the "dominance of industry in lieu of services exacerbates resource requirements."[15]

With a very significant share of the world's resources lying under the ground in the developing world, China's National Development and Reform Commission, Ministry of Commerce and Foreign Ministry, mobilized Chinese firms to "go out" and purchase resources around the world. Thus, in 2004 they promulgated a "Guidance Catalogue on Countries and Industries for Overseas

**Table 3.1   Share of Net Exports to Gross Domestic Product Growth in China, 2003–2007 (in percent)**

| Year | GDP | Net Exports as Share of GDP Growth |
|------|-----|-----------------------------------|
| 2003 | 10.0 | 0.1 |
| 2004 | 10.1 | 0.6 |
| 2005 | 10.4 | 2.6 |
| 2006 | 11.1 | 2.3 |
| 2007 | 11.4 | 2.7 |

*Source:* Asian Development Bank (ADB).

Investment" which listed resources and industries that the state saw as the appropriate targets for foreign investment.[16] The list included 68 countries, with 23 in Asia, including all 10 Association of Southeast Asian Nations (ASEAN) countries, 13 African countries, 15 countries in Europe, 11 in the Western Hemisphere, and 5 in Oceania. Key industries included farming, forestry, mining, oil drilling and refining, natural gas, and manufacturing, particularly textile and electronic manufacturing, as well as service industries, such as construction and shipping. If one looks at the lists attached to each country, the key target states are Thailand, Myanmar (Burma), Vietnam, the Philippines, Malaysia, India (for manufacturing), Pakistan, Saudi Arabia, South Africa, Nigeria, Australia, Canada, and Russia. States not on this list, but key targets nonetheless, would include Iran, and other energy-rich states listed below. What makes the list significant is the enunciated policy that "any enterprise that complies with the Guidance Catalogue and holds an overseas investment approval certificate . . . shall have priority to enjoy preferential treatment under policies of the State in respect of funding, foreign exchange, tax, customs, and import and export, etc."[17]

The guidelines were promulgated in response to an instruction by the Chinese State Council to "strengthen coordination and guidance for overseas investment," which wanted to avoid competition and duplication by domestic Chinese firms, expand and diversify trade, enhance the quality of such trade, and get the Chinese to fully use domestic and foreign markets. The dramatic jump in foreign trade and firms going abroad probably was affected by this policy. (Table 3.2 shows the growth in the number of firms going overseas and in the number of companies that Chinese firms are establishing overseas.) But even as early as the mid-1990s, the State Economic and Trade Commission had selected 120 "national champions" to lead China's engagement with the world and to prepare these firms for the global competition that accession to the WTO would entail.[18]

Interestingly, the Ministry of Commerce issued new guidelines in April 2009, which supplied important information about the laws in the various countries in which Chinese firms might be looking to invest. The guidelines were intended to cover more than 160 countries and regions around the world. The information was supplied by the business departments of Chinese embassies and consulates around the world, suggesting a much more systematic policy of "going out." The guidelines also pointed out the types of problems that firms might face, all the while suggesting solutions for such problems.[19]

China's external FDI shows a pattern similar to the data on Chinese firms going overseas (Table 3.2). China's outbound FDI rose from US$2.8 billion in 2003 to US$26.5 billion in 2007, a tenfold increase in five years. It then doubled in 2008, and as of April 2009 was on course to double again.[20] The annual average for 1990–2000 was US$2.2 billion, indicating an enormous jump in the past few years. Investment in the developing world has increased concomi-

**Table 3.2    Chinese Companies Going Overseas, 2002–2007**

|                                          | 2002  | 2003  | 2004  | 2005  | 2006   | 2007   |
|------------------------------------------|-------|-------|-------|-------|--------|--------|
| Number going out                         | n.a.  | n.a.  | 3,000 | 4,000 | 5,000  | 7,000  |
| Number of overseas enterprises established | 6,960 | 3,439 | 5,163 | 6,426 | 10,000 | 10,000 |

*Source:* Ministry of Commerce of China, 2007 Statistical Bulletin of China's Outward Foreign Direct Investment, available at http://hzs2.mofcom.gov.cn/accessory/20080928 /1222502733006.pdf, and other years. Thanks to Daniel Rosen for his assistance on this data.
*Note:* Some companies establish more than one enterprise overseas, so that by end of 2007, 7,000 enterprises had established over 10,000 companies. n.a. = not available.

tantly, particularly in Africa and Asia (Table 3.3). However, as a share of total FDI, the developing world does not get the lion's share. In fact, in 2007, half of China's total overseas investment went to Hong Kong (US$13.7 billion). Still, much of that money could have been invested in the developing world by mainland Chinese firms. Also, while investment in Africa increased fifteenfold in five years, investment in Latin America has not increased so rapidly.

What drives this overseas investment? While Aaron Friedberg, a hardline realist, sees "going out" as part of an undisclosed "grand strategy" for global dominance,[21] Philip Saunders believes that "China's increasing demand for economic inputs and for access to export markets follows a logic and geography independent of strategic concerns."[22] Friedrich Wu believes that Chinese firms, facing fierce domestic competition and declining domestic revenues, "go out" in search of new sales and distribution networks, cutting-edge technology, manufacturing know-how, and global brands.[23] And while Wu recognizes that the government was pushing its national champions to secure access to overseas resources, he sees increased Chinese investment overseas as boosting the global economy, allowing China to recycle its massive foreign exchange holdings and massive domestic savings, and promoting the world's poorer economies.

Yet both the "Guidelines" and surveys show that Chinese firms are seeking to penetrate the developing world with their exports. A World Bank survey of 132 Chinese firms that were investing abroad in 2005 found that the dominant reason for going overseas was the search for markets. Among numerous explanations deemed to be "most important" or "very important" for going out, 85 percent were seeking markets, 41 percent were making use of domestic production capacity, 39 percent wanted to enhance their efficiency, while 36 percent were tariff-jumping, that is, manufacturing in the host countries in order to avoid import duties. Finally, 12 percent of firms reported that they were investing abroad because of pressure from domestic competitors.[24] Also,

Table 3.3   Regional Shares of China's Outward Foreign Direct
            Investment, 2003–2008 (US$million)

|                | 2003 | 2004 | 2005 | 2006 | 2007 | 2008 |
|----------------|------|------|------|------|------|------|
| Asia[a]          | 1,505.0 | 3,013.9 | 4,484.1 | 7,663.2 | 16,593.2 | n.a. |
| Africa[b]        | 74.8 | 317.4 | 391.6 | 519.8 | 1,574.3 | n.a. |
| Latin America[c] | 1,038.1 | 1,762.7 | 6,466.1 | 8,468.7 | 4,902.4 | n.a. |
| North America  | 57.7 | 126.4 | 320.8 | 258.0 | 1,125.7 | n.a. |
| Europe         | 145.0 | 157.2 | 395.4 | 597.7 | 1,540.4 | n.a. |
| Oceania        | 33.8 | 120.1 | 202.8 | 126.3 | 770.1 | n.a. |
| Total          | 2,854.6 | 5,497.9 | 12,261.1 | 17,633.9 | 26,506.1 | 52,150 |

*Sources:* 2006 data were from the Ministry of Commerce of China, "2006 Statistical Bulletin of China's Outward Foreign Direct Investment," pp. 17–20, 53–57. 2007 data are from the State Statistical Bureau website. 2008 data are from *People's Daily Online,* February 20, 2009, http://english.peopledaily.com.cn/90001/90776/90884/6597575.html.
*Notes:* a. As of 2006, China's outward direct investment (ODI) to Asia mainly includes Hong Kong, Indonesia, Iran, Japan, Kazakhstan, Laos, Mongolia, Saudi Arabia, Singapore, and Vietnam.
    b. As of 2006, China's ODI to Africa mainly includes Algeria, Congo, Nigeria, South Africa, Sudan, and Zambia.
    c. As of 2006, China's ODI to Latin America mainly includes Cayman, British Virgin Islands, Cuba, and Venezuela.
    n.a. = not available.

51 percent of these companies were searching for strategic assets, and 39 percent said they were "resource seeking." A similar survey in 2003 by Roland Berger Strategy Consultants found that the search for "new markets" motivated 56 percent of industry-leading firms; 20 percent were securing resources, and 16 percent were obtaining technology and brand names. However, the search for technology and brand names is unlikely to play a role in China's ties to developing countries.[25]

The behavior of these overseas firms can be contentious, as Chinese firms have not always followed global norms in their treatment of local workers. Reports have circulated of problems in Peru, the Philippines, and especially in Zambia.[26] Thus, consulting firms, such as Price Waterhouse Coopers, train Chinese corporate executives before they head overseas.

Chinese companies have developed much more independence under a public policy that promotes "resource diplomacy." When Chinese leaders go abroad on trips, they now are often accompanied by a coterie of business leaders, whose interests are seen to be one and the same as those of the Chinese state. Leaders, such as Wen Jiaobao, offered important foreign aid to the Kenyan government to help the Chinese oil firms win contracts for oil extraction.

But some Chinese scholars do not see this symmetry of interests, particularly when the businesses are engaged in activities in "pariah" states, and worry that Chinese diplomacy has been "hijacked by the oil companies."[27]

Zhu Feng, professor at Beijing University's Centre for International and Strategic Studies, has written that some state-owned enterprises, such as the oil company Petro-China, are now very powerful interest groups. "They even hijacked China's foreign policy in Sudan."[28] Zhai Kun, of the China Institute of Contemporary International Relations in Beijing, said that while large state companies are driven by "economic considerations. . . . more and more regulations should now be created by the government to constrain their behavior overseas."[29] In 2007, Zhang Yunling, of the Chinese Academy of Social Sciences, dispatched a team of international relations specialists to Sudan to prepare a report on China's conduct in the country. "The companies feel great pressure as a result of being linked to politics," he said. "They don't care a lot about politics but it cannot be avoided. This kind of situation will emerge in many other places as well."

Thus, while many Western scholars see a centrally controlled mercantilist strategy as the core of China's "going out strategy," both Western and Chinese scholars wonder whether the "dog is wagging its tail, or if the tail is wagging the dog." According to Zha Daojiong, the main direction of influence is that the national oil companies (NOCs) push the government to help them compete with foreign oil companies, rather than government pushing oil firms to go overseas.

> For over a decade China has lived without a central ministerial agency to oversee the country's energy industry. . . . [It is] difficult to ascertain whether a particular oil/gas venture overseas is the result of the Chinese government dictating its state-owned energy company to carry out a governmental mission or the domestic energy industry seeking diplomatic assistance from the government.[30]

Similarly, Xin Ma and Philip Andrew-Speed see only tacit encouragement coming from the Chinese government in support of the expansion and diversification of the NOCs. "In most cases, there is little evidence to suggest that the government is doing [anything] other than support an initiative led by the NOC, develop associated economic activities and provide a coordination role."[31] Still, while the Foreign Ministry may face problems justifying ties to globally isolated governments, such as Sudan and Zimbabwe, Chinese firms still appear to be following the overall directive outlined by the state: accumulate resources.

## Searching for Energy in the Right and "Wrong" Places

The search for energy has played a major role in expanding China's economic links with the developing world. In 1993, China became a net importer of oil and natural gas, and by 2007, was the world's number three importer of oil.

And despite a wealth of coal, China became a net importer of coal as well. To resolve this growing dependence on imported energy, China's NOCs have moved out into the world to get the nation the energy it needs.[32]

According to the *Economist*, in many parts of the developing world (as well as Canada), Chinese firms are gobbling up oil, gas, and coal; paying for the right to explore for them; or buying up firms that produce them.[33] Before the 2008 global recession, African and Latin American economies grew at their fastest pace in decades, thanks largely to heavy Chinese demand for their resources, which promoted that growth.

The sources of China's oil imports in 2007 (as shown in Table 3.4) show both the dominance of the developing world and the diversification of China's energy security policy. "The turning point in China's energy strategy was the Iraq war," said Tong Lixia, an energy expert at the Chinese Academy of International Trade and Economic Cooperation, which is affiliated with China's Commerce Ministry. "After 2003, both the companies and the government realized China could not rely on one or two oil production areas. It's too risky."[34]

Still, almost half of China's oil imports come from the Middle East, of which Saudi Arabia provides 16.6 percent and Iran provides 12.9 percent, and supplies from the Middle East are expected to expand in the coming years. Africa supplied 32.2 percent of China's oil imports in 2007, with Angola topping the list. Sudan supplied 6.5 percent; China has poured billions into Sudan, developing its oil industry, making it one of the fastest-growing countries in Africa.

In Latin America, the US backyard, China has become quite active in Venezuela, with over 1.5 percent of China's oil imports in 2005 coming from Venezuela; and imports from Venezuela are on an upward trajectory. In fact, China replaced some US oil producers in Venezuela because they accepted a minority equity share of 40 percent as proposed by Venezuela's nationalistic president, Hugo Chávez. China is also busy in Central Asia; the first oil pipeline from overseas brings oil into China from Kazakhstan.[35] According to Adam Blinick, while the total amount of oil in the pipeline is not very significant, China looms as an alternative source for oil exports that can give countries in Central Asia, such as Kazakhstan, room to maneuver outside Russia's orbit. Natural gas purchases also contribute to China's growing ties with the developing world, as most natural gas is found in Qatar, Iran, Saudi Arabia, and the United Arab Emirates, with Russia the only major source of natural gas that is not a developing nation.[36]

Many Chinese oil purchases are sweetened with foreign aid, which fosters economic development in these developing countries. Throughout Africa, Latin America, and Central Asia, concrete bridges constructed with Chinese capital build political and economic bridges. For example, since 2002, China, which supported the losing side in the Angolan civil war, has tried to improve ties with the victorious Popular Movement for the Liberation of Angola

**Table 3.4  China's Crude Oil Imports, Major Suppliers, 2007**

|  | Oil Imported (tonnes) | Percentage of Total |
|---|---|---|
| **Middle East** | | |
| Saudi Arabia | 26,332,088 | 16.59 |
| Iran | 20,536,769 | 12.94 |
| Oman | 13,677,798 | 8.62 |
| Kuwait | 3,632,297 | 2.29 |
| United Arab Emirates | 3,650,908 | 2.30 |
| Yemen | 3,236,839 | 2.04 |
| Iraq | 1,412,108 | 0.89 |
| Total Middle East | 72,478,807 | 45.66 |
| **Africa** | | |
| Angola | 24,996,499 | 15.75 |
| Sudan | 10,306,048 | 6.49 |
| Congo | 4,801,420 | 3.02 |
| Equatorial Guinea | 3,280,093 | 2.07 |
| Libya | 2,906,872 | 1.83 |
| South Africa | 2,327,152 | 1.47 |
| Algeria | 1,612,828 | 1.02 |
| Nigeria | 895,179 | 0.56 |
| Total Africa | 51,126,091 | 32.21 |
| **Southeast Asia** | | |
| Indonesia | 2,284,087 | 1.44 |
| Thailand | 1,101,774 | 0.69 |
| Vietnam | 496,358 | 0.31 |
| Total Southeast Asia | 3,882,219 | 2.45 |
| **North and South America** | | |
| Venezuela | 4,115,231 | 2.59 |
| Brazil | 2,315,485 | 1.46 |
| Argentina | 1,566,434 | 0.99 |
| Colombia | 842,216 | 0.53 |
| Peru | 1,178,139 | 0.74 |
| Canada | 469,459 | 0.30 |
| Ecuador | 234,595 | 0.15 |
| Total North and South America | 10,721,559 | 6.75 |
| **Russia and Central Asia** | | |
| Russia | 14,526,283 | 9.15 |
| Kazakhstan | 5,997,948 | 3.78 |
| Total Russia and Central Asia | 20,524,231 | 12.93 |
| **Total** | 158,732,907 | 100.00 |

*Source:* General Administration of Customs, People's Republic of China, *China Customs Statistical Yearbook 2007* (Beijing: General Administration of Customs, People's Republic of China, and China Customs Journal, 2008), pp. 216–221.

(MPLA) through more than US$5 billion in low-interest loans; in return, China was able to replace the French oil company Total in several oil fields.

Western states express concern about China's energy diplomacy. But according to the International Crisis Group's 2008 report entitled *China's Thirst for Oil,* China should not be faulted for this massive drive for energy acquisition. According to their data, heavy industry makes up over two-thirds of China's energy demand, which "is mostly driven by the manufacturing of goods sold on global markets. . . . Much energy in China is dedicated to the creation of infrastructure factories, roads, and ports—that makes possible an economy that supports overseas consumption."[37] In other words, China's energy and resources hunger is largely driven by the Western firms that go to China for its lower production costs.

Still there is little doubt that China's largesse to the developing world has allowed many authoritarian governments to persist in political oppression and corruption. Angola is a case in point. The MPLA leadership has formed a predatory ruling class that systematically steals funds from the state coffers to invest overseas. Under pressure from the International Monetary Fund (IMF) and the West to open its books and explain the disappearance of US$4.2 billion in 1997–2001, Angola reneged on the deal once China came up with a US$2 billion loan.[38] However, despite concerns commonly heard in the West that China has proposed that a "Beijing Consensus," which ignores government misbehavior, replace the "Washington Consensus" that dominated commerce since World War II, the *Economist* argued that

> concerns about the dire consequences of China's quest for natural resources are overblown. China does indeed treat some dictators with kid gloves, but it is hardly alone in that. Its companies do not always uphold the highest standards, but again, many Western firms are no angels either. Fifty years of European and American aid have not succeeded in bringing much prosperity to Africa and other poor but resource-rich places. A different approach from China might yield better results. At the very least it will spur other donors to seek more effective methods.[39]

Moreover, some of China's sharpest critics saw a significant shift in 2007–2008, as China began to pressure its resource suppliers, such as Sudan and Iran, to respond to Western concerns about human rights and nuclear proliferation.[40]

## Competing with the Developing World for FDI?

To promote economic development and technological upgrading, Chinese policy is remarkably hospitable to FDI, making China the number two country in the world for foreign investment, after the United States. Developing countries, such as India, are amazed by the level of FDI in China, which is about ten times the levels coming into India.[41] Moreover, that growth in FDI—average annual FDI in 1990–2000 was US$30.1 billion, but reached US$72.4 billion in 2005—could have serious implications for the developing world if China's magnetism draws FDI away from other developing countries.

After the 1997 Asian financial crisis, leaders in Southeast Asia worried that FDI that had been flowing their way was moving to China, and the aggregate data supported that argument. Whereas in the early 1990s, the ASEAN attracted around 30 percent of the FDI coming into developing Asia, by 2000, ASEAN's share had dropped to 10 percent.[42] However, UN Conference on Trade and Development (UNCTAD) data show that despite remarkable growth in the level of FDI flowing into China between 1995 and 2007, the flow of FDI into Southeast Asia also increased significantly (Table 3.5).[43] In fact, the annual rate of growth of FDI into Southeast Asia between 2002 and 2007 was far higher than it was for China. Therefore, it is impossible to argue that Southeast Asia suffered any loss of FDI due to China's attractiveness to foreign investment.

Also, according to UNCTAD, India—the largest recipient of FDI in South Asia—and most member countries of ASEAN also attracted larger inflows, as did postconflict countries and Asian less developed countries, such as Afghanistan, Cambodia, Sri Lanka, and Timor.[44]

Moreover, much of the FDI going to China came from Hong Kong and Taiwan, and included a great deal of mainland capital that first went to the Grand Cayman Islands or the Grand Bahamas, before returning to China as overseas capital, making it eligible for the preferential policies given to foreign investors. Thus, much of China's FDI is actually mainland capital that is engaged in "round tripping." On the other hand, Thailand, Malaysia, Indonesia, and the Philippines actually received five times as much FDI from the United States as China in the year ending March 2001. The totals were US$2.6 billion to US$512 million, respectively. This finding reflects

**Table 3.5    FDI Inflows for China and the Developing World, 1995–2007 (US$ billion)**

| | 1995–2000 (Annual Average) | 2002 | 2003 | 2004 | 2005 | 2006 | 2007 |
|---|---|---|---|---|---|---|---|
| China | 41.8 | 52.7 | 53.5 | 60.6 | 72.4 | 72.7 | 83.5 |
| Southeast Asia | 28.0 | 18.1 | 24.6 | 35.2 | 39.1 | 51.2 | 60.5 |
| Africa | 9.0 | 14.6 | 18.7 | 18.0 | 29.5 | 45.8 | 53.0 |
| Latin America and Caribbean | 72.9 | 57.8 | 45.9 | 94.4 | 76.4 | 92.9 | 126.3 |

*Source:* UNCTAD, *World Investment Report 2008: Transnational Corporations and the Infrastructure Challenge* (New York and Geneva: United Nations, 2008), annex table A.I.16.

an important qualifier to the reality that China has displaced Southeast Asia as the target for most FDI into Asia. The bulk of "overseas" capital heading into China originates from Hong Kong and Taiwan. Some of it represents factories moving from those territories into the mainland in search of lower labour costs or less restrictive environmental regulations. The money going into Southeast Asia tends to be in more capital-intensive, niche areas where China is not yet competitive—higher-end electronics, pharmaceuticals or auto parts.[45]

Thus the great "sucking sound" that everyone is so nervous about is just that, nervous anxiety. Moreover, China's economic growth is positive for Southeast Asia; as demand in the United States and Japan drops, China absorbs many exports from the developing countries of Southeast Asia.

## China: Importing from the Developing World

As a "trading nation," China is open for imports from developing countries, albeit mostly natural resources rather than manufactured goods, and despite charges that it employs a mercantilist strategy, China lowered tariffs significantly through the 1990s, even before joining the WTO.[46] Almost every time former president Jiang Zemin traveled to an ASEAN meeting, he slashed tariffs as a goodwill gesture. While overall tariffs were at 55.6 percent in 1982, and at 42.9 percent in 1992, they nosedived from that time forward, hitting 23.6 percent in 1996, 17.6 percent in 1997, and 12.3 percent in 2002. Moreover, if one averages out the official tariffs that were on the books by the value of imports in each of China's major import categories, the "weighted" tariff level in 2002 was only 6.4 percent.[47]

In truth, China is one of the developing world's best customers.[48] In 2003, imports from Latin America increased by 81 percent and from Africa by 54 percent; as of 2004, China was the third largest importer of developing country exports after the United States and the European Union.[49] According to Kharas, 45 percent of China's US$400 billion in imports in 2002 came from developing countries, rising by another $55 billion in 2003. While some worry that China's demand for commodities has inflated resource prices, Kharas sees this as a positive factor.

> Chinese demand for basic commodities (produced primarily in poorer countries) is so strong that it has pushed up prices for food staples and industrial raw materials such as aluminum, steel, copper, cotton, and rubber. For the millions of farmers around the world who depend on revenue from these products, the global price boom has come at just the right time, reversing decades of slumping prices.[50]

Several newspaper articles in May 2008 focused on how China's hunger for food led it to pour money into the agricultural sector around the world.[51]

UNCTAD data documents China's role in helping the developing world grow. China's imports from developing economies in the Western Hemisphere rose fivefold between 2000 and 2007, from US$5.2 billion in 1999, to US$11.63 billion in 2003, US$23.24 billion in 2005, reaching US$35.54 billion in 2007. Imports from the least developed countries doubled between 1999 and 2003, from US$2.67 billion to US$4.37 billion, almost doubled again by 2005 to US$7.80 billion, and then more than doubled again by 2007, reaching US$14.18 billion.[52]

The impact of China's resource hunger on Africa has been huge and largely positive.[53] China has suddenly become Africa's third trading partner, behind only the United States and France. The *Financial Times* cites the wide-scale impact of China's purchases of commodities beyond the oil sector, including cotton, cocoa, and phosphate.[54] To get these commodities to sea, China has built new harbors and railroads, promoting widespread economic development in a region of the world that has severe need for infrastructure investment.

### Deepest Impact on East Asia

While China is having an important impact on the world's economy, its regional impact is even greater, as a unique pattern of trade flows has emerged. The export-oriented growth strategies of the emerging Asian economies have been reflected in a steady increase of their share of world trade, reaching 34 percent in 2006, up sharply from 21 percent in 1990. Thus, it is not surprising to find that China's imports and exports with "developing Asia" have grown significantly.

But much of this trade is with the rapidly developing territories of East Asia, which ships parts for assembly to China, which then exports those assembled goods to the developed world. China, therefore, has become the core to a multiplicity of networks for the manufacture of electronics and other manufactured goods whose high-level components are first produced in more advanced Asian economies and then assembled in China. Table 3.6 shows what the IMF refers to as the "China Hub."[55] To facilitate the flow of goods, China has established a free trade agreement with ASEAN, as well as free trade agreements with other countries of the region.

### The Downside of China's Growth on the Developing World

China's impact on developing countries depends in part on whether Chinese goods compete directly with their exports. Businesspeople in El Salvador feared Chinese competition in textiles and towels.[56] But the case of China's im-

**Table 3.6 The China Hub: Direction of Exports**

| Exporting Region or Country | Direction of Exports | | | | |
|---|---|---|---|---|---|
| | NIEs[a] | ASEAN5[b] | China | Industrial Asia | Rest of the World |
| NIEs | 14.0 (1.7) | 12.2 (3.7) | 25.4 (17.5) | 8.3 (–5.1) | 38.3 (–18.7) |
| ASEAN5 | 21.6 (0.3) | 9.7 (5.4) | 11.1 (8.9) | 16.0 (–10.9) | 39.6 (–5.1) |
| China | 22.8 (–18.4) | 4.6 (1.7) | — | 11.5 (–3.8) | 59.7 (19.1) |
| Industrial Asia | 21.4 (2.6) | 8.9 (1.1) | 14.8 (12.5) | 6.6 (–0.7) | 46.9 (–16.2) |

*Source:* IMF Direction of Trade Statistics, and staff circulations.
*Note:* First number is share of the direction of exports in 2006, and number in parenthesis is change in the shares from 1990 to 2006.
a. NIEs = newly industrialized economies.
b. ASEAN5 = Indonesia, Malaysia, Philippines, Singapore, and Thailand.

pact on global trade in textiles and garments is complicated. As long as the Multi-Fibre Arrangement (MFA) was in effect, China's exports of textiles was limited by quotas, which distributed imports to the United States and the European Union among different countries, particularly some poor countries in Africa. Chinese firms, therefore, moved their plants to those countries to take up the quota of allotted sales to the developed world. But the MFA expired on January 1, 2005, affecting 87 percent of US quotas and 73 percent of the EU's, and now that the global system of quotas has disappeared and Chinese firms can return to the mainland, garment workers in countries such as Bangladesh and Cambodia, whose jobs and wages depend on protected markets, are being hurt. According to Ian Taylor, African textile and clothing manufacturer exports to the United States fell by 16 percent from 2004–2005, while US imports from China went up by 44 percent and EU imports from China went up by 78 percent.[57] But again, much of the exporting to the developed world before the end of the MFA was by Chinese firms that had relocated to the African continent.

Similarly, maquiladora industries in Central America that exported to the United States under special agreements that are now deemed unfair trade are already exiting the market, fearing the coming competition with China. Figure 3.2 shows which countries are China's direct competitors and therefore are likely to be hurt by China's growing exports. Mexicans are deeply concerned because they produce half of Latin America's exports. Assembly plants there are moving to China, Chinese products are flooding Mexican markets, and China has now surpassed Mexico as the second largest supplier to the United States.

Similarly, Barry Eichengreen and Hui Tong find that China has had a positive impact on resource exporters, such as Australia and Brazil. Countries such as Peru, Chile, Angola, and Congo have also seen positive results, al-

**Figure 3.2    Export Competition with China for Selected Countries, 2000–2005**

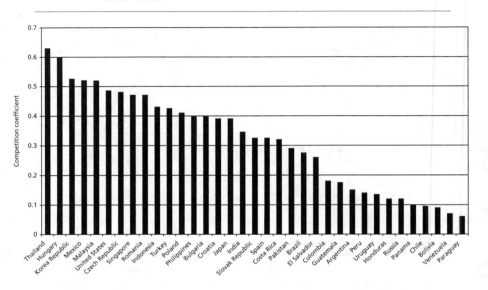

Source: *Latin American Economic Outlook 2008,* OECD Development Centre (2007).
Note: Export competition is measured by comparing the trade structure of each country with China's. A high measure indicates a high degree of similarity in export structures, as determined by specialization and conformity coefficients, and vice versa.

though in these countries, China may be perpetuating the use of low-quality labor for resource extraction, in return for the importation of Chinese manufactured goods.[58] Also helped are countries that produce components that fit into the production networks for the manufacturing of electronic components, such as Malaysia or Singapore. But China creates serious problems for countries such as Bangladesh, Pakistan, or Vietnam that compete with it directly in the production of goods like shoes or textiles.

China's export drive has also depressed the price of many manufactured goods, hurting the economies of other developing countries. According to Mary Amiti and Caroline Freund, many of China's gains to trade are from extensive growth—exporting more of the same goods at cheaper prices, thereby increasing China's world market share—rather than expanding the number of new product lines.[59] Thus, while China appears to be dramatically changing its comparative advantage by increasing its level of specialization, in fact, it continues to specialize in labor-intensive goods. The result is downward pressure on prices of a wide array of goods, generating serious implications for the developing world. Thus, between 1997 and 2005, most of China's export growth was in existing varieties, allowing the importing countries—mostly developed economies—to benefit from lower import prices. Indeed, between 1997 and 2005, the average prices of goods exported from China to the United States fell by an average of 1.5 percent per year, whereas the average prices of these products from the rest of the world to the United States increased on average by 0.4 percent per year.[60]

## Competing with Developing Countries for the US Market

One of the most important markets in the world is the United States. Sales to the United States powered Japan's growth in the 1960s as well as Asia's Four Little Dragons (Hong Kong, Singapore, South Korea, and Taiwan) since the 1970s. And while inter-ASEAN trade has surpassed trans-Pacific trade in the past few years, the battle over the US market is critical to the growth of developing countries around the world. So Mexicans have reason to worry now that in 2003, China replaced Mexico as the second largest source of imports for the United States. Yet according to Neil Hughes, it is often US firms who are bringing the US market to the Chinese, not Chinese who are aggressively seeking to export to the United States:

> Almost 60 percent of Chinese exports to the United States are produced by firms owned by foreign companies, many of them American. These firms have moved operations overseas in response to competitive pressures to lower production costs and thereby offer better prices to consumers and higher returns to shareholders. US importers with dominant positions in China, such as Wal-Mart and Hallmark, have the power to compel Chinese suppliers to keep their costs as low as possible. . . . So who is really "to blame" for China's "exporting deflation" and for the surge of Chinese exports? American importers, the American consumers who buy their Chinese goods at very low prices, and their American shareholders who demand results.[61]

In fact, a large part of China's export drive is powered by foreign firms that have relocated to China from the developed world or from other countries, such as Korea, Japan, or Mexico. Table 3.7 shows the important role of foreign-invested firms in China's exports.

A good example of a sector where China has drawn business away from both developed and developing countries is the computer equipment industry. According to Wayne Morrison and Marc Labonte, imports of computer equipment have shifted from other countries in East Asia to China.[62] In 2000, Japan was the largest foreign supplier of US computer equipment (19.6 percent of total shipments), while China ranked fourth (12.1 percent share). In just seven years, Japan's ranking fell to fourth, the value of its shipments dropped by over half, and its share of shipments declined to 7.0 percent (2007). Mexico and Singapore have also lost out to China, but Malaysia's exports between 2000 and 2007 have more than doubled (Table 3.8). Still, China was by far the

**Table 3.7   China's Exports and Imports by Foreign-Invested Enterprises in China, 1986–2007**

| Year | Annual FDI (US$ Billion) | Exports by FIEs | | Imports by FIEs | |
|---|---|---|---|---|---|
| | | US$ Billion | Percentage of Total Exports | US$ Billion | Percentage of Total Imports |
| 1986 | 1.9 | 0.6 | 1.9 | 2.4 | 5.6 |
| 1990 | 3.5 | 7.8 | 12.6 | 12.3 | 23.1 |
| 1995 | 37.5 | 46.9 | 31.5 | 62.9 | 47.7 |
| 2000 | 40.7 | 119.4 | 47.9 | 117.2 | 52.1 |
| 2001 | 46.9 | 133.2 | 50.0 | 125.8 | 51.6 |
| 2002 | 52.7 | 169.9 | 52.2 | 160.3 | 54.3 |
| 2003 | 53.5 | 240.3 | 54.8 | 231.9 | 56.0 |
| 2004 | 60.6 | 338.2 | 57.0 | 305.6 | 58.0 |
| 2005 | 60.3 | 444.2 | 58.3 | 387.5 | 57.7 |
| 2006 | 63.0 | 563.8 | 58.2 | 472.6 | 59.7 |
| 2007 | 75.0 | 695.5 | 57.1 | 559.4 | 58.5 |

*Source:* Morrison and Labonte, "China's Currency," p. 25.

largest foreign supplier of computer equipment in 2007 with a 51.5 percent share of total US imports. While US imports of computer equipment from China rose by 436 percent over those seven years, the total value of US imports from the world of these commodities rose by only 26 percent.

## The Problems of a Trading Nation

China has emerged as a major global economic force whose rapid development has enormous implications for the Third World. China is both partner and competitor. Its demand for resources and raw materials translates into investment that cranks up the economies in much of the developing world. Its overseas investment has brought life to mines and oil fields that languished due to the high cost of extraction. Its cheap products have allowed poorer people in many parts of the world to dress better and maybe even enjoy their lives more fully. Yet China's growth also challenges many developing countries as China's lack of trade unions and its coercive local state keep wages low, bringing many new enterprises to China. China's ability to attract so much FDI comes, in part, at the expense of other developing countries, which see their share of new FDI falling.

Still, while China has maintained it comparative advantage over much of the developing world, the rising price of its labor has pushed some products to

Table 3.8   Major Sources of US Computer Equipment Imports, 2000–2007 (US$billion)

|  | 2000 | 2002 | 2004 | 2006 | 2007 | Percent Change, 2000–2007 |
|---|---|---|---|---|---|---|
| China | 8.3 | 12.0 | 29.5 | 40.0 | 44.5 | 436.1 |
| Malaysia | 4.9 | 7.1 | 8.7 | 11.1 | 10.9 | 122.4 |
| Mexico | 6.9 | 7.9 | 7.4 | 6.6 | 6.6 | –4.3 |
| Japan | 13.4 | 8.1 | 6.3 | 6.3 | 5.0 | –62.7 |
| Singapore | 8.7 | 7.1 | 6.6 | 5.6 | 4.3 | –50.6 |
| Total | 68.5 | 62.3 | 73.9 | 83.8 | 86.3 | 26.0 |

*Source:* Morrison and Labonte, "China's Currency," p. 26.
*Note:* Ranked by top five suppliers in 2007.

Vietnam, India, and other low-wage countries. This process has been at work since 1998 (Figure 3.3). Great concerns in China have emerged, even among government officials in the republic, as the new labor code, introduced in 2008, which insures fairer treatment for Chinese factory workers, further undermines China's dominant position as the "workshop of the world."[63] Fortunately for China, its infrastructure (particularly transport facilities), energy supply, and skilled workforce help it compete with countries such as the Philippines or South Africa, whose labor costs are now below those in China. Serious trade competition also exists with Mexico, given Mexico's geographic advantage over China in terms of access to the US market.

But the dilemmas do not end there. As a newly emerging trading nation, China must deal with the world as it is—that is, it must compete within an economic structure dominated by the United States, Japan, and the European Union. Several ironies emerge from this situation. First, with the West so dominant in the energy sector, and China's external energy dependence expanding daily, China has been forced to turn to states deemed "pariahs" by the United States and the European Union to gain energy more easily. These are often countries from which the West, or particularly the United States, has withdrawn. Hence China's close ties to states such as Venezuela, Sudan, and Iran, and its willingness to protect them from UN sanctions. Despite Western opprobrium for such foreign policy behavior, China feels a great need to maintain such bilateral ties. Second, since many resource-rich developing countries are, at best, illiberal democracies or are dominated by thuggish authoritarian regimes, China, if it wishes to fuel its economic growth and maintain social employment and stability, finds it must bring development projects and capital to these countries, even though it perpetuates dictatorship. Moreover, these rulers laud China as an alternative model of development (hailing a "Beijing

**Figure 3.3    Average Rise of Wages in China Compared to Other Low-Income Countries, 1995–2005**

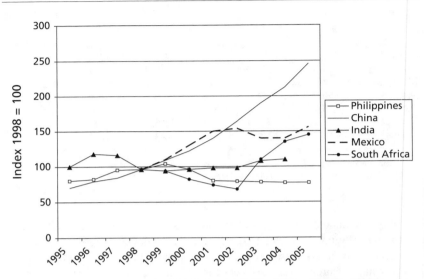

*Sources: China Statistical Yearbook 2005,* People's Bank of China, ILO (the Philippines, South Africa), IBGE (Brazil), Banco de Mexico, Ministry of Statistics and Programme Implementation (India); exchange rates from *IMF International Financial Statistics.*

*Notes:* Internationally comparable average wage rates have been used. Wages are average wages for China, the Philippines, and South Africa, average private sector wages in Brazil, and manufacturing wages for India and Mexico. Wages for 1998–2000 for the Philippines have been estimated using observed wages from 2001 and projecting them backward using GDP per capita growth rates.

Consensus") that can challenge the "Washington Consensus"—free trade, democracy, and government transparency—which challenges their political power. These ironies color China's ties to much of the developing world, all the while complicating its ties to the West.

## Notes

1. Deng Xiaoping, "Why China Has Opened Its Doors," *Foreign Broadcast Information Service, Daily Report: China,* February 12, 1980, p. LI-5.
2. Richard N. Rosecrance, *The Rise of the Trading State: Commerce and Conquest in the Modern World* (New York: Basic Books, 1986).
3. Ibid.
4. Robert Wade, *Governing the Market: Economic Theory and the Role of Government in East Asian Industrialization* (Princeton, NJ: Princeton University Press, 1990).

5. Alice Amsden, *Asia's Next Giant: South Korea and Late Industrialization* (New York: Oxford University Press, 1989).

6. Robert Gilpin, *The Political Economy of International Relations* (Princeton, NJ: Princeton University Press, 1987).

7. Nicholas R. Lardy, *Integrating China into the Global Economy* (Washington, DC: Brookings Institution Press, 2002).

8. Di Yingqing and Zheng Gang, "What Does China's Joining the WTO Actually Imply with Regard to China's Long-Term Interests?" *Gaige neican* [Internal Reference Material on Reform], no. 9 (May 5, 1999), pp. 34–38, and "The Key Is to Control the Initiative in Economic Development: An Analysis of the Problem of China's Joining the WTO," *Gaige neican*, no. 11 (May 20, 1999), pp. 35–39, translated in *The Chinese Economy: China and the WTO, Part II*, vol. 33, no. 2 (March–April 2000), pp. 23–32 and 19, respectively.

9. The World Bank, *The East Asian Miracle: Economic Growth and Public Policy* (Washington, DC: The World Bank, 1993).

10. Homi Kharas, "Lifting All Boats: Why China's Great Leap Is Good for the World's Poor," *Foreign Policy* (January–February 2005): 55.

11. Eswar Prasad, ed., *China's Growth and Integration into the World Economy*, Occasional Paper No. 232 (Washington, DC: International Monetary Fund, 2004).

12. Albert Keidel, "Assessing China's Economic Rise: Strengths, Weaknesses and Implications," paper for the conference on *China Rising: Assessing China's Economic and Military Power,* Foreign Policy Research Institute, Asia Program (March 12, 2007).

13. Andy Rothman, "China Eats the World: The Sustainability of Chinese Commodities Demand," Credit Lyonnais Securities Asia, March 2005.

14. Rothman, "China Eats the World."

15. Barbara Stallings, "China's Economic Relations with Developing Countries," Brown University, December 12, 2007, unpublished paper.

16. Available at www.mofcom.gov.cn/article/200407/20040700251628_1.xml. Translated by a law firm in Hong Kong.

17. Ibid.

18. Peter Nolan, *China and the Global Economy: National Champions, Industrial Policy, and the Big Business Revolution* (New York: Palgrave, 2001).

19. "China Issues Guidelines for Overseas Investment," *People's Daily Online,* April 10, 2009, http://english.peopledaily.com.cn/90001/90776/90884/6634477.html.

20. "China Expands Overseas Investment in First Quarter," *People's Daily Online,* April 15, 2009, http://english.peopledaily.com.cn/90001/90776/90884/6637964.html.

21. Aaron Friedberg, "'Going Out': China's Pursuit of Natural Resources and Implications for the PRC's Grand Strategy," *NBR Analysis* 17, no. 3 (September 2006).

22. Philip Saunders, *China's Global Activism: Strategy, Drivers, and Tools*, Occasional Paper No. 4 (Washington, DC: Institute for National Strategic Studies, National Defense University, 2006), p. 1.

23. Friedrich Wu, "The Globalization of Corporate China," *NBR Analysis* 16, no. 3 (December 2005).

24. Joseph Battat, *China's Outward Foreign Direct Investment* (Washington, DC: Foreign Investment Advisory Services, The World Bank, 2006).

25. Wu, "The Globalization of Corporate China," p. 18.

26. John Reed, "China's African Embrace Evokes Memories of the Old Imperialism," *Financial Times*, September 28, 2006.

27. Richard McGregor, "Chinese Diplomacy 'Hijacked' by Companies," *Financial Times*, March 17, 2008.

28. Ibid.

29. Ibid.

30. Zha Daojiong, "China's Energy Security: Domestic and International Issues," *Survival* 48, no. 1 (Spring 2006): 179–190.

31. Xin Ma and Philip Andrews-Speed, "The Overseas Activities of China's National Oil Companies: Rationale and Outlook," *Minerals and Energy*, no. 1 (2006): 17–30.

32. David Zweig and Bi Jianhai, "China's Global Hunt for Energy," *Foreign Affairs* 84, no. 5 (September–October 2005): 25–38.

33. "A Ravenous Dragon," *The Economist,* March 15, 2008, p. 4.

34. Peter S. Goodman, "Big Shift in China's Oil Policy: With Iraq Deal Dissolved by War, Beijing Looks Elsewhere," Washington Post Foreign Service, July 13, 2005.

35. Adam Blinick, "The Kazakh-Chine Pipeline: 'A Sign of the Times,'" Center on China's Transnational Relations, Working Paper No. 21 (Hong Kong: The Hong Kong University of Science and Technology, 2007).

36. "Worldwide Look at Reserves and Production," *Oil & Gas Journal* 104, no. 47 (December 18, 2006), pp. 22–23.

37. International Crisis Group, *China's Thirst for Oil*, Asia Report No. 153, June 9, 2008, p. 3.

38. John Ghazvinian, *Untapped: The Scramble for Africa's Oil* (Orlando, FL: Harcourt, 2007).

39. "A Ravenous Dragon," p. 4.

40. Stephanie Kleine-Ahlbrandt and Andrew Small, "China's New Dictatorship Diplomacy," *Foreign Affairs* 87, no. 1 (January–February 2008): 38–56.

41. Comments by Lois Dougan Tretiak at a meeting of the Canadian Chamber of Commerce in Hong Kong, 1999.

42. Asia Pacific Foundation of Canada, "China versus Southeast Asia in the Race for Investment," *Asia Pacific Bulletin No. 31*, November 2, 2001, Vancouver, Canada.

43. UNCTAD, *World Investment Report 2008: Transnational Corporations and the Infrastructure Challenge* (New York and Geneva: United Nations, 2008), annex table A.I.16.

44. UNCTAD, *World Investment Report 2008*, p. 10.

45. Asia Pacific Foundation, "China Versus Southeast Asia."

46. Lardy, *Integrating China.*

47. Prasad, *China's Growth and Integration*, p. 10. Based on reports by Chinese authorities; UN Conference on Trade and Development; World Bank; WTO; and IMF staff estimates.

48. Kharas, "Lifting All Boats."

49. Prasad, *China's Growth and Integration.*

50. Kharas, "Lifting All Boats."

51. Jamil Anderlini, "China Eyes Overseas Land in Food Push," *Financial Times*, May 8, 2008, and Associated Press, "China Farms the World to Feed a Ravenous Economy," May 4, 2008.

52. UNCTAD Handbook of Statistics 2008, retrieved from http://stats.unctad.org/Handbook/TableViewer/tableView.aspx.

53. Barry Sautman, "Friends and Interests: China's Distinctive Links with Africa," *CCTR Working Paper No. 12,* Center on China's Transnational Relations, Hong Kong University of Science and Technology, 2006.

54. Javier Blas and Matthew Green, "Africa-China Trade 2008, Commodities: Feeding an Insatiable Appetite," *Financial Times*, January 23, 2008.

55. Paul Gruenwald and Masahiro Hori, "Asian Exports: Intra-regional Trade Key to Asia's Export Boom," *IMF Survey Magazine: Countries & Region,* February 6, 2008.

56. Interviews by the author in December 2005.

57. Ian Taylor, "China's New Role in Africa," lecture presented at the Center on China's Transnational Relations, Hong Kong University of Science and Technology, May 2009.

58. Barry Eichengreen and Hui Tong, "How China Is Reorganizing the World Economy," *Asian Economic Policy Review* 1, no. 1 (2006): 73–97.

59. Mary Amiti and Caroline Freund, *An Anatomy of China's Export Growth* (Washington, DC: National Bureau of Economic Research, 2008).

60. Ibid.

61. Neil C. Hughes, "Trade War with China?" *Foreign Affairs* 84, no. 4 (July–August 2005).

62. Wayne M. Morrison and Marc Labonte, "China's Currency: Economic Issues and Options for US Trade Policy," *Congressional Research Service* (Washington, DC: May 22, 2008).

63. "Costs Driving US Manufacturing Firms out of China," American Chamber of Commerce in Hong Kong, http://news.yahoo.com/s/afp/20080428/pl_afp /chinausbusiness_080428140905&printer=1;_ylt=Al2iLXFWgJ6PIUNakreQvLit OrgF.

# 4

# China and Southeast Asia: A New Regional Order in the Making?

## Jörn Dosch

Predicting China's future position in the region has exercised an un-counted number of pundits. While some believe that China's military potential is significantly overestimated, others see China as a military superpower in ten to twenty years time. Regardless of the likelihood or soundness of the latter scenario, there can be little doubt about the fact that both the United States and most Southeast Asian governments are preparing themselves for a more as-sertive China. As Martin Stuart-Fox concludes in his outline of some two mil-lennia of contact between China and Southeast Asia,

> the ASEAN ten will do all in their power not to provoke China. What they want is to both slow and ease the changing power balance. They want the United States to remain a powerful presence, serving as a balancing force in the regional power equation, and have made this known; but they do not want to be part of any balance-of-power coalition. At the same time, they also want to make room for China.[1]

In other words, the Association of Southeast Asian Nations (ASEAN) has stayed true to its unwritten core principle of keeping its international options open and never leaning too heavily toward one big power. This strategy served ASEAN well during the Cold War and it seems to be working under the cur-rent structural circumstances, too. Most Southeast Asian states hedge against China primarily by accepting the need for a US role in the region. At the same time the acceptance of Chinese leadership among the Southeast Asian govern-ments is growing.

The People's Republic of China (PRC) increasingly exerts regional lead-ership by setting the rules and organizing a growing network of bilateral and multilateral relationships in economic and security (with regard to both tradi-tional and nontraditional security) fields. Just as in the cases of Pax Britannica and Pax Americana, the (re-)emerging Pax Sinica is characterized by the creation and enforcement of rules that favor the dominant state at the center of the regional order. At the same time, the policies of China as a preeminent power on the horizon also bring economic, security, and stability benefits to the states in its zone of influence. Thus, relations between China and Southeast Asia potentially take the form of a positive- rather than a zero-sum game.

Robert Sutter links China's rise to the potential emergence of "an 'inside-out' model of regional governance [which might be] displacing the past half century's 'outside-in' model led by the United States through its regional allies."[2] While such a model has not emerged yet as China is still predominantly a one-dimensional power, based first and foremost on economic strength, that cannot match the multidimensional power (hard and soft power) of the United States, the materialization of such a scenario is already looming large. In the current three-way competition among the United States, Japan, and China for regional influence in Southeast Asia, China appears to be the most proactive power. China has already started to act like a traditional big power, proactively drawing up its own blueprints for regional order and pulling smaller neighbors along in its wake. "China is making big loans for big projects to countries that used to be the sole preserve of the World Bank, the Asian Development Bank, the United States and Japan."[3] The ASEAN-China Free Trade Agreement (ACFTA), which was formally launched in 2002 and is projected to be fully implemented by 2010, is another example of China's increasing leverage over the international relations of the Asia-Pacific. In May 2009, the PRC agreed to contribute US$38.4 billion (the same amount as Japan and significantly more than South Korea and the ten ASEAN members, which are the other involved states) to a US$120 billion emergency currency pool to boost liquidity and help the region overcome the 2008–2009 global financial crisis.[4]

With the rapid growth of its economy, China has become increasingly involved in Southeast Asia's traditional security affairs as well. Beijing has established military links with Thailand, the Philippines, Indonesia, Singapore, Myanmar (Burma), Cambodia, and Malaysia. This extends not only to military aid and loans, bilateral talks on military issues, joint production of military equipment, and joint training exercises; it also includes participation in regional security forums and the signing of defense memoranda of understanding. The view among Southeast Asian elites that ASEAN and China share the profits of security management in an overall situation of a positive-sum game (or win-win situation according to the official Chinese term)[5] has been growing, particularly since the beginning of the Hu Jintao–Wen Jiabao era in 2002–2003. The foreign policy of the so-called fourth-generation leadership (after those led by Mao, Deng, and Jiang) has put strong emphasis on the fostering of friendly and mutually beneficial relations with neighboring states.

Leadership in international relations can only emerge and be institutionalized if the dominant regional power is willing to assume the responsibilities associated with it, is capable (in material terms of both hard and soft power) of establishing primacy, and is acceptable as a regional leader in the eyes of the subordinated states. In the following, I will try to provide empirical evidence that, while several conflicts and disputes (mainly with regard to border and territorial issues) remain unresolved in China–Southeast Asia relations, the PRC scores increasingly well in all three categories of leadership. I will begin with a brief elaboration on Chinese approaches to regional conflict management using the example of the South China Sea. This will be followed by a discussion of Beijing's attempts to increase energy security for itself by strengthening bilateral and multilateral relations with its Southeast Asian neighbors in the Greater Mekong Subregion (GMS). In the third steps, I will delve into a so far under-researched development: China's emergence as an international donor in the region. I conclude the chapter with some reflections on, first, the question as to whether ASEAN-centered regional cooperation in the region mediates a potentially emerging Pax Sinica and, second, the level of regional acceptance of Chinese preeminence and the limitations to it.

I deliberately avoid the term *hegemony* to characterize China's rise in Southeast Asia. The Chinese translation of *hegemony* as *ba dao* has a noxious moral connotation as "unjust domination." It is in this context that Zhou Enlai once said "we will never be hegemons," a statement later echoed by Deng Xiaoping and many other Chinese leaders. For example, Li Peng confirmed in 2001: "China is opposed to hegemonism and will never seek hegemony itself."[6] This part of the Maoist legacy seems to be unchanging. While the linguistic problem could be countered to some extent by stressing that the term *hegemony* has no normative connotation if based purely on Western international relations terminology, any discourse on Chinese hegemony would inevitably provoke an analogy with US hegemony. However, the central question is not as to whether China is able and willing to assume the role that the United States has played in the Asia Pacific over the past decades. The following discussion does not primarily focus on China's relative power vis-à-vis the United States or Japan in the region but considers structures and processes that have contributed to the strengthening of the PRC's position in Southeast Asia in absolute terms.

## Joining the Chinese Bandwagon: The Spratly Islands

Until recently, China, with the exception of the Mongol Yuan dynasty and a short period in the early Ming dynasty, was a land-oriented empire and not a maritime power. During most of Chinese history, the most dangerous threat came from nomadic powers in Inner Asia, which diverted Chinese strategic attention toward the northern and western frontiers. In addition, as agriculture provided the basis of Chinese economy in the premodern times, China did not need to develop a powerful navy or conquer maritime territories to secure its access to resources. All this has changed with the programs of modernization following the defeat of Qing China at the hands of maritime powers. The largest threat now came from the southeastern coasts, and a modernizing China's growth and stability would depend in large part on its connection with the world market and overseas resources, primarily through the East and South China Seas. It was in this context that in the early twentieth century Chinese authorities began to assert Chinese sovereignty over the Paracel Islands in the South China Sea. This triggered protest by the Vietnamese court at Hue, which had established its control over the islands well before the French conquests of Vietnam. In the 1930s, while China began to publish maps declaring its territorial claims in the South China Sea, French authorities in Indochina also began to set up weather stations on and send garrisons to the Paracel and the Spratly Islands.[7] The PRC and successive governments controlling South Vietnam, including the Hanoi regime since 1975, inherited this dispute from Nationalist China and French Indochina. Today, as China's participation in world trade and its demand for overseas energy and raw materials are both large and increasing, the South China Sea becomes more important for China.

At the heart of territorial disputes in the South China Sea lay the Spratly Islands—a collection of mostly barren coral reefs, atolls, and sandbars, many of which disappear at high tide, covering an area of some 70,000 square miles. This area is claimed, in whole or in part, by China, Taiwan, Vietnam, Malaysia, Brunei, and the Philippines. The other major area of dispute in the South China Sea concerns the Paracels, which are claimed by China and Vietnam. With the exception of Brunei, all of the disputants maintain a military presence on some of the islands. Since 1978, when the Philippines set out its exclusive economic zone formally including the island Kalayaan claimed by Manila, the parties in the dispute have held generally consistent claims. However, the controversy itself lay relatively dormant until 1988 when China and Vietnam clashed over Fiery Cross Reef. Since then, hostilities in the South China Sea have regularly erupted, most prominently between China and the Philippines. The Philippines considers China's occupation of Mischief Reef in 1995 and repeated Chinese incursions into Scarborough Reef since 1997 as direct assaults on the Philippines's territory.[8] Although a resolution of the disputes is not in sight, the ASEAN Declaration on the South China Sea of 1992 (signed by China in 2002) is often praised as a first step toward a peaceful settlement. Though nonbinding and from a formal institutional point of view not even a code of conduct, politicians and many scholarly observers alike hope that the agreement will nevertheless oblige the Southeast Asian claimants and China to avoid any activity that would damage or complicate their relations. In a very optimistic liberal-institutionalist scenario, the declaration constructively contributes to the avoidance of armed clashes among the parties over their conflicting claims on the sovereignty of the Spratly Islands[9] and the "declaration's confidence-building measures have appeared to appease claimants."[10]

One has to remain skeptical, however, that ASEAN's multilateral approach based on consensus building and voluntary, nonbinding commitment to the principle of nonuse of force will provide a sustained institutional framework for security management, particularly since the Declaration on the South China Sea lacks any specific provisions on how to resolve the conflict. Samuel Sharpe's finding that ASEAN has not been able to establish sufficient leverage in seeking a wider code of conduct with China is still valid.[11] The more-effective strategy for maintaining peace in the South China Sea is based on bilateral and multilateral negotiations initiated and facilitated by the PRC. Most important, Vietnam signed a land border treaty with China in 1999, and another treaty on the demarcation of the Gulf of Tonkin in 2000 that came into effect in June 2004 after more than three years of negotiations on how to implement the agreement (the demarcation itself was still ongoing in mid-2009). These treaties have narrowed down the scope of territorial disputes at least between these two countries relating to the Paracel and Spratly archipelagos.

In September 2004 the Philippines jumped on the Chinese bandwagon with the signing of an agreement for joint marine seismic exploration in the South China Sea for possible undersea oil. Vietnam joined the agreement in March 2005, when the Vietnam Petroleum Corporation (PetroVietnam), the Philippines National Oil Company, and the China National Offshore Oil Corporation finalized a tripartite agreement in Manila to jointly exploit oil and gas resources in the South China Sea. Philippines Foreign Minister Alberto Romulo and Vietnamese Foreign Minister Nguyen Dy Nien praised the deal as a significant measure to strengthen ASEAN-China cooperation and possibly pave the way for settlement of the South China Sea dispute. Beyond the political rhetoric, the agreement does not reflect core ASEAN values and norms but rather mirrors a new strategic setting in which the Southeast Asian claimants compete for the most favorable bilateral or multilateral agreements with China as the driving force behind the creation of regional order. This perception corresponds with the views of a Chinese government official who was involved in the negotiations.

> When we signed the agreement with the Philippines in 2004 it meant that Vietnam had fallen behind. And although Vietnam joined the agreement later, we are still more advanced in our negotiations with the Philippines. We are also speaking to Malaysia but these talks are less developed than those with the Philippines and Vietnam. A very important achievement in our relations with Vietnam is our joint maneuvers with the Vietnamese navy in the Beibu [Tonkin] Gulf.[12]

In late April 2006, the Chinese Navy began its first-ever patrols with a foreign ally, sending ships to patrol with Vietnamese warships in the Gulf of

Tonkin. According to the Chinese Ministry of National Defense, the joint patrols were intended to strengthen joint cooperation and maintain security of fishing fleets and oil exploration. The PRC is strengthening its naval power—driven at least partly by the concern that any disruption to energy shipments through the major sea lanes of communication would act as a brake on the nation's economy (in 2003, China surpassed Japan as a consumer of petroleum, moving into second place behind the United States): "China is pursuing sea power—measured by the Mahanian indices of commerce, bases, and ships—and it is building up a powerful navy with dispatch."[13]

Furthermore, in the wake of an apparent pirate attack on a Chinese fishing vessel in the Spratlys also in 2006 that left four crewmen dead and three wounded, China, the Philippines, and Vietnam announced plans to strengthen security cooperation in the Spratlys to address piracy, smuggling, and transnational crimes. So far the emphasis of the Vietnamese and Philippines governments on bilateral and trilateral diplomacy in the South China Sea, particularly in relations with China, has not been in open contradiction with collective ASEAN approaches. Yet, this diplomacy takes place outside the ASEAN framework and is a visible indication of a bandwagoning approach toward the PRC. Hanoi's and Manila's foreign-policy efforts might even place the countries in the South China Sea dispute in a more favorable position vis-à-vis China than some of their fellow ASEAN members, especially Malaysia. Despite occasional sabre-rattling—such as a brief diplomatic row between Beijing and Manila in the first half of 2009 over the sovereignty of the Spratlys—provocative acts between China and the Philippines and Vietnam respectively in the South China Sea have declined in the past decade.

## Positive-Sum Games in the Management of Resources?

As in the case of the Spratly Islands, the management of security in the Mekong valley first and foremost follows China's blueprint for order maintenance based on its national interest, particularly as far as access to resources is concerned. An increasingly important aspect of China's interests toward Vietnam, Laos, Cambodia, and Myanmar is the enhancement of the former's energy security. This is particularly visible within the context of the Greater Mekong Subregion. The GMS is a core element of Beijing's policy outlook. The PRC has been represented geographically in GMS by Yunnan Province since 1992. In December 2004, Guangxi Zhuang Autonomous Region was formally included in the GMS.

The Mekong River is the world's twelfth-largest river and Southeast Asia's longest waterway. It originates in Tibet and flows through the Chinese province of Yunnan before continuing southward, touching the territories of six countries (China, Cambodia, Laos, Myanmar, Thailand, and Vietnam) and ending in the South China Sea. The GMS covers some 2.3 million square kilometers and contains a population of about 245 million. The post–World War II history of cooperation within the Mekong valley dates back to 1957 when the Mekong Committee was established at the initiative of the UN Economic Commission for Asia and the Far East (ECAFE) and four riparian countries of the lower Mekong Basin (Cambodia, Laos, Thailand, and Vietnam). For more than three decades, however, the implementation of subregional integration was halted by the prevalence of cold-war structures, or more accurately hot wars and armed conflict, in the region. The process only gained momentum in 1992 when, with the assistance of the Asian Development Bank, the six riparian states of the Mekong River (Cambodia, China, Laos, Myanmar, Thailand, Vietnam) entered into a program of formalized subregional cooperation.

The GMS program has been directed to the management of nontraditional security arenas such as the facilitation of sustainable economic growth and improvement of the standard of living in general and the management of environmental and energy security in particular.[14] The sustainable utilization of water and natural resources in the Mekong Basin is directly and inevitably linked to human survival in the region. Energy security is mainly related to the promising but not uncontroversial issue of hydroelectric power. Compared with rivers of a similar size like the Nile and the Mississippi, the Mekong is still relatively untouched. The first Mekong bridge (between Thailand and Laos) was opened only in 1994, and the first mainstream dam, the 1,500 megawatt Manwan, was completed only in 1995 in Yunnan. Since then the development of hydropower has been among the main priorities of the GMS project and resulted in the two Laos-based power plants, the Theun Hinboun Hydropower Project, which started commercial operation in March 1998, and the Nam Leuk Hydropower Development that was completed in May 2000.

With international conflicts over river water becoming more frequent, there is concern that the Mekong could become a serious source of tension unless the six states can agree on rules for developing the river. The most valuable achievement to reduce the potential for conflict is a technical cooperation agreement achieved in 2002 between China and the Mekong River Commission (MRC, founded in 1995), grouping Thailand, Cambodia, Laos, and Vietnam. The agreement commits China to sending twenty-four-hourly water level and twelve-hourly rainfall data to the MRC to help forecast floods. The design of an early flood warning strategy ranks very high on the agenda of both policymakers and international donor organizations. While China has duly provided the required information since the agreement's implementation in 2003, other key data—most decisively on water quality and pollution—are kept strictly confidential. Various attempts by the lower Mekong states, particularly Vietnam, to get access have failed.[15]

On issues that would impact national decisionmaking authority, such as dam building in the Chinese stretch of the Mekong, China steadfastly refuses to share information. The uncoordinated construction of power plants and irrigation systems by the upper Mekong countries, particularly China, which plans to build more than a dozen power plants (although on the Mekong's tributaries and not the main stream), poses a serious challenge to subregional stability. The construction could result in a potentially explosive competition between the upper and the lower Mekong states for water resources. Politicians and senior officials from the lower Mekong states, mainly Thailand, Vietnam, and Cambodia, have regularly expressed concerns about China's proposed dam-building activities, albeit more indirectly and in private than openly and in official intergovernmental meetings. Some perceive China's ambitious hydropower plans as a zero-sum game in which the PRC's economic gains would be paid for by the lower Mekong states' environmental costs, such as rising salinity levels in Vietnam's agriculturally indispensable Mekong Delta.

Official Chinese interests in the Mekong region can roughly be divided into two realms of importance: domestic and foreign policy. The domestic interest consists of the development of China's landlocked western provinces and the promotion of border trade with the adjoining countries of Myanmar, Laos, and Vietnam. A further domestic strategy aims at narrowing the gap between the ethnic Chinese Han population and ethnic minorities. Furthermore, the government envisions that an economically emerging west will reduce internal migration from western China to the booming coastal cities. In a more general strategic sense, Beijing seeks to put its relations with Southeast Asia on an amicable basis in order to counterbalance US influence in the region.[16] The PRC is able to play a preeminent role in the Mekong valley, partly because it imposes its will on the lesser states in terms of setting the stage for, but also the limits to, cooperation, and partly because the other members benefit from China's cooperation and thus accept China's leadership.

Energy security offers a good example of the emergence of reciprocally beneficial linkages between China and the states in its zone of influence. Since September 2006, China has been supplying electricity to Vietnam through a cross-border 220-kilovolt power transmission line to ease Vietnam's chronic power shortage problems. Further transmission lines are under construction or being planned. China (through the state-owned company, China Southern Power Grid) is also involved in the building of electricity generation facilities in Vietnam, Laos, and Myanmar, enabling the Southeast Asian GMS members to deliver electricity to China's western provinces when it will be much needed in only a few years' time to further fuel rapid industrialization. The electric power trade between Yunnan and Vietnam has reached some US$100 million in 2007.[17] In February 2009, the Chinese Guangdong Nuclear Power Group announced its interest in helping Vietnam build its first nuclear power plant, comprising two 1,000-megawatt reactors to be located in the southern coastal province of Ninh Thuan.[18] The trend toward ever-closer ties between China and Vietnam, which is not necessarily directly facilitated but at least underpinned by the two countries' shared political ideology, also serves the wider interests of both communist parties vis-à-vis the United States. Despite strengthening US-Vietnam economic and diplomatic ties, Vietnam is keen to avoid aligning itself too closely with the United States, while China is equally eager to counter the growing influence of the United States in Vietnam.

Relations between China and Myanmar are another case in point for the growing benefits of cooperation on energy security.[19] China is playing a key role in the construction of large dams on rivers in Myanmar, such as the Salween River. There are at least fourteen Chinese companies involved in approximately forty hydropower projects in Myanmar.[20] Chinese investors have become increasingly dominant in the energy, mining, and to some extent manufacturing sectors in Myanmar.[21] The rapid growth of China's economy has resulted in an increasing demand for energy resources, particularly oil and gas. Although the country itself is rich in energy resources on an absolute basis, China is poorly endowed on a per capita basis. The widening gap between China's oil supply and demand and the projected gap between natural gas supply and demand mean the country will increasingly become reliant on imported oil and gas. The government encourages the biggest Chinese state-owned oil companies, including Sinopec, China National Offshore Oil Corporation (CNOOC), and China National Petroleum Corporation (CNPC), to find and develop new fields at home and abroad and has heavily invested in the construction of pipelines and the exploration of oil and gas fields, including in Myanmar. This meets the interest of the Burmese military junta that needs external support to facilitate the exploitation and development of the country's energy resources. The cooperation with China offers potential areas to foreign investors while maintaining a tight control over the extraction, distribution, and sale of its resources. Some observers claim that significant output of petroleum for example is not expected until after 2010.[22] Nevertheless, it is obvious that the Chinese government believes in the profitability of investments in Myanmar's energy sector. After all, Myanmar's energy reserves are said to be abundant, with proven recoverable reserves of 510 billion cubic meters out of a total 2.54 trillion cubic meters estimated (but not currently recoverable) reserves of offshore and onshore gas. In addition, its recoverable crude oil reserve is estimated to have 3.2 billion barrels.[23] China has at least 17 onshore and offshore oil and gas projects in Myanmar. Key investors are Sinopec, CNPC, and CNOOC, which signed MoUs (memos of understanding) with MOGE for the exploration and the sale of natural gas.[24]

China's involvement in Myanmar provokes questions beyond energy security: Has the PRC's eminent role in Myanmar's economy and—at least indirectly—the fact that this role has provided a lifeline to the Burmese generals been strengthened or even facilitated by the European and US pullout from the country? And in a more general sense, with potentially far-reaching implications, does China's "no strings attached" approach to international cooperation challenge the core principle of Western and Japanese official development assistance in Southeast Asia?

## China's Emergence as an International Donor

In 2007, the total official development assistance (ODA) from members of the OECD Development Assistance Committee (DAC) fell by 8.4 percent in real terms to US$103.7 billion. The combined ODA of the fifteen members of the DAC that are EU members—which represents 60 percent of all DAC ODA—declined by 5.8 percent in real terms to US$62.1 billion. Among the most decisive developments has been the downward trend in Japan's ODA. Japan tumbled to fifth place among the world's twenty-two major aid donors in 2007, its lowest ranking since 1972. The country's net ODA was US$7.7 billion, representing 0.17 percent of gross domestic product (GDP) and a 30.1 percent fall in real terms year-on-year. The four largest donors in 2007, by volume, were the United States, followed by Germany, France, and the United Kingdom. The only countries to exceed the United Nations target of 0.7 percent of GDP were Denmark, Luxembourg, the Netherlands, Norway, and Sweden.[25]

The global decline in DAC ODA payments in general and Japan's contributions in particular were in part due to a decrease in debt relief operations, which had been exceptionally high in 2005 and 2006. Although figures for total ODA worldwide—DAC and non-DAC—do not exist, empirical evidence suggests that development assistance of so-called emerging donor countries, such as China, Brazil, India, Indonesia, Malaysia, Mexico, South Africa, and South Korea, has been significantly growing while the boundaries between donor and recipient countries have become increasingly fuzzy. This is particularly the case in Asia where most of the "new donors" are located, with China being the most important one. Partly due to the successful development of China's economy, the Japanese government informed Beijing that it wanted to end its ODA yen loan program to China by 2008.[26]

At the same time, the development aid strategies and policies of OECD donors have markedly changed in recent years. In addition to the Millennium Development Goals (MDGs),[27] the promotion of democracy, good governance, and respect for human rights and for the rule of law occupy center-stage on the development agenda. However, the governance focus of the European Union and the United States is in stark contrast to Japan's (still) predominantly mercantilist approach to ODA and China's "no strings attached" ODA policy based primarily on national resource interests. The possible clash between OECD and Chinese concepts of development assistance toward the African continent has recently been the growing focus of academic and practical-political discourses. Yet, East and Southeast Asia have received relatively little attention, even though the seeming contradictions between European,

Chinese, and Japanese ODA policies and the potential long-term implications of increasing competition among donors are nowhere more obvious than in Asia. China's rapid transformation from an ODA recipient to a main donor in Asia especially has not been researched yet.

Since the 1950s, Japan had been successfully implementing regional foreign and foreign economic policies through the generous provision of economic and financial and above all official development assistance. Japan's *keizai gaiko* (economic diplomacy) was the country's most efficient and effective foreign policy tool contributing to peace and stability in the region and creating the environment and preconditions for stable relations between Japan and its neighboring countries in East and Southeast Asia.

Japan's rapid economic growth in the 1960s, 1970s, and 1980s enabled Tokyo to dedicate significant financial resources to the economic development of East and Southeast Asia, while at the same time consolidating and expanding its political and economic influence and position in the region. To be sure, as a country highly dependent on the import of raw materials (due to the lack of natural resources in Japan), establishing stable and mutually beneficial relations with countries rich in natural resources in Asia (and beyond) was a necessity for Japan and its own economic development. At the heart of Japan's foreign economic policy was the country's strategy to use its wealth and economic capabilities to help create a politically stable neighborhood beneficial to its own economic and political position and standing in the region.[28]

From the early 1980s onward, Japan greatly increased its contributions to the World Bank and International Monetary Fund. In addition to its multilateral efforts, Japan raised its share of ODA giving among members of the DAC from 12 percent in 1980 to about 20 percent in 1998. In 1998, Japan's ODA per capita was roughly three times that of the United States. For many years, Japanese aid has been concentrated in the region of Asia. Indeed, Asian countries received an average of 60 percent of total Japanese ODA during the 1980s and 1990s, an amount greater than any other region.[29]

China in particular but also South Korea and a number of developing countries in Southeast Asia profited immensely from Japan's support and promotion of regional economies. Recently, however, Japan has begun to decrease its ODA payments in East and Southeast Asia and further cuts are likely in the coming years in view of Japan's rising public debt and fiscal problems. On the one hand, the Japanese government has been facing pressure from within Japan to curtail its spending on ODA. On the other hand, the international community (particularly the developing nations) expects Japan to continue to provide a high level of development assistance. The Japanese government is therefore being exposed to competing pressures from the domestic and international communities, and under these conditions it will likely find its continued active promotion of ODA much more difficult than originally anticipated.[30]

The reduction of Japan's ODA payments to Southeast Asian countries suggests that Tokyo is prepared to let China fill the vacuum left by the cutback of Japanese ODA and other forms of economic and financial support. Despite being still a developing country itself (by official classifications), China has in recent years developed proactive and visible foreign economic policies that in some ways resemble the Japanese version of the same policies in the 1970s, 1980s, and 1990s.

A Japanese 2006 ODA White Paper claimed that contributions by China, India, and other emerging donor nations had "become significant enough for developing countries to influence them. . . . It is quite difficult to grasp the whole picture of aid activities by such countries. They should make their activities more transparent and follow international rules."[31] Indeed, China has been accused of

- unethical and string-free support for "rogue" or "pariah" states;
- providing unconditional aid and opaque loans that are said to undermine European and multilateral efforts to persuade governments to increase their transparency, public accountability, and financial management (governance agenda);
- "free-riding" Western debt relief efforts and undermining individual countries' external debt sustainability and disregarding the multilateral framework for debt sustainability;
- intensifying global economic and strategic competition to secure energy supplies;
- using its self-interested strategies in dealing with developing countries, trying to assert influence, and using its soft power in order to support its own development without any coordination with Western countries, often even aggressively confronting them; and
- neglecting environmental and social standards.[32]

In the Philippines, the Chinese government has spent US$1.8 billion on development projects and will provide US$6 to 10 billion in loans over the next three to five years to finance infrastructure projects in that country.[33] China's growing support for the Philippines comes at a time when the European Union is considering terminating its development assistance for the country given the lack of progress in key development areas. In the case of Cambodia, Southeast Asia's most aid-dependent country where China has emerged as the largest foreign donor, Beijing provided at least US$800 million in 2005 and 2006 with a focus on infrastructure and hydropower projects. The influence of other donors has inevitably declined. OECD donors are worried about their dwindling leverage over key reform areas such as tackling corruption and strengthening good governance in Cambodia. "China has offered aid unconditionally, a policy line that has created tensions among parts of the donor community."[34] In a similar vein, the PRC has increased its presence in Laos and established itself particularly in sectors, such as agriculture, forestry, and infrastructure development, where other donors have reduced their role. Some donors perceive Laos as needing support to avoid being simply taken over by China. However, as Lao government officials point out, it is difficult to differentiate between Beijing's ODA and FDI as most of the funds are channeled through Chinese state companies.[35]

According to the EU's Development Cooperation Instrument (DCI) of 2006, European development cooperation with Asia is, inter alia, intended to consolidate and support democracy, the rule of law, human rights and fundamental freedoms, good governance, gender equality, and related instruments of international law.[36] These priorities seem to be at odds with China's presumed self-interest-driven motivations to extend ODA to the region. If the PRC's attempts at regional leadership already extend even to the highly normative domain of development cooperation, it is hard to imagine that growing Chinese preeminence would go unchallenged.

## The Role of ASEAN, Multilateral Cooperation, and Regional Integration in Mediating the Emerging Pax Sinica

"Everyone wants ASEAN to be in the driver's seat of regional co-operation because ASEAN's leadership is more acceptable in the region than China's or Japan's." This remark by Valérie Niquet, the Director of the Asia Center at the French Institute of International Relations in Paris[37] reflects the general perception that the key role in the search for, and maintenance of, multilateral arrangements in the region has been played by ASEAN ever since the organization took the initiative to apply its well-established model for regional security on a wider Asia-Pacific basis in the early 1990s. ASEAN was founded in 1967 and is often referred to as the most successful regional cooperation scheme outside Europe. The ASEAN dialogue mechanism, a set of various forms of official and informal consultation, coordination, and networking at different levels of decisionmaking, worked effectively enough to produce peaceful conflict management. Perhaps the most valuable achievement of the ASEAN security model is that it has successfully managed to keep residual conflicts between the members (especially territorial disputes) from leading to armed confrontation. Recent developments suggest that the peace dividend of the so-called ASEAN Way of regional cooperation might be successfully extended to relations between Southeast Asia and China. At least at first glance, empirical evidence seems to suggest that ASEAN has been successfully engaging China, thereby significantly contributing to order-building, security, and stability in the Asia-Pacific. When the process of ASEAN identity formation seemingly expanded into the wider East Asian or Asia-Pacific region, academic analysis followed suit: The focus is now on East Asian community building, and the assumed effects are similar to the observed empirical reality within Southeast Asia. The more the idea of community takes hold in East Asia, the more stable and secure the region will become, so the argument goes. China's integration in such a community is seen as key to the emergence of a peaceful international order, and ASEAN has regularly received credit for its leadership abilities and presumed success in engaging China in a growing network of regional consultative fora such as the ASEAN Regional Forum, the ASEAN+3 Meeting, and the East Asian Summit.

However, as the example of the ASEAN-China Free Trade Agreement shows, it was primarily China that engaged ASEAN, not the other way around. Chinese Premier Zhu Rongji first proposed a trade agreement at the ASEAN+China meeting in November 2000 in response to the Asian economic crisis and regional concerns about the impact of China's then-imminent WTO membership. Under the Framework Agreement on ASEAN-China Comprehensive Economic Cooperation, which was officially announced and signed in November 2002, ASEAN and China envision the liberalization of 99 percent of their bilateral trade in stages—by 2010 for the ASEAN-6 and China, and 2015 for Cambodia, Laos, Myanmar, and Vietnam.[38]

Yet this proposal "also arose out of an acute sensitivity toward the need to maintain relations with as many states as possible in order to constrain American power under a global system defined by the struggle between 'one superpower, many great powers.'"[39] Since China's admission into the WTO, the proposed free trade agreement has further contributed to the enhancement of Beijing's position as a preeminent regional power, not only in relation to the United States but also at the expense of Japan. Tokyo reacted with alarm to the plan and subsequently entered into talks on a Japan-ASEAN FTA within the framework of the so-called Japan-ASEAN Comprehensive Economic Partnership. Within ASEAN, China is perceived as an engine of growth, a distinction that previously belonged to Japan. ACFTA, accompanied by the offer of an early harvest, has strengthened China's status as a benevolent regional leader. Strategic, security, and political objectives are essential elements of Beijing's economic outreach. For example, according to one of the PRC's most senior economists, Ma Hong, "the pattern of setting up a free-trade region is a favorable direction for China to develop the relationship of regional grouping and *regional alliance*.[40] China's proposal of a "strategic partnership" with ASEAN that was made at the ASEAN foreign ministers' meeting in Phnom Penh in June 2003 has to be seen in the same context. Multilateralism in ASEAN-China relations has developed to a degree where Beijing is setting the regional agenda.[41] A European senior diplomat confirms this for meetings between the European Union and China. "China is very pro-active on political issues and increasingly open to agendas that used to be taboo only a short while ago, including regionalism, monetary integration, and even democracy and civil society. Beijing is constantly testing new ideas. Anything goes as long as Taiwan, Tibet and Falun Gong are not mentioned."[42]

The first East Asian Summit in Kuala Lumpur in December 2005 is another case in point. The meeting was attended by the ten ASEAN members, China, Japan, South Korea, India, New Zealand, and Australia. Japan's suggestion that Washington at least be invited as an observer made no headway mainly as the result of Beijing's effort to exclude the United States. Behind ASEAN's closed doors, Indonesia and Vietnam were especially critical of Washington's exclusion but did not want to challenge Beijing. According to Abdul Razak Baginda,[43] "there is now this feeling that we have to consult the Chinese. We have to accept some degree of Chinese leadership, particularly in light of the lack of leadership elsewhere."[44] China has both an interest and the capabilities (in terms of hard power and, most important, soft power as the example of ACFTA demonstrates) to provide regional leadership. However, this does not mean that China always gets its way. For example, prior to the first East Asian Summit, China's offer to host the second meeting was rejected by ASEAN.[45] China was equally unsuccessful in lobbying the Vietnamese government for the exclusion of Taiwan from the Asia-Pacific Economic Cooperation (APEC) Summit in November 2006 in Hanoi and the right of sitting next to the host at the summit meetings (the seating was instead arranged in alphabetical order as at previous APEC summits).[46]

## Conclusion and Outlook

If community building and identity formation take place in the Asia Pacific in general and in Sino–Southeast Asia relations in particular, they are not the prime driving forces behind growing regional stability but rather mask, or perhaps ease, the effects of China's increasing international preeminence. From a neorealist perspective it can be argued that relative order and peace in the formerly war-prone region have not derived from ASEAN's leadership in engaging China but are mainly due to the rising concentration of Chinese power in Southeast Asia. When one state possesses considerably more economic, military, and political power resources than the other states in a system of states, it can use that power to coerce the other states or provide them with selective incentives in order to induce cooperation. In this manner, the dominant state increases the costs of defection and decreases the risks of cooperation, thereby making peace and stability possible.[47]

On the one hand, the PRC's foreign policy since the early 1990s is characterized by a "gradual acceptance of a multilateral approach towards Southeast Asia"[48] and "a more vigorous approach to multilateralism at both the international and regional level."[49] On the other hand, there can be little doubt that Beijing is challenging ASEAN's trademark role as the architect of multilateral cooperation in the post–Cold War Asia-Pacific and, partly as the result of ASEAN's weaknesses and partly due to China's quest for preeminence, has more and more assumed the position of first among equals in the existing multilateral frameworks. While China's active integration in multilateral activities has seemingly improved Sino-ASEAN relations, relative stability and peace between the two sides are not primarily the result of institution building and community formation, an eastward extension of the ASEAN way of diplomacy, or an emerging liberal peace deriving from tighter networks of economic cooperation. As the South China Sea disputes, cooperation in the GMS, and the PRC's rapidly growing role as a donor demonstrate, China is increasingly assuming a regional leadership role that sets the rules because this role is perceived as being favorable to the enhancement of the PRC's national interest. Furthermore, and equally important, Beijing's leading role as a manager of regional order is acceptable to key players in Southeast Asia as they see their own benefits as the result of cooperation with China. While China does not promote its system of governance abroad—in the way that OECD donors tie development aid to good governance or the United States has followed the credo of manifest destiny in the transfer of political norms and values—the Deng and post-Deng reform process provides an attractive model in some parts of Southeast Asia and particularly to Vietnam and possibly also Laos.[50]

While the Spratly Islands disputes remain unresolved and concerns over China's use of the Mekong's resources have not been entirely eliminated, the perception among Southeast Asian elites that ASEAN and China share the profits of regional order management in an overall situation of a positive-sum game has been growing. China *has integrated ASEAN* into a regional order that, while not hostile to multilateralism, mainly reflects hard strategic thinking on Beijing's part and is primarily based on rules established by the PRC. Unthinkable only a decade ago, the acceptance of regional Chinese leadership in the management of security has grown. ASEAN diplomats have begun turning to Chinese colleagues for guidance during international meetings. Only a short while ago, Chinese diplomats were viewed as outsiders by their Southeast Asian counterparts.[51]

As the PRC's growing preeminence in the management of regional order is accepted and even perceived as beneficial for the region by key governmental elites in Southeast Asia, the international relationship between China and ASEAN will increasingly generate stability. Due to the reciprocal nature of this system, which generates benefits for both the dominant and the lesser actors, and in the absence of clear systemic alternatives, "no state believes it profitable to attempt to change the system," as Robert Gilpin put it in general terms.[52] China–Southeast Asia relations might not have reached a state of complete equilibrium as a result, but they are more stable than they have ever been before.

Is this too simplistic a view? Do Beijing's growing security and economic links with Southeast Asia and proactive role in multilateral fora indeed attest to China's ever-increasing regional influence and leadership? Or are we easily blinded by a highly successful mix of Chinese "win-win" rhetoric and China hype? Certainly, it should not be ignored that there are limitations to the Southeast Asian embrace of Chinese preeminence. For example, a sense of resentment toward China, emanating from historical legacies, persists within much of Vietnam's political elite, as remained the case with a proportion of the wider Vietnamese population. A low point in diplomatic relations was reached in December 2007 when thousands of Vietnamese took to the streets of Hanoi and Ho Chi Minh City to protest against what they viewed as China's incursions into Vietnamese territory in the South China Sea (the first rally in half a century in communist Vietnam).[53] Anti-China protests resurfaced in December 2008 but were quickly overwhelmed by the Vietnamese government forces. This is where the United States reenters the scene. No two sets of bilateral relationships are more important to Vietnam than its relations with China *and* the United States. Maintaining the best possible balance in its relations with the two powers has emerged as the cornerstone of Vietnam's foreign relations in the post–Cold War era. All Southeast Asian governments (with Myanmar being the only notable exception) hedge against China by sustaining their links with the United States, because "Washington is seen as the 'least distrusted power' in Southeast Asia with no territorial or other ambitions directly at odds with ASEAN states' interests."[54] In the 1990s, Singapore, Thailand, Indonesia, and Malaysia signed military access arrangements with the United States, followed in 1999 by the implementation of the US-Philippines Visiting Forces Agreement. These arrangements form part of a broader set of military cooperation and training activities in Washington's relations with Southeast Asian states that follow a new approach of a "places not bases" policy in the region. In 2003, the United States granted Philippines and Thailand "major non-NATO ally" status, which entitles the two governments to special access to US intelligence, among other privileges. In 2005, Singapore and the United States signed a Strategic Framework Agreement for closer partnership in defense and security cooperation based on the explicit premise that "a strong United States military presence is vital for regional peace and stability."[55]

Beyond long-term strategic considerations, both the United States and ASEAN states consider a US military presence as a decisive—probably the most important—contribution to securing the commercial routes in the region. US military power in the Asia-Pacific is based on the presence and mission of the Seventh Fleet, the largest of the Navy's forward-deployed fleets, including 40–50 ships, 200 aircraft, and about 20,000 Navy and Marine Corps personnel. As for US soft power in Southeast Asia, US exports to ASEAN in 2008 are more than twice as large as US exports to China. Thailand, the Philippines, and Indonesia are among the top twenty-five trading partners of the United States. Furthermore, the United States is by far the largest overall investor in

Southeast Asia, followed by Japan and the United Kingdom. Washington has signed trade and investment framework agreements with Brunei, Cambodia, Indonesia, Malaysia, the Philippines, Thailand, and Vietnam and is negotiating FTAs with Thailand and Malaysia. Preliminary free trade talks have been conducted with the Philippines and Vietnam. While "the United States has used FTAs as political rewards for countries that support US foreign and security policies,"[56] the strategy works because it is a two-way street. US and Southeast Asian views on the mutually reinforcing links between economic and security gains overlap. Recent developments suggest that the United States will not drastically change its strategic approaches toward Southeast Asia. Absent irrational leadership or a catastrophic attack, the most likely midterm scenario for the US role in the region is a continuation of bilateral patterns in economic and security relations characterized by economic partnerships and free-trade agreements on the one hand and defense arrangements with a growing number of Southeast Asian states on the other. Furthermore, opposition to the US international role has been relatively low-key in Southeast Asia in recent years, even during the Iraq War. Yet, if any single actor was to challenge the well-established US position as a primus inter pares among the external powers in Southeast Asia, China is the most likely candidate. For the time being and to the extent that their limited autonomy toward regional order building allows, the Southeast Asian governments—individually and collectively through ASEAN—keep their international options open and pursue a double hedging strategy that is aimed at taking maximum advantage of both Beijing's and Washington's strong involvement in the region while trying to prevent the (re-)emergence of any type of hegemony, be it US or Chinese.

## Notes

1. Martin Stuart-Fox, *A Short History of China and Southeast Asia: Tribute, Trade and Influence* (Crows Nest, Australia: Allen & Unwin, 2003), p. 240.

2. Robert Sutter, "China's Rise, Southeast Asia, and the United States: Is a China-Centered Order Marginalizing the United States?" in E. Goh and S. W. Simon, eds., *China, the United States, and Southeast Asia. Contending Perspectives on Politics, Security, and Economics* (New York and London: Routledge, 2008).

3. Jane Perlez, "China Competes with West in Aid to Its Neighbors," *New York Times*, September 18, 2006.

4. Stephen Coates, "ASEAN, China, S Korea Finalise Crisis Fund Pact," *Agence France Press*, May 3, 2009.

5. "China will pursue a 'mutually beneficial win win' strategy in its opening up to the outside world in the next five years . . . ." Chinese Communist Party (CPC), Beijing (October 18, 2005), http://china.org.cn.

6. "Deepening Understanding, Fostering Friendship and Strengthening Cooperation," Speech by Chairman Li Peng of the Standing Committee of the National People's Congress at Indian International Centre, January 13, 2001, http://in.chinaembassy.org/eng/zyjh/t61434.htm (last accessed November 3, 2008).

7. Monique Chemillier-Gendreau, *Sovereignty over the Paracel and the Spratly Islands* (The Hague: Kluwer Law International, 2000). Nguyen Nha, "Thu dat lai van de Hoang Sa [Reconsidering the Paracel Islands Issue]," *Su Dia* [History and Geography], no. 29 (1975). Jinming Li and Li Dexia, "The Dotted Line on the Chinese Map of the South China Sea: A Note," *Ocean Development & International Law* 34 (2003): 287–295.

8. Liselotte Odgaard, "The South China Sea: ASEAN's Security Concerns About China," *Security Dialogue* 34, no. 1 (2004): 16.

9. Joseph Yu-Shek Cheng, "The ASEAN-China Free Trade Area: Genesis and Implications," *Australian Journal of International Affairs* 58, no. 2 (2004): 259.

10. "Philippines 'All Parties' to ASEAN Declaration on Spratlys Urged to Observe Peace Principles," Thai Press Reports, March 17, 2009.

11. Samuel Sharpe, "An ASEAN Way to Security Cooperation in Southeast Asia?" *The Pacific Review* 16, no. 2 (2003): 1–50.

12. Author interview with a Chinese senior government official in Shanghai, May 2006.

13. James R. Holmes, Andrew C. Winner, and Toshi Yoshihara, *Indian Naval Strategy in the 21st Century* (New York: Routledge, 2009), p. 128.

14. As of December 31, 2006, Asian Development Bank (ADB) had extended loans totaling almost US$1.92 billion for 28 loan and grant projects with a total project cost of $6.8 billion. These projects are in transportation (18 projects), energy (4), health (3), and tourism (3). GMS governments and development partners have provided about $2.2 billion and $2.7 billion, respectively, for these 28 projects. The ADB claims that between 1990 and 2003, the proportion of people living in the GMS on less than $1 a day fell from 46 to 33.8 percent in Cambodia, 33 to 13.4 percent in the PRC, 52.7 to 28.8 percent in Laos, 10.1 to less than 1 percent in Thailand, and 50.7 to 9.7 percent in Vietnam (ADB, Greater Mekong Subregion, Development Effectiveness Brief, Draft, July 18, 2007).

15. Author interviews conducted in the GMS states between June 2006 and September 2008.

16. Jörn Dosch and Oliver Hensengerth, "Sub-Regional Cooperation in Southeast Asia: The Mekong Basin," *European Journal of East Asian Studies* 4, no. 2 (2005): 263–285.

17. "First Sino-Vietnamese Joint Power Station to Start Construction," *SinoCast China Business Daily News,* November 13, 2007, p. 1.

18. Tom Grieder, "China to Assist Vietnam in Building Its First NPP," *Global Insight,* February 24, 2009.

19. The following findings on China's activities in Myanmar are based on a dissertation by Daphne Berenice Pels, "The Sino-Burmese Friendship: Origins, Development and Motivations," submitted to the Department of East Asian Studies, University of Leeds, in May 2008.

20. Earth Rights International, "China in Burma: The Increasing Investment of Chinese Multinational Corporations in Burma's Hydropower, Oil & Gas, and Mining Sectors," Burma Project, September 2007.

21. Toshihiro Kudo, *Myanmar's Economic Relations with China: Can China Support the Myanmar Economy?* Institute of Developing Economies Discussion Paper 66, Japan External Trade Organization (JETRO), 2006. "China: Hungry for Energy: Beijing Hunts for a Coherent Policy As It Gets Hooked on Foreign Oil," *Business Week,* December 24, 2001.

22. Energy Information Administration, "World Oil Markets Analysis to 2030: Petroleum and Other Liquid Fuels," in *International Energy Outlook 2007* (Washington, DC: EIA, 2007).

23. Maung Aung Myoe, *Sino-Myanmar Economic Relations Since 1988,* Asia Research Institute, National University of Singapore, Working Paper Series 86, 2007, p. 15.

24. Earth Rights International, "China in Burma," p. 3.

25. OECD DAC statistics, http://stats.oecd.org/wbos/Default.aspx?usercontext=sourceoecd.

26. Reinhard Drifte, "The End of Japan's ODA Yen Loan Programme to China in 2008 and Its Repercussions," *Japan aktuell—Journal of Current Japanese Affairs,* no. 1 (2008): 3–15.

27. The MDGs, among other objectives, aim at the eradication of poverty, achieving universal primary education, and promoting gender equality.

28. Axel Berkofsky, "True Strategic Partnership or Rhetorical Window Dressing? A Closer Look at the Relationship Between the EU and Japan," *Japan aktuell—Journal of Current Japanese Affairs*, no. 2 (2008): 22–37.

29. John P. Tuman and Jonathan R. Strand, "The Role of Mercantilism, Humanitarianism, and Gaiatsu in Japan's ODA Programme in Asia," *International Relations of the Asia-Pacific* 6, no. 1 (2000): 61–80.

30. A. Kusano, "Japan's ODA in the 21st Century," *Asia-Pacific Review* 7, no. 1 (2000): 38–55.

31. Quoted from *The Daily Yomiuri*, Tokyo, November 20, 2006.

32. Bernt Berger and Uwe Wissenbach, *EU-China-Africa Trilateral Development Cooperation: Common Challenges and New Directions* (Bonn: German Development Institute, 2007), p. 3.

33. *BusinessWorld* (Manila), January 3, 2008.

34. Elizabeth Mills, "Unconditional Aid from China Threatens to Undermine Donor Pressure on Cambodia," *Global Insight,* June 7, 2007.

35. Author interviews with bilateral and multilateral donors and Lao government officials in Vientiane, September 2008.

36. European Union, http://eur-lex.europa.eu/LexUriServ/LexUriServ.do?uri=OJ:L:2006:378:0041:0071:EN:PDF.

37. Author interview in Jeju, South Korea, October 2007.

38. Yukiko Fukagawa, "East Asia's New Economic Integration Strategy: Moving Beyond the FTA," *Asia-Pacific Review* 12, no. 2 (2005).

39. Christopher R. Hughes, "Nationalism and Multilateralism in Chinese Foreign Policy: Implications for Southeast Asia," *Pacific Review* 18, no. 1 (2005): 127.

40. Cited in Ronald C. Keith, "China as a Rising World Power and Its Response to 'Globalization,'" *Review of International Affairs* 3, no. 4 (2004): 514 (emphasis added).

41. Hughes, "Nationalism and Multilateralism," p. 120.

42. Author interview in Singapore, April 2006.

43. Abdul Razak Baginda is the executive director of the Malaysian Strategic Research Center.

44. Quoted in Edward Cody, "China's Quiet Rise Casts Wide Shadow," *Washington Post*, January 26, 2005.

45. Susumu Yamakage, "The Construction of an East Asian Order and the Limitations of the ASEAN Model," *Asia-Pacific Review* 12, no. 2 (2005): 3.

46. Author interview with a Vietnamese journalist who covered the APEC summit and its preparations, Hanoi, April 2007.

47. Norrin M. Ripsman, "Two Stages of Transition from a Region of War to a Region of Peace: Realist Transition and Liberal Endurance," *International Studies Quarterly* 49 (2005): 669–693.

48. Hughes, "Nationalism and Multilateralism."

49. Keith, "China as a Rising World Power."

50. Jörn Dosch and Alexander Vuving, *The Impact of China on Governance Structures in Vietnam* (Bonn: German Institute for Development, 2008).

51. This assessment is based on author interviews with senior government officials conducted in Vietnam, Indonesia, Malaysia, Thailand, and Laos and at the ASEAN Secretariat in 2008 and 2009.

52. Robert Gilpin, *War and Change in World Politics* (Cambridge: Cambridge University Press, 1981), p. 10.

53. Alexander L. Vuving, "Vietnam. Arriving in the World—and at the Crossroads," in *Southeast Asian Affairs 2008* (Singapore: ISEAS 2008), pp. 375–393.

54. Evelyn Goh and Sheldon W. Simon, "Introduction," in E. Goh and S. W. Simon, eds., *China, the United States, and Southeast Asia: Contending Perspectives on Politics, Security, and Economics* (New York and London: Routledge, 2008), p. 7.

55. Strategic Framework Agreement Between the United States of America and the Republic of Singapore for a Closer Cooperation Partnership in Defense and Security, July 12, 2005, Art. 1a.

56. Eul-Soon Pang, "Embedding Security into Free Trade: The Case of the United States–Singapore Free Trade Agreement," *Contemporary Southeast Asia* 29 (2007): 2.

# 5

# China and South Asia: Strategic Implications and Economic Imperatives

*Lawrence Saez and Crystal Chang*

US policy concerns about the emergence of China and India as potential global powers were voiced in a much-discussed US National Intelligence Council document.[1] The focal point of this analysis, though, is on a global discussion about current literature on the strategic implications of the emergence of China's "peaceful rise" (*heping jueqi*) on US interests.[2] Some scholars have highlighted the importance in China's strategic thinking of the doctrine of Five Principles of Peaceful Coexistence, and subsequent refinements of a "new security concept."[3] Other China analysts have framed the debate about the response to US hegemonic influence by emphasizing the ambivalent security perceptions embraced by the Chinese military leadership[4] and by China's growing use of multilateral institutions to achieve its policy aims.[5] In this light, China's strategic concerns encompass a broad range of military, economic, technological, and political linkages.

Recent policy evaluations of China's peaceful rise have tended to analyze Chinese strategic ambitions regionally.[6] However, surprisingly little focus has been paid to South Asia. For instance, in a study prepared by the Congressional Research Service to study China's foreign policy and application of soft power in South America, Asia, and Africa, there are only eight indirect references to India (mostly listed in a number of countries that have regional interests).[7] Likewise, Pakistan, reputedly China's closest ally in South Asia, receives only two passing mentions. Similarly, academic studies of China's strategic ambitions have either ignored South Asia altogether[8] or relegated it to a marginal status.[9] The assessment by others has been more emphatic, namely that China "does not consider India one of the most important states in the world."[10]

In our view, the declaration of India and Pakistan as nuclear powers, the concomitant emergence of India as a global economic power in recent years,

China's own security needs, and political instability in Pakistan and Nepal suggest that South Asia will likely gain greater attention in Chinese foreign policy discussions for several reasons. First, South Asia is likely to play a more direct role in China's strategy on peripheral stability. As Zhao Gancheng has noted, "Maintaining peripheral stability has been always one of the most important goals of Chinese foreign policy and a serious challenge as well indeed."[11] Furthermore, slogans promoting peripheral stability such as "treating neighbors as friends and as partners" (*yulinweishan, yilinweiban*) have become commonplace in speeches made by Chinese leaders like Premier Wen Jiabao on visits to neighboring countries.[12]

During a May 2008 meeting with a press delegation from the South Asian Association for Regional Cooperation (SAARC), Chinese assistant foreign minister He Yafei emphasized that "China follows the foreign policy of 'fostering an amicable, tranquil and prosperous neighbourhood' (*mulin, anlin, fulin*) and hopes to see a peaceful, stable and prosperous South Asia."[13] Framed within the strategic goal of maintaining peripheral stability, there have been important political changes in the region, notably the revival of anti-Chinese protests in Tibet. We also stress the growing importance of South Asia as a transit point for China's crude oil imports. In addition, although the relationship between China and South Asia is framed in terms of its economic dimensions, we argue that given the economic rise of India, it is likely that China will view South Asia as an important actor in the evolving dynamics of China's economic security. As such, the dimensions of China's political-strategic interests in South Asia have changed.

Although on a global scale, as Lowell Dittmer has argued, China is seeking to reconcile its domestic interests with international norms under an overarching banner of multilateralism, we find that recent transformations among China's neighbors have created an imperative for adopting a more disaggregated regional policy.[14] Accordingly, we argue that Chinese policy in South Asia has shifted subtly and we suggest that China may be experimenting with and pursuing a variety of strategic options, namely by balancing multilateralism with peripheral stability and the pursuance of other security objectives (such as energy security). Building on a previous article by Saez, we argue that with respect to South Asia, China is pursuing a policy of *reluctant competition* with India; *contingent cooperation* with Pakistan, Bangladesh, and Sri Lanka; and *secretive co-optation* with Nepal, the Maldives, and Myanmar (Burma).[15]

This chapter will first provide a historical account of China's relationship with South Asia. Having outlined some of the more important bilateral trends in the relationship, the chapter will then focus on the key elements driving China's relationship with individual South Asian countries today. We will evaluate the likely economic and security linkages that may develop between China and South Asia. Finally, we will offer an assessment of the implications of the growing emergence of China for US policy.

## Historical Background of China's Relationship with South Asia

After the founding of the People's Republic of China (PRC), the Chinese Communist Party began to emphasize its relationships with underdeveloped and developing countries, especially as its relations with the United States and the erstwhile Soviet Union faltered. Premier Zhou Enlai worked to stabilize China's relations with its neighbors, including Mongolia, North Korea, India, Myanmar, and revolutionary forces in Vietnam. Among newly independent South Asian nations, India took the lead in developing diplomatic links with the PRC. For instance, India became the second nonsocialist country to establish diplomatic relations with the PRC in 1950.

As part of China's diplomatic effort to promote solidarity in the developing world, Premier Zhou proposed the Five Principles of Peaceful Coexistence (or *Panchsheel* in Hindi) at a meeting with an Indian delegation in December 1953. These principles were put more formally into writing in the 1954 agreement between China and India in which India recognized China's sovereignty in Tibet. The Five Principles—mutual respect for territorial integrity and sovereignty, nonaggression, noninterference in internal affairs, equality and mutual benefit, and peaceful coexistence—were well received by leaders in other parts of the developing world that were still recovering from Western colonialism.

The Five Principles were further promoted at the 1955 Bandung Conference in Indonesia, which brought together delegates from twenty-nine Asian and African nations. Bandung marked China's ascending leadership role among the countries of the Third World, and paved the way to the creation of the Non-Aligned Movement in 1961 in which Third World nations ostensibly refused to side with either the United States or the Soviet Union in what was emerging as a bipolar world.[16]

China's collaboration with India in espousing a third dimension to an increasingly bipolar international system was a cornerstone of India's foreign policy. The relationship was tinged, within Indian policy circles, with an element of idealism. The slogan *Hindi, Chini, bhai bhai* (Indians and Chinese are brothers) exemplified some of the more uncritical perceptions of Chinese and Indian friendship in the 1950s. On the other hand, there was growing evidence that India and China relations could falter. By 1959, India granted asylum to the exiled Tibetan leader, the Dalai Lama. Moreover, Jawaharlal Nehru, India's first prime minister, also pressed to have a more clearly defined boundary between India and China. The McMahon line, a border drawn during British colonial times, was insufficiently precise, particularly in the Himalayan region. A stalemate on the exact demarcation of the border ensued, and by October 1961, Indian border patrols began to post boundary signs along the fluid India-China border. This policy, often referred to as Nehru's

Forward Policy, eventually helped spark a lightning border war between India and China in October 1962.

The 1962 India-China War proved to be a humiliating defeat for the Indian armed forces. It also proved to be a major boost to China's growing global presence, particularly at a time in which it faced increasing international isolation in the midst of the Sino-Soviet split. China's unilateral cease-fire in November 1962 resulted in substantial territorial gains for China, particularly in the Aksai Chin region. However, as one analyst of China's relations with South Asia has noted, "China's victory in the war did not resolve the territorial argument, and instead produced a legacy of mutual suspicion."[17]

While the 1950s witnessed a somewhat united front between China and other moderate Third World nations like India and Egypt, the 1960s marked the peak of China's sponsorship of more radical communist movements all over the world from Angola to the Philippines. Beijing's military assistance to insurgent groups damaged its relations with many Third World nations, and led many leaders to question China's real commitment to the Five Principles. The 1962 India-China War demonstrated further cracks in the delicate foundation of Third World solidarity.

Nevertheless, at a period of perceived military weakness of India, Pakistan began to develop strong relations with China. By 1963, less than a year after India's defeat, Pakistan ceded over 5,180 square kilometers of Pakistani-held territory adjacent to the newly controlled Chinese sectors of Aksai Chin. A subsequent pact between Pakistan and China later solidified the international legal standing relating to the transfer of this territory. On the other hand, India has vigorously disputed the legality of the cession of this territory to China. Thus, India's claim over Kashmiri territory under Pakistani control would inevitably include the portion of land ceded by Pakistan to China.

During China's post-Mao reform era, the new leadership under Deng Xiaoping began to cast aside ideological components of its foreign policy and replace them with more practical economic considerations. As such, Beijing reaffirmed its commitment to constructive relationships with Third World countries based on equality and mutual benefit. Notably, the Five Principles have resurfaced in China's joint statements with South Asian states. Most recently, direct references to Panchsheel appeared in the January 2008 joint statement between China and India. Part of this statement read as follows:

> The two sides believe that in the new century, Panchsheel, or the Five Principles of Peaceful Co-existence, should continue to constitute the basic guiding principles for good relations between all countries and for creating the conditions for realizing peace and progress of humankind. An international system founded on these principles will be fair, rational, equal, and mutually beneficial, and will promote peace and common prosperity, create equal opportunities, and eliminate poverty and discrimination.[18]

Beginning in 1996, the Chinese government has also gradually repackaged the Five Principles into what it terms "the new security concept" (*xinanquanguan*). In the Chinese government's depiction, "the new security concept is, in essence, to rise above one-sided security and seek common security through mutually beneficial cooperation. It is a concept established on the basis of common interests and is conducive to social progress."[19] The Chinese suggest that, in contrast to the days of the Cold War, the means to seek security are being diversified, with many arenas of cooperation from the economy to the environment. As discussed by Saez, the Chinese government considers its active role in the Shanghai Cooperation Organization and the ASEAN Regional Forum as evidence of its commitment to the new security concept.[20] Nonetheless, given the conflict-ridden past, it is unclear whether the new era of the new security concept will lead to a more secure future in South Asia. As will be discussed below, China's current level of engagement with South Asian countries is guided by specific issues.

## China's Strategy Toward South Asia

Though China has had a long history of tension with its southern neighbors, its relations with each country have been steadily improving over the last decade. (Table 5.1 provides a list of the bilateral state visits by Chinese leaders and their South Asian counterparts.) At the level of official state policy, China's 1950s rhetoric of the Five Principles of Peaceful Coexistence and the promotion of "regional peace, stability, and prosperity" have not changed substantially. If anything, this type of language has regained prominence in China's recent joint communiqués with regional partners. However, although cross-border investment and trade continue to take precedence over past security conflicts, China is taking bolder steps to strengthen its position vis-à-vis the United States across Asia, in particular South Asia.

Not surprisingly, the emphasis of Chinese involvement in South Asia has been centered upon India and Pakistan, the largest two countries in the subcontinent. These two countries share over 4,500 kilometers of border with China and are contiguous, nuclear-armed adversaries. Despite India's proximity and size, according to Susan Shirk, "China does not consider India one of the important states in the world; India is simply not on China's radar screen."[21] However, China's attitude toward India is likely to change going forward as India's growth continues, and as the two countries start to compete for resources and international influence. The primary threat India poses to China today is that it could become an ally of the United States and hence part of a potential containment strategy toward China. In order to prevent India from falling under the US security umbrella, China is putting forth greater effort to maintain friendly relations with its neighbor.

**Table 5.1    Official Visits of Heads of State Between China and Selected South Asian Countries, 2000–2008**

| South Asian Country | Date of Official Diplomatic Relations | Visits to the Country by Chinese Heads of State (1998–2008) | Visits by Heads of State to China (1998–2008) |
|---|---|---|---|
| Bangladesh | 1975 | 1999: Chairman Li Peng visits<br>2002: Premier Zhu Rongji visits<br>2005: Premier Wen Jiabao visits | 2000: Prime Minister Sheikh Hashina visits<br>2002: Prime Minister Begum Khaleda Zia<br>2004: Prime Minister Begum Khaleda Zia<br>2005: Prime Minister Begum Khaleda Zia |
| India | 1950[a] | 2002: Premier Zhu Rongji visits<br>2005: Premier Wen Jiabao visits<br>2006: President Hu Jintao visits | 2000: President K. R. Narayanan visits<br>2003: Prime Minister Atal Bihari Vajpayee visits<br>2008: Prime Minister Manmohan Singh visits |
| Nepal | 1955 | 2006: Chinese State Councilor Tang Jixuan visits | 2001: King Birendra visits<br>2002: King Gyanendra visits |
| Pakistan | 1951 | 1999: Chairman Li Peng visits<br>2001: Premier Zhu Rongji visits<br>2006: President Hu Jintao visits | 1998: Prime Minister Nawaz Sharif visits<br>1999: Prime Minister Nawaz Sharif visits<br>2001: President Pervez Musharraf visits<br>2002: President Pervez Musharraf visits<br>2003: Prime Minister Mir Zafarullah Khan Jamali visits<br>2003: President Pervez Musharraf visits<br>2004: Prime Minister Shaukat Aziz visits<br>2006: President Pervez Musharraf visits<br>2008: President Pervez Musharraf visits |
| Sri Lanka | 1957 | 2001: Premier Zhu Rongji visits | 2005: President Chandrika Bandaranaike Kumaratunga visits<br>2007: President Mahinda Rajapaksa visits<br>2008: President Mahinda Rajapaksa visits |

*Sources:* Ministry of Foreign Affairs of the PRC, Embassy of the PRC in Bangladesh, Embassy of the PRC in India, Embassy of the PRC in Nepal, Embassy of the PRC in Pakistan, and Embassy of the PRC in Sri Lanka.

*Note:* a. India and China broke off ambassadorial-level relations from 1961 until 1976.

Nevertheless, there is a noticeable difference in the conventional military capabilities of China and India. As Table 5.2 shows, China has a greater number of active military personnel than India. China enjoys comparative supremacy over India in terms of most types of submarine forces and combat-capable aircraft. India, however, has one aircraft carrier, whereas China does not yet possess one. There is also a striking difference between China and India's strategic missile forces. As Table 5.2 shows, at present, India does not have intercontinental ballistic missile capabilities. China also clearly outnumbers India in terms of its capabilities in intermediate-range ballistic missiles and short-range ballistic missiles.

Moreover, it is also worth highlighting that as part of its effort to modernize its military capabilities, China has substantially strengthened its defense expenditures in recent years. In aggregate terms, there is a growing gap between the aggregate military expenditures of China and South Asia. As Figure 5.1 shows, as early as the year 2000, China and South Asia had comparable levels of military expenditures. Seven years later, China's military expenditures have nearly tripled, showing a more rapid rate of increase than all of South Asia's military expenditures combined.

The most problematic facet of China's relations with South Asia is India's deployment of a nuclear arsenal and the potential for a nuclear conflict between India and Pakistan. Likewise, prominent Indian government officials articulated a more muscular response to China. For instance, a week before India

**Table 5.2   Comparative Troop Strength, Naval Forces and Aircraft, and Strategic Missile Forces for China and India, 2008**

|  | China | India |
|---|---|---|
| Troop strength |  |  |
| Army (active) | 1,600,000 | 1,100,000 |
| Navy (active) | 225,000 | 55,000 |
| Air Force (active) | 250,000 | 125,000 |
| Paramilitary (active) | 1,500,000 | 1,300,000 |
| Reserve forces | 800,000 | 1,155,000 |
| Naval forces and aircraft |  |  |
| Aircraft carriers | — | 1 |
| Strategic ballistic missile submarines | 3 | — |
| Tactical submarines | 59 | 16 |
| Air force combat capable aircraft | 1,762 | 565 |
| Naval combat capable aircraft | 792 | 34 |
| Strategic missile forces | 806 | 42+ |
| Intercontinental ballistic missiles | 46 | — |
| Intermediate-range ballistic missiles | 35 | 12+ |
| Short-range ballistic missiles | 725 | 30 |

*Source:* International Institute for Strategic Studies, *The Military Balance,* 2008.

**Figure 5.1    Aggregate Military Expenditures of China and South Asia, 2000–2007**

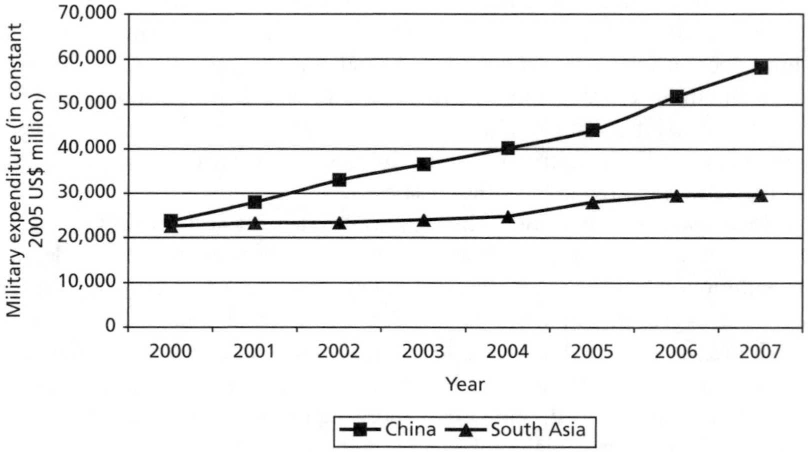

*Source:* SIPRI (2008).
*Note:* Aggregate military expenditures for South Asia include India, Pakistan, Bangladesh, Sri Lanka, and Nepal. Military expenditures for the Maldives and Bhutan were too insignificant.

conducted its first round of nuclear tests in 1998, George Fernandes, then India's defense minister, publicly stated that China is India's "potential threat number one."[22]

Although China has proven that it could swiftly overcome Indian military capabilities in conventional terms, the prospect of a nuclear armed India has been met with growing alarm in Beijing. As some observers have noted, China initially responded with a great deal of restraint to India's first round of nuclear tests conducted on May 11, 1998.[23] However, China's reaction soured once it became public that India had articulated concerns about China as the reason for conducting the nuclear tests. Prior to the second round of nuclear tests carried out by India on May 13, 1998, Prime Minister Atal Bihari Vajpayee wrote a private letter to US president Bill Clinton in which he explained the reasoning for India's decision to conduct the nuclear tests. The letter, which became public on the same day of India's second round of underground nuclear tests, implicitly made direct reference to China. In an obvious reference to China, Vajpayee wrote: "We have an overt nuclear weapon state on our borders, a state which committed armed aggression against India in 1962. Although our relations with that country have improved in the last decade or so, an atmosphere of distrust persists mainly due to the unresolved border problem."[24] Vajpayee then implicitly criticized China's support for Pakistan. He wrote: "To add to the distrust that country has materially helped another neighbor of ours to become a covert nuclear weapons state."[25] The following day, the Chinese government countered that India has "maliciously accused China as posing a nuclear threat to India. This is utterly groundless."[26]

As argued by many scholars, South Asia has traditionally not been a critical focus of Chinese strategic thinking. Nevertheless, South Asia is likely to emerge as an important focal point for China's future strategic thinking as it will be more difficult for China to maintain peripheral stability, one of its key foreign policy goals. It is, in this limited role, that "South Asia is the region with increasing importance in China's perception of periphery."[27] One of the principal reasons for this shift in perception is driven by the carrying out of nuclear tests by India and Pakistan in 1998. According to Zhao Gancheng, "since the outbreak of the Kargil conflict, China has been increasingly aware of the danger of a potential large-scale conflict that would give a severe blow to China's goal of maintaining a stable periphery."[28]

India's claim that it carried out its 1998 nuclear tests to respond to China and its support for Pakistan places China in a delicate diplomatic position, because while China would like to maintain close relations with Pakistan (its staunchest ally in South Asia and perhaps all of Asia), it also appears to show growing concern for peripheral stability. In this sense, China appears to be at a strategic crucible, on the one hand attempting to serve as an external balancer but on the other hand trying to pursue a pragmatic policy of peripheral stability. As such, China appears to be downplaying its bilateral relationship with Pakistan in recent years and pressing for greater regional balance. For example, China has shifted away from its former policies of siding with Pakistan on the Kashmir dispute. Moreover, during the 1999 Kargil conflict between India and Pakistan, China notably did not support the Pakistani incursion, emphasizing instead the necessity to resolve the Kashmir dispute through negotiations rather than military means.

The growing primacy of peripheral stability as a strategic guide for China vis-à-vis its neighbors is also motivated by China's own concerns about a domestic Uighur insurgency in Xinjiang province. The Chinese government has grown increasingly concerned that the Islamist insurgency in Pakistan could spill over into the Xinjiang region, particularly as the province is linked directly to Pakistan through the Karakoram highway. The Karakoram highway, an important trade route linking China to Pakistan, has become an increasing source of tension between the two countries.[29] On the one hand, China and Pakistan are planning to link the Karakoram highway to the Gwadar port through the Chinese-aided Gwadar-Dalbandin railway, which extends up to Rawalpindi. On the other hand, the Chinese suspect that the Karakoram highway is also being used as a corridor for insurgent Uighur groups traveling between China and Pakistan. Although the details concerning these activities are not publicly transparent, officials at the US State Department and Chinese officials claim that the East Turkistan Islamic Movement (ETIM), a militant Uighur separatist group, receives training and funding from Osama bin Laden's terror network, especially its cells inside Pakistan.[30] Though some experts assert that China has exaggerated the ETIM's links to Al-Qaida to gain US support for its crackdowns in Xinjiang, there is evidence that insurgent groups are traveling back and forth across borders. For example, the ETIM leader, Hahsan Mahsum, was killed in raids on Pakistani camps linked to Al-Qaida in 2003.[31] Moreover, the Chinese government is also concerned about drug trafficking through the Karakoram Highway and its possible link to the financing of Islamist militant groups.[32] Though the Chinese government has yet to officially close the Karakoram highway, the road continues to pose security risks.

Some analysts, like Sean Roberts, have stressed that "while there is no evidence that Pakistani political groups have given Uighur nationalists within Xinjiang any direct monetary or arms support, there has been no lack of moral support."[33] Nevertheless, at the official level there have been some efforts to curb potential incursions by Taliban-trained Uighur insurgents through Pakistan, particularly from the ETIM and East Turkistan Liberation Organization (ETLO). To that effect, in 2003, China and Pakistan signed an extradition to repatriate ETIM and ETLO members who had sought safe haven in Pakistan. These steps suggest that China is wary about political instability in Pakistan.

Additional diplomatic efforts have also underscored Chinese perceptions about the impact of political instability in Pakistan on Chinese interests abroad. For instance, on February 19, 2006, President Pervez Musharraf began a five-day visit to Beijing not only to celebrate the 55th anniversary of the establishment of China-Pakistan relations, but to sign a range of agreements regarding bilateral economic and security cooperation (ultimately thirteen documents in all). A few days prior to Musharraf's arrival in China, three Chinese engineers were gunned down near the Gwadar port. Unidentified local Baluchi tribal insurgent groups unhappy with the construction of the Gwadar project are believed to be responsible. The incident caused a great deal of consternation in both countries and was a reminder to Chinese leaders that Islamabad cannot fully protect their interests within Pakistani borders, as this was not the first time Chinese workers in Pakistan had been targets of brutal attacks.[34] Due to these and other regional security concerns, Chinese officials placed particular emphasis on the bilateral effort to combat terrorism and resolve border disputes during Musharraf's visit. Accordingly, highlighting security concerns, Chinese foreign ministry spokesperson Qin Gang, speaking at a press conference just after the shooting incident, stressed the fact that both countries are cooperating to combat "the three evil forces"—terrorism, separatism, and extremism.[35]

China's concerns about the internal political unrest in Pakistan were further discussed on February 20, 2006, during Musharraf's meeting with the chairman of the National People's Congress, Wu Bangguo. Chairman Wu reiterated China's support to Pakistan on counterterrorism and said his country wished to see greater Sino-Pakistani cooperation in promoting peace and development in the region. During Musharraf's meeting with President Hu Jintao on the same day, President Hu specifically called for a peaceful settlement of the Kashmir dispute.[36] The statements about joint Sino-Pakistani cooperation to combat terrorism, linked to China's own territorial claims elsewhere, were in evidence when Musharraf carried out a follow-up visit to China in April 2008, just a few months before he was ousted from power. During his itinerary, Musharraf also visited Urumqi, the capital of the Xinjiang Uigur Autonomous Region, where he visited provincial political and business leaders. In the bilateral joint statement that marked the visit, "Pakistan reiterated its full support for the One China Policy and the return of Taiwan to motherland as well as its condemnation and rejection of the three evil forces i.e. secessionism, separatism, and terrorism."[37] In our view, these developments support the theory that China's leadership now considers peripheral stability in South Asia an important priority.

As noted by some analysts, such as Rollie Lal, this apparent transformation in China's strategic thinking vis-à-vis South Asia could be an indication that "positive relations with India may increasingly be more critical to its interests than maintaining the status quo with a smaller and weaker Pakistan."[38] Nonetheless, we think that China's actions may be guided by an effort to sustain peripheral stability, rather than to seek the support from India. Likewise, we note that China is continuing its military assistance to Pakistan, perhaps in part motivated to gain access to Pakistan's strategic proximity to the Persian Gulf (e.g., the deep-water seaport at Gwadar).

In sum, China faces a number of difficult choices as it attempts to balance its geopolitical and economic objectives in South Asia. The way in which it handles these competing priorities—especially its delicate and complex relationships with India and Pakistan—will have a significant impact on the overall stability of the subcontinent. After a half century fraught with unresolved territorial disputes, nuclear rivalry, and shifting alliances, the region has been witnessing a thawing of tensions. Nevertheless, China has had very limited engagement with the other countries in South Asia, namely Nepal, Bhutan, Bangladesh, Sri Lanka, and the Maldives. Whether this trend is temporary or represents a significant and durable shift in politics of the region is still unclear.

China's concerns about peripheral stability have to be balanced out against other global strategic imperatives. At an aggregate level, China's foreign policy principles are formally guided by improving relations with the developed countries, strengthening friendly relations with neighboring countries, enhancing cooperation with the Third World, actively participating in multilateral diplomacy, adhering to exchanging and cooperating with other parties and political organizations, and extensively developing people to people exchanges.[39] Pursuing this strategy at a regional level, China has been engaged with South Asia's principal regional organization, SAARC. In 2007, for instance, China was accorded observer status and attended the Fourteenth SAARC Summit in Dhaka in that capacity. Prior to his arrival in Dhaka, Chinese Foreign Minister Li Zhaoxing argued that the reasons for China's active engagement with SAARC were motivated by the premise that "the fundamental objective of China's policy towards South Asia is stability, development and good neighbourly relations."[40]

Our research, though, suggests that beneath China's official slogan of peaceful coexistence lies an unofficial program of commercial diplomacy[41] and strategic military objectives—or the so-called string of pearls strategy. Although the Chinese government's focus on commercial relations could provide the foundation for greater regional stability, it does not constitute a coherent, regionwide foreign policy. On the contrary, our view is that China's engagement with each South Asian country will continue to be guided primarily by its desire to reduce US influence in the region and secondarily by specific bilateral issues and ad hoc regional military objectives. Absent a unified and more explicit South Asian foreign policy, China's impact on South Asian security will remain vulnerable to flare-ups of age-old, unresolved bilateral tensions. What is more, any move by China that appears to contradict the Five Principles of Peaceful Coexistence could be looked upon with suspicion and fear by those both inside and outside the region.

In addition, the global market for natural resources is one arena in which China's actions are being carefully watched. Securing energy supply—particularly crude oil and natural gas—has become vital to the sustainability of China's economic growth. Though China was East Asia's largest petroleum exporter in 1985, it became a net importer in 1993. By 2004, China overtook Japan to become the second largest oil importer after the United States, due in large part to the country's dramatic increase in automobile production and private car ownership.

China is now the world's third largest automobile producer and second largest automobile market. In 2007, China's passenger car sales alone jumped 22 percent to about 6.3 million and will likely rise 16 percent in 2008 to about 7.3 million. China is expected to boost vehicle output by a million units a year for the next decade to reach 20 million a year by 2017, according to the China Association of Automobile Manufacturers.[42] In order to fuel all of the new vehicles on the road, China must constantly search for new sources of petroleum.

Today, roughly 70 percent of China's oil imports come by sea from the Middle East and Africa.[43] Yet China has always felt vulnerable to the US Navy's projection of power in the vital sea lanes that connect East Asia to the Middle East. To increase the security of its tankers through these treacherous waters, China has been not only modernizing its blue-water navy, but actively strengthening diplomatic ties, building naval bases and ports, and constructing airfield projects from the littorals of the South China Sea to the Arabian Sea and Persian Gulf.

So far, China's development of strategic geopolitical nodes—the string of pearls strategy—has been nonconfrontational, with no clear evidence of imperial or neocolonial ambition. The development of the string of pearls is not a strategy explicitly guided by China's central government. On the contrary, a 2004 report titled "Energy Futures in Asia" produced by defense contractor Booz Allen Hamilton for the US Department of Defense is responsible for coining the term, and for generating alarm and concern around the Pentagon about China's increasing influence and presence in South Asia. The US Joint Forces Command's 2008 *Joint Operating Environment* report hints that China may be pursuing a string of pearls strategy and maps out the location of ports, surveillance facilities, and airfields that have considerable Chinese political influence or military presence.[44] Nevertheless, in an analysis about impending rivalry in the Indian Ocean, Robert Kaplan is far more categorical and suggests that "the Chinese government has already adopted a 'string of pearls' strategy for the Indian Ocean, which consists of setting up a series of ports in friendly countries along the ocean's northern seaboard."[45]

The Chinese foreign ministry vehemently denies the existence of a string of pearls strategy. In their view, Chinese involvement in building infrastructure projects throughout the region is part of their desire to help countries, like Pakistan, develop impoverished areas. According to China's foreign ministry, China has no military or strategic intentions in the ports of neighboring countries. China's official policy is that it does not set up military bases abroad. After all, in its view, China's own development requires a peaceful and cooperative environment. In contrast, the Chinese government views US suspicions of a string of pearls strategy as reminiscent of a Cold War mentality based on speculation and unfounded assumptions. In any case, the Chinese government argues, it is the US Navy's Fifth Fleet—not the Chinese Navy—that dominates the sea lanes around the Persian Gulf and surrounding waters.

Nonetheless, some US observers view increased Chinese activity in the waters between the South China Sea and the Persian Gulf with unease. According to the Booz Allen Hamilton report, each "pearl" in the string of pearls constitutes a node of growing Chinese geopolitical influence along this sea route. Table 5.3 highlights some of the sample nodes mentioned in the Booz Allen Hamilton report and the facilities allegedly located there.

Table 5.3 also shows the location and facilities available at various naval sites across Asian seaways. The numerous economic benefits of Chinese infrastructure aid are an enticement for countries to facilitate China's strategic ambitions in the region. However, there is a hidden danger that the improvement of China's energy supply links in the Indian Ocean could harm China's simultaneous aim of maintaining peripheral stability, particularly as it brings China into direct competition with India.

**Table 5.3   China's Alleged "String of Pearls" Strategy**

| Pearl or Node in China's "String of Pearls" Strategy in South and Southeast Asia | Details About the Facilities at the Node |
| --- | --- |
| Hainan Island, China | Upgraded military facilities |
| Woody Island, one of the Paracel Islands | An upgraded airstrip |
| Chittagong, Bangladesh | A container shipping facility |
| Sittwe, Myanmar | A deep-water port is under construction |
| Gwadar, Pakistan | A naval base and modern port are under construction |
| Hambantota, Sri Lanka | A modern industrial port is under construction |

*Source:* Perhson (2006).

China's uneasy balancing of strategies is evident with respect to the construction of the deep-water port in Gwadar, Pakistan, arguably the most important pearl for the Chinese so far. For China, the strategic value of Gwadar is its 240-mile distance from the Strait of Hormuz, the only sea passage to the open ocean for many of the petroleum-exporting Persian Gulf states, and hence one of the world's strategically important chokepoints. With a strong presence in Gwadar, China can provide safer passage for its oil tankers, and at the same time monitor US naval activity in the Persian Gulf and Indian activity in the Arabian Sea.

Establishing a modern port facility at Gwadar is also considered a strategic asset by Pakistan, since its main port at Karachi is vulnerable to blockade due to its proximity to India. During the 1971 India-Pakistan War, India's blockade of Karachi had a serious impact on the Pakistani economy. More recently, during the 1999 Kargil conflict, India threatened to, once again, blockade the Karachi port. Fortunately for Pakistan, China is securing its future access to the port by funding a majority of the US$1.2 billion project and by providing the technical expertise of hundreds of Chinese engineers. As noted earlier, though, Chinese involvement in the construction of the port at Gwadar has also generated an internal backlash by Islamist insurgents.

From India's perspective, though, any evidence of Sino-Pakistani collaboration is viewed critically. Thus, the developmental incursions into the Indian Ocean, coupled with China's naval modernization, have been met with some alarm in Indian strategic circles. The presence of Chinese-built ports across the Indian Ocean region has generated a newly created prospect of a long-term strategic encirclement of Indian seaways and a likely competition for power projection by the Chinese navy. One influential analyst has noted that although current Chinese interests in the Indian Ocean appear to be primarily governed by energy security considerations, "the so-called strategic encirclement of

India by China needs to be countered. We might not be able to match the Chinese investment in the region, but overall we should have sufficient hold to ensure that China does not get any blanket clearance for operations from the territory of littorals."[46]

## Evaluation of Current Level of Economic Cooperation Between China and South Asia

China does not designate an explicit foreign policy for each South Asian country, or the region for that matter.[47] Rather, its official policy toward all countries continues to be guided by the rather broad and flexible rhetoric of the Five Principles of Peaceful Coexistence. Within that framework, China particularly emphasizes that each bilateral relationship is not intended to affect its grand vision of an "independent foreign policy of peace."[48] With respect to developing countries, Jiang Zemin argued that China "will continue to enhance its solidarity and cooperation with other Third World countries, increase mutual understanding and trust and strengthen mutual help and support. We will enlarge areas of cooperation and make it more fruitful."[49]

As we have discussed so far, the historical relationship between China and individual South Asian countries has been fraught with challenges and been motivated by specific strategic concerns. We have argued that although three South Asian countries (India, Pakistan, and Nepal) share nearly 6,000 kilometers of border with China, it would be accurate to suggest that, as a composite, South Asia is not currently viewed as central to China's strategic concerns.[50] In this section we will offer an assessment of the probability that China will alter its stance toward South Asia, particularly in the economic sphere.

In evaluating the potential for economic cooperation between China and South Asia it is worth noting first that in strictly commercial terms, China trades little with South Asian countries. At the end of 2007, the entire region of South Asia amounted to only 8.7 percent of China's exports to Asian countries and 2.8 percent of China's overall exports globally. The volume of South Asian imports to China is equally small. In 2006, South Asia accounted for 4.4 percent of China's imports from Asia and 1.6 percent of China's imports worldwide.[51]

In aggregate terms, it is evident that China's bilateral trade with individual South Asian countries has grown in recent years, albeit from a very low starting point. As Figure 5.2 shows, the aggregate trade volume between China and South Asia has increased from US$7.9 billion in 2000 to nearly US$52 billion in 2007.

As Figure 5.2 also shows, since 2004, the level of exports from China to South Asia has outpaced the level of imports from South Asia to China. Accordingly, China is beginning to develop growing trade surpluses with most South Asian countries. The growing trade imbalances between China and

**Figure 5.2   Trade Volume Between China and South Asia, 2000–2007**

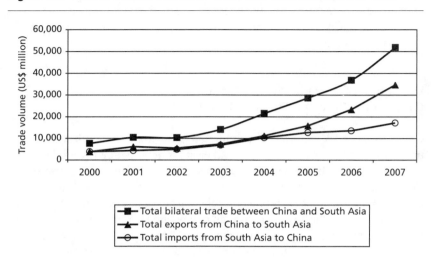

*Source:* International Monetary Fund, *Direction of Trade Statistics, 2008.*
*Note:* Aggregate trade volume figures for South Asia include India, Pakistan, Bangladesh, Sri Lanka, Nepal, and the Maldives. Bilateral trade volume figures with Bhutan are excluded because the available figures are too insignificant and Bhutan has not engaged in bilateral trade with China since 2004.

Bangladesh, Sri Lanka, and Nepal are particularly acute. In 2007, the ratio of Chinese exports to these three South Asian countries relative to their imports to China was 28.7 to 1.[52]

For a brief period, the single exception to China's growing trade imbalance vis-à-vis individual South Asian countries was India. As Figure 5.3 shows, in the year 2000, trade between China and India was very limited. Between 2003 and 2005, India built a slight trade surplus with China. After 2005, the pattern of trade relations between China and India was dramatically reversed, as China began to develop significant trade surpluses with India. An analysis of the types of commodities that are being traded between China and India suggests that there was a dramatic increase in the level of exports of iron ore and steel from India to China.[53]

The increased trade gap after 2005 developed as a result of a rapid increase in Chinese exports to India in the form of manufactured products, namely electrical and electronic equipment and nuclear reactor boilers and maintenance. Inversely, the bulk of China's exports to India come in the form of raw materials, specifically iron ore and steel, cotton, and organic chemicals. These three commodities account for nearly 65 percent of Indian exports to China.[54]

The global financial crisis of 2008 and its effect in reducing global trade flows have certainly alerted the Chinese leadership about potential vulnerabil-

**Figure 5.3    Trade Volume Between China and India, 2000–2007**

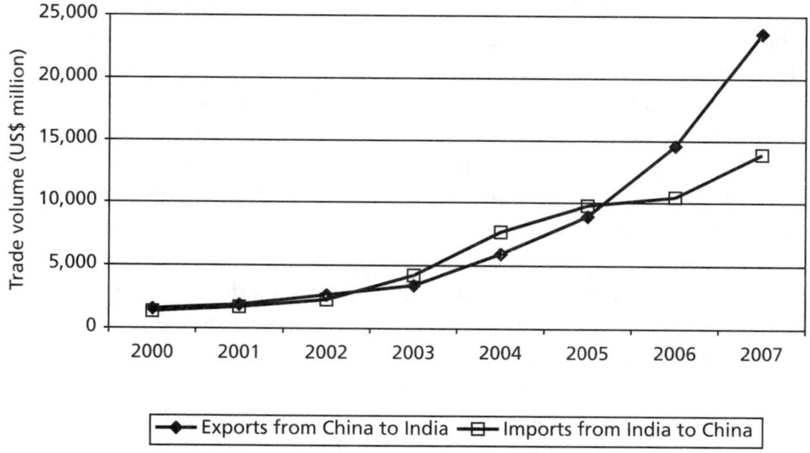

*Source:* International Monetary Fund, *Direction of Trade Statistics, 2008.*

ities in China's export-led growth strategy. We anticipate that the occurrence of such exogenous shocks is likely to prompt China to further diversify its export markets to developing countries. Under these conditions, the high level of growth in recent levels of Indian iron ore and steel exports to China combined with China's large level of absorption of raw materials suggests that it is highly probable that bilateral trade between India and China is likely to grow, albeit in a fairly skewed direction favoring China. At present, there is a greater level of concentration in the types of commodities (namely raw materials) that China imports from India, than the level of concentration of Chinese exports to India (mostly in the form of manufactured products).

Along with bilateral trade, the amount of cross-border investment between China and India has also grown in recent years. In 1990, Chinese outward foreign direct investment to India was only US$124 million. By 2000, this figure had increased to US$1,859 million. The most recent available figures (2006) show that Chinese outward foreign direct investment (FDI) to India was US$12,964 million. If measured in nominal terms, Chinese outward FDI to India has grown dramatically, particularly from a low starting point. However, if measured as a proportion of China's aggregate outward investment, India is not at present a choice destination. For instance, in 2006, India represented only 0.1 percent of Chinese outward FDI stock.[55]

We have argued that China has framed South Asia within the context of its policy regarding peripheral stability. The nature of this relationship has been altered by the emergence of India and Pakistan as nuclear armed states.

In addition, although the relationship between China and South Asia is framed in terms of its economic dimensions, we argue that given the economic rise of India, it is likely that China will view South Asia as an important actor in the evolving dynamics of China's economic security. In our view, the emergence of India as a potential market for Chinese manufactured exports suggests that South Asia is likely to become more central to China's strategic concerns. As we outlined earlier, though, Chinese policy in South Asia has developed from a set of unique historical circumstances. Nevertheless, we also note that China—given the changing military capabilities of India and Pakistan as well as the growing importance of the Indian Ocean as a conduit for the transport for China's energy supplies—appears to be experimenting with and pursuing a variety of strategic options. Nevertheless, it appears that China is differentiating its strategy vis-à-vis specific South Asian countries based on an ambiguous calculation of expected benefits and relative economic and military strengths of different South Asian countries.

Beyond the cursory language of the Five Principles of Peaceful Coexistence, China's bilateral relationships in South Asia continue to be driven by specific institutional constraints. Saez has argued that in asserting its global position, the emergence of China has important implications for the theoretical debate between hegemonic decline and systemic stability. Saez has argued that China gives the semblance of departing from a traditional security paradigm, one that stresses multilateral consensus with a range of international actors that are minor players in the international system. Saez argued that although voicing multilateralism, China adapts to specific regional circumstances, partly motivated by the pursuit of peripheral stability and other specific security concerns. Building on these arguments, we propose that China is pursuing a policy of *ambivalent competition* with India, *contingent cooperation* with Pakistan, Bangladesh, and Sri Lanka, and *secretive co-optation* with Nepal, the Maldives, and Myanmar.[56]

We suggest that the nature of China's relationship with India combines various strategic and economic concerns. At present, there is some uncertainty as to whether this relationship will be cooperative or conflictual. On this basis, we term this ambiguous relationship as a policy of *reluctant competition*. The specific contours of this policy are shaped by a number of concerns. For instance, China is keen to prevent India from developing a closer relationship with the United States (and becoming part of any US containment policy). In line with its policy of internal peripheral stability, China also wants to ensure that India does not change its official position on China's rightful sovereignty over Tibet. Finally, given the recent dynamics of the trade relationship, China appears to be eager to increase bilateral trade and establish a strong foothold in India's large and growing domestic market.

We argue that China's relationship with Pakistan, Bangladesh, and Sri Lanka is one of *contingent cooperation*. This policy is premised on the view that China seeks to forge relationships with these countries based on the achievement of very specific goals for China. This is not to suggest that bilateral relations with China cannot be cordial—quite the contrary. The nature of this relationship is often cordial and cooperative, but only driven unilaterally and not based on reciprocity. We have illustrated the construction and development of a network of deep seawater ports along the Indian Ocean as an example of China's efforts to secure its energy supply. More concretely, we have also shown, though, that China can unilaterally alter its position should its strategic interests be jeopardized (as has been the case with respect to the rise of Islamist extremist attacks on Chinese civilian workers) or should it perceive that there may be a decline in peripheral stability.

At a bilateral level, China is also pursuing country-specific strategies. In its relations with Pakistan, China seeks to maintain the relationship with its close regional ally and prevent the country from establishing closer ties to the United States. To that effect, China is likely to build up its military presence at the deep seawater port at Gwadar, primarily to protect the safe passage of its oil tankers and container ships as well as to monitor US naval activities in the Persian Gulf. However, as we discussed earlier, as part of its broader strategy of peripheral stability, China is also interested in preventing Pakistan from flaring up its fragile relationship with India.

China's relationship with Bangladesh is far more restricted in scope. China's primary concern is to secure access to the Chittagong port, Bangladesh's largest maritime port and a strategic point along the vital sea lanes between the Middle East and China. At a broader level, China seeks to maintain Bangladesh's commitment to the One China policy. Likewise, China's strategic objectives with Sri Lanka are fairly limited, namely, the construction of a billion-dollar deep seawater port in Hambantota, Sri Lanka. Some press reports have suggested that in exchange for enabling it to construct a refueling and docking station in Hambantota, China has become Sri Lanka's biggest foreign donor, has substantially increased arms sales to Sri Lanka, and has encouraged Pakistan to do the same.[57] Though the Chinese claim that its activities at Chittagong and Hambantota are strictly commercial, others in the region—namely India—are dubious of China's motives. In January 2008, India's head of the navy, Admiral Sureesh Mehta, said, "Each pearl in the string is a link in a chain of the Chinese maritime presence." Mehta also expressed concern that Chinese naval forces operating out of ports established by the Chinese could "take control over the world energy jugular."[58]

Finally, we argue that China's relations with other South Asian nations are one of *secretive co-optation.* In this sense, the level and nature of China's engagement with Nepal and the Maldives (and with Myanmar, if one includes it as part of South Asia) is not readily evident in conventional terms. A peculiar feature of Chinese relations with these specific countries is that China appears to exert its power covertly without the outward use of blunt policy instruments typically associated with displays of hard power projection, such as displays of military might or economic coercion. Another defining feature of the covert co-optation relationship is that there is a very pronounced power asymmetry between China and these specific countries. The magnitude of this power asymmetry enables China to quietly signal its intentions with tacit agreements.

Using an approach of covert co-optation, the type of engagement exhibited by China is aimed at the enhancement of certain strategic capabilities. The policy appears to follow a basic pattern of covert engagement and to build upon that existing engagement in order to attain specific military objectives. For instance, there have been unconfirmed reports that in 2001 (following the visit by the Chinese premier to the Maldives), the Maldives leased an atoll in Marao, Maldives, to China. Reports suggest that the atoll was initially used as a maritime traffic management and listening post.[59] However, in the specific case of the Marao atoll, there are also unconfirmed reports that the atoll is now being used as a submarine base. Very little is known about the actual level of usage of this atoll as a submarine base facility. A report from an Indian defense think tank argues "that although the Marao island story is a fabrication, high profile talks are taking place between China and Maldives. Furthermore, there are well founded reports that the Chinese may get their wish to establish a military base in the Maldives by 2010."[60] As such, Chinese naval presence in the Indian Ocean is imperceptible, but growing from a similar pattern.

Likewise, the level of collaboration between China and Nepal is fraught with secrecy. At a general level, China's policy toward Nepal is guided by the expectation of maintaining Nepal's position as a neutral buffer between China and India and ensuring Nepalese cooperation in the management of Tibetan refugee movement to India. In an expression of pragmatism, China has officially maintained a stance on neutrality on Nepal's long-standing civil war. Throughout the conflict, China favored a preference for political stability in Nepal and did not support Maoist rebel troops who were fighting the monarchy. Instead, during King Gyanendra's reign in Nepal, China had pledged support in fighting the country's Maoist rebels, an outfit that had been waging an insurgency to overthrow the constitutional monarchy since the mid-1990s. Rather than displaying ideological affinity with the Maoist rebels, who ostensibly share the same intellectual origins, the Chinese government was much more concerned with securing King Gyanendra's commitment to the One China policy and the principle that Tibet is an indisputable part of China. For instance, during a 2005 visit by Chinese foreign minister Li Zhaoxing to Kathmandu, King Gyanendra stated that "Nepal firmly supports the One China policy of your government and will never allow any anti-China activities in Nepal's territory."[61]

Recent radical changes in Nepal's domestic political system are likely to lead to a reevaluation of Chinese involvement in Nepal. On April 10, 2008, to the surprise of many in the international community, the Nepalese Maoist rebels won the largest number of seats in Nepal's Constituent Assembly elections, took control of government, and abolished the monarchy. Though it is not yet clear how the country's new leadership will manage its vital but delicate relationship with China, it appears that the new government is already under strong pressure from Beijing to also support the One China policy. Since the Maoist rebels seized control of the Nepalese government, the Chinese government has been making quiet inroads with the Maoist leadership in control of Nepal's government. The covert pressure appears to be paying some dividends, and Nepal's Maoist leadership is now strongly aligned with Beijing. For instance, by May 2009, Nepal's Maoist prime minister, Pushpa Kamal Dahal (aka Prachanda), is reported to have threatened to scrap the 1950 Indo-Nepal Treaty of Peace and Friendship (the cornerstone of Indo-Nepalese collaboration) and to replace it with an equivalent China-Nepal treaty.[62]

Moreover, of paramount importance to China is the prevention of the usage of Nepal as a base from which Tibetan dissidents can launch anti-Chinese protests. To that effect, the Chinese government has acted directly to address its concerns with Tibetan dissidents based in Nepal. For instance, prior to the 2008 summer Olympic Games, some press reports suggested that undercover Chinese security police patrolled on the Nepalese side of the border town of Liping in order to monitor the activities by Tibetan dissidents.[63] However, the extent of these cross-border activities is not fully understood. In addition, during the summer of 2008, as Tibetan antigovernment demonstrations in China were mounting, the new Nepalese government ordered the arrest of more than 400 Tibetans who were protesting in front of the Chinese embassy in Kathmandu. In sum, it appears that the Chinese government has adapted quite quickly to political changes in Nepal.

## Conclusion

This chapter has made the argument that there has been little attention paid to China's relationship with South Asia. In the chapter, we have framed China's relationship with South Asia within the scope of China's own policy pronouncements about its development of a new security concept and its advocacy of collaborative South-South dialogue. From a strategic point of view, we have also emphasized China's long-standing policy of maintaining peripheral stability as one of the core elements of its foreign policy.

By analyzing key patterns in China's historical bilateral relationship with individual South Asian countries, we have shown that China is gradually shifting its pattern of strategic responses to emerging military and economic changes in the region. The authors have argued that China has experimented with and developed a range of tactical options, ranging from *reluctant competition* to *secretive co-optation*.

China's increased engagement with South Asia, especially its rapidly expanding maritime presence in the Indian Ocean, has several implications for US interests. First, the US Navy's dominance and influence in the sea lanes between the Persian Gulf and the South China Sea will at some point in the near future be challenged by an increasingly sophisticated Chinese Navy. Whether the United States will choose to improve its relationship with China by increasing the number of joint maritime exercises in the region or attempt to balance China by stepping up its exercises with India is unknown. In our view, maritime cooperation among these three countries would be the most productive way to ameliorate mutual suspicion and potential military conflict.

Second, the United States may want to consider shoring up its own relationships in South and Southeast Asia, particularly with Bangladesh, Sri Lanka, and Myanmar. If the United States does not actively engage these countries and fortify its own naval and diplomatic presence in these countries, it will become more and more difficult to monitor or balance Chinese and Indian maritime activities and growing influence in the region.

In sum, China's relationship with South Asia has important regional and global implications. Regionally, we anticipate that China will continue to strengthen its economic and trade links with individual South Asian countries, but particularly with India. Nevertheless, it is important to note that the multiplicity of China's strategic aims at a global level (i.e., the new security concept) may come into conflict with unresolved territorial disputes with individual South Asian countries. In light of a decline in US hegemonic influence, China's relationship with South Asia also represents new global realignments.

## Notes

The authors would like to thank Gabriel Boc for his invaluable research assistance. The authors would like to thank Chris Alden, Lowell Dittmer, Shabana Fayyaz, Chris Hughes, Li Mingjiang, Ian Talbot, George Yu, and David Zweig for offering valuable comments on earlier drafts of this chapter.

1. US National Intelligence Council, *Mapping the Global Future* (Washington, DC: National Intelligence Council, 2004), p. 47. Available at www.foia.cia.gov/2020/2020.pdf.

2. See, for instance, John Ikenberry, "The Rise of China and the Future of the West: Can the Liberal System Survive?" *Foreign Affairs* 87, no. 1 (January–February 2008): 23–37; Zheng Bijian, "China's 'Peaceful Rise' to Great-Power Status," *Foreign Affairs* 84, no. 5 (September–October 2005): 18–24.

3. See, for instance, Yi Ding, "Upholding the Five Principles of Peaceful Coexistence," *Beijing Review* (February 26–March 4, 1990), pp. 13–19.

4. See, for instance, David Shambaugh, "China's Military Views the World: Ambivalent Security," *International Security* 24, no. 3 (Winter 1999–2000): 52–79.

5. See, for instance, Lowell Dittmer, "China's New Internationalism," in Guoguang Wu and Helen Landsowne, eds., *China Turns to Multilateralism* (London:

Routledge, 2008), pp. 21–34; Marc Lanteigne, *China and International Institutions: Alternate Paths to Global Power* (London: Routledge, 2005).

6. See, for instance, Shanghai Institute for International Studies, *China and Asia's Security* (Singapore: Marshall Cavendish, 2005); Michael Brown, Owen Coté, Sean Lynn-Jones, and Steven Miller, eds., *The Rise of China* (Cambridge, MA: MIT Press, 2000).

7. US Senate Committee on Foreign Relations, *China's Foreign Policy and "Soft Power" in South America, Asia, and Africa*, 110th Cong., 2d sess., April 2008.

8. See, for instance, Shambaugh, "China's Military Views the World."

9. See, for instance, Russell Ong, *China's Security Interests in the Post–Cold War Era* (London: Curzon, 2002).

10. Susan Shirk, "One-Sided Rivalry: China's Perceptions and Policies Toward India," in Francine Frankel and Harry Harding, eds., *The India-China Relationship* (Washington, DC: Woodrow Wilson Center Press, 2004), p. 75.

11. Zhao Gancheng, "China: Periphery and Strategy," in Shanghai Institute for International Studies, *China and Asia's Security* (Singapore: Marshall Cavendish, 2005), p. 67.

12. Please see Wen Jiabao's statement during the Third Summit of the Greater Mekong Subregion on March 31, 2008. In the statement, Wen emphasized that China sticks to its foreign policy of "treating neighbors well and as partners" and remains an active participant and promoter of subregional cooperation and a more harmonious and prosperous community. Wen's statement can be found on the PRC's Ministry of Foreign Affairs website, available at www.fmprc.gov.cn/chn/zxxx/t419795.htm.

13. He Yafei's full statement during the SAARC meeting can be found on the PRC's Ministry of Foreign Affairs website, available at www.fmprc.gov.cn/chn/zxxx/t439116.htm.

14. Dittmer, "China's New Internationalism," pp. 21–34.

15. The theoretical framework of these concepts is developed in Lawrence Saez, "China's Global Emergence and the Theoretical Linkages Between Multilateralism and Peripheral Stability," *Daxiyangguo*, no. 13 (2008): 93–112.

16. See, for instance, Derek Mitchell and Carola McGiffert, "Expanding the Strategic Periphery: A History of China's Interaction with the Developing World," in Joshua Eisenman, Eric Heginbotham, and Derek Mitchell, eds., *China and the Developing World: Beijing's Strategy for the Twenty-First Century* (Armonk, NY: M. E. Sharpe, 2007), pp. 3–28.

17. Rollie Lal, "China's Relations with South Asia," in Eisenman, Heginbotham, and Mitchell, eds., *China and the Developing World*, p. 136.

18. This excerpt was translated from the original text of the China-India Joint Statement signed by President Hu Jintao and Prime Minister Manmohan Singh in Beijing on January 14, 2008. The full text can be found on the website of the Chinese embassy in India at www.chinaembassy.org.in/eng/.

19. This quote was taken from China's Position Paper on the New Security Concept, found on the website of the PRC's Permanent Mission to the United Nations. The full text of this document can be found at www.fmprc.gov.cn/ce/ceun/eng/xw/t27742.htm.

20. Saez, "China's Global Emergence," pp. 101–105.

21. Shirk, "One-Sided Rivalry," p. 75.

22. "China Is India Enemy Number One: George," *Indian Express*, May 4, 1998. Full text is available at www.indianexpress.com/res/web/pIe/ie/daily/19980504/12450024.html.

23. See, for instance, Amardeep Athwal, *China-India Relations: Contemporary*

*Dynamics,* (London: Routledge, 2008), p. 27; John Garver, "The Restoration of Sino-Indian Comity Following India's Nuclear Tests," *The China Quarterly,* no. 168 (December 2001), p. 867.

24. "Nuclear Anxiety: Indian's Letter to Clinton on the Nuclear Testing," *The New York Times,* May 13, 1998, p. A12.

25. Ibid.

26. "Chinese Government Strongly Condemns Indian Nuclear Tests," *Xinhua News Agency,* May 14, 1998.

27. Zhao Gancheng, "China: Periphery and Strategy," p. 71.

28. Ibid.

29. For an analysis of the political significance of this highway to Sino-Pakistani relations, see Ziad Haider, "Sino-Pakistan Relations and Xinjiang's Uighurs: Politics, Trade and Islam Along the Karakoram Highway," *Asian Survey* 45, no. 4 (July/August 2005): 522–545. Also see Berenice Guyot Rechard, "The Karakorum Highway: Opportunities and Threats," available at the Institute of Peace & Conflict Studies website at www.ipcs.org/newKashmirLevel2.jsp?action=showView&kValue=2109&subCatID=null&mod=null.

30. Holly Fletcher and Jayshree Bajoria, "The East Turkestan Islamic Movement (ETIM) Backgrounder," Council on Foreign Relations website, updated July 31, 2008. Full text available at www.cfr.org/publication/9179/.

31. P. S. Suryanarayana, "Chinese Terrorist Killed by Pakistan Army," *The Hindu,* December 26, 2003. Full text available at www.hindu.com/2003/12/26/stories/2003122600891500.htm.

32. Rechard, "The Karakorum Highway."

33. See, for instance, Sean Roberts, "A Land of Borderlands: Implications of Xinjiang's Transborder Interactions," in Frederick Starr, ed., *Xinjiang: China's Muslim Borderland* (Armonk, NY: M. E. Sharpe, 2004), pp. 216–240.

34. Further incidents have highlighted the concern that Chinese civilian workers are being specifically targeted by terrorists in Pakistan. For instance, a car bomb in May 2004 killed three Chinese engineers helping to build the Gwadar seaport. Five months later, kidnappers abducted two Chinese engineers working on a dam construction project in South Waziristan province and threatened to kill the Chinese unless several Al-Qaida members held by Pakistan were released. One Chinese engineer was freed and the other died in a rescue operation. Further details about these events are available at the *CNN News* website, at www.cnn.com/2006/WORLD/asiapcf/02/15/pakistan.china/.

35. Embassy of the People's Republic of China in the Independent State of Papua New Guinea. Available at http://pg.china-embassy.org/eng/fyrth/t235847.htm.

36. Embassy of the People's Republic of China in the Islamic Republic of Pakistan website, "Pakistani President General Musharraf Visits China." Further details available at http://pk.china-embassy.org/eng/zbgx/t236948.htm.

37. Embassy of the People's Republic of China in the Islamic Republic of Pakistan website, "Joint Statement Between the Islamic Republic of Pakistan and the People's Republic of China (April 15, 2008). Full text available at http://pk2.mofcom.gov.cn/aarticle/bilateralvisits/200804/20080405489467.html.

38. Lal, "China's Relations with South Asia," p. 147.

39. For instance, see Jiang Zemin's report delivered at the 16th Party Congress, November 8, 2002, Beijing. Full text available at http://english.people.com.cn/200211/18/eng20021118_106985.shtml.

40. Su Qiang, "China Makes First Visit to SAARC," *China Daily,* April 3, 2007. Full text available at www.chinadaily.com.cn/china/2007-04/03/content_842112.htm.

41. Ellen Frost has characterized China's emphasis on economic relationships as

a form of commercial diplomacy. Her definition of *commercial diplomacy* refers to the use of commercial power such as market access or technology transfer to influence noncommercial decisions in the political or even the security realm. The exercise of commercial diplomacy relies on "positive-sum" economic incentives rather than "zero-sum" military build-ups. For more on commercial diplomacy, please see Ellen Frost, "China's Commercial Diplomacy in Asia: Promise or Threat," in William Keller and Thomas Rawski, eds., *China's Rise and the Balance of Influence in Asia* (Pittsburgh, PA: University of Pittsburgh Press, pp. 95–117).

42. See, for instance, Mark Shenk, "Emerging Market Oil Use Exceeds US as Prices Rise," *Bloomberg News,* April 21, 2008.

43. Christopher Perhson, "String of Pearls: Meeting the Challenge of China's Rising Power Across the Asian Littoral." Strategic Studies Institute of the US Army War College, Carlisle Papers in Security Strategy, July 2006, p. 6.

44. US Joint Forces Command, *2008 Joint Operating Environment: Challenges and Implications for the Joint Future Force* (Norfolk, VA: US Joint Forces Command, 2008), p. 28.

45. Robert Kaplan, "Center Stage for the Twenty-First Century Power Plays in the Indian Ocean," *Foreign Affairs* 88, no. 2 (March–April 2009): 22.

46. Commodore Sanjay Sachdeva, "Great Wall at Sea: Strategic Imperatives for India," Naval Despatch (December 2006), p. 30. Full text available at http://indian-navy.nic.in/NavDespatch06/Chapter%203.pdf.

47. China's Ministry of Foreign Affairs does not have a separate department devoted to South Asia. Instead, the Ministry has a Department of Asian Affairs, which includes all Asian countries (ranging from Afghanistan to Vietnam), including those from South Asia.

48. Jiang Zemin speech.

49. Ibid.

50. See, for instance, Susan Shirk, "One-Sided Rivalry."

51. International Monetary Fund (IMF), *Direction of Trade Statistics Yearbook, 2007* (Washington, DC: International Monetary Fund, 2008). Data calculated by the authors.

52. In 2007, the ratio of Chinese exports to Pakistan relative to Chinese imports from Pakistan was 5.2 to 1. Data calculated by the authors from data provided by the IMF, *Direction of Trade Statistics.*

53. In 2003, the trade value of iron ore and steel exports from India to China amounted to about US$2.3 billion; by 2005 the trade value of those exports nearly tripled to US$6.3 billion. Commodities trade data has been calculated by the authors from the United Nations Commodity Trade Statistics Database (UN Comtrade), New York. Data available at http://comtrade.un.org/.

54. Data calculated by the authors from UN Comtrade.

55. Figures about Chinese outward FDI calculated by the author from data available in the UNCTAD World Investment Report, available at www.unctad.org.

56. The application of these categories to China's relations with South Asia were developed in an earlier setting relating to the theoretical underpinning behind China's global emergence in Saez, "China's Global Emergence," pp. 107–110. However, the exact terms used in the previous formulation are slightly different in wording: *reluctant competition, selective engagement,* and *covert co-optation.*

57. Jeremy Page, "Port in a Storm: How Chinese Billions Funded Army's Battle to Break Tigers," *The Times* (London), May 2, 2009, p. 39.

58. "India, China Jostle for Influence in Indian Ocean," *The Associated Press,* June 8, 2008. The article can be found at www.msnbc.msn.com/id/25024945.

59. This pattern is similar to the reports regarding the construction of Chinese lis-

tening posts across various sites in Myanmar (e.g., at Man-aung, Hainggyi, Zadetkyi Island, and the strategically important Coco Islands).

60. "Democracy and Development in Maldives," *Peace and Conflict* 9, no. 6 (June 2006): 29.

61. "China Is Nepal's Reliable Friend: Nepali King," *Xinhua News,* March 18, 2005, available at http://news.xinhuanet.com/english/2006-03/18/content_4314868.htm.

62. "Nepal Political Crisis & Indo-Chinese Tensions," Kuwait Times, May 6, 2009. Full text available at www.kuwaittimes.net/read_news.php?newsid =ODUwODg3MzI4. As of the time of the writing of this chapter, Prime Minister Dahal tendered his resignation in protest over the decision by Nepal's president, Ram Baran Yadav, to veto Dahal's recommendation to fire Nepal's army chief, Roomangud Katawal. Dahal believed that the army chief was too strongly aligned with India.

63. "China Seals Off Tibet's Pathway to Nepal," Associated Press, April 17, 2008, www.msnbc.msn.com/id/24185262/.

# 6

# China and Greater Central Asia: Economic Opportunities and Security Concerns

## Niklas Swanström

China has recently been much noted in the media about its engagements with, or more correctly, the lack of pressure toward, certain so-called rogue states such as Sudan, Myanmar (Burma), and Uzbekistan. There is a great deal of suspicion from the West of Chinese engagements in the developing world and with states with weak democratic credentials. This especially as China has increased its economic contacts with these states without reservation and gained generous advantages, according to its critics. Moreover, following the media, one could easily get the impression that China has *recently* begun to engage the developing world and regions outside of the Western hemisphere in an attempt to decrease democratic and Western influence. Nothing could be more wrong. First of all, the People's Republic of China (PRC) has been heavily engaged with the developing world since the republic's creation in 1949. In fact, China has seen itself as the leader of the nonaligned states and a protector of the developing states.

Today this view is not without problems in a world where China is far from the weak state it used to be, and in many ways has taken over the position of Western "imperialists" in terms of investments, production, and counsel. The Chinese view this relationship as being more of a partnership, but the reality still persists that China is far more powerful than many of its partners—politically as well as economically—and this is very strongly felt in many states and regions. It has even been argued that China has taken somewhat of a neocolonial position in certain regions.[1] Second, the situation is far more complex than simply being about limiting Western influences or preventing political change (regime change), even if this can at times be important components.

The history of Chinese engagement in many of these regions goes far beyond the creation of the PRC in 1949. One very classical case is the maritime contacts that Zheng He conducted from 1405 to 1433; trips that brought China to the eastern coast of Africa and possibly even farther and established Chinese influence and maritime trade links for a time until the emperor reversed the country's maritime policy. Another example is the trade along the Silk Road to Persia, India, the Middle East, and Europe. In fact, trade with the outside world, political relationships in the form of the tributary system, and an exchange of technical inventions have built the China we see today—much with peaceful means but in no way only depending on this. Chinese expansions into today's minority areas and even outside of its current borders have been frequent events in history, but also losing territory and power to the "barbarians" of primarily the north and east have shaped the current state and its mentality. The most recent significant loss of land was the large part of the northern territories that were ceded to Russia, and then the loss of Mongolia. The Chinese engagement with the outside world has been a rollercoaster of gains and losses. For most of its history, China has been engaged with the outside world—and has even been under the control of external actors—but has, at times, also shielded itself from foreign influence.

The PRC's engagement in the developing world has not been evenhanded over time, and initially Beijing was even very reluctant to engage internationally due to its own weakness. This quickly changed to become more of an interventionist strategy where the PRC supported Communist and Maoist organizations around the world in the struggle against imperialists and enemies of the people, a position that often put it in conflict with many of the developing states that stood on the US or Soviet sides in the Cold War. This confrontational policy changed with the Five Principles of Peaceful Coexistence, and then especially the policy of nonintervention. The PRC has increasingly been reluctant to overtly intervene in internal affairs of foreign states and to impact political stability negatively, even if this has (by no means) slowed down economic interaction and for China positive trade balances, and in certain states economic domination. Instead of supporting foreign revolutionaries, China has shifted to support its own businesses in expanding outside China and to ensure political stability (in contrast to regime change) in the states that are deemed strategically important. This has led China to become both an economic and political partner for many developing and developed states. The European Union's most important trading partner is now China. Southeast Asia and Africa, not to mention Greater Central Asia, have also increasingly become dependent on Chinese trade and investments. The 2008–2009 financial crisis seems to have strengthened the Chinese position both in real figures and relative strength. According to Russian sources, the Chinese trade with Kazakhstan has increased 28 percent from 2007 to 2008 to US$15.9 billion.[2]

## The Silk Road Back and Forward

Chinese engagement in Greater Central Asia[3] is everything but new, and it predates the founding of the current Central Asian states by millennia, as well as predating the Russian influence in the region, which was only felt in the fifteenth and sixteenth centuries.[4] Much of the fear of a possible Chinese expansion into this area rests on the very fact that China has been deeply engaged in the region—arguably too engaged at times according to some academics and policymakers, a position that often is slightly unfair as the expansion has been in both directions. However, it should be noted that the Chinese adventures of today into Greater Central Asia have little to do with the current state formations as the "history of [Central Asia] is primarily one of oases, large and small."[5] A similar argument could be used in Mongolia, which has been divided much after and before the great Genghis Khan. The Chinese interaction was with Zhungharia, Torghuts, Khoshot, and Derbet—tribes and empires that only exist in the memory of the Greater Central Asians and Chinese people, even if not always in the distant past. This is not to say that the territories and peoples of Greater Central Asia have not been important for the Chinese. In fact, it could be argued that the tribes and empires that today form the states in Greater Central Asia have been heavily involved in the very formation of China and its current political, military, and economic outlook. It could even be argued that modern China was built on the very existence of the Greater Central Asian people's engagement, both negative and positive. The Great Wall is only one example of defensive creations that were constructed to keep the northern and western barbarians out of China, many of whom today are minorities within China, such as Mongolians, Manchu, Uighur, and so forth, or who live at the borders of China, such as in Mongolia, Kazakhstan, Kyrgyzstan, and so on.[6]

The interaction between China and its eastern neighbors in Greater Central Asia was often a positive interaction, all but excluding the very backward and poor Europe for a long time. Silk, metals, porcelain, and other valuable trade goods are what the Silk Road often brings to mind when one thinks about the continental interaction between Central Asia, China, Mongolia, Russia, the Middle East, Persia, India, and (on the margins) Europe. Often forgotten, however, is that the threat from the west and northwest (Mongols, Turks, and other steppe people) forced China to integrate and construct defenses against the "foreign devils" and barbarians. China engaged in a policy of loose reign (Jimi) where frontier trade was a national security matter that would supplement the military preparations.[7] The Great Wall, one of the world's greatest structures, was built to protect the Chinese interior against marauding steppe people. China did also attempt to forward the lines of defense by pushing the barbarians out of China's near periphery, an attempt that extended its empire to include today's Mongolia and parts of Russia, but also Tibet, Xinjiang, and other regions that today are integral parts of China. Moreover, there was a cultural export that tied the Greater Central Asian states to China in a deeper and more profound way. The millennium-old adventure to build defenses and fight barbarians cost enormous sums of money and took an almost unimaginable amount of human resources and a well-developed bureaucracy to accomplish. This forced China to become a very centralized state with a great focus on its eastern and northeastern borders and to no small degree forced China to become the continental power it still is. What today is Mongolia and Xinjiang (East Turkestan) eventually became integrated parts of the Chinese empire, and the Mongols and later the Manchus even ruled China during the Yuan dynasty (1271–1368) and the Qing dynasty (1644–1911). This even as China or Chinese areas had already been ruled relatively frequently by barbarians from the west and northwest.

The military interaction between China and its neighbors was characterized by plunder and preventive war. More important, however, is that the riches that were (and still are) transferred over the region have come to benefit all different forms of political constellations and regimes. Trade has simply been too lucrative and important not to engage in. Similarly, it has been too tempting not to try to control or plunder the very same trade. The route through Greater Central Asia and China was the very vein for international trade until maritime trade was made secure enough to compete with the Silk Road. This made Greater Central Asia less important as a trading hub until it nearly vanished with the Russian occupation that cut Central Asia off from the world. Much of the ancient interaction between the Greater Central Asian entities and China has thus been to stimulate increased trade and possibly increase its civilizational influence over the "barbarian" part. With the Soviet demise, all states in the Greater Central Asian region are once again directly relevant for Chinese trade, especially in terms of transit trade and as a resource base.

The failure of China to use this region as a transit route during the Russian occupation of Central Asia did not only decrease its profits and hamper the development potentials of China's western regions, but it also forced China to rely on the more expensive and unreliable (due to the US control of such) sea lanes, which, in turn, also presented a major security challenge. Today, this is most apparent in terms of energy transit, but historically silk, tea, and rhubarb were strategically important commodities.

The economic interaction among China, Persia, India, Afghanistan, and Central Asia over land peaked during the Tang dynasty (618–907) and reached a low point during the Qing dynasty (1644–1912) (due to internal weakness) and was gradually reduced to virtually no interaction at all up to 1991. This was both due to the decline of the Chinese empire, the growth of the sea lanes as a trade route, and the Russian occupation of Central Asia in the nineteenth century, which finally ended in 1991. The Russian occupation cut all contacts between China and the Central Asian states, although some cross-border trade was allowed with the initiation of glasnost in the 1980s. Mongolia and Afghanistan were largely left outside this equation, even if Russian/Soviet influence quickly became much more important in these states than Chinese influence. The Soviet invasion of Afghanistan in 1979 (and the decade-long conflict that followed) together with Russian/Soviet close cooperation with Mongolia, minimized the Chinese influence in both states until the breakdown of the Soviet Union in 1989. In 1991, the Central Asian states were forced to leave the Soviet Union. In contrast to popular perceptions, all the Central Asian states were heavily in favor of keeping the Union of Soviet Socialist Republics intact, but Moscow was simply not interested in letting the Central Asian states remain within a confederation. Russia seems to have changed this policy toward a more traditional tsarist strategy with semi-independent neighboring states closely tied to Russia. Central Asia, and then especially the energy-rich states, will be at risk in this Russian strategy as it could put them in a position of unwanted attention. The revival of the Russian interest was mostly felt before the financial crisis in 2008–2009 and has been reduced in intensity as the crisis has unfolded.

## Political-Strategic Dimensions

The demise of the Soviet Union was the trigger for increased Chinese influence in Greater Central Asia, due largely to the fact that Russia could not sustain the economies of Central Asia and Mongolia alone but also because these states were interested in diversifying and reducing their reliance on Russia. This quickly transformed into a more complex and diversified foreign policy with a greater number of partners, as they did not want to exchange one overlord for another.[8] This was most notable in the cases of Kazakhstan and Mongolia, who developed strategies of reliance on third neighbors instead of relying on China as a counterbalance to Russia only. Initially these changes played in favor of the Chinese, but as the Chinese influence has been increasingly strong, all states have attempted to reduce both Russian as well as Chinese influence, albeit to differing degrees. The states fearing China the least are not surprisingly the states least impacted by Chinese influence—Afghanistan and Turkmenistan. Conversely, the states sharing borders with China, such as Mongolia and Kyrgyzstan, are most concerned about the increasing Chinese influence.

In 1991, it came as no shock to the leaders in Beijing and Xinjiang that they would have to fight an uphill battle to gain influence, acquire economic advantages, and to tackle the joint security challenges across the Central Asian borders. Initially, China was not primarily interested in energy—which today has become one of the most important issues—but rather in border security issues and to stabilize its own minority provinces, that is, Xinjiang. Resolving the outstanding border issues as well as increasing military and security cooperation with the bordering states thus became the foremost concerns, especially as there are large Uighur populations in Central Asia and a popular support for a sixth Central Asian "Turkestan" state. Only after these primary concerns had been dealt with did it become possible for China to focus on its economic and energy interests in the region. Similarly, when the Taliban regime fell in Afghanistan, China's immediate concern was to protect its security interests and limit the Taliban and Al-Qaida's influence in Xinjiang, and defer the pursuance of economic interests until stability had been achieved. Only after the United States and the North American Treaty Organization managed to stabilize parts of the country did it become attractive for the Chinese to increase economic, cultural, and political exchanges and to deepen overall relations. Even though insecurity is running high, and to a certain extent increasing, in Afghanistan, the Chinese investments have risen significantly, and Beijing has extended increased cooperation with Kabul in a variety of fields.[9]

China enhanced its cooperation with Central Asia both bilaterally and multilaterally in the mid-1990s. This was primarily manifested with the establishment of the Shanghai Five organization in 1996 (including China, Russia, Kyrgyzstan, Tajikistan, and Kazakhstan), which later transformed into the Shanghai Cooperation Organization (SCO) with the inclusion of Uzbekistan in 2001. The motives for China to engage Central Asia through a multilateral organization were many, but it is clear today that security issues were imperative in the initial stages. Beijing also realized that many issues could be better handled multilaterally, especially considering Russia's preference to monitor China's activities with the Central Asian states within an established framework. Virtually all treaties adopted in the early years of this organization also had paragraphs that referred back to the minority and terrorist questions, something that has changed slightly in today's interaction, which is more economic in its language. SCO aimed, therefore, at the security issues in its first years, a focus that was problematic considering that the Central Asian states did not work well with each other and none was interested in pooling sovereignty to an intergovernmental organization. With the Russian invasion of Georgia and the declaration of independence of South Ossetia and Abkhazia, the security issues, especially separatism and foreign intervention, are once again of utmost importance.

Thus, as the Central Asian states gained independence, China felt it was crucial to improve security along its borders, both internal and external. Political strategic factors are still the most important motivators behind China's strategy toward Greater Central Asia. It is also the most analyzed, and as a consequence, the security focus will be more limited here. The Central Asian borderlands became the foremost focus, both because Afghanistan was too much in disarray to deal with while Mongolia already was relatively stable and the tension within Mongolia had little potential to spill over into China. It was also felt that the immediate independence period presented a golden opportunity to deal with the border issues, since Russia had pulled out of the region due to its own weakness while the Central Asian states simultaneously were desperate for other economic and political partners. Moreover, Beijing believed that speedy action on the issue was essential to stabilize national affairs and the western borderland regions. Xinjiang had been mentioned as the potential sixth Central Asian state—East Turkestan—and Beijing wanted to shore up support from the Central Asian states directly to thwart separatism. There are an estimated 300,000 Uighurs living in Kazakhstan and Kyrgyzstan who could potentially be a problem to China. In contrast to expectations, China did not feel too confident in the negotiations and neither did it gain as much territory as often is claimed. It was, and has often been, a direct strategy to compromise and give each of the bordering states enough to accept the Chinese demands to support and prevent terrorism, separatism, and extremism (the so-called three evils). As a result, all Central Asian governments, but specifically the ones that border China, are strongly supporting China's struggle against separatists, that is, Uighurs. Recently, the Olympic Games accentuated the question, and the SCO member states were instrumental in thwarting any attempt from Uighur nationalists to disrupt the games.[10] This is not to say that the populations of the Central Asian states support their governments' view. On the contrary, there is quite a bit of support for Uighur independence in Central Asia.[11] Beijing is fully aware of this and therefore has been rather strict in its demands to the SCO members to assist in China's struggle against the three evils.

At the same time, it would hardly be enough for the Chinese government to kindly ask the Central Asian governments for support to combat the Uighurs, as the policy is at times unpopular, not least considering the perception that "fellow Muslims are persecuted by Chinese communists." To improve the situation and make it easier for the governments in Central Asia to back China, Beijing has been a loyal supporter of the sitting governments in Central Asia, which often suffer from the same problems as China with the three evils. This is not a difficult decision for China as it has no interest in assisting in overthrowing the current secular governments in favor of potentially more religiously oriented regimes that would most likely put greater emphasis on its religious kinship with the Uighurs and possibly be more anti-Chinese. In this, China and the sitting governments share a great deal of interest, especially as certain parts of Greater Central Asia have experienced a revival of more fundamentalist forces, such as in the Ferghana Valley and in Afghanistan.

Military cooperation has as a result increased significantly between China and the Central Asian states, although it is still modest between China and Mongolia and Afghanistan, respectively. Despite some attempts at multilateral cooperation, especially in combating terrorists, this has so far been more for media consumption than effective counter-responses, as the real cooperation still is mostly bilateral in nature. Beijing has focused very much on the antiterrorist (read "the three evils") activities and is mostly concerned with how China's cause can be assisted, but also how to stabilize the bordering states, and through this increase its own security. The military-to-military cooperation is still very sensitive for Russian concerns and China has refrained from being too active in Central Asia militarily. As a consequence we can see that the Chinese military sales to Central Asia are very low at this time, and it will not threaten the Russian arms sales to the region in the foreseeable future— this despite an overall trade level that is very high. China has also refrained from openly expressing an interest in establishing military bases in any of the states. Despite this tension, China and Russia do share many interests in the region, especially in consolidating and stabilizing the national governments and minimizing external (i.e., Western) influence.

Instability in the region is a constant headache for China; the chaos in Afghanistan created a safe-haven for fundamentalists and terrorists until the United States dealt with the Taliban and Al-Qaida. There is also a constant fear that any political changes in the region will most likely pull toward the more extremist sides, that is, Islamic fundamentalists. Therefore, the status quo and hopefully improved stability is preferred. The disdain for instability and chaos lies deep in the Chinese psyche due to millennia of disorder and chaos at the border but also due to the track record of internal chaos, such as the Cultural Revolution. Therefore, any Chinese government would go far in stabilizing its own borders and bordering states, much to the benefit of the governments in Greater Central Asia.

Moreover, it is not in the interest of China to assist the international community or civil society, what small pockets of civil society are left, in the Greater Central Asian states to transform the current more authoritarian-oriented governments toward more democratic ones, which so often are demanded by Western activists and scholars. Beijing would first dispute, correctly, whether these states would have any success in establishing democracy under the current conditions (excluding Mongolia). If not, political changes and turmoil would benefit fundamentalist or criminal organizations.[12] Second, it remains to be explained why China, or for that matter Russia, should assist in creating a political system that is pro-Western and anti-authoritarian. That would only decrease their own influence in the region, and if the Greater Central Asian states should gravitate toward China and Russia due to lack of interest and action from the West, so much the better for Beijing. Therefore, there seem to be very few reasons for China to work for increased democratization, and at this political juncture, the governments in Greater Central Asia and China appear to have much in common. The recent tensions in Mongolia and the declaration of martial law is one example of this—a type of action that always is questioned by the West, but never questioned by the government in

China. This policy of noninterference is reducing the political influence of Europe and the United States in Greater Central Asia, while China and Russia are perceived as not being a threat to the interests of the smaller states. This is not to say that they would actively destabilize or counter democratic movements. This is left to domestic forces, but there is a preference for stability and like-minded governments. The financial crisis in 2008–2009 has further tilted the Greater Central Asia governments toward China, as dependency seems to have increased.

The trend of decreasing influence is also accelerated by the direct strategy of China to field its soft power in Greater Central Asia.[13] The creation of Confucius Institutes is especially noticeable in these states in combination with a more coordinated and encouraged policy of exchanges, ranging from military and politics to economic and cultural. China is increasingly perceived as a good neighbor, even if many difficult scars, imagined or real, from past history of occupation, expansion, and cultural hegemony still are visible. This is made easier by the fact that China's engagement "comes with none of the pesky human rights conditions, good governance requirements, approved-project restrictions, and environmental quality regulations" that characterize Western engagements.[14] This has been crucial, as China has not always been seen with a good eye in the region. This is especially true in Mongolia and Kyrgyzstan, which both perceive China as a potential threat, not only for historical reasons, but also due to their increased dependence both politically and, more importantly, economically on China. Beijing has committed generous resources to improving its reputation in all Greater Central Asian states. Financial, diplomatic, and cultural resources at the highest level have been employed in this endeavor, and the result is now evident. It would take a great deal of effort for any state to reverse this. The only danger China faces is itself and a return to the old ethnocentric attitudes that could alienate other states.

## Economy, Trade, and Energy

The most visible and evident improvement in the bilateral and multilateral relations between China and Greater Central Asia is the dramatic trade increase, which is often in favor of China. It is undeniable that China has increased its trade greatly, and it has long been an official policy to try to boost trade relations with Mongolia, Afghanistan, and especially the SCO members in Central Asia.[15] It has never been a PRC policy to militarily occupy any of the states in this region, nor arguably any other state, but financially it has had a direct policy of economic expansion and influence toward the region. The central government in China has actively directed all border regions to increase trade with its neighbors, which it has done with great ease and engagement. In one example, the local government in Sichuan was informed by the central government that it should double its trade with Central Asia between 2001 and 2002. In response, it increased its trade thirteen times that single year.[16] The reason behind this strategy is not only to secure natural resources, increase trade-related economic gains, and establish transregional trading links (primarily with the Middle East and Europe), but also to influence and secure friendly governments in the region. This is not completely unlike strategies used by Europe, the United States, and India, but the success has been more tangible, while other states have failed to assert their influence.[17]

China and the Central Asian states did "hit it off" very well economically directly after the dissolution of the Soviet Union. This was in no way a coincidence. The poor state of the Russian economy and the low Chinese prices (and quality) did effectively offer an attractive alternative for the Central Asian states. If the Central Asian states were interested in consumer goods from China, the Chinese were even more interested in the natural resources of Central Asia, primarily oil and gas. The economic interaction picked up pace, and it has been estimated that some 700,000 Central Asians legally visited Urumqi in 2006 alone, the number of illegal visitors are claimed to be even higher than the legal. Similarly, Chinese traders and migrants are in great numbers seeking their ways into the Greater Central Asian states. In fact, Chinese migration to the Greater Central Asian states, most notably Mongolia and Kazakhstan, could create tension. The situation is not unlike the one in the Russian Far East. Many poor Chinese, many of whom are unemployed Chinese construction workers, work for less and longer hours than the native populations and are accused of taking the jobs of the local population. The situation in Mongolia is telling, where Chinese construction workers dominate the market. Moreover, a few very visible Chinese natives have made fortunes in the region, and this creates tension, as they are seen as exploiting the local population. How many Chinese migrants there are in Greater Central Asia is difficult to estimate as many move back and forth and the numbers are notoriously unpredictable. The perceptions from the local populations are, however, that there are too many Chinese and that restrictions on migrant workers should be imposed.

During the 1990s, China increased its trade incrementally, much due to the lack of institutions and infrastructure to facilitate trade between Central Asia and China. The trade picked up pace in the 2000s, when major infrastructural investments were made on the Chinese side to enlarge trade, but also through Chinese investments in Central Asian infrastructure. China has made serious efforts in improving the 616-kilometer Karakoram highway linking Gwadar port in Pakistan with Xinjiang, the Osh-Sary-Tarsh-Irkeshtam road, and the Atasu-Alashankou pipeline between Kazakhstan and China.[18] According to the Chinese Customs Statistics, the total trade volume, including barter trade, went from approximately US$465 million in 1992 to US$17.794 billion in 2007.[19] This meant that China has approached the levels of the Russian trade with Central Asia for the first time. A vast majority of this trade is with

Kazakhstan (US$13.9 billion in 2007 and according to unofficial statistics US$15.9 billion in 2008); it is to a large extent oriented toward the energy sector, but also includes infrastructural investments.[20] The trade with Kyrgyzstan is however the fastest growing trade, and the trade volume reached US$2.26 billion in 2007, up a whopping 128.6 percent from the previous year. Much of this is oriented toward infrastructure, minerals, and energy.[21] Trade with all states in Greater Central Asia has exploded, and for nine years in a row China has been the largest trading partner of Mongolia, with trade of US$2.08 billion, growing 43.24 percent from last year. Sino-Afghan trade reached US$317 million in 2005–2006.[22] Trade with Uzbekistan exceeded US$1 billion in 2007 (one-fourth of Russian trade with Uzbekistan), while trade with Tajikistan reached US$524 million in 2007.[23] Even the trade with the remote Turkmenistan shows signs of rapid increases since the leadership succession in that state. Chinese statistics claim that the trade exchange with Turkmenistan in 2005 amounted to approximately US$110 million, from which export to Turkmenistan was US$90.8 million and import from Turkmenistan was US$19 million.[24] With the latest oil and gas deals with Turkmenistan in 2008, this figure will be greatly enhanced. This trend has made China the single fastest growing trading partner in the region, and in many cases the dominant trading partner. The Chinese trade with Russia has followed a similar pattern and in 2007 came up to US$48.2 billion, and despite a decrease of Chinese imports from Russia in 2007, it has doubled over the past four years.[25] The financial crisis does not seem to have affected the trade relations negatively; on the contrary, despite being a detraction of the Chinese economy, Sino-GCA trade has shown positive tendencies.

As noted, the bulk of this trade is directly invested in the energy market and infrastructure, but not an insignificant portion is also spent on preventing instability in the region. China fears the possible religious instability in the region that could originate from Afghanistan, Tajikistan, and possibly the Ferghana Valley. In much of the trade China conducts with the Greater Central Asian states, there is the promise of creating political stability in the region, with the exception of Mongolia and Kazakhstan, both of which have proven to be relatively stable politically. Increasing trade, potentially can prevent the escalation of extremism in the region. It has been realized that the stability of the governments in the region is very much linked to economic progress, a progress that has disappeared in corruption and political mismanagement in all states but Kazakhstan and Mongolia. This has increasingly become a problem for China, which is satisfied with the political systems, or at least does not object. The corruption and mismanagement reduces the profitability of trade and creates domestic tension in each of these states that could threaten China if it continues to destabilize individual states or the whole region. For example, increased instability would increase transaction costs, especially for energy due to increased risk for attacks against relevant infrastructure, but could also increase the prevalence of Muslim fundamentalism that could work in favor of the Uighur nationalists in China.

SCO has been an important tool for China to increase its trade and political stability but also to leverage its soft power in the region. The initial results from the infrastructural developments and improved interdependence are already evident in the increase of trade volumes and transit trade in Greater Central Asia.[26] In 2007, bilateral trade between China and the five other SCO members reached US$66 billion, up more than 360 percent from the launch of the organization.[27] To be fair, much of the increase in trade volume would have occurred without SCO, but it has become an increasingly important tool in the process. Not least to create a normative base and discuss multilateral solutions to trade barriers.

Not included in these statistics is the informal economy, both gray and black. Much of the bazaar trade in Central Asia is conducted with merchandise smuggled from China into Central Asia, as well as precursors for the refinement process in the narcotics industry in Afghanistan. Also, increasingly, narcotics (primarily heroin) are smuggled from Afghanistan to China through Central Asia.[28] The smuggled consumer goods from China to Greater Central Asia are substantial, some estimates by local police estimate it to be 10–15 percent of the total licit trade.[29] Moreover, the illegal precursor trade to sustain the heroin production in Afghanistan is in itself one of the largest trades in the region. Both the illicit trade in consumer goods as well as narcotics-related products follow the same transit routes, such as the Wakhan corridor, Kulma Pass, Torughart, and Khorgos, to name a few, which are all increasingly used to smuggle heroin into China and precursors and consumer goods into Central Asia and Afghanistan for the refinement process.[30] Organized crime is an old phenomena in China and is seen in the coastal areas as well as in the center of China. These old centers for organized crime are increasingly dwarfed by the inflow of narcotics from Afghanistan to China. While the trade from Myanmar has decreased significantly, Afghanistan, according to UN figures, is producing well over 94 percent of the world's heroin—China's drug of choice. This, in combination with a rapid economic development, has resulted in China becoming one of the emerging markets for heroin sales from Afghanistan. Although China and the Central Asian states on paper and in joint declarations claim to share the struggle against organized crime, the reality looks very different. China has not prioritized the question of curbing the sales of illegal consumer goods to Greater Central Asia, even if they have tried hard to handle the illegal trade in precursors. On the other side, the Chinese government is eager to combat the transit of narcotics to China, a mission that is in practice not shared by many governments in the region, or at least not by important segments of the government and border units, which are directly involved in the trade and effectively prevent any effective counternarcotics response. In Afghanistan, Tajikistan, and Kyrgyzstan, large segments of the economy are controlled by organized crime, and without the illegal economy these states would not function. In fact, much of the social security net is controlled or paid for by persons directly involved in or connected to organized crime. This makes it virtually impossible to fight the problem without far-reaching multilateral solutions. All states that border China, as well as China itself, have problems with organized crime, but not to the same extent. The result is that the illegal economy creates a skewed picture where little is accomplished due to the collisions and disharmony among local, national, and international interests.

The possibility of economic linkages between Europe and China are a far more positive factor in Sino–Central Asian relations, but also in its relations to Mongolia and Afghanistan. Central Asia has increasingly become a new transport hub, one that potentially can compete and outperform the present one through Mongolia and Russia. The current revitalization of the Silk Road and development of the continental transport corridor, "the Second Eurasian Land Bridge," running from China's east coast to Europe, are here expected to bring massive gains to the landlocked countries of Central Asia should trade obstacles be tackled, but even more so for China.[31] The estimates on these gains are highly speculative and range from an increase of 13 percent of the Chinese gross domestic product (GDP) according to Chinese estimates, 50–100 percent increase of the economies in Central Asia over a ten-year period according to the UN Development Programme (UNDP), while estimates by the Organization for Economic Cooperation and Development (OECD) run up to a 2.3 percent increase of the GDP per annum in the region.[32]

It has become evident that the transport corridor running from China's coast in Lianyungang to Rotterdam via the Xinjiang Province in China's west and Greater Central Asia has attracted increased interest, due greatly to these positive calculations. This is a result of infrastructural development in Greater Central Asia and China, but primarily due to the fact that it could cut transport time between Asia and Europe considerably. For example, in comparison to the sea journey from China to Europe, which takes twenty to forty days, cargo on railway from Lianyungang to Rotterdam via the second Euro-Asia land bridge could cut transport time down to a startling eleven days according to the Asian Development Bank.[33] The booming trade volumes between Europe and China forecasted to increase from 300 million tons in 2000 to 460 million by 2015 also promise enormous transit gains for the landlocked countries in Greater Central Asia if existing trade obstacles are tackled. This projection of the future is strengthening the ties between China and Central Asia and stabilizing the governments. As the sea-lines of communication are becoming increasingly congested, overland transports will become more and more of an option for forwarders and transporters, which also will reduce dependency on the Russian corridor and spur healthy competition.[34] This does not only concern Central Asia; if the full potential of continental trade could be used, primarily across the South and Central Asia divide, Afghanistan will find itself in the middle of a continental market stretching east-west from Lianyungang to Rotterdam and north-south from Moscow to Delhi. This will raise the prospects for long-term prosperity in this pivotal country and directly link its trade to China.

It has become apparent for both China and the Greater Central Asian states that if they can cooperate economically and create sufficient stability to attract business, it will benefit all actors in the region. Despite tension in the military-political field, there is less tension in the economic field, with the exception of an understandable fear of Chinese economic domination. China has increasingly become aware of this and has moved away from its neoliberal parlance of free trade and accepted the concerns of the local populations. However, actual policy changes seem distant and it remains to be seen how much goodwill the Chinese enterprises will destroy before new policies are implemented. The danger is that Chinese businesspeople continue to refuse to hire local workers and out-perform local businesses. Moreover, the local population often views the Chinese traders and workers as arrogant. This has often changed a positive view to a more negative one.

## Bilateralism vs. Multilateralism: A Quest for the Future?

Despite some signs of increased multilateralism in Greater Central Asia and China, the bulk of the interaction is still done on a bilateral basis, and more importantly, the significant agreements are still mainly bilateral in nature. This is natural due to the lack of trust between the different actors, not just between China and the smaller states but also between the smaller states themselves and increasingly between Russia and the Central Asian states. The Central Asian states refuse to work closely together and look toward outside forces to assist them in their internal affairs, due largely to the outstanding identity issues that still plague Central Asia. The weakness of the state apparatuses inhibits deep and institutionalized contacts, as sovereignty is still the primordial instinct of the states in the region, especially in states such as Afghanistan and Tajikistan. China is the driving force for increased multilateralism, arguably due to its own relative strength, but other actors try to inhibit further multilateralism. The insecurity in the region is increasingly transnational in nature, however, requiring multilateral responses, whether it is terrorism (three evils), environmental issues, trade, or energy security.

To counter this insecurity, China has worked hard to create a regional structure that could solve this and be controlled by China. Shanghai Cooperation Organization has emerged as the rising star on the Sino–Greater Central Asian skyline and much of the improvements in the relations are results of the SCO. However, it is still the case that most of the interaction is either dealt with through bilateral relations or can be overridden by bilateral agreements. Even the much-cited border delimitation between China and the Central Asian states that was credited to SCO was in essence bilateral agreements between the concerned states. The reality is that the creation of a truly multilateral organization in the region with far-reaching powers is neither in the smaller states' nor China's short-term interest. Over time, it makes much more sense for China, Mongolia (currently observer status), Kazakhstan, and possibly Uzbekistan to increase the strength of SCO in order to control the smaller states. However, it will be unlikely that the stronger states could utilize SCO in this way due to the very informality of the organizations and the demand for consensus—the very traits that make it more of a discussion club than an effective multilateral structure. In all fairness, SCO was never intended to be anything more, but this makes it difficult to resolve the very difficult issues the region faces.

SCO is not the first or the only multilateral structure that has been proposed or is in action. China developed a strategy for energy security termed the "Pan-Asian Continental Oil Bridge" that would tie Japan, South Korea, and China together with the Middle East. This adventure was terminated because it would give China control over the system.[35] On the other hand, China would not allow SCO to come under the control of another state. Much of the failure in the energy field traces to lack of the kind of trust between the actors that is needed for effective multilateralism.[36] Similarly, there have been attempts to create multilateral structures to handle military affairs, mostly in SCO, but all are showpieces rather than structures that could be used in effective military scenarios.

It is not only smaller states that create problems in the region. In terms of increased multilateralism, especially in SCO, the Sino-Russian relations are to a high degree determining the future. Despite some overlapping interests, there is an overriding conflict over interest in the region. Russia has already or is in the process of losing economic control of the region. Despite Russia's military, political, and particularly cultural influence, China has made impressive inroads, and over the long term, it seems unlikely that Russia will be capable to controlling the hearts and minds of the Greater Central Asians without controlling their wallets. The Russian invasion of Georgia and its effective division of Georgia has made it difficult for the Central Asian states to stand by Russia.

*Multilateralism* is in no way a dead word in Greater Central Asia, but due to the weakness of many of its members and the problems that the region faces today, it is unlikely that we will see effective regional structures in the short term. However, the foundation that SCO has planted puts the region well positioned to boost the growth of multilateral structures when Greater Central Asia is ready to do this.

## Problems and Potential Gains: Moving Forward

China has expanded its presence in all Greater Central Asian states, especially in strategically important states such as Kazakhstan, and there has been no slowdown in the pace of this expansion. China views the region as an important link in its economic and political security strategy. By opening up Greater Central Asia for Chinese influence and investments, China will increase its transit possibilities and economic profits as well as its internal security. Still, the question of internal security, and by extension, border security, is the prime target of China's interest in Greater Central Asia, as can be seen in the Chinese policy related to the Olympic Games and the Yanda (Strike Hard) campaign that China initiated in 1998 to pacify Xinjiang. This campaign has cost a great deal of financial resources and a disproportionate amount of military resources, for debatable gains. Opening up economic links to Central Asia, Mongolia, and Afghanistan would greatly benefit Xinjiang, and there is hope in some circles in Beijing that the economy will fare better than military solutions have done.

China and the Greater Central Asian states share the political denominator, with the partial exception of Mongolia, and it seems very likely that as long as the states in question are more authoritarian, and the West vigorously is working against such systems, China will benefit greatly from its political position. Strengthening the political systems, and effectively stabilizing the governments in the region, is not a problem per se as long as it does not strengthen the criminal structures found in the regional states. China is relatively unaffected by corruption and political co-option by criminal networks that characterize many of the weaker states in the region. Therefore, China could function as a positive example not only in economic terms, but also as a political example at least as long as the Western states continue to put excessively difficult demands on the regional states to transform overnight to full-fledged democracies.

It is apparent that China, and especially Xinjiang, is benefitting greatly by the impressive economic and political impact China has on the region. It should, however, be noted that the economic gains from Greater Central Asia are only secondary to the economic prize on the horizon: Europe and the Middle East. By linking China and Europe, transaction costs would decrease significantly. As mentioned earlier, the impact on GDP could be as high as 13 percent according to some Chinese estimates. Adding the value from energy imports and cheaper transit routes for Middle Eastern and Iranian oil and gas, it is without a doubt a great benefit to open up the transport routes westward. As the Malacca straits are becoming increasingly congested and easily blockaded, a new pipeline system over Central Asia would make sense not only economically, but also in terms of diversification for China.

This said, if there weren't any problems, there would already be an established infrastructure that binds the region together. The problems of further cooperation and possibly integration are both internal and external. The Russian factor is one important obstacle to further Chinese economic integration and political and military cooperation with the region. Russia is, naturally, not keen on letting China dominate what it views as its own backyard. China, on the other hand, argues that Russian occupation and influence in the region is an anomaly given a much-longer Chinese presence. The Sino-Russian struggle over influence will be the determining factor in China's success in the region. However, neither holds the Central Asian region as their primary focus, as both Russia and China have their focus primarily on Europe and the United States, respectively.

Before anything can be accomplished in terms of economic interaction, the question of safety and transparency of transport needs to be handled. Currently there is too much political and military instability in the region, and transports, especially pipelines, are exposed to terrorist attacks. China is especially threatened in Xinjiang, but all transit states need to handle their own internal security as they are all vulnerable, and it seems unlikely that the problems in, for example, the Ferghana Valley should easily be solved. Afghanistan is the most apparent case where tension will remain for a long time to come and the creation of necessary infrastructure will be very difficult to manage. Regardless if security could be obtained, there is a lack of transparency and predictability in the trade transactions.

There is also a plethora of regulations and legal restraints that has made cooperation in all fields very difficult. The protection of sovereignty has taken preeminence over all other interaction. In the political-military field, this both makes sense due to the situation of the involved states and will take a long time to change. However, in the economic field there is a need to overlook tariffs, infrastructural bottlenecks, and investment regulations, as they are not as politically sensitive as other issues, and most importantly, the security of the states involved depends on economic development. When considering tariffs and infrastructure, the problem is not the connection to China but rather the relations within Central Asia and with Afghanistan. There is a lack of both effective infrastructure and a willingness to improve it due to the lack of trust between the smaller states. Before China can take the full benefit from trade with the region, it will need to convince other states to establish better transport between center and periphery but also between regions and states.

The future for the relations between China and the Greater Central Asian states looks positive, despite a few dark clouds in the sky. Trade has integrated the region to a great deal, despite some problems, and the political factor seems to strengthen both the bilateral as well as the multilateral relations. The weakness is Chinese arrogance, Sino-Russian competition that could risk stalemating SCO, intraregional weakness, and especially the failure of the Central Asian states to fully cooperate. China is determined to overcome or at least decrease the impact of these weaknesses, not from the goodness of its heart, but very much due to the possible economic returns and improvements to its own national security.

## Notes

1. Klas Marklund and Karin Odqvist, "Perspectives on Africa Today: A Swedish-Chinese-African Dialogue," report on a conference organized by the Institute for Security and Development Policy and the Dag Hammarskjöld Foundation, Uppsala and Stockholm, Sweden, February 14–15, 2008, www.isdp.eu/files/publications/cr/08/Marklund0804.pdf.

2. V. Paramonov, A. Strokov, and O. Stolpovskii, "Ekonomicheskoe prisutstvie Kitaia v Kazakhstane" [China's Economic Presence in Kazakhstan], May 29, 2009, www.ia-centr.ru/expert/4811/.

3. The Central Asian states are here defined as Turkmenistan, Uzbekistan, Tajikistan, Kyrgyzstan, Kazakhstan, as well as Mongolia and Afghanistan, which historically were a part of the very same cultural, economic, political, and military sphere. Eastern Turkestan (today's Xinjiang) could also be seen as a part of the historical Central Asia and China's gate to modern Central Asia.

4. Peter Perdue, *China Marches West: The Qing Conquest of Central Eurasia* (Cambridge: The Belknap Press of Harvard University Press, 2005).

5. Richard Frye, *The Heritage of Central Asia: From Antiquity to the Turkish Expansion* (Princeton: Markus Wiener Publishers, 2001), p. 13.

6. James Millward, *Eurasian Crossroads: A History of Xinjiang* (New York: Columbia University Press, 2007); Perdue, *China Marches West*. Morris Rossabi, ed., *Governing China's Multiethnic Frontiers* (Seattle: University of Washington Press, 2004); Dru Gladney, *Dislocating China: Muslims, Minorities, and Other Subaltern Subjects* (Chicago: The University of Chicago Press, 2004).

7. Perdue, *China Marches West*, p. 268.

8. Niklas Swanström, "China and Central Asia: A New Great Game or Traditional Vassal Relations," *Journal of Contemporary China* 14, no. 45 (2005): 569–584.

9. Niklas Swanström, Nicklas Norling, and Li Zhang, "The New Silk Roads: Transport and Trade in Greater Central Asia," in Frederick Starr, ed., *The New Silk Roads* (Washington, DC, and Stockholm: Central Asia Caucasus Institute and the Silk Road Studies Program, 2007), pp. 383–422.

10. "82 Suspected Terrorists Targeting Olympics in Xinjiang Detained," *China Daily,* July 10, 2008.

11. It should be noted that the separatist forces in Xinjiang are neither strong in numbers nor strong in weaponry. Uighurs do complain about the treatment in their "own" land, but most are more than willing to stay within China, as this is where the money is.

12. Niklas Swanström, "Political Development and Organized Crime: The Yin and Yang of Greater Central Asia?" *China and Eurasia Forum Quarterly* 5, no. 4 (2007).

13. Niklas Swanström, "China's Role in Central Asia: Soft and Hard Power," *Global Dialogue* 9, no. 1-2 (2007): 79–88; Joshua Kurlantzick, *Charm Offensive: How China's Soft Power Is Transforming the World* (New Haven, CT: Yale University Press, 2007).

14. Congressional Research Service, *China's Foreign Policy and "Soft Power" in South America, Asia, and Africa* (Washington, DC: Library of Congress, 2008), p. 9.

15. Swanström, "China and Central Asia."

16. "SW China Provinces Eyes Central Asian Market," *Xinhua News Agency,* June 9, 2003; "Foreign Minister Urges Chinese Businessmen to Invest in Kazakhstan," *BBC Monitoring Central Asia*, May 11, 2002.

17. Swanström,"China's Role in Central Asia."

18. "Circumventing the Bear. Stratfor, December 16, 2005," Xinjiang Autonomus Region, PRC: Trade Facilitation and Customs Operation Project, Draft Technical Assistance Consultant's Report, November 2005, p. 31. Intergovernmental Kyrgyz-Chinese Commission on Trade and Economic Cooperation, www.mvtp.kg/main.php?lang=en&p=7.21 (accessed March 24, 2006).

19. Nicklas Norling and Niklas Swanström, "The Virtues and Potential Gains of Continental Trade in Eurasia," *Asian Survey* 47 (2007): 351–373; Xinjiang Autonomous Region, PRC, "Trade Facilitation and Customs Cooperation Project, Draft Technical Assistance Consultant's Report, November 30," *China Statistical Yearbook 2006*, Chapter 18-8, "Volume of Imports and Exports by Countries and Regions (Customs Statistics)," June 26, 2008, www.stats.gov.cn/tjsj/ndsj/2006/indexeh.htm. The 2008 statistics had not been released as of the writing of this chapter, and this study is limited to the 2007 official statistics.

20. Ministry of Commerce of the People's Republic of China, "China Trade in Services," June 26, 2008, http://64.233.183.104/search?q=cache:iJCXIr37dEwJ:tradeinservices.mofcom.gov.cn/en/a/2008-06-03/44262.shtml+china+kazakhstan+trade+2007&hl=sv&ct=clnk&cd=8.

21. "China, Kyrgyzstan Pledge to Boost Economic Ties," *China Daily,* June 26, 2008, www.chinadaily.com.cn/china/2007-08/15/content_6028643.htm.

22. "Steady Growth in China-Mongolia Trade, Economic Co-op," *Window of China,* June 26, 2008, http://news.xinhuanet.com/english/2008-06/19/content_8399506.htm. Tariq Mahmud Ashraf, "China Seeks an Afghan Stepping-Stone," *Asia Times Online,* June 26, 2008, www.atimes.com/atimes/China/JE16Ad03.html.

23. "Uzbekistan: Tashkent Strives to Diversify Its Trading Partners," *EurasiaNet Business,* June 26, 2008, www.eurasianet.org/departments/insight/articles/eav031908.shtml. *China Invests in Central Asian Stability Through Tajikistan, China Briefing News,* June 26, 2008, www.china-briefing.com/news/2008/05/22/china-reconnects-with-tajikistan.html.

24. Jan Šír and Slavomír Horák, "China As an Emerging Superpower in Central Asia: The View from Ashkhabad," *China and Eurasia Quarterly* 6, no. 2 (2008).

25. "China-Russia Bilateral Trade Hits $48 bln in 2007," *Russian News and Information Agency Novosti,* June 26, 2008, http://en.rian.ru/business/20080522/108086671.html.

26. Nicklas Norling and Niklas Swanström, "The Shanghai Cooperation Organization, Trade, and the Roles of India, Pakistan, and Iran," *Central Asian Survey* 26, no. 3 (2007): 353–357.

27. Author's own calculations based on Chinese Customs statistics including barter trade.

28. Niklas Swanström and Yin He, eds., *Introduction in China's War on Narcotics: Two Perspectives* (Stockholm: Institute for Security and Development Policy, 2007); Swanström, "Political Development and Organized Crime"; Niklas Swanström, "The Narcotics Trade: A Threat to Security? National and Transnational Implications," *Global Crime* 8, no. 1 (2007): 1–25.

29. Interviews in Greater Central Asia and China, 2006–2008.

30. Niklas Swanström, "The New Opium War in China: New Threats, New Actors and New Implications," in Swanström and He, eds., *Introduction in China's War on Narcotics.*

31. Swanström, Norling, and Li Zhang, "China: The New Silk Roads."

32. Institute of Spatial Planning and Regional Economy, State Development Planning Commission P.R.China, "Study on the Development and Opening-Up of the New Asian-Europe Continental Bridge Area (China's Side)," www.ecdc.net.cn/events/asian_europe/; "Quantitative Assessment of the Benefits for Trade Facilitation," OECD TD/TC/WP, 2003.31, Paris, 2003 (Unclassified), Table 5, p. 16; UNDP, "Bringing Down Barriers: Regional Cooperation for Human Development and Human Security," *Central Asia Human Development Report*, 2005.

33. Asian Development Bank, 2005. Xinjiang Autonomous Region, PRC, Trade Facilitation and Customs Cooperation Project, Draft Technical Assistance Consultant's Report, November, p. 30; Norling and Swanström, "The Virtues and Potential Gains."

34. For an official view on this, see, for example, European Conference on Ministers of Transport–Council of Ministers, "Globalisation: Europe-Asia Links," CEMT/CM (2005) 1.

35. Gaye Christoffersen, "Problems and Prospects for Northeast Asian Energy Cooperation," paper presented at IREX, March 23, 2000.

36. Niklas Swanström, "An Asian Oil and Gas Union: Prospects and Problems," *China and Eurasia Quarterly* 3 (2005): 81–97.

# 7

# China's Africa Policy: South-South Unity and Cooperation

*George T. Yu*

South-South unity and cooperation, formerly known as relations with the Third World, has long constituted a core component of Chinese foreign policy. Dating back to the Cold War era of the 1960s and 1970s, Mao Zedong and Chinese leaders proclaimed that the world was divided into three primary units: The First World led by the United States and the former Soviet Union; the Second World consisting of Australia, Canada, Europe, and Japan; and the Third World, the "new" South, made up of Africa, Asia (except Japan), and Latin America. China was part of and supported the Third World. China has since replaced the former Three-World theory (considered an outdated Cold War view) with a new emerging three-world configuration: the superpower United States, the rising European Union, and the developing world, or the new South.

China declared that it stood with and supported the South, that South-South relations enhanced common interests and self-development.[1] Indeed, China recognized its obligation, nay, responsibility, for unity, cooperation, and mutual dependence with the international forces of anti-imperialism, anticolonialism, and antihegemonism of the South. This, proclaimed China, has been its primary foreign policy objective originated by Mao, implemented by Zhou Enlai, continued by Deng Xiaoping, and supported and operationalized by China's succeeding leadership. And China, as the leading country of the South, has occupied a special global and regional role to ensure the establishment of a just international political and economic order.

China's South-South policy has been influenced by diverse forces and has been subject to change. A significant influence upon China's foreign policy has been its domestic policies and developments; the relationship between domestic and foreign policies has been closely linked. China's "opening and reform" policy beginning in the late 1970s and early 1980s had an equal impact upon

129

its domestic *and* external policy. In the case of foreign policy, the shift from a political/ideological to a political/economic policy thrust has had a major consequence on China's international role and upon global and regional politics. However, not all elements of Chinese foreign policy had changed; China has continued to declare its adherence to certain "core" principles, for example, noninterference in the domestic affairs of other nations, however controversial.

The declaration of China's political and economic objectives in the context of its South-South relations has been supplemented with deeds. To be certain, depending upon the circumstances and the situational-environmental context of time and place and China's capabilities and needs, China has committed to and engaged in a vast range of activities, employing a diversity of "hard" and "soft" foreign policy tools, from military support of African liberation movements to railway, road, and port constructions; from grants and loans to export credit guarantees; from medical and educational assistance to construction of sports facilities; and from direct capital investments to the establishment of special economic zones and engaging in international peacekeeping operations. China has utilized varied tools, depending upon time, place, and need, to achieve its foreign policy objectives.

Nowhere was China's South-South policy better illustrated than in Africa.

## The African Initiative

China's South-South policy was well represented in its African initiative, China's first major independent foreign policy operation outside Asia. Beginning with contacts with African liberation movements and states in the late 1950s to early 1960s, establishing a political presence in Africa in the 1960s and 1970s, a lull in activities while China adjusted to its new "opening and reform" policies in the 1980s and 1990s, and a surge in Sino-African political and economic relations in the early 2000s, China endured a series of challenges and experiences during its fifty plus years of interaction with Africa. Out of China's continued African venture, an ever-evolving policy emerged, influenced by both the international environment and China's internal political and economic developmental changes and needs.

China's African policy can be depicted by three dominant characteristics: continuity, flexibility, and commitment. While these characteristics have served Chinese interests, China has also encountered unfamiliar cultures and experiences such as operating in alien and more-open political and economic environments and, as its presence in Africa increased, attracting African, Chinese, and international scrutiny. In discussing China's African policy, China's domestic development—politically, economically, and socially—has occupied a critical role in each major stage of interaction. Internal and external developments and policies have been closely tied.

## Continuity

China's surge of interest and activities in Africa in the early years of the twenty-first century drew much international attention. Academic, journalist, and policy studies abound focused on China's new foreign policy venture, including a lively discourse questioning China's role in Africa and an emphasis upon China's search for energy and other commodity resources.[2] While there was no doubt of an immediate interest in and need for Africa's oil and abundant mineral resources, given its massive economic developmental requirements, China's relations with Africa were founded on both a broader and deeper political and economic relationship.

Contemporary Sino-African relations date back to the late 1950s and early 1960s. Over a period of half a century, China's commitment to its relations with Africa has been directly related to its international political status and domestic economic stages of development. In the early years following its founding in 1949, especially during the Cold War era, the political and ideological component of China's African policy was primary. China's foremost foreign policy objective was to break out of international "isolation," fostered by the United States beginning in the 1950s and followed by the former Soviet Union following the outbreak of the Sino-Soviet conflict in the 1960s. Subsequently, Africa became a battlefield between China and the Western forces led by the United States and the former Soviet Union for China to gain international recognition, including from the newly independent African states. China described the battle in ideological terms as one against the forces of "imperialism, colonialism, and revisionism."

On another political front, the ever-important sovereignty and unification issue was contested throughout the continent, represented by the controversy between China and Taiwan. China's triumph over Taiwan was achieved when it replaced Taiwan as the sole representative of China in the UN in 1971, with strong support from the African states. China has insisted that each African state adopt and adhere to the One China policy.[3] In 2007, Malawi became the latest of the African states to reject Taiwan and recognize Beijing as the sole legal government of China. From the beginning of Sino-African relations in the 1960s, Africa has served the important functions of gaining China international recognition, acceptance of the One China policy, and membership in international organizations.[4]

The formal beginnings of China's African policy were proclaimed during Zhou Enlai's visit to ten African countries in 1963–1964.[5] Known as China's "Five Principles Governing the Development of Relations with Arab and African Countries," they included support for Africa's anti-imperialist and colonial movements, support for African liberation movements, support for Africa's nonalignment policy, respect for Africa's sovereignty, and opposition to any form of (foreign) invasion and interference in Africa's affairs. During

Zhou's visit, he also announced China's "Eight Principles of Economic Assistance" (which will be discussed in a subsequent section). Thus began China's African initiative.

China has continued to reiterate its foreign policy toward Africa, in addition to adding to and revising the basic guidelines.[6] At the Twelfth Congress of the Chinese Communist Party in 1982, the principle of "Independence, Full Equality, Mutual Respect, and Non-interference in the Internal Affairs (of other nations)" was incorporated as a basic foreign policy principle. In 1996, during former president Jiang Zemin's African visit, he added to China's policy toward Africa the "Five Proposals": Sincere Friendship, Mutual Respect, Mutual Interests, Strengthen Consultations, and Look to the Future. And in 2004, President Hu Jintao announced that China's basic policy toward Africa included maintenance and further development of China-African traditional friendship, respect for African democracy, mutual support at the global and regional levels, mutual respect, equality, and continued assistance to the African states, seeking common development. During his fourth visit to Africa in 2009, President Hu restated China's solidarity with Africa and called for the furthering of "mutual trust" to "cement the political foundation for traditional friendship."[7]

In January 2006, China issued an official White Paper, "China's Africa Policy," further clarifying and reiterating its policy toward Africa.[8] Five primary principles were resummarized: (1) friendship and equality and support for Africa's "independent" developmental path; (2) mutual benefit and China's and Africa's common development and prosperity; (3) mutual support and close international cooperation in the UN and other international organizations; (4) common development in culture, education, health, and science to assist Africa on the road to sustainable development; and (5) that the One China policy was the "political" foundation for the establishment and development of relations with China. These principles, according to China, "will establish and develop a new type of strategic partnership with Africa." After half a century of growing relations, China was looking forward to ever closer continued relations with Africa. A new era in Sino-African relations was initiated.

The main body of the official paper focused on steps for the operationalization of China's African foreign policy, to further strengthen relations among and between the parties. Four primary areas were highlighted: (1) political, including high-level visits and exchanges at all government and political-party levels; (2) economic, including an increase in Chinese assistance and debt reduction and relief, promotion of trade and private investment and financial cooperation, and heightened Chinese-African cooperation in the infrastructure sector; (3) cultural, including education and health, student and people-to-people exchanges, science and technology and medical health cooperation, and environmental cooperation; and (4) security, including military and police cooperation.

Clearly during the half century of Sino-African relations, China had greatly diversified and expanded its foreign policy and arena of interest and operations. However, while adding to and expanding its policy, China has largely retained what can be summarized as the core operating principles first formulated in the 1960s, namely, equal treatment, mutual benefit, noninterference, and respect for sovereignty. In short, China's policy toward Africa has undergone changes, notably an operational shift from primarily political and symbolic considerations to a focus on more pragmatic political, economic, and social objectives, but its core policy has remained the same.

The continuity of China's foreign policy toward Africa has had important implications for both China's African policy and our understanding of Chinese foreign policy generally. First, China's foreign policy toward Africa has to be considered in its entirety, that is, the half century of evolving relations. It should be apparent that China's policy included multiple facets and varied periods, beginning with state-to-state relations, support for national liberation movements, and international consultation and cooperation to increased economic relations, common development, and cultural exchanges. China's foreign policy, similar to the foreign policies of other major international actors, was complex and multidimensional. Second, while China's African policy had focused upon a specific activity during a given period, for example, China's search for energy and mineral resources during the early years of the twenty-first century, one must not exclude other policy objectives, for example, increased international cooperation with the African states to insure success of its One China policy and enhanced international role.

Finally, the question can be asked, through engagement with Africa and the international community, how has China over time, expanded its foreign policy from bilateral, to multilateral, to regional, and to global? And in the process, what impact has enhanced relations had upon China's African policy, as it progressed from state-to-state interaction to relations with regional and global international institutions, governmental and nongovernmental organizations, and the nonstate commercial sector. China's unfolding circle of relationships with Africa has no doubt impacted China's foreign policy as much as it has affected Africa.

## Flexibility

Continuity was one important factor in China's African policy, through which China's presence and influence over the course of one half century has continued and expanded on the African continent. But longevity alone does not explain China's perseverance. An equally critical quality has been the flexibility of China's policy, resulting in the greater acceptance and depth of policy. Consider, for example, the role of ideology in China's domestic and foreign policies. Until the introduction of Deng Xiaoping's "pragmatic" policies of "opening and reform" in the late 1970s, China endured a series of domestic ideological battles, from the Great Leap Forward of the 1950s to the Cultural Revolution of the 1960s and 1970s.

On the foreign policy front, the ideological battles were no less intense, rhetorically and operationally. As previously mentioned, in the 1960s and 1970s, China had described its foreign policy toward Africa in ideological terms, as a battle against the forces of "imperialism, colonialism, and revisionism." China directly linked its ideological stand to its African policy.

This was especially prominent in China's struggles with the former Soviet Union in Africa, with regard to who were the true socialists, namely, supporters of national liberation movements.[9] China charged the former Soviet Union with seeking hegemony and being "counter-revolutionary" and seeking colonial domination and exploitation while opposing African national liberation movements. Clearly, China claimed, no true socialist country could advocate and support such ideas.

China's strong stand against the former Soviet Union was a direct result of the Sino-Soviet conflict, which was fought on several fronts, including military border disputes, economic disruptions, and the battle, ideological and otherwise, for leadership of the Communist world. China and the former Soviet Union each proclaimed to be the true "socialist" leader. For China, a consequence of the struggle was to further harden its ideological stand, namely, to support the battle against the Soviet Union by discrediting it on the international front, that it no longer stood for and represented the global Communist world and advancing the claim that China was now the world's Communist leader. In the process of the Sino-Soviet conflict, China assumed an even greater ideologically purist position, domestically and internationally.

China's rigid ideological stand not only impacted its relations with the former Soviet Union but also defined and limited its relationships with African states and political groups and parties.[10] During the 1960s and 1970s, China's ruling Communist Party repeatedly rejected requests by African political parties to establish relations, based upon the latter's stand toward the Soviet Union. It was reported that on three separate occasions, China refused to consent to entering into relations with the Congolese Labour Party because the latter was not considered "Communist." Similarly, China also refused to enter into diplomatic relations with "revisionist" African states.

A sea change occurred in China's African policy in the late 1970s, concurrent with the introduction of China's "opening and reform" policy. In July 1977, at the request of the Chinese Communist Party leadership, following a meeting with a delegation from Mozambique, the International Liaison Department of the Chinese Communist Party and the Ministry of Foreign Affairs of the Chinese government were directed to conduct a study on the question of relations with African governing political parties. A report was submitted in November 1977 entitled "Request for Instructions on the Issue of Governing Parties of Nations of Black Africa and Other Regions Seeking to Establish Relations with Our Country (China)." In December, the Political Bureau of the Chinese Communist Party approved the report, which recommended the separation of China's African policy from the past ideological orientation and the expansion of relations with Africa's governing political parties. As other studies have noted, with the ideological constraints removed, the only major remaining condition for relations with African states was that they adhere to the One China policy.[11]

The liberation from ideological constraints immediately freed China to pursue expanded and deeper relationships on the foreign policy front, similar to freeing China domestically to adopt and follow new market economics and social policies. With regard to China's relations with Africa, there was an immediate increase and expansion of exchanges with African states and political parties and groups; it was reported that between 1978 and 1990, no fewer than 230 delegations from sub-Saharan Africa visited China, while 56 delegations from the Chinese Communist Party visited the 39 African states. In 2005, the exchanges continued with 24 visits to China by African political parties and 19 Chinese Communist Party delegations to Africa. No doubt the visits and exchanges made possible by China's "pragmatic," less ideological orientation enhanced and furthered China's relations with Africa.

Changes in China's relations with Africa were not confined to ideology. While political objectives continue to drive China's African policy, supporting its global rise and increased influence, a shift to a more pragmatic political/economic policy became a primary objective. This has been due to both Africa's and China's developmental goals and needs. Africa required financial and human resources to support its greater overall economic and social development; China sought markets for its products and energy, mineral, timber, and other resources, to further its growing economy.

Changes in relations with Africa also required a new organizational arrangement to oversee the bilateral and multilateral interaction with the African states. China's new expanded relationship with Africa demanded more coordination and a new administrative structure. In October 2000, the Forum on China-Africa Cooperation (FOCAC) was founded to serve as the primary mechanism for China-Africa engagement. The emphasis was upon mutual benefits and development. This signaled the further importance of Africa to China.

An interagency unit consisting of twenty plus government departments, the FOCAC was jointly administered by the ministries of Commerce and Foreign Affairs; the new agency was assigned the responsibilities of coordination and implementation of China's foreign policy toward Africa. It met in Addis Ababa in December 2003 and in Beijing in November 2006. Another meeting was scheduled in Egypt in the fall of 2009.

During the initial years of operation, the primary known function of the FOCAC had been to review past interactions between China and Africa, to reiterate policies, and to announce new projects. It is instructive to follow in some detail the November 2006 FOCAC meeting in Beijing, as an example of China's heightened African policy *and* the increased scope and range of activities.[12] The 2006 Beijing meeting coincided with the fiftieth anniversary of Sino-African relations; to celebrate the occasion and attend the FOCAC meeting, a total of forty-eight African states were present, of which thirty-five of the delegations were led by African heads of state. President Hu Jintao of China opened the meeting by announcing an eight-point program of how China intended to advance relations with Africa. Included among the "new" programs announced: to double China's 2006 official assistance to Africa by 2009, to establish a US$5 billion China-Africa development fund, to provide US$3 billion of preferential loans to African states, to cancel additional debts owed by poor African states, to further open China's domestic markets to African states, to train 15,000 African professionals in various fields, to increase the number of scholarships for African students in China from 2,000 to 4,000, to dispatch 100 senior Chinese agriculture experts to Africa, and to build a conference center for the African Union. By any measurement, the program constituted a major economic and educational initiative, especially the creation of a US$5 billion China-Africa development fund.

On the second and final day of the FOCAC meeting, China and the attending African leaders agreed to a four-point agenda: (1) Sino-African economic, political, and cultural cooperation was both practical and satisfied mutual interests; (2) the two sides agreed to mutual support and cooperation on international and regional issues; (3) they agreed to build up the forum and strengthen the collective dialogue; and finally, (4) President Hu Jintao reiterated that China was a developing nation and that cooperation and unity with developing nations was the foundation of China's foreign policy.

In 2008, China's African policy was defined as "friendship, peace, cooperation, and development." China's foreign policy objectives represented a major modification from the previously ideologically based policy. The pragmatic policy shift was also reflected operationally, especially in China's use of a multiplicity of old and new foreign policy tools, with an emphasis upon trade, investments, and other commercial activities. China has referred to the new relationship as a "new model" for South-South cooperation.[13]

## Commitment

Nowhere in China's African policy have the changes been more prominent and profound than in the levels, scope, and range of foreign policy tools utilized and the extent of commitments delivered and promised. This has been especially evident in the enlarged use of cultural, economic, and technical tools to serve political and economic objectives and needs. During the half century of relationship with African states, China's commitments have steadily increased and become more ambitious.

China's basic principles of foreign aid were first announced by Zhou Enlai during his African visit in 1964.[14] Known as the "Eight Principles of Economic and Technical Assistance," they included: (1) "the principle of equality and mutual benefit in providing aid to other countries," (2) "respect for the sovereignty of the recipient countries," (3) "economic assistance in the form of interest-free or low-interest loans," (4) "the purpose of (Chinese aid) is . . . to help (the recipient countries) . . . on the road to self-reliance," (5) "in giving technical assistance . . . to see to it that the personnel of the recipient countries fully master such techniques," and other guidelines. These principles have remained constant during the course of Chinese-African relations.

From the beginning of Sino-African relations in the 1960s, the use of foreign policy tools to achieve and support China's ideological, economic, political, and other objectives was an integral part of its African policy. China, similar to France, Japan, the Nordic states, the United States, and other international players, realized and accepted the need for an "aid" component in its foreign policy operations, especially in relations with Africa and other developing nations of the South.[15] The question for China, depending upon the objective(s) and timing and its own capabilities and need(s), has been a cost-benefit issue. Consider, for example, China's extensive use of official bilateral aid packages, grants and loans, economic, medical, and military assistance to gain African diplomatic recognition in the 1960s and 1970s. One estimate calculated that from 1956 through 1977 Chinese aid commitments to Africa totaled no less than US$2.4 billion. Major benefits gained by China included recognition from Africa states who had relations with Taiwan and gaining entry, with African support, into the UN in 1971.

China's effectual utilization of official economic assistance as a foreign policy tool was also demonstrated by China's funding and construction of the Tanzania-Zambian railway (TAZARA) in the 1960s.[16] The TAZARA project was important as a case study in Chinese foreign aid on several levels, including political/ideological, economic, and trade, providing an early example of the operationalization and multiple objectives of Chinese aid. First, the project demonstrated China's support for Tanzania and Zambia, two frontline African states and Africa's struggle for national liberation, against the refusal by the West to assist Africa to undertake the project. China supported Africa's liberation and development. Second, China extended to Tanzania and Zambia a more than US$500 million interest-free loan, notwithstanding its limited economic capacity in the 1960s. In addition, China also supplied the necessary construction manpower; in 1972, at the peak of the construction phase, 13,500 out of the 51,500 of the workforce was made up of Chinese personnel. Thus, a joint Chinese-African workforce worked on the Chinese-funded project. Finally, trade was also a factor in the TAZARA project. To defray locally incurred costs, funding for part of the expenses was paid through the sale of imported Chinese consumer goods, from footballs to mosquito nets and most everything in between. Chinese goods were advanced on credit to Tanzanian and Zambian state trading corporations, and the proceeds from selling the products were then used to pay local costs. The successful linkage of trade to aid represented a triumph of China's aid operations.

From the early successful usage of economic and social foreign policy tools to serve political and developmental objectives and needs, China in the twenty-first century, with increased national wealth following its "opening and reform" policy beginning in the early 1980s, has greatly expanded the range and scope of its international programs and commitments to Africa.[17] The growth of new approaches and the increased commitments of aid have been due both to China's rising international activism and the role, demands, and requirements of its domestic economic development. As we have discussed, a new command structure, FOCAC, was created to coordinate China's new role and new approaches and tools devised to achieve the sought objectives.

As the principle initiator of the relationship, it has been China's role to supply the resources—financial, human, and otherwise—and structure the relationship. This has included a reconceptualization and refocusing of China's aid program and a wide range of new tools to accomplish the tasks. China, for example, has stressed Africa's weak infrastructure, overwhelming debt, and lack of foreign aid as sectors requiring appropriate attention. Furthermore, in its post-2000 engagement with Africa, China has mobilized the institutions and resources of both the government and private enterprises. The latter, though, should still be considered a foreign policy "tool," subject to the direction and/or influence of the state, given the nature of China's political system and society.

In 2009, China did not have a central aid agency; different government units administered disparate tasks. Indeed, China has created a whole new set of institutions to administer economic relations with Africa. A vast and diffused structure provided support for the diverse range of Chinese aid.[18] At the government level, China extended aid in terms of grants, interest-free loans, and concessional loans. These constituted the basic official Chinese foreign-policy aid tools.

China continued to extend traditional official aid in the form of grants and interest-free loans that began in the 1960s. Disbursed in kind on a bilateral basis, such traditional aid packages had included funding for construction of sports complexes, agricultural and office equipment, and support to establish educational and research institutions. In the vast majority of grant aid, China had simply "delivered" the project to the African state, assuming complete responsibility for planning, construction, and equipment. A Chinese-funded US$12 million vocational college project was completed in Ethiopia in 2008.

Consider also concessional financing, an increasingly utilized financial foreign policy tool, whereby a Chinese government agency extended a below-market-rate loan, with the difference between the below market rate and the market rate assumed by the Chinese government. The Export-Import Bank of China (EXIM Bank), a government financial institution, was the sole provider of concessional loans, financing infrastructure development projects ranging from a US$2 billion loan to improve Angola's transportation infrastructure in 2004 to a US$300 billion loan to assist Mozambique's dam-building project in 2005; lesser loan projects included a US$12 million package to Djibouti to develop the telecommunications sector in 2003 and a US$25 million loan to Zimbabwe for agricultural equipment in 2006. The bank had supported more than 300 projects in Africa through mid-2007.

Especially important has been the EXIM Bank's role in financing Chinese construction and investment projects in Africa, such as investing in oil, gas, and mining projects in Nigeria (oil) and Zambia (copper) and other sites. In 2008, the bank announced China's largest resource investment in Africa, a US$800 million iron ore mining and infrastructure project (railway, ports, and hydropower plants) in Gabon. A joint project between the China National Machinery and Equipment Import and Export Corporation, representing China, and the Gabonese government, the joint venture was established to construct and run the Belinga iron ore reserves and support infrastructures for twenty-five years, providing China's booming economy with a continued supply of much-needed iron ore imports. The Export-Import Bank of China would finance the entire project.[19] While such projects could not be defined simply as Chinese aid, the assistance has showcased a heightened China presence in Africa's economic development. The projects, of course, were designed to meet China's growing energy, mineral, and other domestic needs.[20] The "aid" model of "infrastructure for commodities" also applied to China's relations with Angola, the Democratic Republic of Congo, and other African states.

An important new tool in Chinese foreign policy had been the extension of financing on commercial terms, to African state and private institutions and Chinese firms engaged in businesses in Africa. The approach gave new meaning to and provided new opportunities for China's role in financially resource-poor Africa. Foremost, it permitted China to expand and gain influence in Africa's civil and commercial sector, supplementing its political linkages with Africa.

A new foreign-policy instrument was created to assist Chinese businesses gain entry into the African market. In May 2007, the Chinese state China Development Bank was appointed manager of the US$5 billion China-Africa Development Fund (which China claimed to be the largest global African development fund, with an initial capitalization of US$1 billion), announced at the 2006 FOCAC meeting. The fund was considered a "new" type of aid. According to Bo Xilai, China's Minister of Commerce, "Unlike other types of (Chinese) government aid to Africa, the CADF (China-Africa Development Fund) 'will be an independent business but with a business target limited to breaking even or making a marginal profit.'"[21]

The primary purpose of the fund was to support African development projects *and* finance China's market entry into Africa, including supporting Chinese companies, for example, Sino-Steel Group, the China Building Material Company, and the Shenzhen Energy Company, to engage in projects in Africa. This included funding at commercial rates African infrastructure projects; building airports, railroads, and highways in Angola; improving energy infrastructure in Mozambique, South Africa, and Zimbabwe; and developing mining projects in Congo and Zambia. The dual objectives were seen as complementary, satisfying both Africa's and China's commercial, development, and political objectives. The fund was expected to commit US$1 billion to investments in Africa by the end of 2008.[22]

Other forms of Chinese investment were initiated. In 2007, the state-run Industrial and Commercial Bank of China purchased a 20 percent stake in South Africa's Standard Bank for US$5.5 billion, the largest foreign direct investment in South Africa.[23] The two banks would also establish a US$1 billion private equity account to fund joint investments in emerging markets. Through 2007, China's direct investment in Africa was reported to have totaled US$1 billion.[24] Furthermore, China was considered a potential partner and investment source by international firms. Rio Tinto, the world's second largest iron ore producer, was reported seeking partnership with Chinese companies to jointly develop an iron mine in Guinea.[25]

Concurrent with the growth in Chinese investments, Chinese-African trade has also witnessed a significant increase. Variously referred to as "commercial diplomacy," "coalition engagements," and other terms to denote a state-business collaborative approach to achieve foreign policy goals, China has utilized trade as a tool to advance its global power and presence. Beginning with less than US$5 billion in 1995, increasing to US$10 billion in 2003, Chinese-African bilateral trade exceeded US$100 billion in 2008, two years earlier than predicted.[26] Despite the rapid growth, Chinese-African trade accounted for less than 5 percent of China's total foreign trade in 2008. China ranked third in trade with Africa, after the United States and France.

The growth in Chinese-African trade was primarily the result of China's need for Africa's abundant oil and mineral reserves and to support China's consumer and industrial and other developmental requisites. Oil made up the bulk of African exports to China, comprising some 80 percent of total exports, followed by logs, diamonds, cotton, and iron ore (57 percent of Africa's oil is exported to the United States and Europe, with only 14 percent exported to China). The largest African exporter to China was Angola (37 percent), followed by South Africa (14 percent), Congo (10 percent), Equatorial Guinea (9 percent), and the Sudan (7 percent).[27] African imports from China consisted mainly of manufactured products, including machinery and equipment, appliances, and apparel, clothing, and footwear. The largest African importers of Chinese products were South Africa (22 percent of total Chinese exports to Africa), Egypt (11 percent), Nigeria (11 percent), Algeria (7 percent), and Morocco (6 percent).

Angola was China's most important African trading partner.[28] In 2007, trade between China and Angola totaled US$14.11 billion, with more than 70 percent of the trade represented by Angola's oil exports to China. Angola had replaced Saudi Arabia as the largest exporter of oil to China; meanwhile China has supplanted Portugal as the foremost exporter to Angola (about US$900 million in 2007), Portugal's former colony. According to Zhang Polun, China's ambassador to Angola, "With the development of China in recent years, our energy demands are very high. Angola is rich in oil so from China's perspective, Angola is one of our most important partners." It was reported that more than twenty Chinese state-owned enterprises and thirty or so Chinese private companies were present in Angola. The exact number of Chinese in Angola was unknown, but the ambassador believed the figure to be 20,000–30,000 and growing.[29]

South Africa was China's second-largest African trading partner. While the value of China's trade with Angola ranked first, the vast majority of the recorded trade consisted of Angola's oil exports to China. On the other hand, China's trade with South Africa, Africa's biggest economy, represented both a more "balanced" trade pattern *and* China's success in gaining a new market. From a low of US$2 billion total trade between China and South Africa in 2000, trade between the two partners had grown to US$9.8 billion by the end of 2006.[30] In the first quarter of 2008, China replaced Germany as South Africa's largest import market.

China and South Africa enjoyed a generally balanced trade relationship through 2002; beginning in 2003, a trade imbalance began to develop, with Chinese exports to South Africa exceeding China's imports from South Africa.[31] In 2007, major Chinese exports to South Africa included apparel and clothing (33 percent of the total), machinery and equipment (23 percent), electrical and mechanical appliances (12 percent), motor vehicle parts and tires (16 percent), and shoes (9 percent). It should be noted that low-cost consumer products constituted only about 40 percent of China's exports, while more than 50 percent of China's exports to South Africa were made up of machinery, electrical, and other industrial products (an emerging Chinese trade pattern with Africa). China's major imports from South Africa consisted of oil (16 percent of the total imports), diamonds (11 percent), and various commodities— copper, iron ore, platinum, manganese (61 percent).

To further investments in and trade with Africa, China has also proposed the establishment of special economic zones in eight African countries to serve as Chinese commercial and production centers. The centers were to be established in Angola, Egypt, Ethiopia, Mauritius, Mozambique, Nigeria, Tanzania, and Zambia. The first such center, the Zambia-China Economic and Trade Cooperation Zone, was founded in northern Zambia in February 2007.[32]

It was reported that the new Chinese economic zone had secured US$70 million of Chinese funds for infrastructure development and that the zone was expected to "bring in 50 enterprises with a total investment of over US$800 million by 2011 and create more than 20,000 jobs for locals." According to Wang Yu, commercial counselor of the Chinese Embassy in Lusaka, Zambia, the economic zones represented China's "new aid model of investment." In 2009, while Chinese investments were expected to continue, Chinese-African trade was predicted to decrease, due to the global financial crisis.[33]

China's unilateral economic commitments to Africa have been significant, in scope and range. They had brought international attention to Africa's developmental status and needs *and* China's activism and presence on the vast continent. However, African needs have yet to be fully met, and China still trails the West (e.g., the European Union, France, and the United States) in the level of aid to Africa. In 2006, whereas China distributed US$4.6 billion in aid, during the same period development assistance by the West's Development Assistance Committee members totaled US$43.4 billion in aid to Africa.[34]

The impact of the 2009 global economic crisis upon China, including the decline of its economic growth to 6.1 percent, falling exports and imports, plus China's own considerable internal economic requirements, introduced an element of uncertainty in regard to future economic relations with Africa. Africa's vast developmental needs remained. Indeed, the global economic crisis had not spared the continent from economic woes, whether it was urgently needed assistance for economic development and reconstruction or declining commodity prices (falling revenue) due to diminishing demands and the closing or suspension of mining operations in Zambia and elsewhere.[35] Angola, for example, was reported seeking additional economic assistance for reconstruction from China.[36] Meanwhile, China was reported to be waiting for the international markets to turn favorable prior to making investments in Guinea.[37]

President Hu's visit to Africa in 2009 was in part to reassure the African continent of China's continued support. In Mali, President Hu declared that "China will continue to increase aid to Africa despite the impact of the current financial crisis. . . . China and Africa will weather the difficult times together."[38]

For China, the global economic crisis was both a challenge and an opportunity. China pledged to honor its aid commitments; it also encouraged Chinese domestic firms to invest abroad, even issuing a guidebook for overseas investments.[39] At the 2009 G-20 meeting in London, China responded to the call and needs for support of the International Monetary Fund. China contributed US$40 billion to the fund to ease the global financial crisis.[40] The crisis was also an opportunity for China to explore and acquire African energy and commodity resources, utilizing its massive foreign exchange, more than US$2 trillion in 2009.[41]

Yet another tool used by China has been cultural diplomacy, a distinctive "soft power." Variously described as "the ability to change what others do and/or shape what they want" and "the capacity to persuade others to adopt the same goals," the scope and range of cultural activities as a tool of Chinese foreign policy have been equally diverse and significant. The tools of cultural diplomacy have included people-to-people exchanges, academic exchanges, performance delegations, publications, moral leadership, and other "cultural" instruments.

China's deployment of cultural diplomacy dates back to the beginning of Sino-African relations; during the half century of interaction, it has been increasingly used to establish, maintain, and sustain the near- and long-term cooperative relationship.[42] Cultural exchanges were used as the first stage to establish formal diplomatic relations in the 1960s. In sum, China has used cultural exchanges as an initial step to break out of "containment" and international isolation.

In the 1960s, Chinese-Tanzanian interaction was the model of China's successful cultural diplomacy.[43] Through repeated exchange visits, President Julius Nyerere and the Tanzania political leadership were greatly impressed with China's support for national liberation movements, national development, organization, discipline, and revolutionary spirit. President Nyerere was even supportive of the Cultural Revolution, considering it a means to ensure that the next generation would carry forward the revolution. Indeed, China was the model of a successful political, economic, and social revolution, a transformation that the Tanzanian (and other African) leadership sought for its (their) own society.

At the mass level, China sought also to "influence" Africa, whether through cultural delegations, acrobatic and performing delegations, or scholarships to study in China. Even the display in Africa of the *Peking Review, China Pictorial, Quotations of Chairman Mao,* and other Chinese publications, such as in front of Kampala's main post office in the 1960s and 1970s, were intended to showcase China and "influence" the African man on the street. In such instances, it was difficult to determine whether the intended results were achieved, but the use of such tools was certainly proof of China's "presence" in Africa!

Since the 1980s, cultural diplomacy has been employed to counter the advocates of a "China threat" while advancing China's positive international image, its peaceful rise and development and call for a "harmonious world."[44] A major development has been the creation of a new institutional network to advance China's "peaceful rise" and new international role through the teaching of Chinese language and culture.

In 1987, the Chinese Language Council International, also known as Hanban, was established by the Ministry of Education to assist foreign educational institutions in teaching Chinese, conduct cultural exchanges, and enhance cooperation. Funding was provided to foreign institutions to found a distinct unit, known as the Confucius Institute, whose mission was "to help the world understand Chinese language and culture . . . (and) contribute to the building of a harmonious world."[45] The first Confucius Institute was established in

South Korea in 1987. By 2007, 210 institutes were operational, with a target of establishing a total of 500 worldwide by 2010. Through 2007, Chinese expenditures on the new institutional network reached US$26 million.

Ten Confucius Institutes had been established in Africa in 2009, with an additional eleven planned. Through 2008, China had allocated more than US$3 million to establish and support the institutes.[46] The first institute in Africa was established at the University of Nairobi, Kenya, in December 2005. A new Confucius Institute was launched at the University of Liberia, Monrovia, in December 2008. Other Confucius Institutes were located in Cameroon, Egypt, Madagascar, Nigeria, Rwanda, South Africa (two), and Zimbabwe. Each institute's main task was "to promote the teaching of Chinese as a foreign language and (engage in) cultural exchanges and co-operations." Aside from introducing Chinese as a new language to Africans, the language was perceived to provide an introduction to China and facilitate the entry of Chinese enterprises in and products to Africa.

Concurrently, China's Ministry of Culture supported a separate cultural diplomacy program, in addition to two cultural centers, one each in Benin and Mauritius. In 2007, the ministry administered a Cultural Visitor Programme, inviting distinguished cultural leaders from each of ten African nations on all-expense-paid visits to China. Those nations were the Republic of Congo, Benin, Botswana, Ethiopia, Madagascar, Mali, Senegal, Tanzania, Uganda, and Zambia.

Without question, China's commitments and the scope and range of foreign policy tools utilized in Africa have been extensive. Consider, for example, the multiple levels and types of Chinese economic and social aid. Consider also the scale of the resource transfer—financial, human, and otherwise, to Africa *and* China—delivered, promised, and planned. However, it becomes necessary to ask how coordinated, how effective, and with what degree of impact has the execution of China's African policy been, especially in light of China's growing activism and presence on this diverse continent. Another question is how are the relationships among the numerous state agencies responsible for China's African policy and the association between the state agencies and China's growing "private" sector in Africa.[47] Finally, with the momentous increase of aid commitments since 2000, how has (and how will) China administer and insure their successful implementation?

## Apprehension and Empowerment

China's growing presence in Africa brought both apprehension and empowerment to China, Africa, and internationally. While China's growing activism brought international attention to Africa and its vast economic and social needs "put Africa on the map," China's enhanced role on the continent has publicized both its achievements and its problems. China has found itself internationally exposed. At the global level, several issues were voiced. Charges were heard that Africa was in danger of being recolonized. Former President Thabo Mbeki of South Africa created an uproar when he warned about the risk of a colonial relationship with China, given the emerging pattern of economic interaction, notably African exports of raw materials to China while importing Chinese manufactured products.[48] There was a danger of "a replication" of Africa's relations with its former colonial masters, he contended. In 2006, the British journal *Economist* featured a lead article entitled "The New Colonialists."[49] China had undermined and replaced the West's effort to "spread democracy and prosperity" in Africa by "coddling dictators" and "despoiling (African) poor countries," it claimed. China's policy was driven by its hunger for African commodities and markets (and "getting even hungrier") to sustain China's economic growth. Others noted that the scale of the Chinese economic presence was a concern for "colonial unease."[50] They also warned President Robert Mugabe of Zimbabwe and other African countries of their relationship with China: "He and other African leaders should think more carefully. There is a danger of their countries becoming a victim of a re-colonisation."[51] The threat of Africa's recolonization was not from the West; it was from the East. China had become Africa's new "colonial" master.[52]

Other expressions of reservation toward China's role in Africa included Germany's warning of China's lending practices in Africa "saddling the continent with a new round of crippling debt,"[53] the European Parliament's accusation of "investments made by China with no strings attached in African countries ruled by oppressive regimes,"[54] and the European Union's attempt in 2008 to meet China's challenge by strengthening its traditional economic relations with Africa through negotiating a series of new economic agreements.[55]

China was also accused of ignoring the violence and genocide in Darfur, Sudan. China was charged with supporting Sudan's oppressive policy toward the Darfur region by being the largest buyer of Sudan's energy resources, an estimated US$2 billion annually.[56] China provided Sudan with three valuable forms of support: commercial and capital investments, support in the UN (Security Council), and the supply of military equipment. A campaign was initiated, led by the actor Mia Farrow and other Western notables, to "shame" China internationally for its role in Sudan, with the expectation that the campaign would lead China to withdraw support from the Sudanese government.

Aside from the immediate value of Sudan's energy resources, its importance to China lay also in a core principle of Chinese foreign policy: respect for sovereignty and noninterference in domestic affairs. In practice, the principle had frequently become an excuse for China's inaction and protection of its economic interests. China did appoint a special envoy on Darfur, who was reported to have said: "China insists on using influence without interference."[57]

China's official principle of respect for sovereignty and noninterference had been challenged and applied variably, especially on issues of governance and human rights. In 2008, China refrained from commenting on Zimbabwe's economic[58] and political crisis while continuing strong support for President Mugabe, including maintaining China's "regular arms trade" with Zimbabwe.[59] However, Africa was not without its own uncertainties regarding China's policy of noninterference. China's "silence" on the massive riots following the Kenyan election in February 2008 was questioned. How could China have remained indifferent in the face of the "causeless bloodletting and irresponsible display of State might"? And how could Ambassador Zhang Ming of China claim "indifferently, that China would not interfere in Kenya's 'internal affairs'"? Meanwhile, it was business as usual for China, "building roads and toilets, when the lives of the users of such facilities are in danger." Ambassador Zhang was unmoved: "My country has [a] non-interference foreign policy, which means we do not interfere with foreign countries' activities."[60]

China's "indifference" was a topic of discussion at the 2008 Sino-Africa Business Forum, held at Arusha, Tanzania.[61] It was noted that China's flawed noninterference policy was "often adopted by China in conflict zones in which it had major investments." The claim that it supported African rogue regimes tarnished China's image. No doubt referring to Sudan, it was suggested that "China's involvement with African regimes in trouble spots reduced pressure on combatants to make compromises and address causes of the conflicts." It was also suggested that China's support of rogue regimes with weak governing structures, such as Zimbabwe, undermined the protection of human rights. Finally, it was declared that China's "non-interference policy undermines Africa's policy into mainstreaming governance into the prosperity agenda."

On occasion, China has not refrained from violating its noninterference policy, when its national interests were threatened. A well-known case centered on China's intervention in Zambia's presidential election in 2006.[62] Two issues central to China's African policy were at potential risk: Zambia's key role in China's African economic policy *and* Taiwan. Zambia was one of China's oldest allies on the continent, having recognized and established diplomatic relations with China three days after independence in 1964. As a frontline state surrounded by Rhodesia, Portuguese-controlled Angola and Mozambique, and South Africa in the 1960s, friendly and cooperative relations between China and Zambia grew, including China's support to build the Tanzania-Zambian Railway. Subsequently in the late 1990s and early 2000s, as part of China's search for mineral resources to support its economic development, access to Zambia's vast copper mines and mineral deposits constituted a rich prize. In 2006, it was reported that Chinese investments had reached US$300 million and growing. In addition, China planned to establish in northern Zambia a special economic (investment) zone, one of eight to be established in Africa, given Zambia's central location in southern Africa and the positive reception Zambia had extended to Chinese investments.

China supported "the good governance policies" of former incumbent

President Levy Mwanawasa.[63] A grant of US$1.3 million "worth of materials," including motor vehicles, would be provided to Zambia to support the 2006 elections. China also announced that it expected to cancel Zambia's US$250 million debt. Finally, China supported Zambia's policies of holding "free and fair elections," commended the Zambian government for "an accommodative approach" toward the opposition, and noted it was natural for the government and opposition parties to have "differences."

During Zambia's 2006 elections, the opposition presidential candidate, former cabinet minister Michael Sata, introduced China as a campaign issue.[64] He criticized Chinese business practices, treatment of Zambian workers, and "poor-paying" businesses in Zambia and threatened to recognize Taiwan if elected. Sata's "anti-China" campaign proved too much for the Chinese ambassador, Li Baodong. The ambassador publicly retorted that Chinese investors were "scared" to invest in Zambia and that China had put on hold further investments in Zambia as a result of Mr. Sata's remarks. Ambassador Li also announced that China might consider cutting ties with Zambia, were Mr. Sata to be elected and establish diplomatic relations with Taiwan. Needless to say, Ambassador Li's pronouncements caused much "anger," seen as a direct interference in Zambian domestic politics. Mr. Sata lost the election and Ambassador Li returned to Beijing.[65] China's cooperative relations with Zambia continued.

China's proactive foreign policy and increased economic and technical assistance programs in Africa have also received attention and review in China. China's assessments of its agriculture aid program provide a useful look into the evolution and evaluation of China's aid to Africa. The agriculture assistance program evolved through three basic stages. In 1959, China began to offer agricultural aid to Africa; until the early 1980s, Chinese aid mainly consisted of the transfer of technologies and practices intended to promote agriculture development. Eighty-seven projects were established in eleven African countries. An adjustment in forms of aid began in 1984, shifting from a unilateral transfer of aid to the operationalization of joint assistance projects, such as technical cooperation and joint management programs. However, while the period on the one hand witnessed a decrease in aid programs, on the other it saw an increase in the number of "trophy," or showcase, projects. A third adjustment of China's aid program to Africa was introduced in 1995. The new program encouraged aid through interest-bearing loans, trade, and joint financial cooperation among Chinese enterprises and between Chinese and local African partners. The Chinese government concluded that Chinese-African agriculture developmental cooperation had finally "matured," that China was ready to expand aid programs and establish a base of operations in Africa, that Chinese-African relations should be considered in the long-term, and that cooperation with Africa could be achieved in the "agriculture, forestry, mining, and petroleum" sectors.[66]

Another report on China's agricultural assistance programs to Africa, 1960s through the 1990s, based upon field investigations, illustrated the doubts, mixed accomplishments, and problems encountered.[67] Without question, international assistance programs were a special feature of the global political economy; China had participated in this vital endeavor in Africa. The 1970s also ushered in the era of mutual assistance and advantage among developing nations. The close relationship between economic and political interests and use of aid to advance a country's political influence and trade expansion was also recognized.

During China's forty years of association with Africa in the agricultural sector, many lessons had been learned and experience gained. One lesson was that while there were no technological difficulties, insufficient attention was given to Africa's economic and social-cultural factors; in addition, there were administrative and management problems relating to project continuity and replication. From 1979 to 1982, China built an agricultural technical assistance laboratory in Guinea. Upon completion in 1982, management of the unit was transferred to the Guineans. Between 1982 and 1999, China continued to fund the laboratory and dispatched four separate groups of experts. But according to resident Chinese experts, the Guineans were more interested in the material products received from and the wages paid by the project. Neither did the Guineans express much interest in expanding the products cultivated and the laboratory's work. In 1999, after twenty years, the laboratory ceased operations, as the Guinean government failed to seek project renewal. Other Guinean assistance projects also failed. However, China was successful in assisting the development of Africa's fishing industry, providing capital, management, and creating joint ventures with local companies to fish and market (primarily to Europe) the catch.

According to the report, the fundamental problem with the agricultural assistance programs was their political nature, namely, the projects were considered political tools (establishing and maintaining diplomatic relations) and to have achieved their objectives. Once the agreements had been signed between China and an African state and once the projects had been transferred to the recipient, Chinese-African cooperation and political friendship had triumphed.

In summary, the report described China's African policy, as illustrated by the agriculture assistance programs, as follows: One mounted the horse quickly, secured (project) achievement speedily, and dismounted promptly. Chinese economic and technical projects mainly served political objectives, requiring projects to be negotiated, become operational, and fulfilled to achieve political objectives, to showcase China's contributions to and presence in Africa. In short, foreign aid had served the short-term interests and needs of Chinese foreign policy.

Yet, China's role in Africa was not exclusively political or symbolic. China possessed the capacity and potential to contribute meaningfully to

Africa's medium- and long-term economic and social development. On the global front, Sino-African economic interaction solicited increased positive attention. Despite Western suspicions of China's motives—"the recolonization of Africa"—the scope and range of China's African policy brought a reexamination of China's role. Beginning in the 2000s, global official financial institutions and development specialists acknowledged and recognized China's contributions, real and potential, to Africa's development. Joint development projects were agreed to between Chinese and global institutions; in December 2007, the World Bank agreed "to work with Chinese development bodies on aid programs in Africa."[68] Nongovernmental agencies also took an interest in China's role in Africa, joining the "global challenge to combat poverty."[69] International development specialists also accepted the thesis that "the positive impact of Chinese investment and skill transfer far outweigh[s] the negatives."[70] China was considered a partner in Africa's development.

African response to China's role was mixed, near unanimous in praise of China at the elite level, varied at other levels. An example of the interest in China's role in Africa's development was the 2007 annual meeting of the African Development Bank Group, held in Shanghai, China. Africa sought to learn directly from China's developmental experiences. According to Louis Kasekende, chief economist of the bank, Africa and China had much to learn from and many experiences to share with one another.[71] Africa, for example, "could benefit from the special relationship through technology transfer and management training." Furthermore, Africa's development could be helped through China's potential for increasing development assistance and "aid-for-trade." On another plane, Mandla Gantsho, vice president of the bank, said that China had created a powerful developmental force through the establishment of the China Development Bank.

At the bilateral level, Chinese-Sudanese energy cooperation had produced exceptional results. With Chinese assistance, Sudan had been transformed from a crude oil importing country into a crude oil exporter. China had established a "unique model of cooperation" with Sudan, "not only providing capital, technology, and equipment to Sudan, but also attaching great importance to Sudan human resource development."[72]

Zambia represented an extreme example of Africa's mixed response to China's presence. As mentioned, Zambia's relations with China dated back to the 1960s; a special relationship was formed resulting from China's support of the then frontline state, symbolized by TAZARA. Beginning in the early 2000s, bilateral cooperative relations were further strengthened with China's additional aid and decision to invest in Zambia's mineral wealth (e.g., copper) and build a special economic zone. China's aid and investment in Zambia's economic development was warmly welcomed by the Zambian political elite.

At the other end of the population spectrum (shopkeepers and workers), reaction to China's presence was less hospitable.[73] Chinese merchants in

Lusaka were accused of buying up Zambian shops, and the Chinese-owned Chambishi mine was charged with lax safety standards. In addition, more than 1,000 Zambian workers were laid off at the Chinese-built Zambian China Mulungushi Textiles, due to Chinese imports. Chinese construction companies were also accused of not employing sufficient Zambian workers.

The late president Mwanawasa called upon Zambians to be "more positive about investment from Beijing," maintaining that "the Chinese government has brought a lot of development" to Zambia. Indeed, between 2000 and 2007, it has been estimated that total Chinese financial assistance to Zambia reached US$1.1 billion.[74] China was a friend and partner in Zambia's development. China had empowered Zambia and Africa!

## Conclusion

Commenting on Africa's increasing encounters with Asia, one African observer put it thus: first it was the Asian tigers, now the world was witness to the Chinese waking dragon. In earlier research, I had described China's presence in Africa as a "Dragon in the Bush."[75] The argument was that while China's presence in Africa was undisputed, it became difficult to assess, observe, and evaluate the exact details and impact of the dragon's full force, separating fact from fiction, reality from myth. Central to the problem was the distinct lack of transparency. Except for major policy and aid pronouncements, such as China's support for African national liberation movements and funding of TAZARA in the 1960s, the declaration of macro categories of economic and social commitments at the 2006 EOCAC meeting, and an indistinct description of aid to Angola administered by the China International Fund in 2007, China did not, and does not, publicly explain and issue micro accounts of aid and other projects. This has been unfortunate, creating unnecessary doubts and misunderstanding of China's role in Africa,[76] limiting acknowledgment of China's full contributions to and maximum impact on Africa's development. A more open and transparent approach to China's commitments to Africa combined with a more multilateral coordinated approach would enhance China's emerging global leadership role, allowing it to participate jointly with less suspicions with other global players in Africa's economic and social transformation.[77]

China, the dragon in the bush, need not be unknown and misunderstood; indeed, Africa had acknowledged and the West had increasingly recognized that China possesses the capacity, experience, and technology to contribute to Africa's economic transformation. China's evolving African policy of half a century, through increased activism and commitment, has the potential to make a greater contribution to Africa's sustained development, unilaterally and multilaterally.

Compared to what China has regarded as the West's short-termed foreign policy, China considers its foreign policy, including its commitments, to be long-termed, exemplified by its relations with Africa.[78] During the half century of relations and future promised aid programs, China has demonstrated its commitment to Africa. However, the question of China's relations with Africa is not limited to commitments. The question lies also in China's ability to meet and support Africa's present and future developmental needs, political and economic, both at the elite and the popular levels. China has largely succeeded with the former but had mixed responses from the latter. Yet, successful, deepening long-term relations depend upon the reception and trust at all levels, the elite and the masses. As one African official has been quoted: "We welcome China's engagement with Africa. We are looking to you for investment, for trade, and for technical cooperation. But we are also looking to you to do what is right for the people of the countries in which you engage, not just the current leaders. . . . You need the support of the people of those countries. The current leaders will not be there forever."[79] Africa, in addition to looking forward to continued commitments, also looks to China for future support on questions of governance, human rights, and other political and social issues.

The question of China's relations with Africa is also a function of the nature of the changing relationship. Namely, while China began its engagement with Africa in the 1960s and repeatedly refers to itself as a "developing nation," during the half century of relations with Africa, China has emerged, especially since the early 1980s, from a state of international isolation and economic underdevelopment to a transformed economic and political global power. In short, the reality of the relationship has changed, becoming increasingly unequal; many Africans regard China as a "superpower." How China manages the relationship, operationally and rhetorically, constitutes a serious challenge, potentially impacting China's present and future role in Africa and Africa's response. On China's part, adjustment to and recognition of its new international role is critical to its long-term successful relations with Africa.

China's economic role in Africa should not be confused with its larger foreign-policy objectives, that of upholding its sovereignty and safeguarding its security. During the half century of relations with Africa, China has emerged as a regional and global power, with regional and global interests and responsibilities. China's search for allies and access to markets and resources, to support its global standing and economic growth, foremost supports its national interests and international role. Africa constituted a key arena in China's foreign policy; in the global context, Africa serves the function of symbolizing China's successful achievements and relations. China's South-South policy has achieved the goal of unity and cooperation with the "rising rest."

## Notes

1. See, for example, Li Shenming, "China and Africa: Strengthen the Solidarity and Cooperation," *West Asia and Africa,* no. 167 (March 10, 2007), pp. 5–7. This was

the opening address by Li, vice-president of the Chinese Academy of Social Sciences, at the "Common Development of China and Africa" international conference, Beijing, December 18–19, 2006.

2. For three examples of recent academic studies, see Ian Taylor, *China and Africa: Engagement and Compromise* (Abingdon and London: Routledge, 2006); Christopher Alden, Daniel Large, and Ricardo de Oliveira, eds., *China Returns to Africa: A Superpower and a Continent Embraced* (London: Hurst, 2008); and Barry Sautman and Yan Hairong, "The Forest for the Trees: Trade, Investment and the China-in-Africa Discourse," *Pacific Affairs* 81, no. 1 (Spring 2008): 9–29. For a journalist report, see Andress Lorenz and Thilo Thielke, "China's Conquest of Africa," *Spiegel Online International,* May 30, 2008, http://speigalde/international/world/0,1518, 484603-4,00.html. For a policy report, see Congressional Research Service, Library of Congress, "China's Foreign Policy and 'Soft Power' in South American, Asia and Africa," a study prepared for the Committee on Foreign Relations, US Senate, Washington, DC, US Government Printing Office, April 2008.

3. According to Ambassador Johannes J. Spies, former director of Greater China at the South African Department of Foreign Affairs, "China sent a clear signal (to South Africa) that diplomatic relations between the two countries would be impossible as long as diplomatic relations with Taiwan existed." South Africa adopted the "One China" policy in December 1997; full diplomatic relations between South Africa and China were established January 1, 1998. Johannes J. Spies, "Experiences and Impression on Diplomatic Engagement with the People's Republic of China: A South African Perspective," in *New Impulses from the South: China's Engagement of Africa* (Matieland, South Africa: Center for Chinese Studies, University of Stellenbosch, 2008), pp. 66–68.

4. China's appreciation for African support on the Taiwan issue was again illustrated during President Hu Jintao's dinner reception in honor of African presidents attending the opening of the 2008 Beijing Olympic Games. President Hu thanked the African leaders for their support of China's sovereignty relating to Taiwan (and Tibet) (*Renmin Ribao,* August 10, 2008). Since the election of Nationalist party member Ma Ying-jeou to Taiwan's presidency in 2008 and the adoption of the "China-friendly" policy, the overt competition between China and Taiwan for international recognition has all but ceased. Speaking in Swaziland, one of Taiwan's few remaining allies in Africa, visiting vice president Vincent Siew of Taiwan declared that "we (Taiwan) will not waste our resources to try to steal diplomatic allies from the other side" and "we hope that in the international arena Taiwan and China will not engage in vicious competition" (*Telegraph,* September 10, 2008, www.telegraaph.co.uk/news/worldnews/asia/taiwan/2776890/tTa).

5. *Dangdai Zhongguo Waijiao* [Contemporary Chinese Foreign Relations] (Beijing: China Social Science Publishing Company, 1987). See especially chapter 11.

6. Li Anshan, "On Changes and Adjustments in China's Policy Toward Africa," *Zhongguo Waijiao* [China's Foreign Affairs], no. 1 (2007), pp. 33–40.

7. "Hu to Africa: Mutual Support Important," *China Daily,* February 16, 2009.

8. See "China's African Policy," *Renmin Ribao,* January 12, 2006.

9. George T. Yu, "Sino-Soviet Rivalry in Africa," in David E. Albright, ed., *Communism in Africa.* (Bloomington: Indiana University Press, 1980), pp. 168–188.

10. See Li Anshan, "On Changes and Adjustments." Li's main findings also are to be found in Li Anshan, "China and Africa: Policies and Challenges," *China Security* 3, no. 3 (Summer 2007): 69–93.

11. Li Anshan, "On Changes and Adjustments."

12. Department of Policy Planning, Ministry of Foreign Affairs, People's Repub-

lic of China, *Zhongguo Waijiao 2007 Nian Ban* [China's Foreign Affairs, 2007 Edition] (Beijing: World Affairs Press, 2007), pp. 44–46.

13. "South-South Cooperation Opens New Vista for World Economic Growth," *Xinhuanet,* April 24, 2008, http://news.xinhuanet.com/english/2008-04/24/content-8043422.htm.

14. People's Publishing House, *YaFei Renmin fandi datuanjie wansui* [Long Live the Great Solidarity of the Asian African People Against Imperialism] (Beijing: Renmin, 1964), pp. 131–132.

15. George T. Yu, "The Tanzania-Zambia Railway: A Case Study in Chinese Economic Aid to Africa," in Warren Weinstein and Thomas H. Henriksen, eds., *Soviet and Chinese Aid to African Nations* (New York: Praeger, 1980), chapter 6.

16. Ibid. For a careful study of the developmental impact of TAZARA, see Jamie Monson, *Africa's Freedom Railway* (Bloomington and Indianapolis: Indiana University Press, 2009).

17. See the useful study by Martyn Davies, *How China Delivers Development Assistance to Africa* (Stellenbosch, South Africa: Center for Chinese Studies, University of Stellenbosch, 2008). I have used extensively the data and findings of the study.

18. Chinese authorities readily admit to the fact "too many units were involved in foreign assistance work" and that there was a shortage of "qualified personnel." Interview, Beijing, November 2007.

19. "Chinese Firm to Develop Iron Ore Project in Africa," *Renmin Ribao,* July 9, 2008, http://english.peopledaily.com.cn/90001/90776/90884/64446.html.

20. Zhao Zhming, executive president of China Petroleum, is reported to have said that China "wish(ed) to increase the imports, oil and gas from Africa from 35 to 40 percent in the next five to 10 years." "China Wants 40 pct of Oil/Gas Imports from Africa," *Reuters,* May 17, 2008, http://uk.reuters.com/articlePrint?articleId=UKL1727982620080317.

21. "$5 Billion African Fund Launched," *China Daily,* June 26, 2007, www.chinadaily.com.cn/china/2007-6/27/content_903361.htm.

22. "Chinese Fund May Pledge $1 Billion in African Investments in '08," *Bloomberg.com,* April 28, 2008, www.bloomberg.com/apps/news?pid-206770001/$refer=asia$si.

23. "China Grabs a Slice of Africa," *Forbes,* October 15, 2007, www.forbes.com/2007/10/25/standard-bank-icbc-markets-equity. Industrial and Commercial Bank of China, "ICBC and Standard Bank Launch Strategic Cooperation," www.icbc.com.cn/e_detail.jsp?column=ICBC+NEWS&infoid.

24. This was reported by Liu Guijin, China's special envoy on African affairs. "China Supports Good Governance Based on Respect over African Countries' Sovereignty, Dignity," *Xinhua News,* June 4, 2008, www.news.xinhuanet.com/English/2008-06-04/content_8312860.htm.

25. "Rio Looks to China to Develop Africa Mine," *FT,* May 14, 2008, http://ft.com/cms/s/4d0599c2-21c0-11dd-a50a-000077b)7658.d.iii "Sino-African Trade to Hit $100 bin in 2008, China Predicts," *People's Daily,* September 3, 2008; "China-Africa Trade to Soar," *Media Club South Africa,* September 8, 2008, www.Mediaclubsouthafrica.com/index.php?option=com_content. See also trade data from Martyn Davies, "The Drivers of China's Engagement of Africa's Infrastructure," presentation to the SAFCEC Conference, Fancourt, South Africa, October 6, 2008.

26. Martyn Davies, "The Drivers of China's Engagement."

27. "Angola: China Expected to Replace Portugal as Biggest Supplier to Angola in 2008," *Macauhub,* July 7, 2008, www.macauhub.com.mo/en/print.php?papeurl=/en/news.php?ID. "Ambassador Insists 'Mutual Benefits Underpin Relations with

Africa,'" *Irish Times,* August 26, 2008, http://irishtimes.com/newspaper/world/2008/0826/1219679952.

28. "Ambassador Insists 'Mutual Benefits Underpin Relations with Africa,'" *Irish Times,* August 26, 2008.

29. Data reported by Liu Guijin, Chinese Ambassador to South Africa. See "China-Africa Trade to Soar."

30. Martyn Davies, "The Drivers of China's Engagement."

31. "China's Assistance to Zambia, 30 Years On," *Xinhua,* March 11, 2008, http://news.xinhuanet.com/english/2008-11/03/content_10298133.htm.

32. "Beijing Says Global Crisis Risks China-Africa Trade," *Africa-Reuters,* October 9, 2008. http://Africa.reuters.com/top/news/usnJOE4980L.X.html.

33. Martyn Davies, *How China Delivers Development.*

34. Elias Shilangwa and Mu Don, "Zambia Feels Effects of Continuing Global Economic Crisis," *Coastweek,* March 1, 2009, http://coastweek.com/xin270209-02.htm.

35. "Angola Eyes More Loans from China," *Reuters,* April 13, 2009. Meanwhile, it was reported that Angola has secured funding from Germany. "Angola Dos Santos Secures Funds from Germany," *Business Day,* March 2, 2009.

36. Lydia Polgreen, "As Chinese Investment in Africa Drops, Hope Sinks," *New York Times,* March 26, 2009.

37. "China Pledges to Increase Aid to Africa," *China Daily,* February 13, 2009.

38. "China Encourages Domestic Firms to Invest Overseas," *People's Daily* (English), April 10, 2009.

39. "A Financial Body in Need of Urgent Reform," *China Daily,* April 9, 2009.

40. "Use of Forex Reserves for Energy Fund Studied," *Xinhuanet,* February 17, 2009, http://xinhuanet.com/english/2009=02/17/content_10830885.htm.

41. I am indebted to the valuable study of China's cultural diplomacy with reference to Africa by Professor Liu Haifang of the Institute of West Asia and African Studies, Chinese Academy of Social Sciences, "Chinese-African Relations Through the Prism of Culture—The Dynamics of China's Culture Diplomacy with Africa," *China Aktuell,* no. 3 (2008): 9–44. For a general discussion of "soft power" by Chinese scholars, see Yan Xuetong and Xu Jin, "Sino-US Comparisons of Soft Power," *Contemporary International Relations* 18, no. 2 (March–April 2008): 16–27.

42. George T. Yu, *China's African Policy: A Study of Tanzania.* New York: Praeger Publishers, 1975. See especially chapter 2.

43. "China's Peaceful Rise Is All About Soft Power," *China Daily,* June 14, 2007.

44. Liu Haifang, "A Study of China-African Relations Through the Prism of Culture."

45. "Confucius Institutes Help Promote Exchange, Co-op Between China and African Countries, Educator," *Xinhuanet,* October 7, 2008, http://news.exinhuanet.com/english/2008-10-07/content_10160650.htm.

46. China's "private" sector in Africa was not limited to nongovernmental enterprises (e.g., construction companies), but included also the new and old immigrant Chinese in Africa (e.g., individual shop owners), estimated to total no fewer than 700,000 in 2008. See "Emerging Chinese Communities in Africa," *The China Monitor,* no. 26, (February 2008).

47. "Mbeki Warns on China-Africa Ties," *BBC News,* December 14, 2006, http://newsvote.bbc.uk/mpapps/pagetools/print/news.bbc.co.,uk/2/hi.

48. "The New Colonialists," *Economist,* May 13, 2006, www.economist.com/opinion. See also "The New Scramble for Africa Begins," *Timesonline,* April 19, 2008, www.timesonline.co.uk/tol/comments/columnsts/matthew_parris.

49. "Africa's New Colonialists?" *Mail & Guardian,* April 5, 2008, www .mg.co.za.

50. "The New Colonial Masters," *Independence,* April 19, 2008, www .independence.co.uk/opinion/leading-articles.

51. For a lively discussion of the "colonial" issue, see Barry Sautman and Yan Hairong, *East Mountain Tiger, West Mountain Tiger: China, the West, and 'Colonialism' in Africa* (Maryland Series in Contemporary Asian Studies, No. 3, 2006), p. 186. The authors conclude that "China is doing well enough in Africa by using ordinary capitalism that it does not need to 'colonize' Africa."

52. "Germany Warns Against China Lending Practices in Africa," *The China Post,* May 20, 2007, www.chinapost.com.tw/news/archives/front/2007520/110087 .htm.

53. "China's Policy in Africa: MEP on the Alert," *European Parliament-News-Press Service,* February 27, 2008, www.europarl.eropa.eu/news/exert/infopress.

54. "Harmony out of Reach at EU-Africa Summit," *International Herald Tribune,* December 9, 2007, www.iht.com/bin/.

55. David Kilgour, "China Aids Darfur Genocide," *The Suburban,* August 30, 2007, http://the suburban.com/dialog_printarticle.jsp?sid.

56. "Confrontation over Darfar 'Will Lead Us Nowhere,'" *China Daily,* July 27, 2007, http://chinadaily.com.cn/china;2007-07/27/content_5444410.htm. The quotation is attributed to Liu Guijin, China's special envoy.

57. Zimbabwe's annual inflation was reported at 100,580.2 percent in February 2008. The government "had asked China for a 25 billion British pound loan to help repair Zimbabwe's shattered economy" ("Mugabe Begs China for £25bn to Fix Economy," *Scotsman.com News,* February 26, 2008, http://news.scotsman.com/world/Mugabe-begs-China-for-.3813818.jp).

58. "China Arms Trade Conforms to Laws, Int'l Obligations," *China Daily,* April 24, 2008, www.chinadaily.com.cn/china/2008-04/24/content_6642333.htm. "China Recalls Zimbabwe Arms Shipment," *FT,* April 24, 2008, www.ft.com/cms/s/b77c7e18 -11e0-11dd-9b49-0000779fd2ac.

59. Okech Kendo, "China Has Proved It's Not a Friend to Count On," *East African Standard,* February 20, 2008, http://allafrica.com/stories/printable/ 200802200922.html.

60. "Don Hits at China Non-interference Policy," *The Citizen,* April 29, 2008, http://allafrica.com/stories/printable/20080429083.html.

61. "China Intervenes in Zambian Election," *FT,* September 5, 2006, www.ft.com/cms/s/d6d5d176176-3d0a-11db-8239-0000779e2340.html, and "Zambia's Close Poll," *Mail&Guardianonline,* September 22, 2006, www.mg.co.za.

62. "Chinese Give Zambia $1m Materials for Polls," *Times of Zambia,* May 18, 2006.

63. Mr. Sata is reported to "have received funds from Taiwan." Following the 2006 elections, he also visited Taiwan. Sautman and Yan Hairong, "The Forest for the Trees," p. 25. In the 2008 Zambian presidential elections, following the death of President Mwanawasa, Sata again ran for office but did not directly raise the Taiwan issue. Sata was defeated by Rupiah Banda, the acting president.

64. In Beijing, Ambassador Li's behavior was explained in terms of his lack of understanding of and experience in the ways of the workings of a political campaign in a democratic society. If Mr. Sata had been elected president of Zambia and recognized Taiwan, China's ambassador to Zambia would undoubtedly have had to assume the responsibility. Interview, Beijing, November 2007.

65. Center for African Agriculture Development (Ministry of Agriculture, Peo-

ple's Republic of China), "Introduction to the Development of Agriculture Cooperation with Guinea," Working Material for Discussion on African Agriculture Development, Paper No. 4, 2000.

66. Yun Wenju, "Questions on Looking at Chinese Agricultural Assistance to Africa from the Perspective of International Development Assistance," unpubl. paper, 2000(?). As a leading member of China's Ministry of Agriculture foreign assistance group with special reference to Africa since the 1990s, Mr. Yun studied extensively China's agriculture assistance programs in Africa. For a Western study of Chinese agriculture assistance programs in Africa, see Deborah Brautigam, *Chinese Aid and African Development: Exporting the Green Revolution* (Ipswich, Suffolk, UK: The Ipswich Book Company, 1998).

67. "World Bank to Work with China in Africa," *FT*, December 17, 2007, http://ft.com/cms/s/e7708f7e-adae-11dc-9386-0000779fd2ac,dw.

68. Penny Davies, *China and the End of Poverty in Africa—Towards Mutual Benefit?* (Sundbyberg, Sweden: Alfaprint, 2007). The report was published by Diakonia, a Swedish nongovernmental development aid organization.

69. "Chinese Fund May Pledge $1 Billion in African Investment in '08," *Bloomberg.com,* April 28, 2008, www.bloomberg.com/apps/news?pid=20670001$ refer=asia$si.

70. "A Continent Without Poverty Is a Possibility," *African Development Bank Annual Meetings, China Daily,* May 16, 2007.

71. "Sudan Oil Minister Says Energy Cooperation with China Fruitful," *Sudanese Media Center,* July 20, 2007, www.smc.sd/en/artopic.asp?aetID=16384&aCK-EA.

72. "Thanks China, Now Go Home," *Mail & Guardian,* February 5, 2007, www.mg.co.za/articlePage.aspx?articleid-297923&area=break.

73. Davies, *How China Delivers Development,* pp. 49–50.

74. George T. Yu, "Dragon in the Bush," *Asian Survey* 8, no. 12 (December 1968): 1018–1026.

75. In 2007, there was a "misunderstanding" over the amount of credit extended to Angola by China. Angola declared that the actual credit was worth US$2.9 billion, as opposed to the anticipated US$9.8 billion. "The World Bank was attracted by the remarks of the Angolan government because it had been interested in the secrecy that had been cast by Luanda and Beijing over the ties between China and Angola." ("Angola Loan Cast Light on Ties with China," *International Relations,* October 21, 2007, http://fsnternationalrelations.worldpress.com/2007/10./21/angolan-loan. See also "Angolan Loan Casts Light on Ties with China," *FT,* October 19, 2007. http://ft.com./cms/s/0/19adee7a-7dce-11dc-9f47-000079fd2ac.)

76. The question of transparency was a difficult one for China, deepening mistrust and suspicions between China and the West. As Gao Xiqing, head of China's US$200 billion sovereign wealth fund, is reported to have said: "Our government has never been transparent for 5,000 years. . . . Now we are told we need to be transparent and we are trying." Regarding the West's distrust and suspiciousness of China, Gao said, "We are regular people. We do not have horns growing out of our heads." John Thornhill, "Chinese Fund Tries to Calm West's Fear," *FT.com,* Asia-Pacific China, June 3, 2008, www.ft.com/cms/s/50946dc8-3198-11dd-b77c-0000779fd2ac,d.

77. For China, transparency also had a different meaning, that of disclosure of what it considered its limited (compared to the West's) foreign aid activities and programs, on the one hand, while on the other, a concern for creating and maintaining a Chinese identity for China's projects. Interview, Beijing, November 2008.

78. Interview, Beijing, November 2007.

79. Philip Karp, "China-Africa Learning on Development—Lessons for and from All Involved," *East Asia and Pacific on the Rise* (The World Bank), June 5, 2008, http://eapblog.worldbank.org/print99.

# 8

## China's Middle East Strategy: In Search of Wells and Power

### Yitzhak Shichor

To some extent, China's Middle East policy resembles a pushmi-pullyu, the two-headed creature from Hugh Lofting's *Dr. Dolittle*. It occasionally reflects contradictory views and attitudes that cannot be easily reconciled, if at all. On the one hand, China rejects US presence in the Middle East as the reincarnation of its encirclement strategy going back to the 1950s and 1960s. On the other hand, Beijing implicitly recognizes the US contribution to regional (and global) stability—a top priority in China's foreign policy and a precondition for its accelerated economic growth. Similarly, while the Chinese admit that they would like to become more involved in Middle Eastern (and global) affairs, at the same time they seem reluctant to become more active in regional and international decisionmaking processes, least of all to lead them. And, although the Middle East is by far the predominant source of easily available crude oil, so essential for China's development drive, Beijing has been trying hard to diversify its oil-supply sources, spreading them thinly all over the world in all continents, only to realize that ultimately there is no long-term substitute for Middle Eastern oil.

Nevertheless, post-Mao China's presence in the Middle East has never been as visible as it is today—politically, militarily, and economically. Since the early 1990s, Beijing has maintained diplomatic relations with all Middle Eastern governments and, albeit modestly, has played a role in policymaking processes related to the Middle East by various international organizations, in particular the UN and its Security Council, but also other outfits like the International Atomic Energy Agency. Beijing has also been present in the Middle East arms markets, as both a supplier and a customer, meanwhile carefully watching and monitoring the Middle East conflicts as a huge laboratory for drawing lessons relevant to its own military modernization. Needless to say, the dimensions of China's economic relations with the Middle East are unprecedented—not only in terms of volume but also in terms of diversification—and appear to underlie Beijing's policy in this region.[1]

Given this post-Mao emphasis in its foreign relations, what are China's objectives in the Middle East and to what extent are political, strategic, and security considerations subordinate to economic ones—if at all? More to the point, what are the relationships between China's growing dependence on Middle Eastern oil and its political attitudes and orientations? Is this dependence a source of weakness—or a source of strength? Could Chinese money buy not only oil but also power and friendship? Evidently, oil is a new and predominant component of post-Mao China's Middle East policy, but to what extent is this policy still affected and determined by historical considerations and precedents? These questions, and others, will be discussed in this chapter. It is divided into four main parts. The first deals with the historical dimension in Mao's time when Beijing's Middle East policy was determined primarily by political and strategic considerations. The next two parts discuss post-Mao China when China's Middle East policy was determined primarily by growth and development considerations, first dealing with the economic dimension and then with the political-strategic implications. Given Beijing's political, economic, and military constraints, the fourth and final part attempts to assess the prospects of its future Middle East policy. For thirty years, from 1950 to 1980, the Middle East had been marginal to China—and vice versa. Then for the next thirty years, from 1980 to 2010, the Middle East has become central for China—and vice versa. What will be China's position in the Middle East in the next thirty years?

## Politics in Command: Mao's China and the Middle East

For approximately thirty years, from the late 1940s to the late 1970s, Beijing's Middle East policy was determined primarily by politics, in the wider sense of the word, both internally and externally. Internal fluctuations reflecting moderation-radicalism cycles led to corresponding upheavals in China's Middle East policy that had little or nothing to do with regional (or global) developments. Perceived external security threats and related ideological considerations underlined, in varying dosage, China's Middle East policy throughout these years.

Pre-1979 Chinese strategy in the Middle East derived almost exclusively from its role as a stepping stone, or a base, in a perceived attack directed at China and as a link in a chain of perceived encirclement. Already in the early 1940s, long before envisioning the occupation of the entire Chinese mainland, some Chinese Communist leaders had been concerned about the possibility that Germany would seize the Middle East on its way eastward to join forces with Japan.[2] In the 1950s, and after the People's Republic of China (PRC) had been established, Beijing was irritated by the systems of alliances set up by the United States and Britain (e.g., the Baghdad Pact and the Central Treaty Organization), supposedly directed at China. In addition, in the 1960s and 1970s— as its conflict with Moscow gathered momentum—Beijing concentrated most of its effort in the Middle East against the Soviet presence.[3] But China's arsenal in this formidable task—driving threatening powers out of the Middle East—was practically empty, in political, military, and economic terms.

There was next to nothing that China could have done to accomplish its foreign policy and strategic objectives in the Middle East indirectly, let alone directly. The PRC was not a member of the UN, not to mention its Security Council, and did not have diplomatic relations with the United States, some of the European countries, and most Middle Eastern countries. Beijing did not have any military presence or bases in or near the Middle East and, depending heavily on Soviet military assistance and later isolated from any external military supply, could not deliver any meaningful quantity and quality of arms or defense technology to Middle Eastern governments. Similarly, as a backward country, China could not provide any meaningful economic assistance or aid to the Middle East, which was marginal to its economic interests. Beijing did not need Middle Eastern oil. From the early 1950s to the early 1970s, China imported oil from Soviet and East European suppliers and then became a net oil exporter until the early 1990s. Thus, there was no way, nor economic need, that Beijing could enter into a competition with Washington, Moscow, or their allies in attempting to win the goodwill of the Arab capitals—let alone to convince them to get rid of their traditional supporters— save one: revolution.

Mao's China's relative and potential advantage in the Middle East was not keeping order, but promoting disorder; not maintaining stability, but sustaining instability; not defending the status quo, but undermining it; not aspiring for rest, but inspiring unrest. Put differently, China's Middle East policy reflected some of Mao's basic principles that stressed constant change, permanent revolution, and ongoing transformation. Stagnation meant a setback and China's only hope in the Middle East was in stirring up trouble and urging a political change that would relieve the external pressure and enable a foothold. This, apparently, would have given China the upper hand as neither the United States and its allies nor the Soviet Union and its allies had been ready to support revolutionary radicalism; but China was, and, moreover, had no choice. This is why in the mid-1960s Beijing began to back national liberation movements and organizations such as the Palestinians, not for their intrinsic "revolutionary" qualities, but because the Chinese assumed that this way they would win the Arab governments' support—something neither Washington nor Moscow could have done. Beijing failed. The only weapon it had misfired. The Arab governments regarded China's intervention in the Arab-Israeli conflict (or in the South Arabia dispute) as a threat to themselves and their own survival. Revolution and radicalism proved to be a double-edged sword for China's Middle East policy, and not for the first time.

The late 1950s' Great Leap Forward domestic radicalization, its ideological fervor and revolutionary mood, propelled Beijing to support Middle Eastern communism, ending in a deterioration of Sino-Arab relations, primarily with Egypt, Syria, and Iraq. These failures reflect a major handicap that characterized China's Middle East policy in the prereform era, namely, its inconsistency that in turn was an outcome of the political fluctuations at home. China's Middle East policy changed every few years from more conventional state-to-state relations emphasizing moderation and relaxation to a more radical subgovernmental relationship (with parties, "revolutionary organizations, and "national liberation" movements) that promoted instability and unrest. For example, a representative of the People's Front for the Liberation of Oman and the Arabian Gulf (PFLOAG), which enjoyed PRC support, admitted: "Most of the working masses tended to shy away from the extremist Chinese-styled ideology which had been the officially sponsored line and which had also lost PFLOAG the friendship of the Soviet Union."[4] Even by its so-called Middle Eastern friends, the PRC was not always perceived as a reliable partner—a legacy that persists.[5]

These parameters of China's Middle East policy had begun to change very slowly and gradually since the late 1960s, a few years before Mao's death. Determined by internal politics (the demise of Cultural Revolution radicalism and violence, the reconstruction of the Chinese Communist Party, and the rehabilitation of the economy), as well as by external politics (the improved relations with the United States, the confrontation with the Soviet Union, and the PRC's admission to the UN), the Chinese foreign policy system began to be restored, including in the Middle East. Ambassadors were now being sent back to their posts, and new diplomatic relations were established with Middle Eastern governments that had heretofore failed to recognize the PRC. Just in 1971, these included Turkey, Iran, Lebanon, Kuwait, and Cyprus (as well as Tunisia, which resumed relations suspended in September 1967). Additional countries included Jordan (in 1977) and Oman and Libya (in 1978).[6]

Notwithstanding these changes, however, in the 1970s China's Middle East policy still followed its "traditional" patterns, reflecting the delicate factional balance of power in Chinese politics between radicals and moderates. Becoming a permanent member of the UN Security Council in October 1971, the PRC was very reluctant to use its new position and very slow in assuming its new international responsibilities. This was an outcome not merely of a difficult learning process and the need to adapt to new forms of international behavior; it was also, or mainly, an outcome of traditional patterns of behavior, trying to avoid involvement in issues and regions that are far away from the immediate Chinese interests and concerns. Consequently, Beijing adopted a policy of abstention and absenteeism, trying to keep clear of offending friends—and associating with former or current adversaries.[7]

While these traditional features of Beijing's Middle East policy—and a few others—are still evident in China's international behavior today, its fundamental assumptions have undergone dramatic changes since the late 1970s. Most important among them is the paramount priority accorded to economic growth, at the apparent expense of time-honored Maoist ideology, military modernization, and social solidarity. Consequently, while China's Middle East policy was governed mainly by political, strategic, security, and ideological considerations in Mao's time, China's Middle East policy in post-Mao China has been governed mainly by economic, pragmatic, particularistic, and practical considerations. These, in turn, have affected Beijing's political, strategic, and security relations with the Middle East.

## Economics in Command: Post-Mao China and the Middle East

As mentioned above, the Middle East was marginal to China's economic interests, and vice versa. There was next to nothing China could trade with the Middle East, either in export or in import, compared to other powers. Similarly, China's aid to some Middle Eastern countries—launched in the 1960s—was not only modest in scale but had also been ultimately motivated by political rather than by economic considerations; it was meant to win the goodwill of the Arab governments and to urge them to get rid of the US "imperialist" and Soviet "social-imperialist" presence. Yet the benefits gained by the Arab governments from their relations with the United States and the Soviet Union by far overshadowed anything that Beijing could offer, in political, economic, and military terms. China's dogmatic either-or demands failed and these lessons were learned, and applied, since the late 1970s.

Still a net oil exporter, at the beginning post-Mao China regarded the Middle East in general, and the Persian Gulf countries in particular, not so much as a potential source of oil but primarily as a huge market for Chinese goods and services, including labor export and construction contracts, and as a potential source of loans and investments in China's infrastructure. It is only since the mid-1980s that Beijing had begun to buy relatively small quantities of crude oil from the Middle East (mainly from Oman and Yemen), and it is only ten years later, after China had become a net oil importer, that the Greater Middle East has become China's principal source of oil import, about 50–60 percent of the total. China's heavy reliance on Middle Eastern oil has affected its overall economic (as well as political and strategic) relations with the Middle East. Therefore, the economic phase in post-Mao China's relations with the Middle East should be divided into two parts: before the early 1990s and afterward. By that time, China's domestic politics as well as international environment had undergone drastic, perhaps irreversible, changes. Politically, the Tiananmen Square massacre underlined the role of the Chinese Communist Party as the ultimate power broker in China. Economically, Deng Xiaoping's trip to the South put an end to earlier debates and underlined China's long-run commitment to modernization, development, and growth. Internationally, the Soviet collapse paved the ground for a new global constellation whereby Beijing's friction with Washington has increased while Beijing's friction with Moscow has decreased.

## Economic Relations in the 1980s

Heretofore marginal in China's international economic relations, as soon as post-Mao reform was launched in the late 1970s, the Middle East became a focus of innovative activities hardly attempted before, definitely not on this scale. These included delivery of arms and military technology, labor export and construction services, and multilateral investments. Trade turnover also increased, yet along more traditional lines, before oil has become the predominant commodity leading to multiplied trade figures following the mid-1990s. In fact, arms sales inflated China's trade figures with the Middle East in the 1980s, according to Chinese Customs Statistics, though not always with the end-user countries.

Apparently, there was nothing new in Beijing's arms transfers. Mao's China had given considerable quantities of arms to North Korea, North Vietnam, and Pakistan, but there are major differences. For one, Mao's China offered arms primarily to its buffer states and based strictly on security considerations. To be sure, small quantities of light arms were also supplied to "revolutionary" organizations, such as the Palestinians, together with elementary military training—based on ideological (and strategic) motivations.[8] For another, Mao's China supplied arms free of charge. Post-Mao China, on the other hand, sold arms (including aircraft, tanks, guns, missiles, and submarines) to countries far away and based mainly on commercial considerations.[9]

This drastic departure from past Chinese behavior was directed at the Middle East, which from the late 1970s to the late 1980s became Beijing's leading arms market (primarily Iraq and Iran, but also Egypt), absorbing over 90 percent of the total. In those years, the Chinese were quick to observe that some Middle Eastern countries, engaged in violent confrontations, had faced difficulties in acquiring the weapons they needed from their traditional suppliers. Exploiting this window of opportunity, Beijing agreed to sell the Middle East arms that by the end of the decade were valued at around US$20 billion. This was an unexpected and substantial bonus for the Chinese as most of the weapons delivered were obsolete surplus equipment. According to China's Customs Statistics, to conceal the end users, the accounting was occasionally done through third countries that provided a clearinghouse (notably, Jordan, for weapons sent to Iraq), so that arms sales obviously had a favorable effect on total trade turnover, leading to inconceivable and unexplained high trade figures with marginal countries. It is quite likely that most of the income from arms sales has been used not strictly for the sake of economics, but more for the sake of defense economics (to supplement military allocations and create extrabudgetary resources used, perhaps, to import advanced military technology and sophisticated weapons and defense equipment, ironically from Israel).[10]

The Middle East became the main market not only for Chinese arms sales, but also for Chinese labor export and construction services. Apparently, there was nothing new in these activities either. Mao's China had been engaged in engineering projects in many Asian and African countries, the Middle East included, but there are major differences—and not only in scale. Most important among them is the fact that while in the past these activities had been politically motivated, in post-Mao China they are primarily (while not only) based on economic considerations and considerably more diversified. China began to compete with international corporations over construction lenders and has managed to win substantial contracts.

Launched in the late 1970s on an experimental and provisional basis and accompanied by ideological debates concerning their conformity to socialism, Beijing's labor export and construction services (which, together with design consultation, have been termed "foreign economic cooperation") have since gathered momentum. As in the case of arms exports (though for different reasons), this new activity was directed first to the Middle East, where there was a shortage of workforce on the one hand, and a surplus of money, on the other. Thus, by the late 1980s, the Middle East (or to be more precise, the Persian Gulf countries) had become China's principal market for labor export at an annual average of 86 percent of the total turnover; construction services accounted for an annual average of 48 percent of the total turnover, altogether an annual average of 56 percent. Most of this activity was concentrated in Iraq (that alone accounted for 70 percent of China's total labor export turnover) and Kuwait.

Kuwait was also one of the countries that provided China with loans, a departure from past experience in which China had not received loans and grants other than from Soviet sources. Yet, despite the huge amounts of money accumulated in the Gulf, the Middle East has been a modest, if not marginal, investor in China—and vice versa. Except for breakthroughs in labor export, construction services, and arms sales, China's economic relations with the Middle East in the 1980s still reflected traditional inertia and, no less important, uncertainty about China's future course, political stability, and the ultimate success of the reform drive. We take it for granted, in a retrospective perspective, that China's post-Mao reform has proceeded in a linear course in an apparently irreversible way; however, in the 1980s people could not have known that the change, dramatic as it was, would last longer than earlier changes that China had undergone. This lack of confidence and uncertainty restricted China's international behavior, including in the Middle East. In fact, it seemed as if some of Beijing's initiatives in the Middle East, in particular arms sales and labor export, were carried out hastily and en masse before a new political upheaval would erupt. Yet, by the early 1990s, it had become clear that rather than slowing down the reform drive, it would be accelerated, perhaps far beyond the imagination and expectations of those who had planned and launched it.

## Economic Relations Since the 1980s

China's economic relations with the Middle East have begun to change since the early 1990s primarily, but not only, because of its growing dependence on oil import. What had singled out the Middle East in China's 1980s international economic relations, in particular arms sales and labor export, has no longer applied to the 1990s and beyond. No less important than the predominance of oil has been the remarkable expansion of China's international economic relations to other regions, thereby dwarfing the Middle Eastern share in these relations. Chinese arms exports to the Middle East, that in the 1980s had reached an annual average of nearly 87 percent of China's total arms export and over 74 percent of the total arms agreements, declined in the 1990s to nearly 32 and 26.5 percent, respectively. In 2000–2008, the average share of the Middle East in China's arms sales stood at about 34 percent, with most of the weapons going to Iran (some 18 percent), Egypt, and Sudan. Similarly, China's share in the total arms supplies to the Middle East, that had reached an annual average of around 8 percent of deliveries and nearly 7 percent of agreements in the 1980s, deteriorated to 1.6 and 1.8 percent, respectively, in the 1990s. From 2000 to 2008, the share of Chinese arms sales to the Middle East reached an average of around 3.5 percent (compared to 48 percent for the United States, 21 for Russia, 17 for France, and 3.6 percent for the UK).[11]

This drop has had nothing to do with oil. It has had to do with combined reasons that included US pressure accusing Beijing of proliferation; the emergence of alternative arms customers in other regions, mostly in South and Southeast Asia; the resumption of deliveries by traditional arms exporters; and the poor performance of China-made weapons in battle, notably during the Iran-Iraq War (1980–1987). However, since the early 1990s, the decrease in income from the loss of Middle Eastern arms markets has been more than compensated for by an annual double-digit increase in military budgets. China's arms sales to the Middle East have by no means stopped completely, but they have now been affected again by strategic and political considerations, notably in the case of Iran, to be discussed later in this chapter. Still, since the 1980s and especially the 1990s, the Chinese have been carefully watching the Middle East as a huge laboratory for state-of-the-art Western military technologies and doctrines that could affect and shape the PRC defense modernization and its security environment.[12]

While China's arms transfers to the Middle East have nosedived, its foreign economic cooperation with the Middle East has increased dramatically: from a 1999 turnover of nearly US$720 million, it had more than doubled to US$1,500 million by 2004, and in 2006 it reached nearly US$4,300 million—an amazing sixfold growth. However, the relative share of the Middle East in China's labor export and construction services—which have expanded so rapidly and extensively—has been rather modest, increasing from 6.4 percent in 1999 to 7 percent in 2004, nearly 9 percent in 2005, and nearly 13 percent in 2007 (or nearly 24 percent if we add Sudan and North Africa). In 2007, among China's ten leading foreign economic cooperation markets, there are only two Middle Eastern countries, the United Arab Emirates (ranks six) and Saudi Arabia (ranks eight). Sudan ranks two and Algeria is number one.[13] In addition to its development drive, Beijing's increased economic activism in the Middle East could also be explained by its wish to offset its skyrocketing expenses on Middle Eastern crude oil.

As mentioned above, Beijing had begun to import relatively small quantities of crude oil from the Middle East already in the 1980s, when China was still a net oil exporter. The decision to start importing oil nonetheless had probably been an outcome of two interrelated considerations. For one, China's economic growth gathered momentum while its oil output was growing at a much slower pace to satisfy further development. For another, some of China's oil had been committed for export (to North Korea and primarily to Japan) by long-term contracts that could not be legally aborted. Yet, the first Chinese choice for oil import had been Southeast Asia and not the Middle East, which was not only too far but also seemed unstable and risky. However, by the early 1990s, Beijing had realized that, given its fast economic growth and the stagnation of domestic oil output, acquiring more energy resources became essential if not urgent. Middle Eastern oil could no longer be ignored or sidestepped.[14]

Still, one of the most fundamental assumptions underlying China's international quest for energy has been that the Middle East is unpredictable and, therefore, not a reliable source of oil in the long run. Consequently, since the early 1990s, China has employed two strategies: one, to diversify its crude oil suppliers as much as possible, and two, to buy oilfield concessions abroad and sign production sharing agreements so as to guarantee future oil supply as independently as possible. To a great extent, China's strategies have apparently succeeded. Since the mid-1990s, the Chinese have managed to acquire the oil they need from as many as thirty or forty different sources—without becoming too dependent on any—switching from one predominant supplier to another every year, or even every month (from Iran to Saudi Arabia and then to Angola, back to Iran, etc.).[15] Yet, China's fundamental oil acquisition assumptions and strategies have proved to be faulty on two accounts.

First, most if not all of China's oil supply substitutes (to the Middle East) cannot cater for long-term needs. They represent relatively limited verified oil reserves (estimated to decline in twenty to thirty years, if not before); technologically difficult extraction and ecological harm; diverse quality and therefore problems in refining; and, last but not least, dubious political reputations related to the abuse of human rights, support of terrorism, and corruption that draw international criticism. Second, Middle Eastern oil is not only practically unlimited, of similar quality, and relatively closer to China (in terms of transportation), but also, just as important, is not as subject to instability or unpredictability as the Chinese (and most others) assume. As a matter of fact—and despite rampant violent conflicts—there have been few, if any, serious disruptions of crude oil supply since October 1973 caused by the *suppliers*. Most, if not all problems in Middle Eastern oil supply have been caused by *customers*, primarily by the United States, that imposed embargoes, sanctions, prohibitions, and other penalties directed at oil suppliers considered "rogue" or part of the so-called axis of evil. Although China is still looking for alternatives to Middle Eastern oil supply (a strategy based, perhaps, not just on necessity but also on choice, to exploit in the short-run whatever resources are available *outside* the Middle East), in the long-run there is no substitute for Middle Eastern oil. If the Chinese have not realized this already, they will shortly.[16]

In the meantime, the share of the Greater Middle East in China's crude oil import has steadily increased from the 1980s, reaching around 50 percent by the mid-1990s and up to 60 percent ten years later (including Sudan and North Africa). Initially, Beijing had imported crude oil mainly from Oman and Yemen, both relatively marginal crude oil producers. More recently, most of China's Middle Eastern oil has been shipped from two main sources, Iran and Saudi Arabia, which together contribute about one-third of all China's oil import. Beijing is fully aware of Iran's role in nuclear proliferation as well as support of terrorism and consequent vulnerability to international sanctions—if not military action. This is one reason why Beijing has spread its oil suppliers all over the world and, more concretely, prepared a fallback position in case crude oil supply from Iran should be disrupted. In a preemptive move, in early 2006 Beijing accepted what amounted to an insurance policy offered by Saudi Arabia. Visiting China, he proposed to provide all of China's oil needs single-handedly, an offer Saudi Arabia had already made in the 1990s. Turned down then to avoid an overwhelming dependence on one supplier, the Saudi proposal was now implicitly accepted. Beijing still wishes to avoid such dependence, but Riyadh's commitment solves not only long-term economic problems but political ones as well.[17] It provides Beijing with greater flexibility toward Iran and makes it less painful to support sanctions with less concern about oil supplies.

## Political and Strategic Implications

China's emphasis on economic growth since the late 1970s has determined its strategy and politics in the Middle East (and elsewhere). Earlier, Beijing's *exclusive* policy had rejected relations with certain "reactionary" governments like Saudi Arabia or Israel—considered too pro-Western or even worse, pro–United States. Occasionally, Beijing had also cooled off relations with "revolutionary" governments, like Egypt, Syria, and Iraq, accused of persecuting communists. Now Beijing has adopted an *inclusive* policy that welcomes relations with *all* governments based on mutual benefit—notwithstanding their political outlook or international orientation. To be sure, although China's system has remained "socialist" and governed by the Chinese Communist Party, its political outlook and international orientation have changed as well. The origins of both these changes, the internal and external, however, go back to the late 1960s when relations with the United States had begun to improve following the end of the radical and violent phase of the Cultural Revolution.

Therefore, post-Mao China's Middle East policy continues and accentuates trends that had begun earlier, especially with regard to the expansion of diplomatic relations and the gradual dissociation from, and disapproval of, national liberation movements and revolutionary organizations. To be sure, Beijing still maintains quasi-diplomatic links with the Palestinian Authority and even recognized the nonexisting Palestinian state in 1988. China has also tried to cultivate relations with the Hamas after it had won the elections in the Gaza Strip and, at least indirectly, with the Hizbullah in Lebanon and the Revolutionary Guards in Iran. Yet, unlike its policy in Mao's time, the Chinese no longer promote revolution, unrest, and instability. Itself affected by terrorism,[18] China tries to distance itself from Middle Eastern acts of radicalism or attempts to settle the Arab-Israeli conflict, or any other, by force—not to mention attempts to subvert and undermine existing and legitimate governments. Instead, Beijing has tried to improve relations with all Middle East governments, without exception.

Some of these governments had rejected diplomatic relations with the PRC before the 1980s on account of its anti-US policy, communist ideology, and hostility to its Muslim minorities and to Islam in general. In those years, Beijing had not been eager either to establish relations with them, but by the 1980s the situation had changed, for all. One example is Turkey. Closely associated with the United States and the only Middle East country that had played an active role in the Korean War along with the UN forces against North Korea and China,[19] Turkey had failed to recognize the PRC until August 1971. By the early 1990s, bilateral relations had been developing rather slowly, but since the mid-1990s considerable progress has been made. While this is an outcome of China's fast economic growth and foreign trade prosperity, it has to do also with the Turkish implicit support of the Uighurs. Turkey had been a source of nationalist inspiration to Xinjiang's Uighurs since the late nineteenth century and a model to be followed. Many East Turkestan Uighurs (like Mehmet Rıza Bekin, a general in the Turkish Army) fled China in the 1930s and 1940s and chose Turkey as a substitute homeland, where some remain to this day. Feeling responsible for the persecuted Uighurs, the Turkish government since the early 1950s had willingly and warmly welcomed Mehmet Emin Bughra and Isa Yusuf Alptekin—the uncrowned leaders of Uighur nationalism—and for many years provided them, their followers, their movement, and Uighur refugees at large with financial support, office facilities, citizenship, housing, and even military training and thereby with a viable base of operation.[20]

By the mid-1990s, however, the situation had changed. Finally understanding that the so-called Uighur separatism is not just "an internal affair"—as they had claimed all along—but had become an international issue that enjoys substantial external support, the Chinese have begun to apply pressure on Turkey. Beijing urged Ankara to restrict the activities of East Turkestan organizations; to deny Uighur refugees—who kept flowing from China to Turkey—citizenship and other benefits; and to forbid, disrupt, and limit Uighur demonstrations against China. These political demands, underlined by visits of high-ranking Chinese leaders, have been accompanied by a dramatic surge in economic relations and trade that leads to a greater Turkish dependence on China.[21] Much more significant—and less known—are Beijing's military relations with Ankara. Launched in the latter half of the 1990s after Washington had refused to sell missiles to Ankara, these relations have focused on multiple launch rocket systems, based on the Chinese WS-1A/B (Turkish designation: *Kasırga*, whirlwind or tornado, or TR-300) and on tactical missiles based on the Chinese B-611 (Turkish designation: *Yıldırım*, thunderbolt or lightning) similar to the DF-11 (M-7 or CSS7).[22] As a result of these economic and military exchanges, Ankara has quietly submitted to Beijing's demands, at the expense of Uighur nationalist activism. Nevertheless, Turkey is still relatively marginal in China's Middle East policy. Driven by its thirst for oil, China's main interest in the Middle East is in the Persian Gulf.

Although it is unlikely that the Chinese had anticipated their future dependence on oil import from the Middle East so early, they concentrated their diplomatic efforts in the Persian Gulf region—where the PRC had still been rejected—soon after the launch of the 1979 reform. In 1984 they established relations with the United Arab Emirates, in 1988 with Qatar, in 1989 with Bahrain, and in July 1990—just a week before Saddam Hussein's invasion of Kuwait—with Saudi Arabia. Chinese explorations and gestures with Riyadh had begun earlier, when China resumed Muslim hajj missions to Mecca following a fifteen-year interruption. Moreover, having been turned down by the United States, the Saudis turned to China to buy long-range missiles. Exposed in 1988, it is China's sale of DF (*Dongfeng,* or east wind)-3A (CSS-2) conventional-warhead intermediate-range ballistic missiles that had finally paved the ground for diplomatic relations between Beijing and Riyadh.[23]

These relations have been especially significant not only because Saudi Arabia was a potential future oil supplier but because of its criticism of Chinese communism in the past, its role in the Muslim world, its long-standing relations with Taiwan (that had to be cut short now), its assumed leadership of the Arab world, and, last but not least, its association with Washington. Saudi Arabia was the last Arab Middle Eastern country to recognize the PRC and to establish diplomatic relations with it. Unlike most, if not all, other similar acts, this one finally legitimized China as a trustworthy newcomer in the Middle East. Paradoxically, it was Riyadh that finally stamped China's presence in the Middle East as "kosher," thereby paving the ground for the formation of Beijing's relations with Israel. It had been inconceivable that China would have formed official relations with Israel before Saudi Arabia.

Although Israel had been the first country in the Middle East to recognize the PRC—as early as January 9, 1950—diplomatic relations were not established until forty-two years later, on January 24, 1992. Initially, this long delay had been caused by Israel's reluctance to move forward following China's implication in the Korean War and the consequent US pressure to avoid official relations with China. Yet, by the mid-1950s, Beijing had begun to realize the quantitative importance of the Arab—and Muslim—countries, the disadvantages of Israel's association with Washington, and Moscow's negative attitude toward Jerusalem. The newly opened PRC foreign ministry archive documents demonstrate that in those years, at least as far as Beijing was concerned, the Sino-Israeli exchanges that had taken place by 1953 were no more than superficial window dressing.[24] Beijing did not intend to establish diplomatic relations with Israel, definitely not in the 1960s and 1970s when it needed Arab (and Palestinian) support against the Soviets and when it was involved in a confrontation with the United States in Asia. Yet, by the late 1970s, Beijing's attitude began to change, slowly and gradually.

Initial signs emerged already in the early 1970s, after Israel's vote (among others) had facilitated China's admission to the UN. Indirectly and implicitly, Beijing disclosed its appreciation for Israel's role in checking Soviet "expansionism" into the Middle East. While still critical about Israel's "aggressiveness" toward the Arabs and the Palestinians, the Chinese began to make a distinction between the "government" (considered negative) and the "people" (considered positive)—a judgment still based on strategic, security, and political considerations. Thus, in the late 1970s, the Chinese approved, again indirectly and implicitly, the Israeli-Egyptian peace settlement—not (yet) because of any sympathy to Israel but because it was done under US auspices to the detriment of Soviet interests. But in the 1980s, China began, still informally, to appreciate Israel's advantages, given the new Chinese emphasis on economic growth, technological development, and overall modernization.

This transformation of China's domestic and foreign policies has allowed, for the first time, bilateral exchanges with Israel even without diplomatic relations, in the fields of tourism, agriculture, communications, academic research, science and technology, and—last but by no means least—defense. Beijing's military system had been watching and monitoring Israel's military achievements, operations, and technologies long before the 1980s. Following two decades of interruption of external military supply and a more recent blunder against Vietnam, China's defense system was in bad shape and in need of resuscitation. Explorations with the West were mostly aborted because China did not have the necessary funds to buy off-the-shelf weapons in quantity nor the will to become heavily dependent yet again on any power. Israel, on the other hand, not only had advanced military technology but was also ready to sell it, unlike Western suppliers.[25] Moreover, Israel had the most up-to-date experience in coping with Soviet weapons, as well as upgrading them. There was no danger whatsoever that the PRC would become dependent on Israel. These considerations had led to the Sino-Israeli arms deals in the 1980s, absolutely inconceivable just a few years earlier.

These arms sales agreements and deliveries were made without US objection and with Washington's knowledge and, possibly, even tacit approval. In those years, before the unexpected collapse of the Soviet Union, Washington had considered Beijing an ally (though undeclared) and a partner in the fight against Moscow, mainly in Afghanistan. Israel thus became a US proxy in a policy intended to make China stronger militarily. Still publicly denied by Beijing, these unofficial Sino-Israeli relations had paved the ground for political and diplomatic exchanges in the latter half of the 1980s, mostly in the UN. Apparently, the Chinese decided to establish diplomatic relations with Israel by the late 1980s, if not before. Israel's rather mild response to Tiananmen was undoubtedly noted in Beijing. By the early 1990s, Beijing had been ready, having gathered enough self-confidence to defy Arab, Palestinian, and Iranian opposition, which had subsided anyway. If some Arab countries, notably Egypt and Jordan, maintained full diplomatic relations with Israel, there was no reason that China should not. In fact, China—as a rising power—wanted to become more involved in Middle Eastern affairs in general, and in the settlement of the Arab-Israeli conflict in particular. Yet China could not act as an "honest broker" without having diplomatic relations with Israel. These relations had been facilitated, though inadvertently, by none other than Saddam Hussein.

Iraq's invasion of Kuwait in early August 1990, shortly after China established official relations with Saudi Arabia, has changed not only the situation in the Middle East but China's attitudes as well. For one thing, Beijing suddenly realized that the Arab-Israeli conflict is not the only one in the Middle East and that for years Arabs had confronted Arabs, no less viciously. For another, Beijing appreciated Israel's restraint in the face of Iraqi Scud missile attacks on its territories. Interested in regional stability for the sake of its economic growth, the Chinese had been concerned that an Israeli reprisal would have complicated the war, undermined the anti-Iraqi alliance, and sucked the entire region into the conflict. Finally, the Chinese—like many others—understood that, as a reward for those Arab countries that supported the US-led anti-Iraqi alliance, the next item on the international and regional agenda following the Gulf War would be to hold an international conference to settle the Arab-Israeli-Palestinian conflict. Indeed, such a conference was held in Madrid in late October–early November 1991, but China did not and could not participate. The next meeting of the peace process multilateral talks was planned to be held in Moscow on January 28, 1992. Beijing wanted to be present and this determined the date of the establishment of Sino-Israeli diplomatic relations: January 24, 1992.[26]

Ironically, soon after diplomatic relations had been established, Sino-Israeli relations ran into difficulties, not because of China's growing dependence on Persian Gulf oil or any bilateral disagreements, but because of the United States. From their very beginning in the early 1950s, the prospects of Sino-Israeli relations have been affected by interests of third parties, primarily the United States, the Soviets, and the Arabs. It is these parties, outside the bilateral nexus, that have actually determined or even dictated the pace and progress of China-Israel relations. US pressure was probably the most significant reason why Israel had failed to establish diplomatic relations with China by the mid-1950s; Arab and Muslim pressure—and the deterioration of Soviet-Israeli relations—was probably the most significant reason why China had failed to establish official relations with Israel since the 1950s. By the 1990s, based on its perceived "China threat" syndrome, the United States began yet again to apply pressure on Israel to stop supplying arms to China. Leading to the cancellation of contracts that had already been signed, this pressure caused a chill in Sino-Israeli relations that have only recently begun to warm again, though by no means in the military field. This chill has been undoubtedly welcomed in Tehran, whose relations with China have begun to look like an alliance.

Indeed, Beijing had targeted Tehran long before it started importing Iranian oil. Iran, as mentioned above, was not only one of China's best arms customers in the 1980s but also a vocal rival of the United States and as such, an implicit ally. Having already undertaken a number of infrastructure projects in Iran, notably Tehran's subway system carried out by Norinco, an armament conglomerate, China has also begun to import crude oil from Iran, which has become a leading oil supplier to China. This perceived dependence on Iran's oil and Beijing's support of Tehran on a number of issues, including nuclear proliferation, created an image of friendship and commitment.[27] This image should be qualified from both sides. As for China, its trade with Iran accounts for less than 1 percent of its overall international trade, oil included. Also, Beijing cannot be very happy with Iran's contribution to terrorism, Islamic radicalism, and regional and global instability. Reiterating Tehran's claims that its nuclear program is only for peaceful uses, Beijing does not want Iran to have nuclear weapons. While the Chinese have been trying to avoid and delay anti-Iran decisions either by the International Atomic Energy Agency or by the UN Security Council, they ultimately supported sanctions against Iran. At the moment of truth—if it comes at all—it is unlikely that China would use its veto power to save Iran. Washington is far more important for Beijing than Tehran. As for the Iranians, they know that China (and Russia) are not to be fully trusted and that their current relationship reflects mutual suspicions. A recent Iranian editorial admitted: China and Russia "adopt positions on the basis of their interests, calculations and considerations, and pinning our hopes on a division of East and West is not an entirely secure bet in safeguarding our national interests."[28] These interests are not always compatible with those of China, whose pro-Iran attitude may change in the future.

## China's Future and the Middle East

"Never make predictions, particularly about the future," said George Bernard Shaw, advice that applies equally to the Middle East as to China. Perhaps, China's future can be more easily predicted, both politically and economically. As a one-party state that enjoys a monopoly of power and widespread legitimization, it is difficult to foresee a domestic threat to its ongoing rule that could not be efficiently, and if needed, brutally, dealt with. All the more so since its legitimization increasingly depends on continued delivery of public goods and its continued commitment to economic growth. Beijing appears to be one of the countries least affected by the current global economic crisis. Given its huge domestic but still little-tapped market, accumulation of capital fed by high rates of savings and foreign trade surplus, accessibility to advanced technology, improved infrastructures and education system, and—probably most important—the availability of a relatively unlimited workforce potential, China's impressive growth rates are expected by economists to continue for the next thirty to forty years—provided China is not militarily targeted by external powers (namely, but unlikely, the United States), and provided China will have enough energy to lubricate and propel its economic prosperity. It is precisely on this issue that the Middle East comes into the picture.

Assuming that no energy-substitutes or renewable energies would significantly reduce its reliance on traditional energy resources in the next three to four decades, the PRC by necessity, rather than by choice, would become even more dependent on Persian Gulf crude oil for a long time to come. China's dependence on Middle Eastern oil import is likely to reach 70 percent by 2015, probably more later on. This is because oil from other sources is expected to decline much faster than Middle Eastern oil, which may lead to a fierce, if not violent, competition. With current foreign exchange reserves of US$1.954 trillion (as of late March 2009), in the future China is expected to stockpile much more and to pay the huge sums of money required for importing scarce oil. The fact that China's current share in the world oil import and consumption is only 6 and 8 percent respectively means only one thing: China still has a long way to go and these percentages will undoubtedly increase.

## Conclusion

Whereas in Mao's time the occasional fluctuations in China's Middle East policy had reflected the domestic ideological and political upheavals, the consistency of China's Middle East policy after Mao reflects the domestic political and ideological stability. Yet it would be a mistake to interpret China's Middle East policy solely in terms of oil needs and economic priorities. China is no longer what many thought since the 1980s (myself included), a regional power with few interests beyond the East Asia perimeter, in a traditional sense. While there is a consensus that China is already a global power in economic terms, there are initial indications that China has begun to take the first steps as a political power—though not yet as a military power. Therefore, Beijing's decision not to become involved politically and militarily in Middle Eastern affairs is by no means the final word. It only means that Beijing does not feel it is ready. The Chinese say they will not play a more active role in the Middle East (and elsewhere) "until China would become stronger."[29] In the meantime, some still perceive the Middle East as marginal to China's foreign policy. Recent studies of Chinese foreign policy tend to underestimate if not ignore altogether the Middle East.[30]

While there is no doubt that other regions figure more prominently in Chinese foreign and security policy (primarily Asia, the United States, and Europe), perceptions of Middle East marginality will necessarily change, both because of China's advantages (its growing economic, political, and perhaps military profile) and because of its disadvantages (its growing need for energy and other commodities). Nevertheless, it is highly unlikely that any Middle Eastern country (or any other) would adopt the so-called China model. A number of studies have recently raised the possibility that the Chinese model would become an attractive option for non-Western countries that welcome the tempting combination of fast economic growth within a nondemocratic framework.[31] Some in the Middle East, including Syria and Iran, have explored this possibility—which has been totally rejected by others. An elaborate Iranian editorial that analyzed the different components of the Chinese economic achievements concluded: "It is useless to expect such miracles from those [rightist conservatives and religious traditionalists] who, after two decades of ruling, instead of creating patterns for the Islamic countries are in a position that the Communist Party of China has become their model. What will happen is like the famous story of the crow, which tried to learn the partridge's style of walking, but forgot its own way of walking."[32]

## Notes

1. There are various definitions of the Middle East. Usually I use a wider definition based on Arab League members that includes African Arab countries. But since Africa will be dealt with in another chapter, this one adopts a narrower definition of the Middle East that excludes North Africa and Sudan but includes Turkey and Iran (that in official Chinese statistics are parts of Asia) and Egypt (that in Chinese statistics is part of Africa). For a wider definition, see Kurt W. Radtke, "China and the Greater Middle East: Globalization No Longer Equals Westernization," in M. Parvizi Amineh, ed., *The Greater Middle East in Global Politics* (Leiden: Brill, 2007), pp. 387–414.

2. Mao Zedong, "A Turning Point in World War II, October 12, 1942," *Selected Readings from the Works of Mao Tse-tung,* Vol. 3 (Peking: Foreign Languages Press, 1965), p. 105.

3. Liu Jing, Zhang Shizhi, and Zhu Li, *Sulian zhongdong guanxi shi* [History of Soviet–Middle Eastern Relations] (Beijing: Zhongguo shehui kexue chubanshe, 1987). More details in Yitzhak Shichor, *The Middle East in China's Foreign Policy 1949–1977* (Cambridge: Cambridge University Press, 1979); Hong Chun and Guo Yingde, *Zhong'a guanxi shi* [A History of Sino-Arab Relations] (Beijing: jingji ribao chubanshe, 2001). See also 'Amr 'Itāni, *Siyasat Bakin izā'a al-Sharq al-'Arabi bayn al-Ams wa'l-Yaum* [Beijing's Policy Toward the Arab East Between Yesterday and Today] (Beirut: Dār al-Farābi, 1972); 'Abdullah al-Khariji, *Al-Ṣin wa'l-Shu'ub al-'Arabiyyah* [China and the Arab Peoples] (Beirut: Dār al-Farābi, 1979).

4. CIA document TDFIRDB-315/03919-73, April 24, 1973, declassified March 2008.

5. Thus, some in Iran, and not only from the opposition, warn against reliance on China, which is not to be trusted. They say that, ultimately, Washington is far more important to Beijing than Tehran. As a matter of fact, Chinese experts reiterate this view. More details in Yitzhak Shichor, "Disillusionment: China and Iran's Nuclear Gamble," *Freeman Report* (Washington, DC: Center for Strategic and International Studies, July–August 2006).

6. For ongoing coverage of China's relations with Middle Eastern countries, see the annual editions by the Department of Policy Planning, Ministry of Foreign Affairs, PRC, *China's Foreign Affairs* (Beijing: World Affairs Press).

7. Yitzhak Shichor, "China and the Role of the United Nations in the Middle East: Revised Policy," *Asian Survey* 31, no. 3 (March 1991): 255–269.

8. On China's military relations with the Palestinians, see Raphael Israeli, ed., *PLO in Lebanon: Selected Documents* (London: Weidenfeld and Nicolson, 1983), pp. 89, 96, 142–143, 293, 296.

9. Anne Gilks and Gerald Segal, *China and the Arms Trade* (London: Croom Helm, 1985); Daniel L. Byman and Roger Cliff, *China's Arms Sales: Motivations and Implications* (Santa Monica, CA: RAND, 1999).

10. On China's arms sales, see Yitzhak Shichor, "Unfolded Arms: Beijing's Recent Military Sales Offensive," *The Pacific Review* 1, no. 3 (October 1988): 320–330; Shichor, "The Year of the Silkworms: China's Arms Transactions, 1987," in Richard Yang, ed., *SCPS Yearbook on PLA Affairs 1987* (Kaohsiung: Sun Yat-sen Center for Policy Studies, 1988), pp. 153–168.

11. Figures from SIPRI *Arms Transfers Database*. See also the annual reports by Richard F. Grimmett, *Conventional Arms Transfers to Developing Nations*, CRS Report to Congress (Washington, DC: Library of Congress).

12. See, for example, Fan Huitao, Wang Qifei, and Bai Xiaodong, "Dui Yilake zhanzheng lun duoquzhi kongquan de junshi shoudu" [On the Military Measures for Achieving Air Superiority in the Iraq War], *Daodan yu hangtian yunzai jishu* [Missiles and Space Vehicles], no. 5 (2003): 5–9; Xu Derong and Xiang Dongmei, "Dui Yilake zhanzheng de zhengzhi junshi fenxi" [A Political and Military Analysis of the Iraq War], *Haerbin Xueyuan Xuebao* [Journal of Harbin University] 25, no. 5 (May 2004): 28–33. See also, Michael S. Chase, "China's Assessment of the War in Iraq: America's 'Deepest Quagmire' and the Implications for Chinese National Security," *China Brief* (The Jamestown Foundation) 7, no. 17 (September 19, 2007): 8–11.

13. All data adapted from *China Statistical Yearbook*, various years. For an analysis of the reason for this decline, see Zhang Jianwu, "Zhongguo dui zhongdong laowu shuchu de qianjing yu duice" [Prospects and Counter-Measures of China's Labor Service Export to the Middle East], *Xiya Feizhou* [West Asia and Africa], no. 6 (2000), pp. 56–60.

14. Jin Jianhua, "Luexi Zhong'A youqi hezuo" [Brief Analysis on Sino-Arab Oil and Gas Cooperation], *Alabo shijie* [The Arab World], no. 6 (2005): 24–29. See also, Wenran Jiang, "China's Growing Energy Relations with the Middle East," *China Brief* (The Jamestown Foundation) 7, no. 14 (July 11, 2007): 12–14.

15. For example, in August 2008, Angola was China's leading crude oil supplier, followed closely by Saudi Arabia and then Iran. Altogether they supplied nearly 50 percent of China's crude import. PRC, *General Administration of Customs*.

16. Zhao Weiming, "China's Energy Strategy Security Moves It Closer to the Middle East," *The Daily Star* (Beirut), May 12, 2008; Li Weijian, "Zhongdong nengyuan yu Zhongguo de heping jueqi" [Middle Eastern Energy and China's Peaceful Rise], *Dangdai shiyou shihua* [Petroleum and Petrochemical Today] 12, no. 9 (September 2004): 26–28, 38.

17. JianJun Tu, "The Strategic Considerations of the Sino-Saudi Oil Deal," *China Brief* (The Jamestown Foundation) 6, no. 4 (February 15, 2006): 3–5; John Calabrese, "Saudi Arabia and China Extend Ties Beyond Oil," *China Brief* 5, no. 20 (September 27, 2005): 3–6; Ali Husayn Bakir, "Oil and the Future of Saudi-Chinese Relations," *Islam Today*, November 7, 2005.

18. Rhetoric notwithstanding, Chinese intellectuals (and policymakers as well) instinctively associate terrorism with Islam. See, for examples, Ma Ting, "Yisilan shiye lide kongbuzhuyi" [Terrorism in an Islamic Perspective], *Journal of the Second Northwest University for Nationalities* 3 (2004): 96–99; Jiao Pei and Xia Lu, "Yisilan shijie: guoji kongbuzhuyi de zongjiao minzu yinsu fenxi" [The Islamic World: An Analysis of the Religious and National Causes of International Terrorism], *Yinshan Academic Journal* 17, no. 3 (May 2004): 81–84. The Chinese are also aware that much of the international terrorism originates in the Middle East. See Zhang Jinping and Xiao Xian, "Dangdai Zhongdong kongbuzhuyi tedian" [Characteristics of Contemporary Middle Eastern Terrorism], *Arab World* 1 (2001): 10–14.

19. See Cameron S. Brown, "The One Coalition They Craved to Join: Turkey in the Korean War," *Review of International Studies*, no. 34 (2008), pp. 89–108; Füsun Türkmen, "Turkey and the Korean War," *Turkish Studies* 3, no. 2 (Autumn 2002): 161–180; Musret Özselçuk, "The Turkish Brigade in the Korean War," *Revue Internationale d'Histoire Militaire*, no. 46 (1980); John Vander Lippe, "Forgotten Brigade of the Forgotten War: Turkey's Participation in the Korean War," *Middle Eastern Studies* 36, no. 1 (January 2000): 92–102. See also Doğu Türkistan Vakfı Başkanı [president of the East Turkestan Endowment], *M. Rıza Bekin'in Anıları* [Reminiscences of M. Rıza Bekin] (Istanbul: Kastaş Yayınavi, 2005), pp. 30–44.

20. This and the following paragraph draw from Yitzhak Shichor, *Ethnodiplomacy: The Uyghur Hitch in Sino-Turkish Relations*, Policy Studies, No. 53 (Washington, DC: East-West Center, 2009).

21. See John C. K. Daly, "Sino-Turkish Relations Beyond the Silk Road," *China Brief* (The Jamestown Foundation) 7, no. 4 (February 21, 2007): 10–13; Mehmet Ögütçü, "Turkey and China," *Perceptions, Journal of International Affairs* 1 (September–November 1996); and Ögütçü, "Sino-Turkish Relations: Preparing for the Next Century," *China Report* 34, no. 3–4 (1998).

22. Information collected from several sources. See, for example, *Turkish Armed Forces* (Land Forces Equipment), www.turkishworld.multiservers.com/equipment .html; *Jane's Strategic Weapons Systems,* www.janes.com/extracts/extract/jsws /jswsa002.html. See also Wu Gang, "Tuerqi: Zhongguo shangpin jinru Ouzhou de 'tiaoban'" [Turkey: Gangway for the Entry of Chinese Commodities to Europe], *World Market* (March 2002), p. 14.

23. Yitzhak Shichor, *East Wind over Arabia: Origins and Implications of the Sino-Saudi Missile Deal*, China Research Monographs 35 (Berkeley: Center for Chinese Studies, University of California, 1989).

24. Xia Liping, "Cong waijiaobu kaifang dangankan 20 shiji 50 nian Zhong Yi jiechu shimo" [Sino-Israeli Contacts as Seen from Declassified Foreign Ministry Files], *Dangdai Zhongguoshi yenjiu* [Contemporary China History Studies] 12, no. 3 (May 2005): 76–82.

25. To some extent, the Chinese look at Israel's defense industries as a model of successful privatization. Admitting that much progress has been made in China's defense industry toward greater competition, they also say: "Still, we can borrow from Israel's experience in how to use both military and civilian resources, how to maximize domestic and international markets, and how to run market mechanisms." Ren Desheng, "Yisilie guofang gongye fazhan ji qi dui Zhonhguo de qishi" [The Development of Israel's Defense Industry and Its Inspiration for China], *Haerbin gongye daxue xuebao (shehui kexue ban)* [Journal of Harbin Industrial University (Social Science Edition)] 7, no. 5 (September 2005): 36–40.

26. For more details, see the book by Israel's first ambassador to China, E. Zev Sufott, *A China Diary: Towards the Establishment of China-Israel Diplomatic Relations* (London: Frank Cass, 1997).

27. For the most comprehensive study, see John W. Garver, *China and Iran: Ancient Partners in a Post-Imperial World* (Seattle: University of Washington Press, 2006).

28. Editorial, "Observations on the Anti-Iranian Resolutions," *Jomhuri-ye Eslami* [Islamic Republic] (Tehran), October 7, 2008.

29. Li Shaoxian, deputy directory of the China Institute of Contemporary International Relations (CICIR), lecture in Jerusalem, 2005.

30. For example, Alastair Iain Johnston and Robert S. Ross, eds., *New Directions in the Study of China's Foreign Policy* (Stanford, CA: Stanford University Press, 2006), fails to mention the Middle East in the index, let alone devote a chapter to this topic. The same goes for David M. Lampton, ed., *The Making of Chinese Foreign and Security Policy in the Era of Reform, 1978–2000* (Stanford, CA: Stanford University Press, 2001).

31. For example, Tian Yu Cao, ed., *The Chinese Model of Modern Development* (London: Routledge, 2005); Randall Peerenboom, *China Modernizes: Threat to the West or Model for the Rest?* (Oxford: Oxford University Press, 2007).

32. Ebrahim Yazdi, "The Chinese Model," *Tehran Sharq* [Tehran East], February 7, 2004, pp. 1, 4.

# 9

## China and Latin America: Development Challenges and Geopolitical Dilemmas

### *Nicola Phillips*

Like all the other regions under consideration here, Latin America has been drawn squarely into China's emerging strategy in the developing world, particularly since the late 1990s. Yet it is at the same time a rather different relationship from the ones that have been articulated with other developing regions. In a sense, Latin America is less significant than regions such as Africa or Asia in the universe of China's engagements. It is overwhelmingly a relationship based on accelerating economic exchange, but one that remains of slight proportions in the overall trade and investment profiles of both Latin America and China. The Latin American region forms part of the focus of Chinese energy-related strategies, but again, in comparison with other developing regions such as Africa or the Middle East, these relationships play only something of a bit part in China's overall strategy. Equally, the relationship has attracted a great deal of attention for the extent to which China may or may not be encroaching politically, militarily, or ideologically on a region that traditionally has been dominated by US power, but there has never been any attempt to construct either an ideologically driven or geopolitically purposeful strategy in Latin America. In this sense, the importance of Latin America to China, and vice versa, must not be overstated.

In a different sense, however, it is a relationship of intriguing significance in both economic and geopolitical terms, particularly when viewed in the context of the "triangle" between China, the Latin American region, and the United States. This chapter puts forward two central arguments in this respect. First, while China (and most Latin American countries) have steered away from any form of engagement that resembles an overtly ideological or geopolitical agenda, the relationship is fundamentally informed and shaped by geopolitical considerations—namely, the Chinese regime's anxiety to avoid any geopolitical consequences or perception of geopolitical threat to the

United States arising from its expansion in the Western hemisphere. The substantial dilemmas that this imperative poses for its strategy in Latin America have not yet been resolved by the Chinese authorities, which have attempted simply to pursue an ostentatiously nonideological approach.[1] The emerging Sino–Latin American relationship thus takes on a particular importance in considerations of the broader geopolitical implications of China's emergence in developing regions, and indeed the manner in which the Chinese authorities seek to handle that dimension of their global strategy.

The second argument is that the implications for Latin American development of the emergence of China can be seen in important revisions of established development thinking, as well as in a further squeezing of already very constrained development spaces for the majority of the region's economies and societies. However, these implications are not related simply to the emergence of a particular bilateral relationship, but rather to the restructuring of the global economy that has propelled the emergence of China and, in turn, been shaped by the growth of the Chinese economy. The consequences for Latin American development can only properly be grasped in this context. Relying, as most accounts do, on merely a snapshot of China's patterns of contemporary engagement in Latin America yields entirely inadequate understandings of both the nature and the significance of China's expansion for Latin America.

In order to elaborate these arguments, the chapter proceeds in three parts. The first section explores the nature and dimensions of the emerging relationship between China and the Latin American region[2] and lays the groundwork for discussion of the economic dimensions of this relationship in the second section. The third section considers—or reconsiders—the implications of the emerging relationship for Latin American development, and the fourth moves on to explore the implications of these dynamics for the political economy of Latin America–US relations. The final section draws together some conclusions.

## Contours of the Emerging Sino–Latin American Relationship

From a historical perspective, interaction between China and much of Latin America is a very recent development, coinciding with the onset of the growth and liberalization strategy from the 1970s onward. There was contact between China and the region in the late sixteenth century in the context of the burgeoning Pacific trade at the time, and some movement of southern Chinese peasants to work in mines and plantations in South America and the Caribbean in the nineteenth century after the abolition of black slavery,[3] but that is about as much as can be said of the historical context before the twentieth century. Equally, following the formation of the People's Republic of China (PRC) in 1949, there was no "relationship" to speak of between China and Latin America. The virulent anticommunism that prevailed in most of Latin America during the Cold War, pursued in its fiercest forms by brutal right-wing military dictatorships, meant that the region as a whole was not fertile ground for Chinese diplomacy; furthermore, the identification of Latin America as the United States' primary "sphere of influence" in this context meant that the region was clearly off limits for any expansion of Chinese engagement.

The one country with which China did have links during this time was Cuba, which was in fact the first country to recognize the PRC in 1960. Indeed, Latin America started to show up on China's radar screen precisely because of the Cuban revolution in 1959, reflected in the establishment of the Institute of Latin American Studies in Beijing in 1961, along with other international studies programs thereafter that incorporated attention to Latin America. This early interest in Latin America was tied directly to Mao's objective of subverting US dominance and supporting movements of national liberation and anti-imperialism across the developing world.[4] Yet the relationship with Cuba was short-lived, interrupted as it was by the Sino-Soviet split, the decision of the regime of Fidel Castro to align itself with the Soviet Union, and the consequent rapprochement between China and the United States. Even when the reform process was initiated under Deng Xiaoping in the late 1970s and economic development was made the first policy priority, the onset of the debt crisis and severe economic recession across Latin America sidelined the region from the attentions of the Chinese authorities, and it remained on the margins of China's global strategy until well into the 1990s.

The relationship that emerged at that time had a number of dimensions, of a military, political, and economic nature. While much has been made of the first two of these dimensions, particularly among observers worried about the "threat" posed by China to US security interests, in reality they have been of slight importance. In terms of the military projection of China in Latin America, attention has been drawn to such issues as the extent of military contacts between China and Latin American countries, the greater number of visits by Chinese defense officials than their US counterparts to Latin American countries, and the sale of nonlethal equipment to countries in the region.[5] Interactions with such countries as Venezuela and Brazil have been noted as indicative of an expanding Chinese military presence in Latin America during the early part of the 2000s. The relationship with Cuba has inevitably occasioned intense speculation in response to reports that the Chinese have been training significant numbers of Cuban military and civilian officers and selling large quantities of military equipment to the Cuban armed forces. Yet it has also been shown that many of the reported accounts of Chinese involvement in Cuba, military and otherwise, are either exaggerated or false.[6]

The problem with these arguments is that they have generally been presented entirely out of context, in a manner similar, as we shall see, to many analyses of the scale of the economic relationship. In fact, it has been argued persuasively that, since 2000, by far the most notable military expansion in

Latin America has been on the part of the United States, not China. Evidence for this contention is marshalled from the huge numbers of staff devoted to the region based at the US Southern Command (SOUTHCOM) in Miami, the numbers of visits by SOUTHCOM personnel to Latin America, increased deployment by SOUTHCOM in the Caribbean and Latin America, and the military resources, training, and other programs provided to Latin America by the United States.[7] By comparison, Chinese military projection in the region can be considered to be insignificant. Equally, the significant sales of armaments to Venezuela by Russia in 2005 and 2006, and sales to countries in the region of a wide range of equipment and arms by the United States, Saudi Arabia, and numerous European countries, prompts skepticism in response to the more overblown, "hawkish" assessments of China's representation in the region's patterns of military interactions.[8]

In broader security terms, the further move by China that has prompted significant apprehension for the United States has been the purchase of leases on two of the four ports along the Panama Canal. This undoubtedly represents an important arena of investment for China, but as yet, again, there is no evidence to indicate that it is seen by the Chinese authorities as a move of any significant geopolitical consequence, and established dimensions of US control over the canal have not been altered by China's investments.[9]

In terms of political and diplomatic engagement, again China does not occupy an especially high profile, although its presence has gradually expanded. China has been granted observer status in the Organization of American States, the Inter-American Development Bank, the UN Economic Commission for Latin America and the Caribbean, the Latin American Integration Association, and the Latin American Parliament, and frequent meetings have been held since the late 1990s with the Rio Group and the Mercosur.[10] Yet for China the key political and diplomatic issue in the region relates to the question of Taiwan. Half of the countries in the world that do not support the One China policy are located in Latin America and the Caribbean, and an aggressive drive to persuade those countries to switch to break ties with Taiwan has formed a key pillar of China's economic diplomacy in the region, along with the search for supplies of natural resources. Perhaps the most visible episode of this kind of economic diplomacy emerged around September 2008, when it was reported that a deal had been struck in secret between China and Costa Rica, under which China would spend US$300 million purchasing Costa Rican bonds in exchange for Costa Rican agreement to shift diplomatic recognition from Taiwan to China. Reported extensively in the world's media, but confirmed only very reluctantly by Costa Rican and Chinese officials, this agreement was taken as an indication of the willingness of Chinese authorities to use the country's US$1.8 trillion in foreign exchange reserves to further their political and diplomatic agenda, despite assurances that they would not do so.[11] The Chen Shui-bian administration in Taiwan also pursued an aggressive agenda of economic diplomacy to try to counter some of this pressure, but the playing field with China was not a level one, and its efforts yielded few tangible results.[12]

It is in this sense that China's emerging economic relationship with Latin America can be seen as driven by the geopolitical agenda of isolating Taiwan. At the same time, its Latin American strategy has been shaped by the need to avoid perceptions of geopolitical consequences in this emerging relationship in the interests of avoiding confrontation with the United States. It is for this reason that China has stayed well away from any serious political engagement with Colombia, for instance, and has also been lukewarm in its approach to countries like Venezuela and Cuba, making efforts to portray these relationships as driven by economic and energy-related interests, not ideological affinities. Equally, most Latin American countries have shown no interest in a relationship founded on political or ideological interests, and instead have seen the agenda almost entirely in terms of opportunities for export expansion. Yet this has been a tricky line to tread for two reasons. First, China's economic agenda is intimately tied to energy-related priorities, including in countries such as Venezuela, and investment initiatives such as those in the Panama Canal necessarily carry strategic and security-related implications in the region. For the United States as well as the rest of the region, questions and concerns relating to energy security and geopolitical stability are consequently inevitable. Second, China's emergence in Latin America has coincided with a generalized surge in anti-US sentiment, along with the election of left-of-center governments in many of the countries of key interest, especially in the Andean and Central American region. Consequently, it has frequently been difficult to draw clear dividing lines between an economic agenda dominated by the search for supplies of natural resources and enhanced export opportunities, and a pattern of engagement that carries ideological overtones and political consequences.

We will return to this bigger picture at the end of the chapter. For now, let us turn our attention to the dynamics of the economic relationship between Latin America and China.

## Emerging Patterns of Sino–Latin American Trade and Investment

At face value, and as indicated in Tables 9.1 and 9.2, the growth in Chinese trade with Latin America can be said to have boomed since the late 1990s. Total trade increased from around US$200 million in 1975 to US$12.6 billion in 2000, US$26.8 billion in 2003, US$50.5 billion in 2005, and US$102.6 billion in 2007. It must be noted, of course, that when a boom starts from a very low base, arresting levels of expansion do not necessarily mean significant

**Table 9.1    Sino–Latin American Trade: Exports to China and Imports from China (percentages of country totals, selected countries)**

| Country | Exports to China | | | Imports from China | | |
|---|---|---|---|---|---|---|
| | 1995 | 2005 | 2008 | 1995 | 2005 | 2008 |
| Argentina | 3.5 | 6.5 | 12.1 | 2.8 | 8.8 | 11.7 |
| Brazil | 2.7 | 6.8 | 12.5 | 3.5 | 8.3 | 11.5 |
| Chile | 3.2 | 8.1 | 15.5 | 2.3 | 11.3 | 11.9 |
| Colombia | 0.7 | 5.6 | 2.7 | 1.3 | 0.9 | 8.5 |
| Mexico | 0.9 | 3.1 | 1.2 | 0.7 | 1.1 | 7.1 |
| Peru | 2.8 | 8.6 | 14.9 | 7.3 | 11.1 | 10.6 |
| Venezuela | 0.5 | 3.8 | 4.9 | 0.0 | 1.7 | 6.5 |

*Source:* Based on data from International Monetary Fund, *Direction of Trade Statistics.*

levels of overall trade—Sino–Latin American flows reach a level equivalent to only some 5 percent of both China's and the Latin American region's total trade. So one must not get carried away with the scale of commercial interactions between China and Latin America, even though the increase and dynamism of bilateral trade are very striking.

Around 60 percent of China's total trade with Latin America is with Mexico, Brazil, and Chile. Mexico is the most significant destination for Chinese exports, absorbing some 25 percent of the total to the region, followed by Brazil at around 20 percent. Again, the annual average growth rates of exports to these countries in the 2000–2005 period were arresting—respectively, 35.5 percent and 31.6 percent.[13] Conversely, the pattern of imports from Latin America is dominated by Brazil, Chile, and Argentina, with Brazil accounting for around 37.4 percent in 2005. Mexico accounted for only 8.3 percent of the total from the region in this year. At the start of 2006, China had become the second largest export market (behind the United States) for Chile, Peru, and Cuba, and the third largest (behind the European Union) for Brazil. Chile signed a free trade agreement with China in 2006—the only country in Latin America to have done so—and by 2007 China had replaced the United States as the major destination for Chilean exports.

In terms of profile, around 75 percent of Latin American exports to China are raw materials, foodstuffs, and natural resource–based manufactured goods, concentrated particularly in copper, iron ore, nickel, soy, pulp, fishmeal, and sugar. In the mid-2000s, copper represented around 44 percent of Chilean exports to China. Around 57 percent of Argentina's exports were oilseeds, and Brazilian exports are dominated by oilseeds and mineral ores, as well as timber and soybeans.[14] The principal export from Venezuela to China is, of course, oil. An array of cooperation agreements and investment projects have

**Table 9.2  Latin America: Export Shares by Main Destination, Region, and Selected Countries, 2000 and 2007 (percentages of total exports)**

| Country/Region | Latin America and the Caribbean | | China | | Asia-Pacific | | United States | | European Union | |
|---|---|---|---|---|---|---|---|---|---|---|
| | 2000 | 2007 | 2000 | 2007 | 2000 | 2007 | 2000 | 2007 | 2000 | 2007 |
| Latin America and the Caribbean | 16 | 18 | 1 | 6 | 6 | 12 | 60 | 42 | 12 | 15 |
| Argentina | 48 | 39 | 3 | 10 | 8 | 16 | 12 | 8 | 18 | 19 |
| Brazil | 47 | 61 | 0 | 1 | 1 | 12 | 24 | 9 | 17 | 6 |
| Chile | 22 | 16 | 5 | 15 | 29 | 36 | 18 | 13 | 25 | 24 |
| Colombia | 29 | 36 | 0 | 3 | 3 | 6 | 51 | 31 | 14 | 18 |
| Costa Rica | 19 | 25 | 0 | 14 | 3 | 24 | 38 | 25 | 21 | 24 |
| Dominican Republic | 4 | 5 | 0 | 2 | 1 | 6 | 87 | 67 | 6 | 17 |
| Mexico | 3 | 6 | 0 | 1 | 1 | 3 | 89 | 78 | 3 | 6 |
| Peru | 22 | 18 | 7 | 12 | 20 | 24 | 28 | 19 | 21 | 18 |
| Venezuela | 20 | 15 | 0 | 4 | 1 | 5 | 55 | 52 | 5 | 9 |

*Source*: Adapted from Economic Commission for Latin America and the Caribbean (ECLAC), *Latin America and the Caribbean in the World Economy 2007, Trends 2008*.

been elaborated to secure Venezuelan supplies for China, and it was estimated that exports of crude oil no less than doubled between 2005 and 2007 to reach over 200,000 barrels a day, with an agreement put in place in mid-2006 to secure 500,000 barrels a day by 2009.[15] In terms of imports from China, an overwhelming proportion—around 90 percent—consists of manufactured products, the bulk of which are labor-intensive, low-technology, and low-value-added.[16] Key products here are textiles and apparel, footwear, machinery, and plastics. However, the technology component of Chinese exports has rapidly increased since the start of the 2000s, and such sectors as automobiles, auto parts, steel, telecommunications, and electronics have become much more significant in the overall export profile of the Chinese economy, as well as in the profile of exports to Latin America.

Sino–Latin American foreign direct investment (FDI) starts from a similarly low base but again has shown a striking increase, if not as dramatic as in the area of trade. Latin American FDI in China appears to have increased significantly, reaching around 13 percent of total FDI flowing into China in 2003. However, the vast bulk of this investment comes from the tax havens of the Cayman Islands and British Virgin Islands, the latter now representing the second most significant source of investment in China. As such, this is not investment by firms and actors from Latin America itself—indeed, it is likely that Hong Kong and Taiwanese investment, channelled through these tax havens, account for the bulk of these flows.[17] This form of investment "round-tripping" is concealed by bilateral figures indicating investment flows from "Latin America" to "China"—they are in fact reflecting flows of Chinese money to tax havens in Latin America, which is then sent back to China disguised as foreign investment and therefore subject to the incentives and preferences governing external investment flows. (Estimates have put this kind of round-tripping investment at around 40 percent of total [global] flows of FDI to China.[18]) Latin American investment in China is, in reality, minimal, as is Chinese investment in Latin America as a share of overall FDI to the region. In 2007, Latin America accounted for only about 0.08 percent of total FDI flowing into China (while the Cayman Islands alone accounted on average for about 2.9 percent between 2002 and 2007).[19] The same qualification must apply to assessments of Chinese investment in Latin America, a large proportion of which is again accounted for by flows to the offshore tax havens in the Caribbean. Chinese investment in Africa, Asia, and North America has also been greater than in Latin America.

Notwithstanding these important caveats, Chinese investments in Latin America have been increasing since the start of the 2000s, particularly in such areas as railways, oil and gas exploration, communications satellites, and construction. Ecuador has been the largest recipient of Chinese energy investment in Latin America since the end of 2005, when the China National Petroleum Corporation (CNPC) and Sinopec, the major Chinese refining company, purchased Canadian-based Encana assets and gave themselves a 12 percent stake in Ecuador's total oil production. By comparison, at the same point in time, CNPC controlled only 1 percent of Venezuela's oil production, although cooperation and investment in both directions have been steadily increasing.[20] CNPC also operates three oil fields in Venezuela and has a presence in Peru, Colombia, and Brazil.[21] In other indicative areas, in 2005 a joint venture company was set up between China's Minmetals Group and the Chilean national oil company Codelco, guaranteeing supplies of copper to China and financing for Codelco's future projects.[22] In 2008, it was announced that China had effectively taken ownership of the vast Toromocho copper ore mines in Peru, which was intended to provide sufficient copper wire for the electrification of the whole of China.[23] These investment deals have been complemented by an array of cooperation agreements and state-supported strategic alliances in the sectors of most significance to the Chinese development plan.

## Implications for Latin American Development

This thumbnail regional sketch tells us rather little about the real significance of China's economic presence in Latin America. The implications vary considerably across the region, given the nature of production structures and economic profiles. Using very broad brush strokes, the region can be divided into two—South America on the one hand, and Mexico and Central America on the other. In both regions, we are seeing signs of what we might call a "revisionism" in established development thinking as a direct consequence of both the restructuring of the global and regional economy implied by the emergence of China and the specific impacts that have manifested themselves in different parts of Latin America. For most of South America, this revisionism is connected with the apparent boon to exports implied by Chinese demand for raw materials, energy, and natural resource–based products and the slightly curious return to a celebration of resource-based export strategies. For Mexico and parts of Central America, given the scale of competition from China, it has involved a rethinking of development strategies based on competitive labor costs and the notion of "geographical advantage." Let us take each of these parts of the region in turn.

### South America

The overall South American profile is one of capital-intensive industry associated with the processing of natural resources and characterized by low levels of domestic value-added.[24] Both recurrent patterns of macroeconomic instability and overvalued exchange rates across the region have long impeded the development of manufacturing and, in most cases, have reinforced a sustained process of deindustrialization.[25] Within this model, countries such as Argentina and Paraguay thus remain largely dependent on agriculture and, mainly, low value-added resource-based manufactures. Chile and most of the Andean countries have export profiles heavily concentrated in natural resources and, in the case of Chile, higher value-added resource-based products in sectors such as copper, minerals, and fishing. In the case of Venezuela, the key is oil and oil-related products. Thus, South American resource-based exports fit well into patterns of emerging Chinese demand, and in general export similarity indices point to complementarity rather than competition between Chinese and the majority of South American exports in third markets.[26]

Brazil is something of an exception given the importance of manufacturing in its production and export profile, and the scale of competition with China is correspondingly perceived to be much greater. It is significant that some 60 percent of Brazilian exports to China are primary products, while these exports represent only 30 percent of its exports to the rest of the world,[27] indicating a lack of competitiveness and lack of market access for Brazilian manufactured exports in China. Factor endowments are crucial in this scenario, above all the vast supply of cheap labor in China, which translates into average wages around three times lower than in Brazil, and the much higher levels of government intervention in the Chinese economy yield high levels of domestic productive investment and easy access to credit from state banks. Despite developmentalist streaks in Brazilian strategies that differentiate it from the majority of other Latin American countries, the extent of Chinese state support for industrialization outstrips any similar promotion measures in a broadly neoliberal region.[28]

Chile is also rather different from much of the rest of South America, given the extent of the export diversification and upgrading that was achieved from the 1980s onward, and the fact that its economy has been the most competitive in Latin America for some years. In this sense, it has been able to position itself rather more effectively than many countries in the universe of Chinese strategic interests and, as mentioned, is the only country thus far to have signed a trade agreement with China. Nevertheless, the Chilean economy has remained dominated by a single export commodity—in the mid-2000s, copper accounted for 40 percent of exports—and its success looks flimsy by comparison with the growth, diversification, and technological sophistication of the East Asian manufacturing economies.[29] As in the case of Brazil, the combination of factor endowments and the model of domestic productive investment in East Asia has left clear blue water, as it were, between the growth and industrial development records of East Asia and Latin America, even in the cases of Chile and Brazil.

The vigorous expansion of exports to China has been welcomed and celebrated by South American exporters and governments, not least for the fact that Chinese demand has pushed up world prices for primary products following decades of decline in prices, with important positive implications for the terms on which the major resource-based economies in South America are participating in world trade. At the same time, other Asian governments appear to be following the Chinese lead in clamoring to secure supplies of raw materials from Latin America and Africa, in particular.[30] The results of this explosion in demand are already evident: The Latin American and Caribbean region achieved the second largest increase in exports in 2005, after China, explained by the South American economies' specialization in commodity exports and flows of trade in oil and oil-related products.[31] It must be noted that the position of Latin America as a supplier of natural resources to China and Asia is marginal compared with that of Africa; even in terms of oil and despite the expansion of exports from Venezuela, Latin America cannot be seen in any sense as a major supplier to China, even while it is much more important as a destination for Chinese oil investments.[32] Yet it is undoubtedly the case that the emergence of China has presented possibilities for export expansion that have been in short supply for much of South America over recent decades, and indeed has improved markedly the terms of trade for the majority of South American economies.

Nevertheless, it is the concentration of these exports in traditional resource-based sectors that represents the more troubling panorama for Latin American development, especially when put in the context of the longstanding inability of the majority of South American economies to compete in global markets for manufactured, high-technology products, as well as the increasing dominance of China in the US and other markets. As shown in Table 9.3, patterns of Chinese demand for exports from Latin America are based almost entirely on primary products, the demand for processed products and resource-based manufactures being focused significantly more on economies of the Association of Southeast Asian Nations (ASEAN). In this sense, South American economies are in the main subject to sharp competition from Asian economies and are locked into the lower value-added ends of commodity and production chains. The higher one goes in the hierarchy of technological content for natural resource–based products, the greater the gap becomes between the representation of ASEAN and Latin American economies in supplying Chinese demand. It must be noted that Asian economies are linked to the Chinese economy in very specific forms of regional production networks, and the bulk of trade is of an intra-industry variety. Conversely, trade with Latin America in general conforms with traditional patterns of comparative advantage, which, as Mauricio Mesquita Moreira notes, may not be of a growth-enhancing nature.[33]

Looking at the relationship from another angle, the countries of South America in general have faced increasing losses in domestic manufacturing markets as a result of accelerating Chinese imports. Significant losses have occurred even in Brazil, particularly in low-tech sectors such as footwear, but

**Table 9.3   Composition of Chinese Trade with ASEAN and LAIA Countries, 2004 (percentage shares of trade flows of each group of products)**

| Category | Group | Imports | Exports |
|---|---|---|---|
| Primary | ASEAN | 9.0 | 9.0 |
| | LAIA | 13.3 | 0.9 |
| Resource-based manufactures | ASEAN | 15.6 | 11.1 |
| | LAIA | 7.8 | 3.4 |
| Low-technology manufactures | ASEAN | 5.0 | 4.1 |
| | LAIA | 2.4 | 2.2 |
| Intermediate-technology manufactures | ASEAN | 6.2 | 8.4 |
| | LAIA | 1.2 | 3.1 |
| High-technology manufactures | ASEAN | 19.5 | 8.3 |
| | LAIA | 0.6 | 1.7 |
| Other | ASEAN | 4.7 | 3.2 |
| | LAIA | 0.6 | 0.5 |

*Source:* Adapted from ECLAC, *Latin America and the Caribbean in the World Economy, 2005–2006,* on basis of data from UN Commodity Trade Statistics Database.
*Note:* ASEAN: Association of Southeast Asian Nations; LAIA: Latin American Integration Association.

also in most high-tech sectors.[34] This competition has also occasioned a disruption of patterns of manufacturing trade. In 2006, for example, Chinese manufactured exports displaced Argentine exports in the Brazilian market, preferential arrangements in the subregional grouping Mercosur notwithstanding.[35] This has led to a sustained pattern of antidumping suits against China and the invocation of other forms of trade remedies, along with general pressures for greater protectionism in the affected countries. While there has been a considerably larger "adjustment cushion" in Brazil as a result of its greater level of trade diversification and huge economies of scale,[36] fifteen antidumping cases were presented between 1995 and 2004.[37] In the same period, thirty-one cases were initiated by Argentina in relation to Chinese mechanics and transport sectors, and rules of origin were invoked on numerous occasions by the Chilean government in sectors such as textiles, metals, plastics, chemicals, and rubber.[38] It can thus plausibly be argued that competition from China in manufacturing could combine with deficiencies in public policy and differential factor endowments to augur a further squeezing of the space for enhancing industrial competitiveness, reinforcing existing structures of dependence on natural resources.

The extent to which this reinforcement will constitute a serious long-term development problem for the region remains a matter for speculation. But it is nevertheless worth noting that debates about development in South America have, for around half a century, revolved precisely around the imperative of breaking the region's dependence on raw materials for export, especially given the dislocating effects of Dutch disease and other structural problems associated with such a model.[39] The celebration of the export opportunities provided by the emergence of China consequently has something of a strange ring to it, inasmuch as most of the long-established anxiety about this form of dependence on raw materials appears curiously to have disappeared from contemporary discourse. Yet, given what we know from both theory and past experience, the new strategy that is crystallizing around Chinese demand for raw materials is potentially inauspicious for the region's economies. At the very least, this new revisionism in development thinking in South America, reflected in wider debates propelled by China's strategy in the developing world, carries with it dangers of facilitating a return to discourses that play down manufacturing and industrial upgrading in favor of traditional "comparative advantage"–style arguments. We know, moreover, that it was precisely by defying these kinds of arguments and their policy stipulations that the newly industrializing countries of East Asia, and indeed China itself, were able to put in place the conditions for their high-growth development performance.[40]

### Mexico and Central America

The development model that was established in Mexico and parts of Central America over the 1980s and 1990s rested substantially on their integration into vertical flows of trade in manufactured goods associated with assembly and export processing activities, with preferential access to and a competitive niche in the US market. Indeed, the northern part of the region is in general marked by a profound dependence on the US market, which in part explains the negotiation of the North American Free Trade Agreement (NAFTA) and the Dominican Republic–Central American Free Trade Area (DR-CAFTA). Table 9.4 offers an indication of the extent of dependence on the United States across the region. Like China, Mexico also came over the 1990s to specialize in temporary imports for processing and reexport, overwhelmingly to the US market. Mexico and parts of Central America thus have export and production profiles that bring these countries into considerably greater competition with China in third markets, to the extent that Chinese economic expansion has carried often profoundly difficult consequences for this part of the region, particularly Mexico. Indeed, the Mexican deficit with China stood at some US$4.5 billion in 2005—by far the highest in the region. Research in the mid-2000s indicated that over 70 percent of Mexico's exports were under some sort of "threat" from China, including, very directly, the majority of Mexico's fifteen most important export products. Furthermore, it suggested a decline in the technological sophistication of Mexican exports as a result of the loss of export competitiveness to China.[41] In July 2005, China also displaced Mexico as the second largest trading partner of the United States (after Canada).

**Table 9.4    Trade Dependence on the United States, 2008 (selected countries)**

|  | Exports to the United States (US$) | Exports to the United States as Proportion of Total Exports (percent) |
|---|---|---|
| Argentina | 5,616,180,000 | 8.1 |
| Bolivia | 478,273,000 | 11.6 |
| Brazil | 29,157,200,000 | 14.6 |
| Chile | 7,856,140,000 | 11.0 |
| Colombia | 12,574,800,000 | 32.5 |
| Costa Rica | 3,808,450,000 | 23.5 |
| Dominican Republic | 3,715,640,000 | 63.1 |
| Ecuador | 8,666,090,000 | 43.8 |
| El Salvador | 2,098,820,000 | 47.0 |
| Guatemala | 3,383,730,000 | 41.6 |
| Honduras | 3,848,730,000 | 64.2 |
| Mexico | 198,260,000,000 | 73.5 |
| Nicaragua | 1,607,820,000 | 60.6 |
| Panama | 365,364,000 | 17.7 |
| Paraguay | 84,363,600 | 19.7 |
| Peru | 5,580,090,000 | 18.9 |
| Uruguay | 235,636,000 | 3.6 |
| Venezuela | 47,828,400,000 | 41.3 |

*Source:* International Monetary Fund, *Direction of Trade Statistics.*

The impact in Mexico of competition from China has been felt primarily in sectors that are intensive in unskilled labor and in which transport costs are cheap, notwithstanding some continued advantage (or at least absence of disadvantage) in sectors where transport costs are more expensive and the principle of geographical advantage finds some expression. The decline of the Mexican manufacturing sector is evident in terms of its share in overall GDP and employment, and some estimates indicate that from 2000 to 2005, around 250,000 jobs were lost in Mexico as maquiladoras relocated to Asia.[42] For some time, Mexico exported more intermediate- and high-technology-intensive manufactured goods than China,[43] and as such the competition between China and Mexico in third markets was concentrated in low-technology products. However, as noted earlier, the rapid increase in the technology component of Chinese exports and the rapid expansion of exports of electronics, steel, and automobiles, as well as garments, footwear, and the other "staples" of Chinese trade, carried highly significant consequences for Mexican competitiveness in critical product lines, particularly in the US market. Over 55 percent of Mexican exports to the United States between 1990 and 2003 were in the electronics, autos, and auto parts sectors—precisely those sectors into which Chinese competition has emerged with most force.[44] Table 9.5 indicates this displacement of Mexico in the US market from 1999 to 2008. At the same time, competition from China in the Mexican domestic market has been severe. Since 2002, China has been the second largest exporter to Mexico (after the United States), particularly in areas such as auto parts, electronics, toys, and footwear, and local producers have been significantly affected.[45]

For Central America, the panorama has been slightly different. While also heavily dependent on the US market, the principal exports from Central American economies are concentrated in agricultural crops such as bananas, coffee, tropical fruits, sugar, and so on. As such, export profiles are much less similar to those of China than in the Mexican case. Chinese penetration of Central American domestic markets has also been much less pronounced.[46] However, one of the arenas in which competition from China has been felt particularly sharply in both Central American countries and Mexico is in the textiles and apparel sectors. China is now the largest exporter of apparel outside the Organisation for Economic Cooperation and Development (OECD), accounting with India for the bulk of apparel exports from non-OECD to OECD countries. Through the 1980s and the 1990s, the Central American and Caribbean textiles and apparel sectors had benefited from the combination of the provisions of the Multi-Fibre Arrangement (MFA) and the strong inclination in the United States toward outsourcing functions at the lower value-added ends of the production chain. But with the ending of the MFA and the gradual lifting of restrictions under the terms of the Agreement on Textiles and Clothing (ATC), the multilateral lifting of import restrictions on Chinese apparel exports under the terms of China's accession in 2001 to the World Trade Organization (WTO), and increased relocations by US textile firms to the special economic zones in China

**Table 9.5   Exports to the United States from China and Mexico, 1999–2008**

| Year | China | | Mexico | |
|------|----------------------|---------------|----------------------|---------------|
|      | Exports (US$ billion) | Change (%) | Exports (US$ billion) | Change (%) |
| 1999 | 42.0  |       | 120.4 |      |
| 2002 | 70.1  | 66.9  | 141.9 | 17.9 |
| 2005 | 163.3 | 133.0 | 183.9 | 29.6 |
| 2008 | 273.1 | 67.2  | 198.3 | 7.8  |

*Source:* International Monetary Fund, *Direction of Trade Statistics.*

and elsewhere, exporters in the Caribbean Basin (including Mexico) have been among the most visible losers in the global textiles and apparel industries.[47] They became exposed increasingly to the full force of competition from textiles from the "giants" of China, India, Bangladesh, Pakistan, and so on—a competition waged primarily on the terrain of labor costs, as Table 9.6 illustrates.

At the end of the ATC in January 2005, US apparel imports from China increased by 64 percent, while imports from Latin America and the Caribbean declined by 1.5 percent.[48] The force of this competition from increased Chinese exports prompted both the United States and European Union (EU) to impose quota restrictions on Chinese apparel imports in late 2005. The side-effect of this protection of US and EU domestic markets was a certain temporary sheltering of the smaller textiles and apparel exporters in Latin America from the potentially devastating effects of a free-trade regime in these sectors. But the issue remains to be resolved, and China's clear objective in the WTO is to achieve full liberalization in the apparel sector. At the same time, bilateral production-sharing arrangements between the United States and parts of Latin America, such as the Caribbean Basin Initiative, are coming to an end. The United States and other retailers consequently have access to direct imports from the big Asian suppliers. For Latin American (and Caribbean) producers, this represents the severe contraction of the niche formerly occupied in supply chains and in the US market. The DR-CAFTA agreement goes some way to protecting the position of Central American countries in the US market, but, taken together with the multilateral elimination of quotas, the terms of the agreement have been calculated to signify a potential 50 percent cut in the expansion of Central American textiles and clothing exports to the United States.[49]

**Table 9.6   Apparel Manufacturing Cost by Country (US$)**

| Country of Origin | Total Manufacturing Cost |
| --- | --- |
| China | 1.12 |
| Nicaragua | 1.50 |
| Dominican Republic | 1.70 |
| Honduras | 1.70 |
| Guatemala | 1.80 |
| El Salvador | 1.85 |
| Costa Rica | 2.00 |
| Mexico | 2.20 |
| United States | 5.00 |

*Source:* Devlin, Estevadeordal, and Rodríguez-Clare, *The Emergence of China: Opportunities and Challenges for Latin America and the Caribbean,* Inter-American Development Bank, 2006, on basis of data from the Institute for the Integration of Latin America and the Caribbean: Integration, Trade, and Hemispheric Issues Division (INT/ITD).

*Note:* Amounts shown assume that it takes 20 minutes to cut, sew, and finish a dress shirt for the US market.

To be sure, not all Central American countries have lost out in such dramatic terms to China, and indeed not all parts of the Mexican textiles sector have been affected so negatively. While countries like El Salvador have fit the pattern described above, Nicaragua, for example has in fact become the second fastest growing exporter of apparel to the United States, assisted by the terms of the DR-CAFTA and the lowest labor costs in the region. Some industrial clusters in Mexico have also retained their market position. But the general pattern is one of a combination of shifts in multilateral rules governing trade in textiles, changes in bilateral arrangements with the United States, and the onslaught of huge competition from China and Asia (which is likely only to grow as pressure increases in the WTO for full liberalization), creating severe competitive pressures for the Latin American textiles sector.

These trends together indicate increasing pressure on a development model based on export-oriented growth and, in large part, low-cost manufacturing, with few clear indications yet of what might take its place. Similar consequences have been observed in the sub-Saharan African textiles industry, undermining the present viability and future prospects for export-oriented manufacturing in that region.[50] At the same time, these trends have called into question the notion of geographical advantage as the foundation for development strategies.[51] In sectors such as the auto industry, Mexico's geographical proximity to the US market has remained of pivotal importance, due to the constraints on transport costs; in other sectors, the advantage has been substantially eroded by the increasing global penetration of Chinese exports. In any case, it has been suggested that transport costs (and hence geography) do not constitute a particular advantage for the region inasmuch as the unit values of goods shipped from China and East Asia tend to be higher than those from Latin America, compensating for much of the difference in transport costs.[52] For the northern part of Latin America, in this sense, the foundations of established development strategies are undergoing a process of potentially significant undermining, exacerbating the pronounced shortcomings of those strategies and already low and precarious levels of overall competitiveness and performance.

## The Latin America–United States Relationship

What does all this mean for the political economy that structures relations between the United States and Latin America? One of the arguments that is often advanced in this respect relates to the way in which the impact on Latin America of the slowdown in the US economy and the weakening of US demand is compensated by the expansion of demand in China and its impact on commodity prices.[53] Other arguments see the surge in Latin American economic interest in China—particularly in South America—as a reflection of the languid state of contemporary relations between the United States and Latin America. Quite apart from the commercial opportunities arising from the opening up of a market of this size and the particular pattern of demand that attends the Chinese model of industrialization, China is often presented as filling a developmental gap left by the United States.[54] US investment in Latin America has been steadily declining as US corporations have focused their strategies predominantly on the emerging markets of Asia (including China), and the burgeoning US deficit situation precludes any serious rectification in the short term of the neglect that many perceive as having characterized US engagement with the region over recent years. In this context, the potential of Chinese investment in infrastructure, in particular, has often been noted as valuable for many Latin American economies. As we have seen, Venezuela and other natural resource–rich countries have been a particular focus in this regard.

Such interpretations of China's importance for Latin America are only very partial, for the simple reason that the economic relationship with the United States remains by far the most important for the region. While aggregate figures for the region as a whole do indeed indicate the offsetting by China of the effects of slowdown in the United States, this mechanism does not work for the majority of the most dependent economies in the north of the region. At the same time, as our discussion has highlighted, Chinese investment in Latin America is still profoundly limited; trade is far more important, but even then China accounts for only some 5 percent or so of total Latin American trade. In short, the notion that China fills either the gaps in US investment in the region or the limitations of access to the US market finds little justification, inasmuch as overwhelmingly the foremost economic relationship for Latin America remains that with the United States, with but a handful of exceptions in the Southern Cone, which have more diversified export and investment profiles.

The most pressing concern, in this light, relates to the potential displacement of Latin American competitiveness in the US market. While the possibilities for export diversification have been celebrated in various countries of South America that operate with relatively less pronounced structures of dependence on the US market (Argentina, Brazil, Chile), as shown in Table 9.4, the competitive threat arising from China in the US market has been felt keenly in many North American economies, manifested above all in the massive displacement of key Mexican exports in the US market. The potential (further) diversion of investment away from the Americas to Asia is also seen as a considerable challenge to Latin American development strategies, and there is certainly enough evidence to suggest that these perceptions are not entirely ill-founded. Nevertheless, China and Latin America do not rely on the same sources of FDI—a key factor in determining the potential for diversion—and for the only two countries that invest significantly in both, the

United States and Japan, available evidence reveals no correlation between expanding flows to China and declining flows to Latin America.[55]

However, this picture becomes more complex when we think beyond stylized depictions of China's economic rise, which miss a crucial point: China's pattern of growth is fueled primarily by the production and investment strategies of companies in the developed world, which in turn are premised largely on demand in markets in the developed world.[56] It is clear that Chinese industrialization has been driven largely by investment from Asia, and particularly from "Chinese Asia." Yet global and regional production structures are much more complex than this statement would suggest. Let us make the point with an example: Around 75 percent of China's computer-related products are produced by Taiwanese companies, and around 70 percent of Taiwanese computer-related products are based on original equipment manufacturing contracts with foreign firms, overwhelmingly from the United States and Japan. As such, we need to understand China's computer industry and other sectors as representing only the final stage in a *global* production process—the assembly hub of a wider regional production network—which is not adequately grasped when one takes at face value the bilateral investment and trade figures that show Taiwan as the source of investment in China, or China as the exporter to the rest of the world.[57]

By focusing on the global production and value chains into which particular parts of the Chinese economy are inserted, and on the global production structures that fuel Chinese export growth, we can draw a more complex but vastly more revealing picture of the implications of China's rise for Latin America, and indeed the emerging dynamics among Latin America, the United States, and China.[58] First, the challenges for Latin American development arise not so much from China as from Latin American economies' modes of insertion into global production structures. Concentrating on China misses a key point about the new demands of competitiveness, which for Latin America and other developing regions relate precisely to their position in global production and value chains. In other words, the key issue is not a "bilateral" relationship, but rather the place that developing regions occupy in the global structures and processes that condition their development prospects, and which have been (and continue to be) restructured by the emergence of key sites of economic activity in China and Asia.

Second, competition from China is fueled, in a variety of sectors, by investment from the "developed" world, including from US firms. Arguments that the emergence of China fills developmental gaps left by the United States are thus simplistic and misleading, inasmuch as US production and investment strategies, in the context of a wider global economic restructuring, are pivotal to the development predicament in which many Latin American and Caribbean countries find themselves. Again, a massively simplified emphasis on a bilateral relationship between the United States and Latin American economies, or between the United States and China, misses entirely the complexity of contemporary production chains and the manner in which all three of these economies and regions are inserted into them. In other words, by focusing solely on statistics measuring direct investment, say, from the United States to Brazil, or from China to Brazil, we have no sense of the chain from which this investment emerged, and the manner in which US investment is deeply embedded in the processes that produce Chinese overseas investment, and vice versa. Arguments that the economic relationship between the United States and Latin America is thus undermined or threatened by the emergence of China are consequently redundant, as are assertions that a relationship with China represents an alternative to traditional forms of economic dependence on the United States, such as those made frequently by President Hugo Chávez of Venezuela and others.

Yet, as we have seen, the question of immediate dependence on the US market is of profound consequence for many parts of Latin America, and it is in part for this reason that many countries across the region have been eager to enter into bilateral trade negotiations with the United States. But the further impact of the emergence of China may well be a contraction of the possibilities for the successful negotiation of bilateral or regional free trade arrangements, inasmuch as one of the visible trends in the United States itself has been a growing decline in public and political support for trade since the start of the decade. The primary reasons for this decline are uniformly cited as the emerging "threat" from the Chinese economy, together with the experience of NAFTA. Undoubtedly, the steady growth in the US trade deficit, which reached record highs in 2005 and 2006 (US$765,267 million in the latter) and is fueled primarily by rising Chinese imports, has sharpened still further the political sensitivity of the trade agenda.[59] An important implication of the emergence of China for Latin America may thus materialize through the mechanisms of *domestic* politics of reactions to China in the United States, with the effect that possibilities for safeguarding the region's most important economic relationship, particularly under the additional pressures of multilateral liberalization commitments, may well be progressively compromised.

## Conclusion

The Latin American region fits squarely into China's global strategy in a number of respects: as a supplier of natural resources and energy, as an export platform for enhanced access to the US market, and as the key arena for diplomatic goals associated with the Taiwan question. We have seen that it is by no means as significant to China's strategy as other developing regions, such as Asia and Africa, and is not an important energy supplier in comparison with regions such as the Middle East or Central Asia. Equally, the emerging relationship with

China has not altered the extent to which the economic and geopolitical structure of the Americas is conditioned by US power and dominance.

Yet this chapter has argued that the relationship is one of key importance for its broader context in two senses. First, it has wrought significant changes, positive and negative, in terms of trade and investment for Latin American economies, and the consequent shifts in development thinking are likely to be of significant long-term consequence for the societies of the region. I have argued here that the impact of the emergence of China and the attendant restructuring of the global economy represents a contraction of development space in both the north and the south of the region, which may carry inauspicious longer-term prospects for a region already characterized by poor development performance and massive social inequalities over several decades. The precise contours of these consequences naturally vary between economies, depending on the nature of prevailing structures, forms, and levels of sectoral competitiveness, and particular distributions of factor endowments. The adaptive capacity of the larger and more diversified economies, such as Chile or Brazil, may for these reasons be rather higher than those of some of the smaller economies, which remain more dependent on raw materials and low value-added resource-based products. Yet we have also shown that, even for these more diversified economies, the prospects for competing effectively with China and East Asia in general, or moreover for fashioning a new, competitive mode of insertion into restructured production and value chains, remain at present highly complicated. Comparatively low levels of domestic productive investment, technological sophistication, and access to credit constitute some of the most salient contrasts between East Asian and Latin American economies, and indeed some of the highest barriers to addressing effectively the new competitive challenges in the changing global economy.

Second, the perceived need to avoid geopolitical consequences that may arouse tension with the United States is indicative of the potentially tricky terrain that Latin America represents for China. Even when occasioned by investment strategies rather than overt political or geopolitical maneuverings, the long-term agenda and consequences of Chinese incursions into the Western Hemisphere have been subject to anxious (and occasionally alarmist) scrutiny in the United States. Latin America in this sense represents an intriguing microcosm of the geopolitical tensions and dilemmas that are intrinsic to China's wider strategy in the developing world.

## Notes

1. Xiang Lanxin, "An Alternative Chinese View," in Riordan Roett and Guadalupe Paz, eds., *China's Expansion into the Western Hemisphere: Implications for Latin America and the United States* (Washington, DC: Brookings Institution, 2008), pp. 44–58.

2. The Latin American region is here defined as including South America, Central America, and Mexico, but as excluding the Caribbean. A detailed account and evaluation of the relationship between the Caribbean and China can be found in Gregory T. Chin, "China and the Small States of the Caribbean: Responding to Vulnerabilities, Securing Developmental Space," paper presented at the Graduate Institute of International Relations, University of the West Indies, Trinidad, February 8, 2008.

3. Jiang Shixue, "The Chinese Foreign Policy Perspective," in Roett and Paz, eds., *China's Expansion*, p. 27.

4. Xiang, "An Alternative Chinese View," p. 47.

5. General Brantz J. Craddock, statement to the hearing on "Fiscal Year 2006 National Defense Authorization Budget Request" before the Armed Services Committee of the House of Representatives, March 9, 2005. Also see June Teufel Dreyer, "The China Connection," China–Latin America Task Force, Center for Hemispheric Policy, University of Miami, March–June 2006, pp. 6–7.

6. William Ratliff, "The Global Context of a Chinese 'Threat' in Latin America," China–Latin America Task Force, Center for Hemispheric Policy, University of Miami, March–June 2006, pp. 12–13.

7. Juan Gabriel Tokatlian, "A View from Latin America," in Roett and Paz, eds., *China's Expansion*, pp. 67–68.

8. Ibid., p. 69.

9. Ibid., pp. 69–70.

10. Jiang, "The Chinese Foreign Policy Perspective," p. 35.

11. See, for example, "Beijing Uses Forex Reserves to Target Taiwan," *Financial Times,* September 11, 2008; "Cash Helped China Win Costa Rica's Recognition," *Financial Times,* September 13, 2008. It was reported by the *Financial Times* that the agreement had included a clause obliging the Costa Rican authorities to take "necessary measures to prevent the disclosure of the financial terms of this operation and of Safe [the State Administration of Foreign Exchange] as a purchaser of these bonds to the public." Under pressure from media attention, statements were eventually issued by the Costa Rican Ministry of Foreign Affairs, which attempted to justify the failure to disclose the information and defend the agreement. See "Aclaración obligada ante información de prensa sobre compra de títulos de deuda interna denominados en dólares por parte de la República Popular China" and "Establecimiento de relaciones diplomáticas con la República Popular China ha resultado beneficioso para el país," statements dated September 10, 2008 (www.rree.go.cr).

12. For a detailed discussion, see Daniel P. Erikson and Janice Chen, "China, Taiwan and the Battle for Latin America," *The Fletcher Forum of World Affairs* 31, no. 2 (2007): 76–80.

13. Enrique Dussel Peters, "What Does China's Integration to the World Market Mean for Latin America? The Mexican Experience," in Diego Sánchez-Ancochea and Kenneth C. Shadlen, *The Political Economy of Hemispheric Integration: Responding to Globalization in the Americas* (Basingstoke, UK: Palgrave, 2008), p. 65.

14. Dussel Peters, "What Does China's Integration Mean?" p. 73.

15. Luisa Palacios, "Latin America as China's Energy Supplier," in Roett and Paz, eds., *China's Expansion*, p. 182.

16. See Sanjaya Lall and John Weiss, "China's Competitive Threat to Latin America: An Analysis for 1990–2002," *Oxford Development Studies* 33, no. 2 (2005): 163–194; Rhys Jenkins, Enrique Dussel Peters, and Mauricio Mesquita Moreira, "The Impact of China on Latin America and the Caribbean," *World Development* 36, no. 2 (2008), pp. 235–253.

17. Shaun Breslin, "Power and Production: Rethinking China's Global Economic Role," *Review of International Studies* 31, no. 4 (2005): 744.

18. Xiao Geng, "Round-Tripping Foreign Direct Investment in the People's Republic of China: Scale, Causes and Implications," Research Paper No. 58, Asia Development Bank Institute, Tokyo, July 2004.

19. Economic Commission for Latin America and the Caribbean, *Economic and Trade Relations Between Latin America and Asia-Pacific: The Link with China*, document prepared for the 2nd Latin America–China Business Summit, Harbin, Heilongjiang, October 21–22, 2008.

20. Palacios, "Latin America as China's Energy Supplier," pp. 178, 185.

21. Ibid., pp. 179–180.

22. Chung-Chian Teng, "Hegemony or Partnership: China's Strategy and Diplomacy Toward Latin America," in Joshua Eisenman, Eric Heginbotham, and Derek Mitchell, eds., *China and the Developing World: Beijing's Strategy for the Twenty-First Century* (Armonk, NY: M. E. Sharpe, 2007), pp. 93, 100–101.

23. John Simpson, "Peru's 'Copper Mountain' in Chinese Hands," *BBC News,* June 18, 2008. The return on this investment is expected to be 2,000 percent.

24. Nicola Phillips, *The Southern Cone Model: The Political Economy of Regionalist Capitalist Development in Latin America* (London: Routledge, 2004).

25. Mauricio Mesquita Moreira, "Fear of China: Is There a Future for Manufacturing in Latin America?" *World Development* 35, no. 3 (2006): 358–359.

26. Robert Devlin, Antoni Estevadeordal, and Andrés Rodríguez-Clare, *The Emergence of China: Opportunities and Challenges for Latin America and the Caribbean* (Washington, DC: Inter-American Development Bank, 2006), pp. 117–123.

27. Rhys Jenkins, Enrique Dussel Peters, and Mauricio Mesquita Moreira, "The Economic Impact of China on Latin America—An Agenda for Research," paper presented at the 7th Annual Global Development Conference, preconference workshop on *Asian and Other Drivers of Global Change*, St. Petersburg, January 18–19, 2006, p. 12.

28. See ibid., p. 359; Phillips, *The Southern Cone Model*, pp. 70–74.

29. Mauricio Mesquita Moreira and Juan Blyde, "Chile's Integration Strategy: Is There Room for Improvement?" IADB-INTAL-ITD Working Paper No. 21, Inter-American Development Bank, Washington, DC, March 2006.

30. Park Yong Soo, president of the state-run Korea Resources Corporation, is reported to have stated that "within a few years there is likely to be a 'war' to develop raw materials . . . [and] China is challenging aggressively," *New York Times*, November 20, 2004.

31. UN Economic Commission for Latin America and the Caribbean (ECLAC), *Latin America and the Caribbean in the World Economy, 2005–2006* (Santiago, Chile: ECLAC, 2006), p. 31.

32. Palacios, "Latin America as China's Energy Supplier."

33. Mesquita Moreira, "Fear of China," p. 369.

34. Jenkins, Dussel Peters, and Mesquita Moreira, "The Impact of China on Latin America and the Caribbean," p. 242.

35. Carol Wise and Cintia Quiliconi, "China's Surge in Latin American Markets: Policy Challenges and Responses," *Politics and Policy* 35, no. 3 (2007): 410–438.

36. Ibid., p. 434.

37. Scott Kennedy, "China's Porous Protectionism: The Changing Political Economy of Trade Policy," *Political Science Quarterly* 120, no. 3 (2005): 413.

38. See Francisco E. González, "Latin America in the Economic Equation—Winners and Losers: What Can Losers Do?" in Roett and Paz, eds., *China's Expansion*, p. 153.

39. *Dutch disease* refers to the process of currency appreciation that is frequently associated with large inflows of revenues from natural resources, leading to declines in the competitiveness of manufacturing sectors, export growth, and overall economic performance. While most commonly used in discussions of natural resources–based economies, the term is used to refer more generally to the implications of significant inflows of foreign currency of whatever provenance.

40. Ha-Joon Chang, *Kicking Away the Ladder: Development Strategy in Historical Perspective* (London: Anthem Press, 2002).

41. Kevin P. Gallagher, Juan Carlos Moreno-Brid, and Roberto Porzecanski, "The Dynamism of Mexican Exports: Lost in (Chinese) Translation?" *World Development* 36, no. 8 (2008): 1365–1380.

42. David Hale, "China y América Latina," *Revista Poder*, June 11, 2005, cited in Daniel Lederman, Marcelo Olarrreaga, and Isidro Soloaga, "The Growth of China and India in World Trade: Opportunity or Threat for Latin America and the Caribbean?" Policy Research Working Paper No. 4320, The World Bank, August 2007, p. 2.

43. Jenkins, Dussel Peters, and Mesquita Moreira, "The Economic Impact of China on Latin America," p. 23.

44. González, "Latin America in the Economic Equation," p. 167, fn 35.

45. Ibid., p. 157. More research is also needed into the connections between penetration of Mexican domestic markets and penetration of the US market, inasmuch as it seems likely that at least a proportion of investment in the former is as a platform stage in the production chain for subsequent export.

46. Ibid., pp. 156–157.

47. Tony Heron, "The Ending of the Multifibre Arrangement: A Development Boon for the South," *European Journal of Development Research* 18, no. 1 (2006): 1–21.

48. Mesquita Moreira, "Fear of China," p. 367.

49. Alvin Hilaire and Yongzheng Yang, "The United States and the New Regionalism/Bilateralism," IMF Working Paper WP/03/206, International Monetary Fund, Washington, DC, October 2003, pp. 15–16.

50. Raphael Kaplinsky and Mike Morris, "Do the Asian Drivers Undermine Export-Oriented Industrialization in SSA?" *World Development* 36, no. 2 (2008): 254–273; for a broader discussion, also see Raphael Kaplinsky, *Globalization, Poverty, and Inequality* (Cambridge, UK: Polity, 2005).

51. On this notion in the Mexican context, see Carol Wise, "Great Expectations: Mexico's Short-Lived Convergence Under NAFTA," Working Paper No. 15, Centre for International Governance Innovation (CIGI), January 2007.

52. Devlin, Estevadeordal, and Rodríguez-Clare, *The Emergence of China*; Robert Devlin, "China's Economic Rise," in Roett and Paz, eds., *China's Expansion*, p. 139.

53. UN ECLAC, *Latin America and the Caribbean*, pp. 27–28.

54. Riordan Roett, "Relations Between China and Latin America/the Western Hemisphere," statement before the Subcommittee on the Western Hemisphere, House International Relations Committee, US Congress, April 6, 2005.

55. Devlin, Estevadeordal, and Rodríguez-Clare, *The Emergence of China*, pp. 159–161; Kevin P. Gallagher and Roberto Porzecanski, "China Matters: China's Economic Impact in Latin America," *Latin American Research Review* 43, no. 1 (2008): 195.

56. Breslin, "Power and Production," p. 745.

57. Breslin, "Power and Production," pp. 744–748.

58. Nicola Phillips, "China and the New Global Economy: Is Development Space Disappearing for Latin America and the Caribbean?" in Andrew F. Cooper and Jorge Heine, eds., *Which Way Latin America? Hemispheric Politics Meets Globalisation* (Tokyo: United Nations University Press, forthcoming).

59. Nicola Phillips, "The Limits of 'Securitization': Power, Politics and Process in US Foreign Economic Policy," *Government and Opposition* 42, no. 2 (2007): 181–212.

# 10

## China's Rise, Global Identity, and the Developing World

### Lowell Dittmer

The People's Republic of China (PRC) began as a utopian experiment in revolutionary socialism and an ambitious innovator in the theory and practice of political-economic development. The developing world very early became a central political reference group in China's national self-definition and has remained so ever since, even as the political relevance of the international Communist movement began to fade in the waning decades of the twentieth century. China's developing world identification has been rhetorically consistent while the political semantics of that identification has evolved over time. It is an interesting question why such an identity should have such a long rhetorical half-life even as both parties distanced themselves over time in diverse ways from the shared empirical experiences on which the bond was originally based. To Beijing, such language is to some degree a performative utterance, encouraging and helping to define a constituency to which it can appeal for support in various international projects requiring international support. Ignored since the Cold War by the self-absorbed advanced democracies, much of the developing world has welcomed Beijing's revival of interest in their development without too much concern about the motives from which it stems. In this book, we have attempted to dissect this language and its political implications as it has been applied to the various components of the new developing world. And without detracting from the sincerity of the rhetoric that has guided the emergent relationship, we have also found interesting variations over time and space.

These concluding reflections about the aggregate import of what we have learned are divided thematically rather than geographically into three sections. In the first, we look at China's approach to the developing world in historical context, seeking to trace its developmental path and to analyze the reasons for its continuing adherence to that path despite periodic course corrections. In the second, we revisit the economic dimension of China's growing integration with the developing economies, illustrating the linkages to domestic economic development as well as to Beijing's theorizing about how the developing world can most efficiently catch up with the developed. Third, we inquire whether there is still a grand strategic political vision informing China's involvement with the developing world linking it to Beijing's perceived material or ideal national interests, as there was during the Maoist era.

## History

The People's Republic of China identified itself as both revolutionary and developing ever since its postliberation appearance on the world stage, embracing a dual identity as member of both the Communist bloc and the Third World.[1] Beijing initially endorsed the bipolar, "two-camp" conception of a world starkly divided between socialism and capitalism first articulated by Andrei Zhdanov and then echoed by John Foster Dulles, but Mao Zedong qualified this as early as 1946 (in an interview with Anna Louise Strong) to include a vast "intermediate zone" of developing, politically indeterminate countries harboring great revolutionary potential. In 1946, Liu Shaoqi, identifying China as "a semi-feudal, semi-colonial country in which vast numbers of people live at the edge of starvation," asserted that many other countries were in the same situation and that the course chosen by China would be the most relevant model for them to adopt to affect their own revolutionary breakthroughs. Three years later, at the Conference of Trade Unions of Asia and Oceania in Beijing, he elaborated further on the international relevance of the Chinese model, urging the people of all colonial and semicolonial countries to embrace the path of armed struggle. The program adopted by the Chinese People's Political Consultative Council in 1949 as the basis for New China's foreign policy called for a struggle against imperialism and for independence, democracy, and peace, asserting that the PRC belonged to the world camp of peace and democracy and was fighting with the revolutionary forces against imperialist aggression for lasting peace. Still frozen out of the UN and other international organizations, China thus identified with this collection of some 130 developing nations (comprising nearly 80 percent of UN General Assembly membership) even before it had become a self-conscious grouping. China's focus was always less on what it was and more on what it could become, perceiving its potential significance as the natural constituency of a world revolution of the "wretched of the earth." There was thus always some normative tension between the Third World as the aggregation of weak, poor, newly independent postcolonial countries that it actually was and as the revolutionary cynosure the PRC wished and hoped it to be.

China was first in the Communist world to recognize and appreciate the ideological and strategic importance of this emergent grouping, defined not only as fellow victims of imperialism, the highest stage of capitalism, but as poor or economically underdeveloped, non-Western, nonwhite, and southern. In the early 1950s, the PRC deemed violent socialist revolution an indispensable gateway to further development. In this sense, China still adhered to the two-camp theory: the Third World might be accredited only to the extent that it graduated into the Second World. Yet by the mid-1950s, Beijing had broadened its ideological horizons. In 1954, China, along with India and Burma, formulated the famous Panchsheel, or Five Principles of Peaceful Coexistence (FPPC): mutual respect for sovereignty and territorial integrity, mutual nonaggression, mutual noninterference in internal affairs, equality and mutual benefit, and peaceful coexistence. The first conference of Afro-Asian countries, held at Bandung, Indonesia, in 1955, endorsed and publicized this formulation, affirming Beijing's solidarity with the developing world. Zhou Enlai now refrained from publicly expostulating the need for violent world revolution, urging the colonial powers to free all their remaining colonies (voluntarily) within fifteen years, even proclaiming his country's willingness to start negotiations with the United States for the exchange of Korean prisoners of war, the status of Taiwan, and other chronic roadblocks.[2] The Eighth Congress of the Chinese Communist Party (CCP) in 1956 officially endorsed the FPPC as the basis for establishing and developing relations with the new nations in Africa and Asia. "There are a number of countries in Asia and Africa which have shaken off their colonial bondage and achieved national independence," the report to the Eighth National Party Congress stated. "These nationally independent countries, our great neighbor India included, have a total population of more than 600 million, or one-fourth of the human race. The overwhelming majority of these countries are all pursuing a peaceful neutral foreign policy. They are playing a growing role in world affairs. . . . The friendship and cooperation between the socialist countries and the nationally independent countries conform not only to their common interest but to the interest in world peace as well."[3] Following this line, the PRC supported the first Indochina War in Vietnam and the Algerian and Cuban national liberation wars, condemned the Anglo-French-Israeli attack on Egypt in the 1956 Suez Crisis, supported the Iraqi Revolution, and endorsed various proposals for replacing the bipolar alliance structure with some form of inclusive collective security. The FPPC have been reaffirmed in the preambles of the 1975, 1978, and 1982 state constitutions.

There were, however, certain unresolved contradictions in Maoist developing world policy, which tended to shift over time from one aspect of these contradictions to another based on the international correlation of forces and Beijing's domestic needs at the time. As noted, one of the central contradictions reflected China's own dual identity: socialist or developing? If the new nation in question were developing and also socialist, the international relationship was "fraternal," based on class solidarity; if it were, however, under-developed but not (yet) socialist, the appropriate PRC policy was "united front" with the regime in the achievement of limited short-term objectives. Of course "fraternal" relations were in the latter case still feasible with the working people of that country, more so with its constituent Communist Party, in pursuit of shared world revolutionary interests. Nevertheless a non-Communist government in even a developing country was considered inherently exploitative, part of a neoimperialist world system and hence ultimately to be overthrown by the indigenous working classes, whom the PRC was bound in principle to support. Support for revolutionaries in a struggle against their government was likely to be viewed by said government as clearly inconsistent with the FPPC. Thus these two formulas for cooperation with developing world countries could clash, as they did in 1965, when Zhou Enlai, on a visit to Dar es Salaam, proclaimed that Africa was ripe for revolution, to the dismay of his hosts and indeed all postcolonial but nonsocialist African governments. China's commitment to world revolution coexisted uneasily with its FPPC pledge to respect national sovereignty and to not interfere in the internal affairs of other countries.

This "contradiction" between revolution and united front cooperation was sharpened by Beijing's increasingly militant international behavior as the Sino-Soviet ideological rift widened in the 1960s and 1970s. World revolutionary policy was of course one of the central issues in the ideological dispute between Beijing and Moscow, as both countries vied to support national liberation wars throughout the developing world. Although China could not hope to compete with the USSR in terms of material assistance to developing nations, it was able to compensate to some extent in the uncompromising purity of its commitment to revolution. Thus, in a break with the more moderate rhetoric of the 1950s (including the FPPC), Beijing decreed in 1962, "It is indisputable that peaceful coexistence is wrong, anti-Marxist, anti-Leninist, for it actually means continuous officious subservience, continuous compromise, continuous concessions to imperialism."[4] In 1964, Mao refined his conception of the intermediate zone between the two "camps" to discriminate between the first tier (developed nonsocialist countries such as France) and the second tier of developing countries, and China's diplomatic policies toward the developing world began to discriminate between "revolutionary" developing regimes (e.g., Nepal, Burma, Laos, Colombia, Angola, etc.) whose national liberation it continued to support, and "revisionist" or pro-Soviet Third World governments (e.g., India, Yugoslavia, Cuba, Vietnam after 1972), which it now repudiated and sought in various ways to undermine.

Now scorning the feasibility of ideological neutrality on which the nonaligned bloc had been premised, China began demanding uncompromising revolutionary commitment. In 1965, Lin Biao wrote his famous article "Long Live the Victory of People's War," conceiving the developing world to be analogous to the world countryside in a revolutionary strategy echoing the Chinese civil war and called for surrounding the (North Atlantic capitalist) "cities" via a class revolution among black, brown, and yellow races.[5] During this period, Beijing endorsed ongoing armed struggles in twenty-four countries, eighteen of which were pro-Western, independent states, while still attempting to build stable state-to-state relations with the rest of the developing world, urging these governments to reject the West.[6] In 1974, in the wake of the Sino-Soviet border clash, Mao once again reformulated his strategic blueprint as "three worlds": the first world now consisted of the two superpowers, the United States and the "social revisionist" Soviet Union; the second, of economically developed middle powers like Japan or France; and the third, of the developing nations.

The consistent ideological thrust of Chinese support for the Third World during the Maoist period was commitment to world proletarian revolution. And indeed, several successes or partial successes could be claimed in this quest (e.g., defense of North Korea from 1950 to 1953, unification of Vietnam in 1975). But clearly, the effort did not eventuate in the envisioned world socialist triumph, due partly to entrenched and effective Western resistance, to a dearth of revolutionary zeal among postcolonial indigenous elites, and to the shifting strategies and tactics adopted by ideologically split (and often competitive) revolutionary forces. Consistent with its emphasis on "self-reliant" development at this time, China's emphasis was on aid rather than foreign trade or investment, in which it had very little involvement. The Chinese aid program officially began in 1956 with the provision of assistance to Cambodia, followed by Nepal, Sri Lanka, Burma, and Indonesia.[7] Chinese arms aid, consisting of small arms bequests and the occasional dispatch of military advisers, was extensive in the case of Vietnam, Malaya (before 1960), Indonesia (before 1965), Congo, Burma, Cuba, and many other countries, though there are (understandably) few public statistics. By the late 1950s, however, Chinese developmental aid had become quite substantial, now including turnkey projects [*chengtao xiangmu*], in which China would provide all aspects of a project, including labor. The most famous of such projects, detailed by Yu, was the 1,200-mile Tanzania-Zambia railroad from the Zambian copper mines to Dar es Salaam.[8]

During his 1963–1964 tour of eleven Asian and African countries, Zhou Enlai laid out eight principles as guidelines for China's aid to developing world countries.[9] By the end of 1978, China had provided developmental aid to sixty-six countries, helping twenty-eight of them build 880 projects, making China by far the largest donor country to the developing world that was not a member of the Organization of the Petroleum Exporting Countries, with a cumulative total of US$9.3 billion in bilateral aid from 1953 to 1985.[10] The amount of Chinese aid varied over time, based not, however, on the business cycle but rather on the *fang-shou* cycle of ideological radicalization and de-radicalization, reaching a high point during the Cultural Revolution (not exactly an economic high tide for China). Certainly one major impetus to Chinese generosity was Beijing's competition with Moscow for leadership of the world revolution, which reached a violent climax in the 1969 border clashes. In 1970, the PRC donated no less than US$709 million in aid to developing countries, nearly twice the amount contributed by the USSR and all other Communist bloc countries combined (namely, US$391 million). By mid-1971, Beijing's offers of aid exceeded US$750 million in soft loans. From 1971 to 1975, China's aid budget was equal to 5.88 percent of its gross domestic product (GDP). In comparison, the highest proportion of gross national product (GNP) any developed nation has ever given for aid barely exceeds 0.5 percent (the US figure at the turn of the millennium was below 0.1 percent). During the late Maoist period, China's reached a high point of 6.92 percent (1973), the highest (in proportional terms) the world has ever known.[11]

Although the altruistic purpose of this aid was of course publicly emphasized, certain short-term political quid pro quos redounded to Beijing above and beyond the satisfaction of contributing to the eventual triumph of worldwide communist revolution. First, China cultivated relations among these countries to shift their ideological loyalties from Washington or Moscow to Beijing. Second, China hoped to induce these countries to switch diplomatic recognition from Taipei to Beijing and hence to garner votes for Beijing's eventual breakthrough into membership in the UN and other international governmental and nongovernmental organizations (in which it consistently disclaimed interest, until it was a fait accompli). Thus it is perhaps not entirely coincidental that the high point of Chinese aid coincided chronologically with China's 1971 displacement of Taiwan to occupy the Chinese seat in the UN (eventually including leading positions in the UN Security Council, the International Monetary Fund, World Bank, the World Health Organization, and other affiliated agencies) (see Table 10.1). Third, although there was probably no explicit quid pro quo on this point, Beijing no doubt appreciated developing world support in blocking censure resolutions on Chinese prison labor and other such issues at the UN Human Rights Commission and its successor organization when they were proposed by various Western countries in the wake of the Tiananmen crackdown.

The introduction of the policy of "reform and opening to the outside world" [*gaige kaifang*] at the Third Plenum of the Eleventh Party Congress in December 1978 has resulted in an adjustment of Beijing's developing world policies consonant with the overall transformation of PRC foreign and domestic policies. The announced end (and official repudiation) of the Cultural Revolution in 1981 was accompanied by a systematic reassessment of late Maoist thinking resulting in the excision of its more anarchic and polarizing aspects and a prioritization of rapid, stable domestic economic development. China thus curtailed its support for national liberation movements in the developing

**Table 10.1  Voting Record on the Question of Chinese Representation in the United Nations General Assembly, 1950–1971**

| Year (Session) | Membership | Pro-PRC | Anti-PRC | Abstentions | Sponsors |
|---|---|---|---|---|---|
| 1950 (5th) | 59 | 16 (27%) | 33 (56%) | 10 | India |
| 1951 (6th) | 60 | 11 (18%) | 37 (62%) | 4 | Moratorium[a] |
| 1952 (7th) | 60 | 7 (12%) | 42 (70%) | 11 | Moratorium |
| 1953 (8th) | 60 | 10 (17%) | 44 (73%) | 2 | Moratorium |
| 1954 (9th) | 60 | 11 (18%) | 43 (72%) | 6 | Moratorium |
| 1955 (10th) | 60 | 12 (20%) | 42 (70%) | 6 | Moratorium |
| 1956 (11th) | 79 | 24 (30%) | 47 (59%) | 8 | Moratorium |
| 1957 (12th) | 82 | 27 (33%) | 48 (59%) | 6 | Moratorium |
| 1958 (13th) | 81 | 28 (35%) | 44 (54%) | 6 | Moratorium |
| 1959 (14th) | 82 | 29 (35%) | 44 (54%) | 9 | Moratorium |
| 1960 (15th) | 98 | 34 (35%) | 42 (43%) | 22 | Moratorium |
| 1961 (16th) | 104 | 37 (36%) | 48 (46%) | 19 | USSR[b] |
| 1962 (17th) | 110 | 42 (38%) | 56 (51%) | 12 | USSR[b] |
| 1963 (18th) | 111 | 41 (37%) | 57 (51%) | 12 | Albania and Cambodia |
| 1964 (19th) | 114[c] | | | | |
| 1965 (20th) | 117 | 47 (40%) | 47 (40%) | 20 | Albania plus 11 nations[b] |
| 1966 (21st) | 121 | 46 (39%) | 57 (47%) | 17 | Albania plus 10 nations[b] |
| 1967 (22nd) | 122 | 45 (37%) | 58 (48%) | 17 | Albania plus 11 nations |
| 1968 (23rd) | 126 | 44 (35%) | 58 (46%) | 23 | Albania plus 14 nations |
| 1969 (24th) | 126 | 48 (38%) | 56 (44%) | 21 | Albania plus 16 nations |
| 1970 (25th) | 127 | 51 (40%) | 49 (39%) | 25 | Albania plus 17 nations |
| 1971 (26th) | 131 | 76 (58%) | 35 (27%) | 17 | Albania plus 22 nations |

*Source: Yearbook of the United Nations, 1950 through 1969; UN Monthly Chronicle, 1970–1971.*
*Notes:* a. Votes from 1951 to 1960 inclusive were on a US motion to keep the question off the agenda. For uniformity, the numbers in the pro-PRC column reflect the votes in favor of the PRC.
b. Two-thirds majority required for adoption.
c. No vote was taken due to financial crisis.

world and forfeited its claim to be a model and leader of international revolutionary development. Under the circumstances it would seem logical to infer, as does Peter Van Ness, that China "seemed to give up entirely on . . . trying to build alliances among the have-nots, but rather sought to join the haves as quickly as possible by making a separate peace with the global status quo."[12] Yet that judgment may have been premature. It is true that China's opening to the outside world initially emphasized the economically advanced economies with large export markets that had been largely inaccessible during the Cold War. China's foreign aid budget thus declined somewhat in proportional terms in the late 1970s, though the degree of decline should by no means be exaggerated.[13]

In giving the Chinese people their first exposure to the advanced industrial economies in the non-Communist world, Deng's "opening" policy inadvertently led many Chinese to infer that their country, however advanced by revolutionary socialist criteria, had fallen far behind economically. Thus China applied for and received subsidized loans and other developmental aid from newly accessible donor institutions. In late 1978, China for the first time requested aid from the UN Development Programme, the world's largest multilateral technical aid organization. China subsequently became the largest recipient of World Bank multilateral aid (about US$3 billion per year). Beijing's applications for aid created an incentive not to advertise any aid it was itself donating to other countries. More consistent with its recipient status were cuts in intergovernmental organization (IGO) dues remittances. Whereas during its postentry Maoist period (1971–1976) China had requested to have its UN assessment rate raised from 4 percent to 5.5 percent (of the total UN budget), an act of unprecedented fiscal generosity for a developing country, in 1979 China asked the UN to decrease its assessment rate from 5.5 percent to 0.79 percent, the lowest assessment rate of any UN Security Council permanent member, below the dues of Mexico or Switzerland (see Figure 10.1).[14] As an aid recipient, China's international role was no longer revolutionary tribunal but indigent supplicant. Yet China's booming growth has been changing that image willy-nilly. In 2006, the year following a proposal by Japan (whose assessment rate was then 17 percent, and the US rate 22 percent) to increase the assessment rates of all UN Security Council members to 3 to 5 percent (which China "firmly opposed" at the time), China volunteered to increase its assessment rate from 2 percent to 2.5 percent for the next three years (still a lower rate than any of the five permanent members but Russia).[15]

In Beijing's eyes, its national identity as a developing country has been undiminished, perhaps even underscored by the shift from radical Maoism to a policy of "reform and opening." This is indicated not only by China's transition from international aid donor to recipient, but by China's continuing resort to "victimization" rhetoric to mobilize patriotism and its increasingly explicit identification with the developing world as a community of fellow

**Figure 10.1** **China's Contribution to UN Regular Budget, 1992–2006 (compared with the United States, Russia, France, as percentage of total budget)**

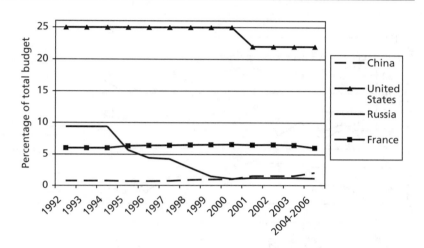

victims. As Samuel Kim has demonstrated based on a time-series analysis of Chinese roll-call voting behavior, the Chinese positive voting record accorded with that of the UN developing world majority on 58.5 percent of the 452 roll-call votes in the UN General Assembly between the Twenty-sixth and the Forty-second sessions (1971–1987), ranking China second only to the Soviet Union in its support of developing world issues among the five permanent members of the Security Council during this period. After the Third Plenum of the Eleventh Party Congress, however, Chinese voting congruence with the developing world majority jumped to 65.9 percent in 1978, to 77.2 percent in 1979, and 86.4 percent in 1987.[16] Despite China's exceedingly rapid economic growth rates, this positive correlation with developing world voting patterns remained above 80 percent through the turn of the millennium, ranging from 88.7 percent agreement in 1991 to 83 percent agreement in 2003. This stands in stark contrast to the strong negative correlation between voting patterns of the developing world and the United States (and most Western developed democracies) (see Figure 10.2).[17]

The Chinese media have (not unreasonably) begun to champion the PRC as the permanent representative of the developing world in the UN Security Council, the halls of the World Trade Organization (WTO), the International Monetary Fund, and other powerful IGOs. China's identification with this grouping became particularly salient around the time of the inauguration of its "independent foreign policy line" (nonaligned from both superpowers) at the Twelfth Party Congress in 1982. Not too surprising in view of their sharply

**Figure 10.2   Percentage of China's Roll-Call Votes in Favor of the Developing World Majority in the UN General Assembly, 1991–2003 (compared with Russia, the United States, and France)**

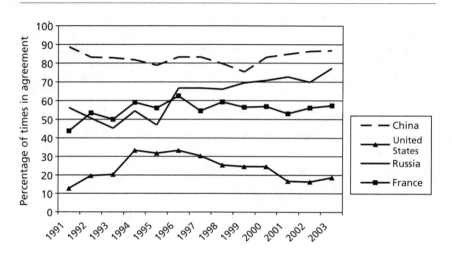

contrasting positions vis-à-vis the developing world, this has entrenched the PRC as a rather consistent opponent of the United States on a wide range of international issues, at least in terms of General Assembly roll-call votes (see Figure 10.3). In one conspicuous display of this, China departed from its usual voting pattern (in which it generally tries to avoid unilateral vetoes) in the latter half of 1981 to block the reelection of the Austrian Kurt Waldheim as secretary-general, creating a stalemate that eventually resulted in the election of compromise candidate Javier Pérez de Cuéllar of Peru.

## Economics

Notwithstanding its higher profile identification with the developing world, China after reform is a quite different place than the poor but revolutionary vanguard of the Maoist era. China forsook the policy of economic self-reliance and quickly became one of what David Zweig calls the world's "trading nations," at first limiting international market exposure to four isolated special economic zones, but eventually, as these experiments proved extraordinarily successful, extending the experience to the entire eastern seaboard. China joined the World Bank and the International Monetary Fund and accepted long-term foreign loans; in 2001, it finally entered the WTO as well, after successfully negotiating stringent accession agreements with existing members.

**Figure 10.3    Percentage of China's Roll-Call Votes in Favor of US Position in UN General Assembly, 1991–2003 (compared with Japan, France, Russia)**

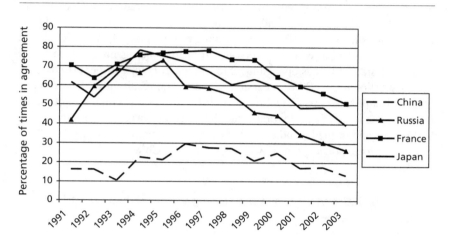

Foreign tourism and intensive Western cultural penetration followed, as hundreds of thousands of China's best students left to study abroad. Though Maoist China had not been entirely bereft of economic achievements, these more flexible policies stimulated the most rapid sustained economic growth the world had ever seen. China's GDP increased fourfold from 1980 to 2000, and by the end of 2008 it had doubled again to become Asia's second-largest economy and third-largest in the world (Asia's largest, and second in the world, by purchasing power parity). With about 10 percent of world GDP, China became an international economic locomotive, contributing one-third of world growth in 2004 and more to growth than any other economy in 2007–2008. Despite growing inequality, poverty was reduced from some 250 million in 1978 to 30 million in 2006, while per capita income increased sixfold and life expectancy rose from 63.2 to 71 years. In 1998, China was officially reclassified by the World Bank from a low-income to a middle-income country, gravitating to the upper tier of developing countries.

China's rise as a trading state has altered the tenor of its relations with the developing countries in at least three significant ways. First, China has increased its trade-to-GDP ratio, most dramatically during the 1992–1997 period, when the country's volume of foreign trade totaled US$1,493.8 billion, exceeding the accumulated total from 1949 to 1991. By 2008, China had become the world's largest trading state. While the most dramatic increase was in trade with the Western advanced capitalist markets, the developing countries have also been beneficiaries of this increase, both in terms of more competitive prices for sale of their raw materials and as a source of relatively affordable consumer imports. Over half of China's exports now go to other emerging nations, and it has emerged as the biggest trade partner of Brazil, Iran, India, Sudan, Vietnam, and many other developing countries. The developing nations have since 1980 been growing more rapidly than the developed economies, so China can look forward to an expanding market (see Table 10.2). Second, China has opened itself to foreign direct investment (FDI), particularly following its 2001 accession to the WTO, resulting in an enormous influx of capital (from US$1 billion in 1985 to $74.86 billion in 2007), attracted by an increasingly favorable tax, labor, and infrastructure regime—and by the prospect of the legendary China market. Beginning in the 1990s, China has begun to export capital as well, encouraging Chinese firms to "go out"

**Table 10.2   GDP Growth Rates in Developing vs. Developed Countries**

| | Percentage Change from Previous Year, Real GDP Growth | | | | | | | |
| --- | --- | --- | --- | --- | --- | --- | --- | --- |
| | Estimate | | | | | | Forecast | |
| | 1960–1980 | 1980–2000 | 2004 | 2005 | 2006 | 2007 | 2008 | 2008–2030 |
| World | 4.7 | 3.0 | 4.1 | 3.5 | 3.9 | 3.2 | 3.5 | 2.9 |
| High income | 4.5 | 2.9 | 3.3 | 2.7 | 3.1 | 2.4 | 2.8 | 2.4 |
| Organization for Economic Cooperation and Development (OECD) countries | | | 3.2 | 2.6 | 3.0 | 2.3 | 2.7 | |
| European Area | | | 1.7 | 1.4 | 2.4 | 1.9 | 1.9 | |
| Japan | | | 2.7 | 2.6 | 2.9 | 2.4 | 2.5 | |
| United States | | | 4.2 | 3.2 | 3.2 | 2.1 | 3.0 | |
| Non-OECD countries | | 6.4 | 5.8 | 5.3 | 4.7 | 4.8 | | |
| Developing countries | 6.2 | 3.4 | 7.2 | 6.6 | 7.0 | 6.4 | 6.1 | 4.0 |
| East Asia and Pacific | 5.5 | 8.5 | 9.0 | 9.0 | 9.2 | 8.7 | 8.1 | 5.1 |
| Europe and Central Asia | 10.7 | 0.6 | 7.2 | 6.0 | 6.4 | 5.7 | 5.5 | 2.7 |
| Latin America and Caribbean | 5.5 | 2.2 | 6.0 | 4.5 | 5.0 | 4.2 | 4.0 | 3.0 |
| Middle East and North America | 5.9 | 4.0 | 4.8 | 4.4 | 4.9 | 4.9 | 4.8 | 3.6 |
| South Asia | 3.7 | 5.4 | 8.0 | 8.1 | 8.2 | 7.5 | 7.0 | 4.7 |
| Sub-Saharan Africa | 4.4 | 2.2 | 5.2 | 5.5 | 5.3 | 5.3 | 5.4 | 3.3 |
| Developing countries excluding China and India | 6.6 | 2.3 | 6.1 | 5.1 | 5.5 | 4.9 | 4.9 | |

*Source:* International Bank for Reconstruction and Development/World Bank, *Global Economic Prospects,* 2007, table 1.1; Chih-shian Liou, forthcoming, "Outsourcing Reform: The Political Logic of Overseas Expansion of China's Central State-Owned Enterprises," chapter 3, Ph.D. dissertation, Department of Government, University of Texas at Austin.

[*zou chu qu*], that is, to invest abroad, often in developing countries (see Table 10.3). Third, China has ameliorated its muscular economic presence with bilateral and multilateral commercial diplomacy and with "soft power" initiatives designed to facilitate achievement of its economic interests and to translate economic power into political gains.

The PRC's identification with the developing world is not only rhetorical but reflects a growing coincidence of material interests as well. Indeed, China *needs* the developing world in a quite elemental sense: It needs its natural resources and, to pay for them without incurring a current account deficit, it needs its markets. This demand is driven partly by domestic consumption as Chinese living standards rise, but much more from investment in China's burgeoning industrial sector, which absorbs an unusually high proportion (45 percent in 2007 and rising 25.5 percent in 2008) of GDP. This export sector surged dramatically after China entered the WTO, in turn stimulating fixed-asset investment. China became the workshop of the world, producing more steel than any other country (from 25 percent of global output in 2000 to 35 percent in 2005), for example; a comparable increase in aluminum output; and about half the global cement output (1.35 billion tons in 2007).[18] This boom stimulated an appetite for raw materials, much of them imported from the developing world. China has since 2000 contributed to two-fifths of the growth in the world's demand for raw materials, driving up the prices of the commodities it now imports in such great quantities. For example, in 2003 nickel hit a thirteen-year high of $13 per ton, while in 2004 zinc reached a seven-year high and platinum a twenty-three-year high of $800 per ounce, with Chinese demand in each case playing a leading role.[19] China has thus overtaken the United States to become the world's leading natural resource consumer. Among the basic commodities (grain and meat in the food sector, oil and coal in the energy sector, and steel in the industrial sector), China now consumes more of each than the United States—except oil, where China still ranks a distant second (yet China's oil consumption doubled between 1994 and 2004, contributing 25 percent of the increase in world demand, while US oil consumption increased by only 15 percent).[20] China's rate of increase in oil consumption is likely to continue to grow at a pace of 4–5 percent per year at least through 2015, compared to a pace of around 1 percent in other industrialized countries. China consumes nearly twice as much meat (67 million tons compared with 39 million tons in the United States) and more than twice as much steel (258 million tons to 104 million). China consumes some 40 percent of the world's coal, 32 percent of its steel, 25 percent of its aluminum, 23 percent of its copper, 30 percent of its zinc, and 18 percent of its nickel. In 2004, exports to China increased by 45 percent in South Africa, 71 percent in Brazil, and 48 percent in Panama. After remaining fairly constant from 1978 to 1991, the proportion of China's trade with the developing countries rose from 34 percent in 1991 to 47 percent in 2005.[21]

While this sudden increase in resource purchases has often incurred at

**Table 10.3  Leading Destinations of China's Outward FDI Flows**

| Country/Region | 2003 Amount (US$100 million) | 2003 Percent of Total | 2004 Amount (US$100 million) | 2004 Percent of Total | 2005 Amount (US$100 million) | 2005 Percent of Total | 2006 Amount (US$100 million) | 2006 Percent of Total | 2007 Amount (US$100 million) | 2007 Percent of Total |
|---|---|---|---|---|---|---|---|---|---|---|
| Hong Kong | 11.5 | 40.40 | 26.3 | 47.80 | 34.2 | 27.90 | 69.3 | 39.31 | 137.3 | 51.79 |
| Cayman Islands | 8.1 | 28.30 | 12.9 | 23.40 | 51.6 | 42.10 | 78.3 | 44.41 | 26.0 | 9.81 |
| British Virgin Islands | 2.1 | 7.40 | 3.9 | 7.00 | 12.3 | 10.00 | 5.38 | 3.05 | 18.8 | 7.09 |
| South Korea | 1.5 | 5.40 | 0.4 | 0.70 | 5.9 | 4.80 | 0.3 | 0.17 | 0.6 | 0.23 |
| Australia | 0.3 | 0.90 | 1.3 | 2.30 | 1.9 | 1.60 | 0.9 | 0.51 | 5.3 | 2.00 |
| United States | 0.7 | 2.30 | 1.2 | 2.20 | 2.3 | 1.90 | 2.0 | 1.13 | 2.0 | 0.75 |
| Russia | 0.3 | 1.10 | 0.8 | 1.40 | 2.0 | 1.60 | 4.5 | 2.55 | 4.8 | 1.81 |
| Indonesia | 0.3 | 0.90 | 0.6 | 1.10 | 0.1 | 0.08 | 0.6 | 0.34 | 1.0 | 0.38 |
| Sudan | — | — | 1.5 | 2.70 | 0.1 | 0.08 | 0.5 | 0.28 | 0.7 | 0.26 |
| Total | 24.8 | 86.70 | 48.9 | 88.60 | 110.4 | 90.06 | 161.78 | 91.75 | 196.5 | 74.12 |

*Sources: China FDI Statistics Report,* Ministry of Commerce and China Statistics Bureau; Chih-shian Liou, forthcoming, "Outsourcing Reform: The Political Logic of Overseas Expansion of China's Central State-Owned Enterprises," chapter 3, Ph.D. dissertation, Department of Government, University of Texas at Austin.

least a temporary negative trade balance, one Chinese expedient has been to accelerate exports to its raw material suppliers, often focusing on apparel, toys, and other light consumer goods. Due to their fairly good quality and very low price (Chinese companies typically operate on margins of 10 percent or less), Chinese products have generally proved highly competitive. The impact on China's domestic industrial structure has been to help sustain those labor-intensive "sunset" light industries even as the state's industrial policy shifts focus to the "sunrise" high-tech and heavy industrial sector for export to developed country markets. (For example, whereas in 1985, 49 percent of China's exports were of primary products and resource-based manufactures, by 2000 non-resource-based manufactures accounted for 88 percent; the share of high-tech exports jumped from 3 to 22 percent over that period.) China now also exports weapons and military technology, though arms sales have declined since their high point in the 1980s.

While in many ways China's approach to development during reform and opening has approximated the newly industrialized country (NIC) model of export-led growth, it has departed from that model (at least the Japanese–pre-1998 Korean variant of that model) in its relatively liberal attitude toward foreign direct investment. China first invited foreign investment within the confines of isolated, experimental special economic zones in the early 1980s and followed that extraordinary success by extending a comparably liberal investment climate along most of the east coast. FDI then surged into the country in three great waves, the first in the mid-1980s, the second in 1992–1994, and the third since 2000. Even during the worldwide high-tech crash in 2001 and 2002, when global flows of FDI fell by a half and a third respectively, they continued to flow into China. Incoming FDI flowed disproportionately into the export sector (largely because the PRC was at first reluctant to allow full access to the China market). And as government incentives targeted high-tech, knowledge-intensive investment, the FDI influx disproportionately built up this sector: Whereas in 1985, 49 percent of exports were primary products or resource-based manufactures, by 2000, non-resource-based manufactures accounted for 88 percent, while the share of high-tech exports jumped from 3 to 22 percent. From 1994 to mid-2003, exports trebled (from US$121 billion to $365 billion), and foreign-invested enterprises (FIEs) accounted for 65 percent of that increase. Whereas in 1996, foreign affiliates accounted for 59 percent of high-tech exports, that share rose to 74 percent in 1998, 81 percent in 2000, and 85 percent by 2003.[22]

Outgoing Chinese FDI began more recently and remains smaller in scale than incoming FDI, though for the past ten years it has been growing more rapidly in percentage terms (from a smaller base). The "going out" or "going global" campaign was launched by Jiang Zemin in 2000 to encourage Chinese investment abroad, particularly in developing world countries from which China hopes to import raw materials. As "workshop of the world" and new regional economic locomotive, China sought to encourage both state and private enterprises to invest abroad, and China subsequently streamlined approval procedures and developed a set of targets and sectors where investment is encouraged, for example, using subsidized loans from the China Import-Export Bank and China Construction Bank.[23] Investment policy is partly linked to imports: It has not escaped the Chinese that their intensified purchases tend to drive up global commodity prices, and so China shifted in the 1990s from purchasing imports on the market to buying equity in the resource, to allow technology transfer, ensure supply in times of economic uncertainty, and protect against price shocks. As of 2005, China's officially recorded total outbound FDI was US$43.9 billion, doubling to US$90.63 billion in 2006 and US$127.6 billion by 2007, according to Xinhua News Agency.[24] Though largely focused on energy and raw materials, China's investments have also included the purchase of millions of acres of farmland to produce staples for consumption in the domestic markets. Chinese FDI was particularly appreciated during the 2008 recession, to prop up falling demand.[25] Whereas Chinese investments generated outsized publicity when going after First World firms (as in Lenovo's acquisition of IBM's personal computer unit, or the less successful cases of China National Offshore Oil Corporation's 2005 bid for Unocal, Minmetals's bid for Noranda in Canada, or Chinalco's 2009 bid for Rio Tinto in Australia), most outgoing FDI has been funneled to Hong Kong (the largest single recipient) or to resource-rich developing countries throughout the world. Southeast Asia has been the largest cumulative beneficiary, though Africa has received the largest recent increment (see Table 10.3). Inasmuch as many of the most attractive properties have already signed long-term contracts with Western firms, Chinese companies have tended to access countries where political conditions limit or preclude competition from Western multinationals (such as Sudan, Iran, Myanmar (Burma), or Zimbabwe). Beijing not only invests in states sanctioned by the international community, but then shields them from censure. China has threatened to use its Security Council veto to protect Khartoum from proposed oil sanctions, for example, and has been able to dilute every attempt to impose sanctions on Sudan for alleged human rights violations in Darfur, from which China imports nearly 6 percent of its oil (Sudan is currently the only country in Africa where oil is produced by Chinese companies, rather than via production-sharing agreements with other companies).[26]

Though host governments have on the whole responded favorably to China's export purchases and incoming FDI, the grassroots feedback has been mixed: Retailers, farmers, and manufacturers object to the inundation of local markets with cheap Chinese products; working conditions in Chinese mines are sometimes criticized by human rights activists; and Chinese infrastructure projects importing up to 70 percent of their workforce from China do not help domestic unemployment statistics. In Zambia, a populist politician named Michael ("King Cobra") Sata ran for president in 2006 on a platform calling for the ejection of Chinese investors (also accusing Beijing of vote tampering via Chinese-made computers), which so annoyed his Chinese targets that the local ambassador, one Li Baodong, threatened to sever diplomatic relations if he won (he did not). To help ameliorate such problems, China has rejoined the ranks of donor nations. In 1995, Beijing restructured its foreign aid program, shifting its emphasis from interest-free loans to providing preferential loans or aid. Most aid is provided through bilateral channels, about half in the form of grants and the other half in loans, typically financed through the China Import-Export Bank for industrial or infrastructure projects.

As for geographical distribution, about half goes to Asia and a third to Africa.[27] Total Chinese loans to Africa in 2004 were equivalent to three times the total development aid provided by the OECD countries that year, and in 2006, China offered three times as much aid as the World Bank.[28] According to a 2007 estimate, China's total foreign aid budget came to US$1.5 to 2 billion.[29] Although China has come under fire for neglecting human rights or good governance considerations (e.g., corruption) in awarding its aid, its principles of aid distribution remain generally consistent with the Eight Points Zhou Enlai first announced in Mali in 1964: mutual benefit ("win-win"), no political conditions, and so forth. While other donor countries have complained, these "no strings attached" arrangements have been much appreciated by recipient governments as a relatively complication-free alternative. Aid often takes the form of large construction projects—trains, roads, ports, dams, soccer stadiums, schools, and other high-profile public works.

Actually "no strings" is not strictly true—certainly one indispensable condition has been China's One-China policy: Any country to recognize the Republic of China on Taiwan will promptly lose not only PRC diplomatic recognition but developmental aid. Otherwise, one might say the strings are not totally absent but implied, now mostly tied to business arrangements rather than politics. Aid is, for example, contingent on its being spent on Chinese imports (as is also true for Japanese or US developmental aid), and large infrastructure projects are often contracted with countries from which raw materials are to be exported, in part to pay for the exports. The Chinese offer package deals that include long-term low-interest loans that Western companies can rarely compete with; countries like Sudan and Zimbabwe have also been sold Chinese weapons (which the West embargoes).[30] Yet there are also spontaneous displays of magnanimity. An early conspicuous display of charity occurred, for example, during the Asian Financial Crisis, when China not only refrained from devaluing its currency, but in 1998 provided some US$5 billion in assistance to Thailand and Indonesia (at a time when the United States was refusing to provide any bilateral aid).[31] At the 2002 ASEAN+3 summit in Phnom Penh, Premier Zhu Rongji announced that China would reduce or write off the matured debts owed China by six Southeast Asian nations. As many researchers have observed, the exact amount of aid dispensed is as yet unclear, perhaps even to the Chinese. According to Chinese figures, Chinese external assistance totaled US$602.77 million in 2002, $630.36 million in 2003, and $731.20 million in 2004—yet this seems to be an underestimate.[32] In response to the tsunami in Southeast Asia at the end of 2004, China made the largest bequest of humanitarian aid in its history (though dwarfed by the contributions of Japan and the United States), pledging some US$63 million in bilateral aid and another US$20 million through multilateral channels. In response to the earthquake in northern India the following year, China offered another US$27 million in emergency assistance.[33] China has been (and continues to be) the largest benefactor of its ally North Korea, reportedly providing around US$500 million annually, mostly in food and heavy oil. Following a Chinese deal to expand the Pakistani port of Gwadar to host Chinese ships (commercial transport only, according to Beijing), PRC assistance to Pakistan increased dramatically in 2003–2004, including nuclear reactors, power plants, and railroad projects. Chinese developmental assistance in Africa includes large grants and loans to oil-producing states such as Angola, Sudan, and Nigeria; China recently announced creation of a US$5 billion China-Africa Development Fund. China even donated a token US$5 million to the United States in the aftermath of Hurricane Katrina.

Analytically distinct from but closely related to the use of economic power to exert influence ("commercial diplomacy"), the PRC has taken note of the concept of "soft" or cultural power, coined by Joseph Nye in 2004, constructing a Comprehensive National Power index that includes soft as well as hard power and making a studied attempt to enhance its own soft power.[34] By 2007, China had constructed 210 Confucius Institutes worldwide to propagate instruction in Chinese language, including at least 12 in Africa; it aims to approve 500 by 2010. Foreign student enrollment in Chinese universities has increased from 85,000 in 2002 to 195,000 in 2007.[35] About 75 percent of the foreign students are from Asian countries, led by South Korea and Japan (in 2004); but China also gives financial assistance to students from the developing countries, resulting in significant increases of students from Africa and South Asia. By 2005, the number of foreign tourists had reached 17 million. Since 2005, these efforts have been placed in the context of "peaceful rise" or "peaceful development" in a "harmonious world." This has encouraged the notion that China might once again serve as an attractive alternative "model" for economic development, a Beijing Consensus to counter the Washington Consensus.[36] Beijing has been careful not to endorse this, though of course it does not exactly shun spontaneous admiration for China's achievements. Perhaps the most successful recent display of China's soft power was the August 2008 Beijing Olympics, the first to be hosted by a developing country since Mexico City.

It would seem that the major impact of China's economic rise on China's policy to the developing world has been to activate a congeries of domestic constituencies with an interest in that relationship in order to constitute a stronger material basis for a "linkage" argument between domestic political interests and foreign policy. Without attempting to draw a precise map of how such emergent interests dovetail with which policies toward which specific objectives or international institutions, the general economic picture that emerges is one in which China is becoming the "hub" and final assembly point of a sprawling multinational manufacturing network. This creates trade and investment interdependencies between China and its partners in both the developed and the developing world, and so long as both sides benefit from such a dependency, it may also be expected to produce political and diplomatic side benefits. How other countries might fit into such a chain will depend on their resource endowment, stage of development, and other factors. To those countries with a similar composition of trade, a rising China represents a serious competitor that, with persistently lower wage costs, can export goods of comparable quality at a lower end-price. China thus threatens to drive a number of developing countries (e.g., Malaysia, South Korea, Bangladesh) out of their foreign (or even domestic) product markets. On the other hand, by joining the multinational manufacturing and assembly chain with its nexus in China, they can export goods or partially fabricated components to China, deemed the most cost-efficient site for final assembly production, and the products can then be exported to third countries or back to domestic markets. The country in question loses market share in the West (for finished products) while being compensated by gaining market share (for parts) in China. This trend has accelerated since the early 1990s, particularly in information technology, and particularly in emerging Asia. Chinese emissaries thus now focus their appeals to such countries on lucrative exports to China or on the prospect of Chinese FDI. To the extent that developing countries have switched from dependency theories to export-oriented growth and are hence bidding for incoming FDI, China represents formidable competition—only partially assuaged, so far, by outgoing Chinese FDI.

The pattern has been that if one firm in a tight market invests in China, then all the competitors must do likewise or risk having their end-price undercut. This has been particularly visible in the case of Southeast Asia: After the Asian Financial Crisis, particularly after China entered the WTO in 2001, foreign investors shifted from Southeast Asia to China.[37] In Chapter 9, Nicola Phillips notes some FDI diversion effect in Latin America as well, though it is much less clear there because of the sub rosa practice of investment "round-tripping": that is, Chinese investors who launder their money and invest it back into China from abroad to take advantage of FDI incentives. (Nor should this be underestimated: Since 2005 the British Virgin Islands, a tiny Caribbean community boasting a population of some 22,000 and a liberal tax and investment climate, has been the world's second or third largest investor in China!) For those countries whose level of development does not permit them to fit into this multinational production and assembly chain, China's demand drives up the international price of commodity exports, but these economies can still thrive by exporting the raw materials that China needs. If, however, their economies are relatively advanced with an export composition overlapping China's but no longer (because of strong unions, higher living standards, etc.) price competitive, they may find themselves trapped in commodity export or some other niche market, Phillips warns. Thus while China continues to identify politically with the developing world and to support it economically through trade and aid flows, patterns of development create different developmental trajectories that will make some relationships more economically attractive than others.

## Strategy

Does China have a coherent strategy toward the developing world, and if so, what is it? The developing world has been an international reference group since liberation, and yet it is an intellectual challenge to descry much continuity in a policy that has undergone so much change over the past half century—from the advocacy of violent revolution to peaceful development, from ideological exclusivity to eclectic ecumenism, from egalitarian poverty to purpose-rational payoffs, from revolutionary idealism to realism, from inter-Communist revolutionary schemes and plots to noninterference in internal affairs. If there is any common theme underlying China's identification, it is a conviction that the underdeveloped countries (like China) represent a new frontier and hence enhance the future prospects of the planet.[38] This conviction seems not to have flagged even as China's economic trajectory has transcended underdevelopment. It has manifested itself not only in foundational documents like the constitution but in China's General Assembly and Security Council voting patterns. Meanwhile, the action implications have changed: Whereas at one time this implied revolutionary rhetoric, military advisers, and weapons shipments, since the Cold War, policy has been deradicalized to fit China's functional needs in economic modernization. Displacing the revolutionary imperative and grand design is a loose set of general strategic guidelines: (1) Try to cultivate good relations with all developing countries in principle, but particularly with those having vital trade complementarities. (2) Have mutual respect for national sovereignty: Do not impose conditions or otherwise interfere in internal affairs or even gratuitously preach ideological or developmental reform, but accept and deal with the host government "as is" (i.e., "international democracy"). (3) Negotiate agreements on matters of clear short-term mutual benefit first while postponing disagreements or troublesome long-term implications for later consideration ("win-win"). (4) Be particularly solicitous to those countries otherwise alienated from the international community, for their isolation may give China a negotiating edge and thus help redress the global power imbalance—beware, however, of prematurely provoking "the hegemon" unnecessarily.

What has remained constant is China's commitment to the developing world, not only in itself, as the emergent driver of world economic development, but for China, to enhance China's leadership role as the self-selected tribunal of developing world interests in the UN, the Group of 20, and other international councils. At the same time, China's strategy has not only deradicalized but become more subtle and discriminating, with variations depending not only on a particular country's resource endowment but on the international and regional power balance. Complementary needs and interests can provide the basis for a mutually profitable relationship, but only so long as international and regional contexts are benign. The international context is an important limiting factor inasmuch as the hegemon is still conceded to retain the requisite military might to crush an explicit antagonist in any given region (situational complications may in practice constrain that capacity, of course). As for geopolitical adaptability, PRC strategy distinguishes between those Asian regions directly adjoining the nation (viz., Southeast Asia, South Asia, and Central Asia), where "neighborhood diplomacy" [*zhoubian waijiao*] applies, from more distant regions in which national security is not immediately at risk. In the regional "neighborhood," Beijing alternates between a forward policy and a more passive, defense posture. In its forward policy, Beijing assumes the role of outside balancer, much as England traditionally played vis-à-vis the European continent, playing upon national enmities, taking the side of the weaker party to balance against the stronger (e.g., supporting Pakistan against India, the Central Asian Republics against Russia). In its more defensive posture, China practices a combination of peripheral stabilizer and strategic denial, striving to minimize possibly contagious instability. The choice between offensive and defensive strategies depends on the stakes in play and Beijing's tolerance for risk, also taking domestic circumstances into account.

Since the 1990s, one new aspect of China's strategy has involved greater reliance on IGOs to supplement bilateral diplomacy in its approach to developing countries (see Figure 10.4). Much of its IGO political capital was acquired following China's admission to the UN Security Council in 1971 (e.g., leadership positions in the World Bank and the International Monetary Fund), but China has since the 1990s been a joiner and leading participant in regional organizations as well. Relatively cautious in affiliating with IGOs explicitly identified with developing world causes, China is now a member of the Group of 77 (formed in 1964 to represent developing-world trade interests) and the WTO's Group of 33, and is an observer in the Nonaligned Movement and the Group of 24. China's multilateral activities have been most conspicuous in its own neighborhood, where it is a founding member of the Shanghai Coopera-

**Figure 10.4    Membership in Intergovernmental Organizations**

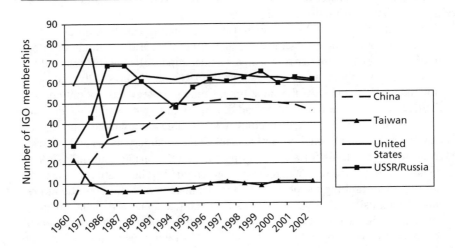

tion Organization (including Russia and the Central Asian republics) and ASEAN+1, the world's largest free trade agreement, which by 2010 will embrace more than two billion people with a combined GDP of nearly US$2 trillion. China is also a member of Asia-Pacific Economic Cooperation, ASEAN+3 (China, Japan, and Korea), the Asian Developmental Bank, the ASEAN Regional Forum, the East Asian Summit, and an observer at the South Asian Association for Regional Cooperation. In Latin America, China has been an observer at the Organization of American States and the Latin American Integration Association, and in January became a member of the Inter-American Developmental Bank and the Caribbean Developmental Bank. In Africa, it is a member of the African Developmental Bank as well as a founding member of the China-Africa Forum, and in the Middle East, it organized the China-Arab Cooperation Forum in 2004 to coordinate relations with the twenty-two-member League of Arab States. China's multilateral approach to regional forums reduces the otherwise intimidating bargaining asymmetry between the two sides, while utilizing bandwagon psychology to promote political-economic cooperation.

## Conclusion

China appears to have retained its identification with the developing world even as it has in many ways transcended that category: Because China has been such a developmental success, one of the questions about the relationship involves the question of authenticity. Is China really still part of the developing world, or is this just a useful international mask, following Deng Xiaoping's famous admonition (borrowed from Sun Tzu) to "hide your capabilities" [*tao guang yang hui*]? Three possibilities have been implicit in the relevant Chinese discourse: (1) *Fundamentalist*: In principle, China belongs axiomatically to the developing world. As Deng Xiaoping put it in 1984, "We have said more than once that China belongs to the Third World. It will still belong to the Third World even in the future, after it is developed. China will never become a 'superpower.'"[39] (2) *Progressivist*: China is currently a developing country, but well on its way to becoming a great power, despite concerted efforts to delay or impede that by certain established powers. After all, "development" is a transitional process toward a desired end-state, not a Sisyphean treadmill. As Communist Party theorist Zheng Bijian put it in 2003: "China's 'peaceful rise' [is] to great-power status."[40] (3) *Nationalist*: China is no longer a developing country but already a great power, and it should do all it can to maintain and if possible enhance that status. Thus in 2003, the Group of 8 organized a North-South Conference to which China was invited, and China accepted. Fully aware of the significance of UN permanent five membership, Beijing has emphasized its faithful representation of developing world interests on the Security Council—but it has not pressed for (indeed, it has been visibly reluctant about) its reorganization to accommodate additional developing countries.

Though there is support for each of these propositions in China, probably the current preponderance of opinion favors the second, progressivist interpretation. Yet the picture is still mixed—per capita living standards rank China between high-end less-developed countries and entry-level newly industrialized countries—Taiwanese expatriates now enjoy a higher living standard in the suburbs of Shanghai than in Taipei—while indices of aggregate power and wealth clearly place China among world powers. In this period of dramatic, tumultuous flux, China seems to be in a bout of uncertainty about its national identity. And this is reflected in the discourse, where different schools of thought take advantage of the ambiguity of its liminal developmental status to draw out their own implications for future development. The question of Third World or First World identity is only one of the riddles. Is China, now widely recognized as a market economy (avidly pursuing official recognition as such among its counterparts in the WTO), a democracy? Emphatically it is not a "bourgeois democracy," the CCP leadership has decreed. Due partly to definitional tergiversation (the PRC Constitution states it is a "People's Democratic Dictatorship"), the answer is surprisingly unclear. In the 1980s, there was some interest among reformers in changing the party's name to the Chinese Social Democratic Party—but this talk seems not to have survived the "Tiananmen Incident." Still, there is a certain tension between the positions that (1) China is currently a socialist democracy that is different from but superior to bourgeois democracy, and (2) due to its chaotic revolutionary heritage and populist immaturity, China is regrettably not yet a democracy, but is well on the way to becoming one. Related but analytically distinct from such national identity issues is the question of what role China should play on the world stage: Should it continue to adhere to Deng Xiaoping's famous admonition to *tao guang yang hui* (hide brightness, nourish obscurity), passively awaiting openings in the international power game to advance its own interests, or should it become a "responsible great power" or "stakeholder," willing and able to articulate its own vision for the reform and reconstruction of the international order? Although Deng's admonitions command very high prestige in Chinese leadership circles, there are growing indications of China's interest in playing a larger role. Beijing convened the six-power talks to help solve the crisis of the North Korean nuclear program, and in late 2008 played an active roll in the Group of 20 meeting convened to reform the world's financial architecture, suggesting a departure from the dollar as international reserve currency in the context of a pointed critique of US fiscal policy. If China acts like a great power and concerts with other great powers on the UN Security Council or via "strategic partnerships," is it not a great power? Yet there is still ambivalence about China's new role, not only in Beijing, but also in Washington and Tokyo.

There are perfectly sensible reasons for such uncertainty. The truth may be that China, like a young adult, is now more confused about its national identity than it was when it was more radical and less developed. To some extent this confusion has affected images of China among other countries as well. Developing countries are generally assumed to be poor; how can it be that China is the largest holder of US treasury bonds and the largest foreign exchange stockpile ever amassed, approaching US$2 trillion? If China is peacefully rising, in its strongest national security position since the Opium War, why does it increase its defense budget by double-digit percentages each year? True, this identity confusion does not seem to have affected China's identification with the developing world, as noted earlier. And fellow developing country leaders reportedly like dealing with a government that is one of them, dragging no imperialist "tail." Yet, it has not escaped their attention that China is bigger, richer, and more powerful than its so-called peers. China now occupies a functional position vis-à-vis much of the developing world more closely analogous to that of the former imperialist countries. It has been assuming the role of banker, landlord, employer, and merchant capitalist. Perhaps it can play this role better than its Caucasian forebears, but the act will be a delicate one. For the developing world as well, the relationship to a patron that is a peer in name but asymmetrically patron-client in fact, while perhaps a useful euphemism diplomatically, may prove sensitive to charges of hypocrisy.

The world has changed since the Chinese revolution. In the dawn of post-colonial national liberation, the developing world claimed greater ideological solidarity, but even then Beijing's path of violent revolution found few adherents. Developing countries are now more diverse both politically and economically than ever before, and it has become more complicated to characterize China's developmental path as well. China is attempting during its dizzyingly swift ascent to balance its past identity against its future, its respect for the travails of the less developed with its responsibilities as a newly industrialized great power. While steadfastly opposed to any effort by the United States or international organizations to impose Western values on Eastern nations, and of course keeping its own national interest clearly in view, China has been quietly responsive to calls to become a "responsible stakeholder." Since first responding to the invitation to participate in UN peacekeeping forces in 2000, the PRC had by 2009 escalated its involvement to more than 2,000 peacekeepers in ten UN peacekeeping operations worldwide. While its financial support remains modest, China is now the second largest provider of peacekeepers among the five permanent members of the Security Council.

Having inherited from its revolutionary heritage a genuine conviction that the future of the world still lies with the less-developed countries, China's renewed economic commitment to that proposition—bolstered, it is true, by its own complementary developmental needs—seems to have shaped a new global dynamic. Like the United States after World War II, China in the wake of the 2008–2009 global financial crisis has been stepping up with its "deep pockets" to claim a unique status not as traditional "great power" but as benefactor and leader of the developing world. As the world economy recovers and the developed and developing world resume their diverging growth trajectories, we may be witnessing the emergence of a new global dynamic.

## Notes

1. See Chapter 2, Mel Gurtov, "Changing Perspectives and Policies."

2. This led to Sino-American ambassadorial-level talks in Warsaw that, without resolving any important issues, were to meet quite regularly for the next decade and a half. See, by way of comparison, Kenneth T. Young, *Negotiating with the Chinese Communists: The United States Experience, 1953–1967* (New York: McGraw-Hill, 1968).

3. Liu Shaoqi, "Daibiao zhonggong zhongyang wei yuan hui xiang di bazi quan guo daibiao dahui di zhenyzki baogao" [Political work report by the Central Committee to the Eighth National Congress of the Communist Party of China], in *Liuo Shaoqi wenti ziliao zhuanji* [Collected materials on the Liu Shaoqi Question] (Taipei: Shanghai Printing Press, 197) pp. 286–287.

4. Schram, Stuart, ed., *Chairman Mao Talks to the People: Talks and Letters, 1956–1971* (New York: Pantheon, 1974), p. 189.

5. For example, compare with Tom Robinson, "Peking's Revolutionary Strategy

and the Developing World: The Failures of Success," *Annals of the American Academy of Political and Social Sciences* 386 (1969): 64–67.

6. Peter Van Ness, *Revolution and Chinese Foreign Policy: Peking's Support for Wars of National Liberation* (Berkeley: University of California Press, 1970), chapters 4 and 6; see also Van Ness, "China and the Third World," in Samuel S. Kim, *China and the World: Chinese Foreign Policy Faces the New Millennium,* 4th ed. (Boulder, CO: Westview Press, 1998), pp. 151–171.

7. Namely, the idea was to emphasize equality and mutual benefit, respect sovereignty and never attach conditions, provide interest-free or low-interest loans, help recipients develop independence and self-reliance, build projects that require little investment and can be accomplished quickly, provide quality equipment and material at market prices, ensure effective technical assistance, and pledge to pay experts according to local standard of living. See Shi Lin, *Dangdai Zhongguo de duiwai jingji hezuo* [Contemporary China's Economic Cooperation] (Beijing: China Social Sciences Press, 1989).

8. George T. Yu, "The Tanzania-Zambia Railway: A Case Study in Chinese Economic Aid to Africa," in Warren Weinstein and Thomas Henriksen, eds., *Soviet and Chinese Aid to African Nations* (New York: Praeger, 1980), ch. 6.

9. George T. Yu, "South-South Unity and Cooperation: China's African Policy," unpublished paper, Ljubljana, Slovenia, 2008.

10. Organization for Economic Cooperation and Development, *The Aid Program of China* (Paris: OECD, March 1987), as quoted in Samuel S. Kim, *The Third World in Chinese World Policy,* World Order Studies Program Occasional Paper No. 19 (Princeton, NJ: Princeton University, Center of International Studies, 1989), p. 37.

11. Shi Lin, *Dangdai Zhongguo,* p. 68.

12. Van Ness, "China and the Third World," p. 156.

13. China's commitment to Africa in particular has been unflagging: According to Deborah Brautigam, China has provided Africa the largest cumulative disbursement between 1960 and 1996. Deborah Brautigam, *Chinese Aid and African Development* (Ipswich, Suffolk, UK: Ipswich Book Company, 1997), p. 447.

14. Samuel S. Kim, "China as a Great Power," *Current History* 96, no. 611 (September 1997): 246–251. There have been subsequent adjustments of China's assessment rate: to 0.9 percent by 1999, and in 2006, after "firmly opposing" a motion by Japan (with an assessment rate of some 20 percent) to force reassessment of all five permanent members, China volunteered to increase its rate to 2.5 percent for the next three years. *China Daily,* online ed., December 26, 2006, http://english.people.com.cn/200612/26/eng20061226_335818.html.

15. *China Daily* (Beijing), December 25, 2006.

16. "This means that China's agreement with the Third World majority increased from an annual average of 58.5% from 1971–1976 to 80.5% during the independent line period (1981–1983), to 84.5% during the peace-development line period (1984–1987)." Kim, *Third World,* p. 15.

17. For example, the United States voted in correlation with the Third World General Assembly 1 percent of the time in 1991, 2 percent in 2003. Compare with Samuel Kim, "The People's Republic of China in the United Nations: A Preliminary Analysis," *World Politics* 26, no. 3 (April 1974): 299–330; I wish to thank Sam Kim for making UN General Assembly roll-call voting data available to me, amplifying his analysis.

18. Jeffrey Logan, "China's Energy Surge," in Mark Mohr, ed., *China's Galloping Economy: Prospects, Problems, and Implications for the United States,* Woodrow Wilson International Center for Scholars, Special Report No. 140 (May 2008), pp. 19–25.

19. "Chinese Whispers Drive Metals Boom," *BBC Online,* November 16, 2004, www.bbc.co.uk/l/hi/business/3265737.stm; "China Drives Surge in Zinc Prices," *BBC Online,* January 2, 2005, www.bbc.co.uk/1/hi/business/4134963.stm; as cited in Chris Alden, "China in Africa," *Survival* 47, no. 3 (October 2005): 147–164.

20. V. P. Dutt, "Crystal Gazing China," *Strategic Analysis* 32, no. 4 (July 2008): 509–526; Lester R. Brown, "A New World Order," *Manchester Guardian*, January 25, 2006, www.guardian.co.uk/print/0,,5382253-108142,00.html (accessed September 26, 2008).

21. Phillip C. Saunders, *China's Global Activism: Strategy, Drivers, and Tools,* Occasional Paper No. 4, (Washington, DC: National Defense University, Institute for National Strategic Studies, 2006), p. 11; Eric Heginbotham, "Evaluating China's Strategy Toward the Developing World," in Joshua Eisenman, Eric Heginbotham, and Derek Mitchell, eds., *China and the Developing World* (Armonk, NY: M. E. Sharpe, 2007), p. 197.

22. See Edward S. Steinfeld, "The Capitalist Embrace: China Ten Years After the Asian Financial Crisis," paper presented at the Conference on the Asian Financial Crisis: Ten Years After, University of California, Berkeley, November 3–4, 2006.

23. "Regulations of Verification Matters in Relation to Overseas Investment for the Establishment of Enterprises," Ministry of Commerce Order No. 16, October 1, 2004; "Guide Catalog of Countries and Industries for Overseas Investment," Ministry of Commerce, July/August 2004; as cited in Saunders, *China's Global Activism,* p. 31, fn. 28.

24. "China Makes More Overseas Investment in 2005, Mainly in Asia," *People's Daily Online* FBIS-CPP 2006021501006, February 11, 2006; Reuters, January 19, 2008.

25. On Chinese oil "loans" (tantamount to purchases, as they are tied to oil export agreements), see Michael Richardson in *Japan Times,* May 29, 2009. China was able to ramp up these purchases during the 2008–2009 world recession because the slump in world demand deflated prices while China had an approximately US$2 trillion cache of foreign exchange reserves that could not easily be spent in domestic markets without inflation.

26. Alex Vines, "China in Africa: A Mixed Blessing?" *Current History* 106, no. 700 (May 2007): 213–219.

27. Michael A. Glosny, *Meeting the Developmental Challenge in the 21st Century: American and Chinese Perspectives on Foreign Aid,* National Committee on United States–China Relations, China Policy Series, no. 21 (August 2006), p. 16.

28. Vines, "China in Africa," pp. 216–218.

29. Carol Lancaster, "The Chinese Aid System," Center for Global Development (June 2007), www.cgdev.org/files/.3953_file_chinese_aid.pdf p. 2 (accessed April 1, 2009).

30. Vines, "China in Africa," pp. 215–217.

31. Saunders, *China's Global Activism,* p. 21.

32. *China Statistical Yearbook*, 2003–2005 editions, as cited in Saunders, *China's Global Activism,* p. 18. These figures fail to take into account the statements of leading officials. For example, attending the 2005 ASEAN+3 summit in Malaysia, Premier Wen Jiabao said that in the past five years, China had provided nearly US$3 billion to ASEAN countries, and that ASEAN countries would receive one-third of the $10 billion in preferential loans and buyers' credits China would offer developing countries in the next three years.

33. Glosny, *Meeting the Developmental Challenge*, p. 7.

34. See Joseph S. Nye, *Soft Power: The Means to Success in World Politics* (New

York: Public Affairs, 2004); and Nye, "The Rise of China's Soft Power," *Wall Street Journal Asia*, December 29, 2005; see also Joshua Kurlantzick, *Charm Offensive: How China's Soft Power Is Transforming the World* (New Haven, CT: Yale University Press, 2007).

35. However, only one-third of these were seeking degrees; see *Chronicle of Higher Education*, September 15, 2008.

36. See Joshua Cooper Ramo, *Beijing Consensus* (London: Foreign Policy Centre, 2004).

37. See Michael A. Glosny, "Stabilizing the Backyard," in Eisenman, Heginbotham, and Mitchell, eds., *China and the Developing World,* p. 159, table 7:4.

38. Although the "future of the planet" is honored more in rhetoric than in policy. Take for example the global climate change issue, which finds China forming a coalition with developing countries to resist higher emission standards. In 2009, China demanded that rich countries cut greenhouse gases by 40 percent (from 1990 levels) by 2020 and help pay for pollution reduction schemes in less-developed countries. The latter are encouraged to curb emissions on a voluntary basis but only if that "accords with national situations." *Financial Times*, May 21, 2009, p. 3.

39. Deng Xiaoping, "We Must Follow Our Own Road in Economic Development as We Did in Revolution" (October 26, 1984), in Deng Xiaoping, *Selected Works*, vol. 3 (Beijing: Foreign Languages Press, 1994), pp. 100–101.

40. The term itself was used in a speech given by former vice principal of the Central Party School Zheng Bijian in late 2003 during the Boao Forum for Asia. It was then reiterated by PRC premier Wen Jiabao in an ASEAN meeting as well as during his visit to the United States. The term, however, then became so controversial that it was modified in leadership speeches to "peaceful development." See, by comparison, Zheng Bijian, "China's 'Peaceful Rise' to Great-Power Status," *Foreign Affairs* 84, no. 5 (September–October 2005): 18.

# Bibliography

Alden, Chris. "China in Africa." *Survival* 47, no. 3 (October 2005): 147–164.

Alden, Christopher, Daniel Large, and Ricardo de Oliveira, eds. *China Returns to Africa: A Superpower and a Continent Embraced.* London: Hurst, 2008.

Allen, Kenneth W., and Eric A. McVadon. *China's Foreign Military Relations.* Washington, DC: Henry L. Stimson Center, 1999.

Amiti, Mary, and Caroline Freund. *An Anatomy of China's Export Growth.* Washington, DC: National Bureau of Economic Research, 2008.

Amsden, Alice. *Asia's Next Giant: South Korea and Late Industrialization.* New York: Oxford University Press, 1989.

Armstrong, J. D. *Revolutionary Diplomacy: Chinese Foreign Policy and the United Front Doctrine.* Berkeley: University of California Press, 1977.

Athwal, Amardeep. *China-India Relations: Contemporary Dynamics.* London: Routledge, 2008.

Battat, Joseph. *China's Outward Foreign Direct Investment.* Washington, DC: Foreign Investment Advisory Services, The World Bank, 2006.

Berger, Bernt, and Uwe Wissenbach. *EU-China-Africa Trilateral Development Cooperation: Common Challenges and New Directions.* Bonn: German Development Institute, 2007.

Berkofsky, Axel. "True Strategic Partnership or Rhetorical Window Dressing? A Closer Look at the Relationship Between the EU and Japan." *Japan aktuell—Journal of Current Japanese Affairs*, no. 2 (2008): 22–37.

Brautigam, Deborah. *Chinese Aid and African Development: Exporting the Green Revolution.* Ipswich, Suffolk: The Ipswich Book Company, 1998.

Breslin, Shaun. "Power and Production: Rethinking China's Global Economic Role," *Review of International Studies* 31, no. 4 (2005).

———. "Supplying Demand or Demanding Supply? An Alternative Look at the Forces Driving East Asian Community Building." Stanley Foundation Policy Analysis Brief (November 2007).

Brown, Michael, Owen Coté, Sean Lynn-Jones, and Steven Miller, eds., *The Rise of China.* Cambridge, MA: MIT Press, 2000.

Bureau of International Cooperation, CASS, Institute of West-Asia and African Studies, CASS and Department for International Development, UK. *The Symposium of China-Africa Shared Development.* Beijing, 2006.

Byman, Daniel L., and Roger Cliff. *China's Arms Sales: Motivations and Implications.* Santa Monica, CA: RAND Corp., 1999.

*Chairman Mao's Theory of the Differentiation of the Three Worlds Is a Major Contribution to Marxism-Leninism.* Beijing: Foreign Languages Press, 1977.

Chang, Ha-Joon. *Kicking Away the Ladder: Development Strategy in Historical Perspective.* London: Anthem Press, 2002.

Chemillier-Gendreau, Monique. *Sovereignty over the Paracel and the Spratly Islands.* The Hague: Kluwer Law International, 2000.

Cheng, Joseph Yu-Shek. "The ASEAN-China Free Trade Area: Genesis and Implications." *Australian Journal of International Affairs* 58, no. 2 (2004): 257–277.

Chicago Council on Global Affairs. "Soft Power in Asia: Report of a 2008 Multinational Survey of Public Opinion." Available at www.thechicagocouncil .org/UserFiles/File/POS_Topline%20Reports/Asia%20Soft%20Power%202008/ Chicago%20Council%20Soft%20Power%20Report-%20Final%206-11-08.pdf.

Chin, Gregory T. "China and the Small States of the Caribbean: Responding to Vulnerabilities, Securing Developmental Space." Paper presented at the Graduate Institute of International Relations, University of the West Indies, Trinidad, February 8, 2008.

Christoffersen, Gaye. "Problems and Prospects for Northeast Energy Cooperation." Paper presented at IREX. March 23, 2000.

Chu Shulong. *Zhongguo waijiao zhanlue he zhengci* [China's Foreign Strategy and Policy]. Beijing: Shishi chubanshe, 2005.

Cody, Edward. "China's Quiet Rise Casts Wide Shadow." *Washington Post.* January 26, 2005.

Collier, Paul. *The Bottom Billion: Why the Poorest Countries Are Failing and What Can Be Done About It.* New York: Oxford University Press, 2007.

Cooper Ramo, Joshua. *Beijing Consensus.* London: Foreign Policy Centre, 2004.

Craddock, General Brantz J. Statement to the hearing on "Fiscal Year 2006 National Defense Authorization Budget Request" before the Armed Services Committee of the House of Representatives. March 9, 2005.

Cranmer-Byng, John. "The Chinese View of Their Place in the World: An Historical Perspective." *The China Quarterly*, no. 53 (January–March 1973).

*Dangdai Zhongguo Weijiao* [Contemporary Chinese Foreign Relations]. Beijing: China Social Science Publishing Company, 1987.

Davies, Martyn. *How China Delivers Development Assistance to Africa.* Stellenbosch, South Africa: Center for Chinese Studies, University of Stellenbosch, 2008.

Davies, Penny. *China and the End of Poverty in Africa–Towards Mutual Benefit?* Sundbyberg, Sweden: Alfaprint, 2007.

"Democracy and Development in Maldives," *Peace and Conflict* 9, no. 6 (June 2006).

Deng Xiaoping. *Fundamental Issues in Present-Day China.* Beijing: Foreign Languages Press, 1987.

———. *Selected Works*, vol. 3. Beijing: Foreign Languages Press, 1994.

Department of Policy Planning, Ministry of Foreign Affairs, People's Republic of

China. *Zhongguo Weijiao 2006 Nian Ban* [China's Foreign Affairs, 2006 Edition]. Beijing: World Affairs Press, 2006.

——. *Zhongguo Weijiao 2007 Nian Ban* [China's Foreign Affairs, 2007 Edition]. Beijing: World Affairs Press, 2007.

Devlin, Robert. "China's Economic Rise." In Riordan Roett and Guadalupe Paz, eds., *China's Expansion into the Western Hemisphere: Implications for Latin America and the United States.* Washington, DC: Brookings Institution, 2008.

Devlin, Robert, Antoni Estevadeordal, and Andrés Rodríguez-Clare. *The Emergence of China: Opportunities and Challenges for Latin America and the Caribbean.* Washington, DC: Inter-American Development Bank, 2006.

Dittmer, Lowell. "China's New Internationalism." In Guoguang Wu and Helen Landsowne, eds., *China Turns to Multilateralism*, 21–34. London: Routledge, 2008.

Dosch, Jörn, and Oliver Hensengerth. "Sub-Regional Cooperation in Southeast Asia: The Mekong Basin." *European Journal of East Asian Studies* 4, no. 2 (2005): 263–285.

Dosch, Jörn, and Alexander Vuving. *The Impact of China on Governance Structures in Vietnam.* Bonn: German Institute for Development (DIE), 2008.

Dreyer, June Teufel. "The China Connection," Paper by China–Latin America Task Force, Center for Hemispheric Policy, University of Miami, March–June 2006.

Drifte, Reinhard. "The End of Japan's ODA Yen Loan Programme to China in 2008 and Its Repercussions." *Japan Aktuell—Journal of Current Japanese Affairs,* no. 1 (2008): 3–15.

Dussel Peters, Enrique. "What Does China's Integration to the World Market Mean for Latin America? The Mexican Experience." In Diego Sánchez-Ancochea and Kenneth C. Shadlen, *The Political Economy of Hemispheric Integration: Responding to Globalization in the Americas.* Basingstoke, UK: Palgrave, 2008.

Dutt, V. P. "Crystal Gazing China." *Strategic Analysis* 32, no. 4 (July 2008): 509–526.

Earth Rights International. "China in Burma: The Increasing Investment of Chinese Multinational Corporations in Burma's Hydropower, Oil & Gas, and Mining Sectors," Burma Project, September 2007.

Economic Commission for Latin America and the Caribbean, "Economic and Trade Relations Between Latin America and Asia-Pacific: The Link with China." Document prepared for the 2nd Latin America–China Business Summit, Harbin, Heilongjiang, October 21–22, 2008.

Eichengreen, Barry, and Hui Tong. "How China Is Reorganizing the World Economy." *Asian Economic Policy Review* 1, no. 1 (2006): 73–97.

Eisenman, Joshua, Eric Heginbotham, and Derek Mitchell, eds. *China and the Developing World.* Armonk, NY: M. E. Sharpe, 2007.

Energy Information Administration. "World Oil Markets Analysis to 2030: Petroleum and Other Liquid Fuels." In *International Energy Outlook 2007.* Washington, DC: EIA, 2007.

Erikson, Daniel P., and Janice Chen. "China, Taiwan and the Battle for Latin America." *The Fletcher Forum of World Affairs* 31, no. 2 (2007).

Frieberg, Aaron. "'Going Out': China's Pursuit of Natural Resources and Implications for the PRC's Grand Strategy." *NBR Analysis* 17, no. 3 (September 2006).

Frost, Ellen. "China's Commercial Diplomacy in Asia: Promise or Threat." In William

Keller and Thomas Rawski, eds., *China's Rise and the Balance of Influence in Asia*, 95–117. Pittsburgh, PA: University of Pittsburgh Press.

Frye, Richard. *The Heritage of Central Asia: From Antiquity to the Turkish Expansion.* Princeton: Markus Wiener Publishers, 2001.

Fukagawa, Yukiko. "East Asia's New Economic Integration Strategy: Moving Beyond the FTA." *Asia-Pacific Review* 12, no. 2 (2005).

Gallagher, Kevin P., Juan Carlos Moreno-Brid, and Roberto Porzecanski. "The Dynamism of Mexican Exports: Lost in (Chinese) Translation?" *World Development* 36, no. 8 (2008).

Gallagher, Kevin P., and Roberto Porzecanski. "China Matters: China's Economic Impact in Latin America," *Latin American Research Review* 43, no. 1 (2008).

Garver, John W. *China and Iran: Ancient Partners in a Post-Imperial World.* Seattle: University of Washington Press, 2006.

———. "The Restoration of Sino-Indian Comity Following India's Nuclear Tests." *The China Quarterly,* no. 168 (December 2001): 865–889.

Garver, John W., and Jon B. Alterman. *The Vital Triangle: China, the United States, and the Middle East.* Washington, DC: Center for Strategic and International Studies, 2008.

Ghazvinian, John. *Untapped: The Scramble for Africa's Oil.* Orlando, FL: Harcourt, 2007.

Gilks, Anne, and Gerald Segal. *China and the Arms Trade.* London: Croom Helm, 1985.

Gill, R. Bates. "Curbing Beijing's Arms Sales." *Orbis* 36, no. 3 (Summer 1992): 379–396.

Gill, Bates, and James Reilly. "Tenuous Hold of China Inc. in Africa." *Atlantic Quarterly* 30, no. 3 (Summer 2007): 37–52.

Gilpin, Robert. *The Political Economy of International Relations.* Princeton, NJ: Princeton University Press, 1987.

———. *War and Change in World Politics.* Cambridge: Cambridge University Press, 1981.

Gittings, John. *The World and China, 1922–1972.* New York: Harper & Row, 1974.

Gladney, Dru. *Dislocating China: Muslims, Minorities, and other Subaltern Subjects.* Chicago: The University of Chicago Press, 2004.

Glosny, Michael A. *Meeting the Developmental Challenge in the Twenty-First Century: American and Chinese Perspectives on Foreign Aid.* National Committee on United States–China Relations, China Policy Series, no. 21 (August 2006).

Goh, Evelyn, and Sheldon W. Simon. "Introduction." In E. Goh and S. W. Simon, eds., *China, the United States, and Southeast Asia: Contending Perspectives on Politics, Security, and Economics.* New York and London: Routledge, 2008.

González, Francisco E. "Latin America in the Economic Equation—Winners and Losers: What Can Losers Do?" In Riordan Roett and Guadalupe Paz, eds. *China's Expansion into the Western Hemisphere: Implications for Latin America and the United States.* Washington, DC: Brookings Institution, 2008.

Grieder, Tom. "China to Assist Vietnam in Building Its First NPP." *Global Insight.* February 24, 2009.

Gruenwald, Paul, and Masahiro Hori. "Asian Exports: Intra-regional Trade Key to

Asia's Export Boom." *IMF Survey Magazine: Countries & Region.* February 6, 2008.

Gurtov, Melvin. *China and Southeast Asia—The Politics of Survival: A Study of Foreign Policy Interaction.* Lexington, MA: D. C. Heath, 1971.

Gurtov, Melvin, and Byong-Moo Hwang. *China Under Threat: The Politics of Strategy and Diplomacy.* Baltimore: Johns Hopkins University Press, 1980.

Haider, Ziad. "Sino-Pakistan Relations and Xinjiang's Uighurs: Politics, Trade and Islam Along the Karakoram Highway." *Asian Survey* 45, no. 4 (July-August 2005): 522–545.

Harris, Lillian Craig. *China Considers the Middle East.* London: Tauris, 1993.

Heron, Tony. "The Ending of the Multifibre Arrangement: A Development Boon for the South." *European Journal of Development Research* 18, no. 1 (2006): 1–21.

Hilaire, Alvin, and Yongzheng Yang. "The United States and the New Regionalism/ Bilateralism." IMF Working Paper WP/03/206, 1–16. Washington, DC: International Monetary Fund, 2003.

Holmes, James R., Andrew C. Winner, and Toshi Yoshihara. *Indian Naval Strategy in the 21st Century.* New York: Routledge, 2009.

Hong Chun, and Guo Yingde. *Zhong'a guanxi shi* [A History of Sino-Arab Relations]. Beijing: Jingji ribao chubanshe, 2001.

Hu Sheng. "On the Establishment of a New International Order on the Basis of the Five Principles of Peaceful Coexistence." *Social Sciences in China* 13, no. 1 (January 1992): 5–12.

Huan Xiang. "On Sino-US Relations." *Foreign Affairs* 60, no. 1 (Fall 1981): 35–53.

Hughes, Christopher R. "Nationalism and Multilateralism in Chinese Foreign Policy: Implications for Southeast Asia." *Pacific Review* 18, no. 1 (2005): 19–35.

Huwaidin, Mohamed Bin. *China's Relations with Arabia and the Gulf.* London: Routledge, 2002.

Ikenberry, John. "The Rise of China and the Future of the West: Can the Liberal System Survive?" *Foreign Affairs* 87, no. 1 (January/February 2008): 23–37.

International Crisis Group. "China's Growing Role in UN Peacekeeping." April 17, 2009. Available at www.crisisgroup.org/library/documents/asia/north_east_asia/166_chinas_growing_role_in_un_peacekeeping.pdf.

———. *China's Thirst for Oil.* Asia Report No. 153, June 9, 2008.

International Institute for Strategic Studies. *The Military Balance, 2008–2009.* Oxford: Oxford University Press, 2008.

International Monetary Fund. *Direction of Trade Statistics Yearbook, 2007.* Washington, DC: International Monetary Fund, 2008.

Israeli, Raphael, ed. *PLO in Lebanon: Selected Documents.* London: Weidenfeld and Nicolson, 1983.

'Itāni, 'Amr. *Siyasat Bakin izā'a al-Sharq al-'Arabi bayn al-Ams wa'l-Yaum* [Beijing's Policy Toward the Arab East Between Yesterday and Today]. Beirut: Dār al-Farābi, 1972.

Jenkins, Rhys, Enrique Dussel Peters, and Mauricio Mesquita Moreira. "The Economic Impact of China on Latin America—An Agenda for Research." Paper presented at the 7th Annual Global Development Conference, Pre-conference Workshop on "Asian and Other Drivers of Global Change," St. Petersburg, January 18–19, 2006.

————. "The Impact of China on Latin America and the Caribbean." *World Development* 36, no. 2 (2008).

Jiang, Shixue. "The Chinese Foreign Policy Perspective." In Riordan Roett and Guadalupe Paz, eds., *China's Expansion into the Western Hemisphere: Implications for Latin America and the United States.* Washington, DC: Brookings Institution, 2008.

Johnston, Alastair Iain, and Robert S. Ross, eds. *New Directions in the Study of China's Foreign Policy.* Stanford, CA: Stanford University Press, 2006.

Kaplan, Robert. "Center Stage for the Twenty-First Century Power Plays in the Indian Ocean," *Foreign Affairs* 88, no. 2 (March–April 2009): 16–32.

Kaplinsky, Raphael. *Globalization, Poverty, and Inequality.* Cambridge, UK: Polity, 2005.

Kaplinsky, Raphael, and Mike Morris. "Do the Asian Drivers Undermine Export-Oriented Industrialization in SSA?" *World Development* 36, no. 2 (2008): 254–273.

Keith, Ronald C. "China as a Rising World Power and Its Response to 'Globalization.'" *Review of International Affairs* 3, no. 4 (2004): 507–523.

Kennedy, Scott. "China's Porous Protectionism: The Changing Political Economy of Trade Policy. " *Political Science Quarterly* 120, no. 3 (2005).

Kharas, Homi. "Lifting All Boats: Why China's Great Leap Is Good for the World's Poor," *Foreign Policy* (January–February 2005): 55.

al-Khariji, 'Abdullah. *Al-Ṣin wa'l-Shu'ub al-'Arabiyyah* [China and the Arab Peoples]. Beirut: Dār al-Farābi, 1979.

Kim, Samuel S. *China and the World: Chinese Foreign Policy Faces the New Millennium,* 4th ed., 151–171. Boulder, CO: Westview Press, 1998.

————. "China as a Great Power." *Current History* 96, no. 611 (September 1997): 246–251.

————. *China, the United Nations, and World Order.* Princeton, NJ: Princeton University Press, 1979.

————. "The People's Republic of China in the United Nations: A Preliminary Analysis." *World Politics* 26, no. 3 (April 1974): 299–330.

————. *The Third World in Chinese World Policy.* World Order Studies Program Occasional Paper No. 19. Princeton, NJ: Princeton University, Center for International Studies, Woodrow Wilson School of Public and International Affairs, 1989.

Kleine-Ahlbrandt, Stephanie, and Andrew Small. "China's New Dictatorship Diplomacy," *Foreign Affairs* 87, no. 1 (January/February 2008): 38–56.

Kudo, Toshihiro. *Myanmar's Economic Relations with China: Can China Support the Myanmar Economy?* Institute of Developing Economies Discussion Paper 66, Japan External Trade Organization (JETRO), 2006.

Kun, Zhai. "Vietnam Thriving on Major-Power Diplomacy." *China Daily* (North American ed.). June 22, 2007.

Kurlantzick, Joshua. *Charm Offensive: How China's Soft Power Is Transforming the World.* New Haven, CT: Yale University Press, 2007.

Kusano, A. "Japan's ODA in the 21st Century." *Asia-Pacific Review* 7, no. 1 (2000): 38–55.

Lal, Rollie. "China's Relations with South Asia." In Joshua Eisenman, Eric

Heginbotham, and Derek Mitchell, eds., *China and the Developing World: Beijing's Strategy for the Twenty-First Century,* 133–149. Armonk, NY: M. E. Sharpe, 2007.

Lall, Sanjaya, and John Weiss. "China's Competitive Threat to Latin America: An Analysis for 1990–2002." *Oxford Development Studies* 33, no. 2 (2005): 163–194.

Lampton, David M., ed. *The Making of Chinese Foreign and Security Policy in the Era of Reform, 1978–2000.* Stanford, CA: Stanford University Press, 2001.

Lancaster, Carol. "The Chinese Aid System." Center for Global Development (June 2007). Available at www.cgdev.org/files/.3953_file_chinese_aid.pdf.

Lanteigne, Marc. *China and International Institutions: Alternate Paths to Global Power.* London: Routledge, 2005.

Lardy, Nicholas R. *Integrating China into the Global Economy.* Washington, DC: Brookings Institution Press, 2002.

Large, Daniel. "Beyond 'Dragon in the Bush': The Study of China-African Relations." *African Affairs* 107, no. 426 (2008): 45–61.

Lederman, Daniel, Marcelo Olarreaga, and Isidro Soloaga. "The Growth of China and India in World Trade: Opportunity or Threat for Latin America and the Caribbean?" Policy Research Working Paper no. 4320, 2. Washington, DC: The World Bank.

Li Anshan. "China and Africa: Policies and Challenges." *China Security* 3, no. 3 (Summer 2007): 69–93.

Li Jinming, and Li Dexia. "The Dotted Line on the Chinese Map of the South China Sea: A Note." *Ocean Development & International Law* 34 (2003): 287–295.

Liang, Wei. "China: Globalization and the Emergence of a New Status Quo Power?" *Asian Perspective* 31, no. 4 (2007): 125–149.

Liou, Chih-shian. "Outsourcing Reform: The Political Logic of Overseas Expansion of China's Central State-Owned Enterprises." Chapter 3 of Ph.D. dissertation, Department of Government, University of Texas at Austin. Forthcoming.

Liu Haifang, "Chinese-African Relations Through the Prism of Culture—The Dynamics of China's Culture Diplomacy with Africa," *China Aktuell,* no. 3 (2008): 9–44.

Liu Jing, Zhang Shizhi, and Zhu Li. *Sulian zhongdong guanxi shi* [History of Soviet–Middle Eastern Relations]. Beijing: Zhongguo shehui kexue chubanshe, 1987.

Liu Shaoqi (Liu Shao-chi). *Internationalism and Nationalism.* Beijing: Foreign Languages Press, 1951.

———. *Ten Glorious Years.* Beijing: Foreign Languages Press, 1950.

Logan, Jeffrey. "China's Energy Surge." In Mark Mohr, ed., *China's Galloping Economy: Prospects, Problems, and Implications for the United States.* Woodrow Wilson International Center for Scholars, Special Report No. 140 (May 2008), pp. 19–25.

Lu Tingen, and Ma Ruimin, eds. *Zhongguo yu Feizhou* [China and Africa]. Beijing: Peking University Press, 2000.

Lum, Thomas, et al. "China's Foreign Aid Activities in Africa, Latin America, and Southeast Asia." Report R-40361. Washington, DC: Congressional Research Service, 2009.

Lum, Thomas, et al. *China's "Soft Power" in Southeast Asia.* Washington, DC: Congressional Research Service, January 4, 2008.

Ma, Xin, and Philip Andrews-Speed. "The Overseas Activities of China's National Oil Companies: Rationale and Outlook." *Minerals and Energy*, no. 1 (2006): 17–30.

Ma Jisen. *Waijiaobu wenge jishi* [The Cultural Revolution in the Foreign Ministry]. Hong Kong: The Chinese University Press, 2003.

Mao Zedong. *The Chinese Revolution and the Chinese Communist Party*. Peking: Foreign Languages Press, 1967.

———. *Selected Readings from the Works of Mao Tse-tung*. Peking: Foreign Languages Press, 1971.

Maung Aung Myoe. *Sino-Myanmar Economic Relations Since 1988*. Asia Research Institute, National University of Singapore, Working Paper Series 86, 2007.

Medeiros, Evan S., and Bates Gill. *Chinese Arms Exports: Policy, Players, and Process*. Carlisle, PA: US Army War College, Strategic Studies Institute, 2000.

Mesquita Moreira, Mauricio. "Fear of China: Is There a Future for Manufacturing in Latin America?" *World Development* 35, no. 3 (2006).

Mesquita Moreira, Mauricio, and Juan Blyde. "Chile's Integration Strategy: Is There Room for Improvement?" IADB-INTAL-ITD Working Paper No. 21. Washington, DC: Inter-American Development Bank, 2006.

Mills, Elizabeth. "Unconditional Aid from China Threatens to Undermine Donor Pressure on Cambodia." *Global Insight*. June 7, 2007.

Millward, James. *Eurasian Crossroads: A History of Xinjiang*. New York: Columbia University Press, 2007.

Ministry of Commerce of the People's Republic of China. "China Trade in Services." June 26, 2008. Available at http://64.233.183.104/search?q=cache:iJCXIr37dEwJ: tradeinservices.mofcom.gov.cn/en/a/2008-06-03/44262.shtml+china+ kazakhstan+trade+2007&hl=sv&ct=clnk&cd=8.

Monson, Jamie. *Africa's Freedom Railway*. Bloomington and Indianapolis: Indiana University Press, 2009.

Morrison, Wayne M., and Marc Labonte. "China's Currency: Economic Issues and Options for US Trade Policy." *Congressional Research Service*. Washington, DC. May 22, 2008.

Mozingo, David. *Chinese Policy Toward Indonesia, 1949–1967*. Ithaca, NY: Cornell University Press, 1976.

Nguyen Nha. *Thu dat lai van de Hoang Sa* [Reconsidering the Paracel Islands Issue]. *Su Dia* [History and Geography], no. 29 (1975).

Nolan, Peter. *China and the Global Economy: National Champions, Industrial Policy, and the Big Business Revolution*. New York: Palgrave, 2001.

Norling, Nicklas, and Swanström, Niklas. "The Shanghai Cooperation Organization, Trade, and the Roles of India, Pakistan, and Iran." *Central Asian Survey* 26, no. 3 (2007).

———. "The Virtues and Potential Gains of Continental Trade in Eurasia." *Asian Survey* 47 (2007): 351–373.

Nye, Joseph S. *Soft Power: The Means to Success in World Politics* (New York: Public Affairs, 2004).

Odgaard, Liselotte. "The South China Sea: ASEAN's Security Concerns About China." *Security Dialogue* 34, no. 1 (2004): 11–24.

Ong, Russell. *China's Security Interests in the Post–Cold War Era*. London: Curzon, 2002.

Palacios, Luisa. "Latin America as China's Energy Supplier. " In Riordan Roett and

Guadalupe Paz, eds., *China's Expansion into the Western Hemisphere: Implications for Latin America and the United States.* Washington, DC: Brookings Institution, 2008.

Paltiel, Jeremy T. *The Empire's New Clothes: Cultural Particularism and Universal Value in China's Quest for Global Status.* New York: Palgrave Macmillan, 2007.

Pang, Eul-Soon. "Embedding Security into Free Trade: The Case of the United States–Singapore Free Trade Agreement." *Contemporary Southeast Asia* 29 (2007): 1–32.

Peerenboom, Randall. *China Modernizes: Threat to the West or Model for the Rest?* Oxford: Oxford University Press, 2007.

Peng Zhen (Peng Chen). *Speech at the Aliarcham Academy of Social Sciences in Indonesia.* Peking: Foreign Languages Press, 1965.

Perdue, Peter. *China Marches West: The Qing Conquest of Central Eurasia.* Cambridge: The Belknap Press of Harvard University Press, 2005.

Perhson, Christopher. "String of Pearls: Meeting the Challenge of China's Rising Power Across the Asian Littoral." US Army War College, Strategic Studies Institute, Carlisle Papers in Security Strategy, July 2006.

Pew Global Attitudes Project. "Global Economic Gloom—China and India Notable Exceptions." June 12, 2008. Available at http://pewglobal.org/reports/display.php?ReportID=260.

Phillips, Nicola. "China and the New Global Economy: Is Development Space Disappearing for Latin America and the Caribbean?" In Andrew F. Cooper and Jorge Heine, eds., *Which Way Latin America? Hemispheric Politics Meets Globalisation.* Tokyo: United Nations University Press, forthcoming.

———. "The Limits of 'Securitization': Power, Politics and Process in US Foreign Economic Policy." *Government and Opposition* 42, no. 2 (2007).

———. *The Southern Cone Model: The Political Economy of Regionalist Capitalist Development in Latin America.* London: Routledge, 2004.

Prasad, Eswar, ed. *China's Growth and Integration into the World Economy.* Occasional Paper No. 232. Washington, DC: International Monetary Fund, 2004.

Radtke, Kurt W. "China and the Greater Middle East: Globalization No Longer Equals Westernization." In M. Parvizi Amineh, ed., *The Greater Middle East in Global Politics*, 387–414. Leiden: Brill, 2007.

Raine, Sarah. *China's African Challenges.* London: The International Institute for Strategic Studies, 2009.

Ratliff, William. "The Global Context of a Chinese 'Threat' in Latin America." China–Latin America Task Force, Center for Hemispheric Policy, University of Miami, March–June, 2006.

Ripsman, Norrin M. "Two Stages of Transition from a Region of War to a Region of Peace: Realist Transition and Liberal Endurance." *International Studies Quarterly* 49 (2005): 669–693.

Roberts, Sean. "A Land of Borderlands: Implications of Xinjiang's Transborder Interactions." In Frederick Starr, ed., *Xinjiang: China's Muslim Borderland*, 216–240. Armonk, NY: M. E. Sharpe, 2004.

Robinson, Tom. "Peking's Revolutionary Strategy and the Developing World: The Failures of Success." *Annals of the American Academy of Political and Social Sciences* 386 (1969): 64–67.

Roett, Riordan. "Relations Between China and Latin America/the Western Hemisphere." Statement Before the Subcommittee on the Western Hemisphere, House International Relations Committee, US Congress, April 6, 2005.

Rosecrance, Richard N. *The Rise of the Trading State: Commerce and Conquest in the Modern World.* New York: Basic Books, 1986.

Rossabi, Morris, ed. *Governing China's Multiethnic Frontiers.* Seattle: University of Washington Press, 2004.

Rothman, Andy. "China Eats the World: The Sustainability of Chinese Commodities Demand." Credit Lyonnais Securities Asia, March 2005.

Saez, Lawrence. "China's Global Emergence and the Theoretical Linkages Between Multilateralism and Peripheral Stability." *Daxiyangguo,* no. 13 (2008): 93–112.

Saunders, Phillip C. *China's Global Activism: Strategy, Drivers, and Tools.* Occasional Paper No. 4. Washington, DC: National Defense University, Institute for National Strategic Studies, 2006.

Sautman, Barry, and Yan Hairong. *East Mountain Tiger, West Mountain Tiger: China, the West, and 'Colonialism' in Africa.* Maryland Series in Contemporary Asian Studies, No. 3 (2006).

———. "The Forest for the Trees: Trade, Investment and the China-in-Africa Discourse." *Pacific Affairs* 81, no. 1 (Spring 2008): 9–29.

Schram, Stuart, ed. *Chairman Mao Talks to the People: Talks and Letters, 1956–1971.* New York: Pantheon, 1974.

Shambaugh, David. "China's Military Views the World: Ambivalent Security." *International Security* 24, no. 3 (Winter 1999/2000): 52–79.

Shanghai Institute for International Studies. *China and Asia's Security.* Singapore: Marshall Cavendish, 2005.

Sharpe, Samuel. "An ASEAN Way to Security Cooperation in Southeast Asia?" *The Pacific Review* 16, no. 2 (2003): 1–50.

Shi Lin. *Dangdai Zhongguo de duiwai jingji hezuo* [Contemporary China's Economic Cooperation]. Beijing: China Social Sciences Press, 1989.

Shichor, Yitzhak. "China and the Role of the United Nations in the Middle East: Revised Policy." *Asian Survey* 31, no. 3 (March 1991): 255–269.

———. "China's Economic Relations with the Middle East: New Dimensions." In P. R. Kumaraswamy, ed., *China and the Middle East: The Quest for Influence,* 178–199. New Delhi and London: Sage Publications, 1999.

———. "China's Upsurge: Implications for the Middle East." *Israel Affairs* 12, no. 4 (September 2006): 665–683.

———. "The Chinese Factor in the Middle East Security Equation: An Israeli Perspective." In Jonathan Goldstein, ed., *China and Israel, 1948–1998: A Fifty Year Retrospective,* 153–178. Westport, CT: Praeger, 1999.

———. "Competence and Incompetence: The Political Economy of China's Relations with the Middle East." *Asian Perspective* 30, no. 4 (2006): 39–67.

———. "Decisionmaking in Triplicate: China and the Three Iraqi Wars." In Andrew Scobell and Larry Wortzel, eds., *Chinese National Security Decision-Making Under Stress,* 191–228. Carlisle, PA: US Army War College, Strategic Studies Institute, 2005).

———. *East Wind over Arabia: Origins and Implications of the Sino-Saudi Missile Deal.* China Research Monographs 35. Berkeley: Center for Chinese Studies, University of California, 1989.

———. *Ethnodiplomacy: The Uyghur Hitch in Sino-Turkish Relations.* Policy Studies, No. 53. Washington, DC: East-West Center, 2009.

———. "Hide-and-Seek: Sino-Israeli Relations in Perspective." *Israel Affairs* 1, no. 2 (Winter 1994): 16–35.

———. "Israel's Military Transfers to China and Taiwan." *Survival* 40, no. 1 (Spring 1998): 68–91.

———. *The Middle East in China's Foreign Policy 1949–1977.* Cambridge: Cambridge University Press, 1979, 2008.

———. "Mountains Out of Molehills: Arms Transfers in Sino–Middle Eastern Relations." *Middle East Review of International Affairs (MERIA)* 4, no. 3 (Fall 2000): 68–79.

———. "Much Ado About Nothing: Middle East Perceptions of the 'China Threat.'" In Herbert Yee, ed., *The China Threat—Perceptions, Myths, and Reality*, 312–331. Richmond, Surrey, UK: Curzon, 2002.

———. "Unfolded Arms: Beijing's Recent Military Sales Offensive," *The Pacific Review* 1, no. 3 (October 1988): 320–330.

———. "The Year of the Silkworms: China's Arms Transactions, 1987." In Richard Yang, ed., *SCPS Yearbook on PLA Affairs 1987*, 153–168. Kaohsiung: Sun Yat-sen Center for Policy Studies, 1988.

Shirk, Susan. "One-Sided Rivalry: China's Perceptions and Policies Toward India." In Francine Frankel and Harry Harding, eds., *The India-China Relationship*, 75–102. Washington, DC: Woodrow Wilson Center Press, 2004.

Simpson, John. "Peru's 'Copper Mountain' in Chinese Hands." *BBC News.* June 18, 2008.

Šír, Jan, and Slavomír Horák. "China as an Emerging Superpower in Central Asia: The View from Ashkhabad," *China and Eurasia Quarterly* 6, no. 2 (2008).

Spies, Johannes J. "Experiences and Impression on Diplomatic Engagement with the People's Republic of China: A South African Perspective." In *New Impulses from the South: China's Engagement of Africa*, 66–68. Matieland, South Africa: Center for Chinese Studies, University of Stellenbosch, 2008.

Strategic Framework Agreement Between the United States of America and the Republic of Singapore for a Closer Cooperation Partnership in Defense and Security, July 12, 2005.

Stiglitz, Joseph E. *Globalization and Its Discontents.* New York: W. W. Norton, 2002.

Stuart-Fox, Martin. *A Short History of China and Southeast Asia: Tribute, Trade and Influence.* Crows Nest, Australia: Allen & Unwin, 2003.

Sufott, E. Zev. *A China Diary: Towards the Establishment of China-Israel Diplomatic Relations.* London: Frank Cass, 1997.

Sutter, Robert. "China's Rise, Southeast Asia, and the United States: Is a China-Centered Order Marginalizing the United States?" In E. Goh and S. W. Simon, eds., *China, the United States, and Southeast Asia. Contending Perspectives on Politics, Security, and Economics.* New York and London: Routledge, 2008.

Swanström, Niklas. "An Asian Oil and Gas Union: Prospects and Problems." *China and Eurasia Quarterly* 3 (2005): 81–97.

———. "China and Central Asia: A New Great Game or Traditional Vassal Relations?" *Journal of Contemporary China* 14, no. 45 (2005): 569–584.

———. "China's Role in Central Asia: Soft and Hard Power." *Global Dialogue* 9, no. 1–2 (2007).

————. "The Narcotics Trade: A Threat to Security? National and Transnational Implications." *Global Crime* 8, no. 1 (2007): 1–25.

————. "The New Opium War in China: New Threats, New Actors and New Implications." In Niklas Swanström and Yin He, eds., *Introduction in China's War on Narcotics: Two Perspectives*. Stockholm: Institute for Security and Development Policy, 2007.

————. "Political Development and Organized Crime: The Yin and Yang of Greater Central Asia?" *China and Eurasia Forum Quarterly* 5, no. 4 (2007).

Swanström, Niklas, and Yin He, eds. *Introduction in China's War on Narcotics: Two Perspectives*. Stockholm: Institute for Security and Development Policy, 2007.

Swanström, Niklas, Nicklas Norling, and Li Zhang. "China: The New Silk Roads: Transport and Trade in Greater Central Asia." In Frederick Starr, ed., *The New Silk Roads,* 383–422. Washington, DC, and Stockholm: Central Asia Caucasus Institute and the Silk Road Studies Program, 2007.

Taylor, Ian. *China and Africa: Engagement and Compromise*. Abingdon, UK: Routledge, 2006.

————. *China's New Role in Africa*. Boulder, CO: Lynne Rienner, 2008.

Teng, Chung-Chian. "Hegemony or Partnership: China's Strategy and Diplomacy Toward Latin America." In Joshua Eisenman, Eric Heginbotham, and Derek Mitchell, eds., *China and the Developing World: Beijing's Strategy for the Twenty-First Century*. Armonk, NY: M. E. Sharpe, 2007.

Than, Mya. "Economic Co-operation in the Greater Mekong Subregion." *Asian-Pacific Economic Literature* 11, no. 2 (1997): 40–57.

Tian Yu Cao, ed. *The Chinese Model of Modern Development*. London: Routledge, 2005.

Tokatlian, Juan Gabriel. "A View from Latin America." In Riordan Roett and Guadalupe Paz, eds., *China's Expansion into the Western Hemisphere: Implications for Latin America and the United States*. Washington, DC: Brookings Institution, 2008.

Tuman, John P., and Jonathan R. Strand. "The Role of Mercantilism, Humanitarianism, and Gaiatsu in Japan's ODA Programme in Asia." *International Relations of the Asia-Pacific* 6, no. 1 (2000): 61–80.

Tun Myint. "Democracy in Global Environmental Governance: Issues, Interests, Actors in Mekong and Rhine Basins." *Indiana Journal of Global Legal Studies* 10, no. 1 (2003): 287–314.

UNCTAD. *World Investment Report 2008: Transnational Corporations and the Infrastructure Challenge*. New York and Geneva: United Nations, 2008.

UN Economic Commission for Latin America and the Caribbean (ECLAC). *Latin America and the Caribbean in the World Economy, 2005–2006* (Santiago, Chile: ECLAC, 2006).

US National Intelligence Council. *Mapping the Global Future*. Washington, DC: National Intelligence Council, 2004.

Van Ness, Peter. "China and the Third World." In Samuel S. Kim, *China and the World: Chinese Foreign Policy Faces the New Millennium,* 4th ed., 151–171. Boulder, CO: Westview Press, 1998.

————. *Revolution and Chinese Foreign Policy: Peking's Support for Wars of National Liberation*. Berkeley: University of California Press, 1970.

Vertzberger, Yaacov. *China's Southwestern Strategy: Encirclement and Counterencirclement.* New York: Praeger, 1985.

Vines, Alex. "China in Africa: A Mixed Blessing?" *Current History* 106, no. 700 (May 2007): 213–219.

Vuving, Alexander L. "Vietnam. Arriving in the World—and at the Crossroads." In *Southeast Asian Affairs 2008*, 375–393. Singapore: ISEAS, 2008.

Wade, Robert. *Governing the Market: Economic Theory and the Role of Government in East Asian Industrialization.* Princeton, NJ: Princeton University Press, 1990.

Whiting, Allen S. *The Chinese Calculus of Deterrence: India and Indochina.* Ann Arbor: University of Michigan Press, 1975.

Wise, Carol. "Great Expectations: Mexico's Short-Lived Convergence Under NAFTA." Working Paper No. 15, Centre for International Governance Innovation (CIGI), January 2007.

Wise, Carol, and Cintia Quiliconi. "China's Surge in Latin American Markets: Policy Challenges and Responses." *Politics and Policy* 35, no. 3 (2007): 410–438.

World Bank. *The East Asian Miracle: Economic Growth and Public Policy.* Washington, DC: The World Bank, 1993.

Wu Baiyi. "The Chinese Security Concept and Its Historical Evolution." *Journal of Contemporary China* 10, no. 27 (May 2001): 281.

Xiang, Lanxin. "An Alternative Chinese View." In Riordan Roett and Guadalupe Paz, eds., *China's Expansion into the Western Hemisphere: Implications for Latin America and the United States.* Washington, DC: Brookings Institution, 2008.

Xiao Geng. "Round-Tripping Foreign Direct Investment in the People's Republic of China: Scale, Causes and Implications." Research Paper No. 58, Asia Development Bank Institute, Tokyo, July 2004.

Xinjiang Autonomous Region, PRC. "Trade Facilitation and Customs Cooperation Project, Draft Technical Assistance Consultant's Report, November 30." In *China Statistical Yearbook 2006,* Table 18-8. "Volume of Imports and Exports by Countries and Regions (Customs Statistics)." June 26, 2008. Available at www.stats.gov.cn/tjsj/ndsj/2006/indexeh.htm.

Yahuda, Michael. *The International Politics of the Asia-Pacific,* 2nd rev. ed. London: RoutledgeCurzon, 2004.

Yamakage, Susumu. "The Construction of an East Asian Order and the Limitations of the ASEAN Model." *Asia-Pacific Review* 12, no. 2 (2005): 1–9.

Yan Xuetong and Xu Jin. "Sino-US Comparisons of Soft Power." *Contemporary International Relations* 18, no. 2 (March–April 2008): 16–27.

Young, Kenneth T. *Negotiating with the Chinese Communists: The United States Experience, 1953–1967.* New York: McGraw-Hill, 1968.

Yu, George T. *China's African Policy: A Study of Tanzania.* New York: Praeger, 1975.

———. "Chinese Arms Transfer to Africa." In Bruce E. Arlinghaus, ed., *Arms for Africa.* Lexington, MA: Lexington Books, 1983.

———. "Dragon in the Bush." *Asian Survey* 8, no. 12 (December 1968): 1018–1026.

———. "Sino-Soviet Rivalry in Africa." In David E. Albright, ed., *Communism in Africa,* 168–188. Bloomington: Indiana University Press, 1980.

———. "The Tanzania-Zambia Railway: A Case Study in Chinese Economic Aid to Africa." In Warren Weinstein and Thomas H. Henriksen, eds., *Soviet and Chinese Aid to African Nations.* New York: Praeger Special Studies, 1980.

Zha Daojiong. "China's Energy Security: Domestic and International Issues." *Survival* 48, no. 1 (Spring 2006): 179–190.

Zhao Gancheng. "China: Periphery and Strategy." In Shanghai Institute for International Studies, *China and Asia's Security*, 67–78. Singapore: Marshall Cavendish, 2005.

Zheng Bijian. "China's 'Peaceful Rise' to Great-Power Status." *Foreign Affairs* 84, no. 5 (September/October 2005): 18–24.

Zweig, David. *Internationalizing China: Domestic Interests and Global Linkages.* Ithaca, NY: Cornell University Press, 2002.

Zweig, David, and Bi Jianhai. "China's Global Hunt for Energy." *Foreign Affairs* 84, no. 5 (September/October 2005): 25–38.

# The Contributors

**Crystal Chang** is a doctoral candidate in the political science department at the University of California, Berkeley. Her research is focused on the political economy of the Chinese auto industry.

**Jörn Dosch** is professor of Asia Pacific studies and head of the Department of East Asian Studies at the University of Leeds, UK. He was previously a Fulbright Scholar at the Asia/Pacific Research Center, Stanford University. Dosch has published some sixty books and academic papers on Southeast Asian politics and international relations, including the monograph *The Changing Dynamics of Southeast Asian Politics* (Lynne Rienner Publishers, 2006).

**Mel Gurtov** is professor emeritus of political science at Portland State University (Oregon) and visiting professor at the University of Oregon (Eugene). He is editor-in-chief of *Asian Perspective* and author, most recently, of *Global Politics in the Human Interest* (5th rev. ed., Lynne Rienner Publishers, 2007) and *Superpower on Crusade: The Bush Doctrine in US Foreign Policy* (Lynne Rienner Publishers, 2006).

**Nicola Phillips** is professor of political economy and director of the Political Economy Institute at the University of Manchester, UK. She is editor-in-chief of the journal *New Political Economy*. Her research focuses broadly on the political economy of development, with a particular regional interest in the Americas. Her most recent books include *Development*, coauthored with Anthony Payne, *Globalizing International Political Economy*, and *The Southern Cone Model: The Political Economy of Regional Capitalist Development*. Recent articles have appeared in, among other journals, *Review of International Political Economy* and *Latin American Politics and Society*.

**Lawrence Saez** is senior lecturer (associate professor) in comparative and international politics in the Department of Politics, School of Oriental and African Studies (SOAS), University of London. He is a political economist with a focus on South Asia. He is the coeditor of *Coalition Politics and Hindu Nationalism,* and author of *Banking Reform in India and China* and *Federalism Without a Center.*

**Yitzhak Shichor** is professor of political science and East Asian studies at the University of Haifa and professor emeritus at the Hebrew University of Jerusalem, where he is a senior research fellow at the Harry S. Truman Research Institute for the Advancement of Peace. A former Michael William Lipson chair in Chinese studies and dean of students at the Hebrew University and head of the Tel-Hai Academic College, his research and publications cover aspects of China's military modernization and defense conversion, China's Middle East policy and labor export, China's international energy policy, East Asian democratization processes, Sino-Uighur relations and the Uighur Diaspora, and the Eastern Turkestan independence movement.

**Niklas L. P. Swanström** is director at the Institute for Security and Development Policy, Stockholm, Sweden. His main areas of expertise are conflict prevention, conflict management, and regional cooperation; Chinese foreign policy and security in Northeast Asia; narcotics trafficking and its effect on regional and national security as well as negotiations. He is the author of four books: *Conflict Prevention and Conflict Management in Northeast Asia; Transnationell brottslighet: ett säkerhetshot?* (Transnational Crime: A Security Threat?); *Regional Cooperation and Conflict Management: Lessons from the Pacific Rim*; and *Foreign Devils, Dictatorship or Institutional Control: China's Foreign Policy Towards Southeast Asia.* He is the editor of *China and Eurasia Quarterly.*

**David Zweig** is chair professor, Division of Social Science, and director of the Center on China's Transnational Relations, Hong Kong University of Science and Technology, Hong Kong. His books include *Internationalizing China: Domestic Interests and Global Linkages, Freeing China's Farmers,* and *Agrarian Radicalism in China, 1968–1981.* He is currently writing a book on China's overseas student diaspora and returnees to the mainland, as well as directing two projects on Hong Kong–mainland relations.

# Index

# About the Book

With China's rise as a major player in international affairs, how have its policies toward developing countries changed? And how do those policies now fit with its overall foreign policy goals? This timely new book explores the complexities of China's evolving relationship with the developing world.

The authors first examine the political and economic implications of China's efforts to be seen as a responsible great power. A series of comprehensive regional chapters then showcase a quid-pro-quo relationship—variously involving crucial raw materials, energy, and consumers on the one hand and infrastructure development, aid, and security on the other. The concluding chapter illuminates China's search for national identity in the context of widespread suspicions of its strategic motives. The result is a thorough, yet accessible, view of an increasingly important topic in global affairs.

**Lowell Dittmer** is professor of political science at the University of California, Berkeley, and editor of *Asian Survey*. His numerous publications include *South Asia's Nuclear Security Dilemma: India, Pakistan, and China* and *China's Deep Reform: Domestic Politics in Transition*. **George T. Yu** is professor emeritus of political science at the University of Illinois. Among his recent publications are *The Emerging East Asian Community* and *Mongolia and Northeast Asia: Economic Development and Regional Cooperation*.